THE AMERICAN

COLONIAL STATE IN

THE PHILIPPINES

AMERICAN ENCOUNTERS/

GLOBAL INTERACTIONS

*A series edited by Gilbert M. Joseph
and Emily S. Rosenberg*

This series aims to stimulate critical
perspectives and fresh interpretive
frameworks for scholarship on the
history of the imposing global presence
of the United States. Its primary
concerns include the deployment and
contestation of power, the construction
and deconstruction of cultural and
political borders, the fluid meanings
of intercultural encounters, and the
complex interplay between the global
and the local. American Encounters
seeks to strengthen dialogue and
collaboration between historians of
U.S. international relations and area
studies specialists.

The series encourages scholarship
based on multiarchival historical
research. At the same time, it supports a
recognition of the representational
character of all stories about the past
and promotes critical inquiry into issues
of subjectivity and narrative. In the
process, American Encounters strives to
understand the context in which
meanings related to nations, cultures,
and political economy are continually
produced, challenged, and reshaped.

THE AMERICAN

COLONIAL STATE IN

THE PHILIPPINES

GLOBAL PERSPECTIVES

Edited by Julian Go and Anne L. Foster

DUKE UNIVERSITY PRESS

DURHAM AND LONDON 2003

© 2003 Duke University Press
All rights reserved
Printed in the United States of
America on acid-free paper ∞
Designed by Rebecca Giménez
Typeset in Adobe Minion by
Keystone Typesetting, Inc.
Library of Congress Cataloging-
in-Publication Data appear on the
last printed page of this book

CONTENTS

ACKNOWLEDGMENTS

This book has a long, rich history, and so we, the editors, have benefited from much assistance, guidance, and encouragement along the way. The project had its genesis in a lively panel at the Association for Asian Studies' annual meeting in Chicago in 1997, organized and chaired by Patricio N. Abinales, with papers by Chiharu Takenaka, Donna Amoroso, Anne Foster, and Julian Go. Glenn A. May provided insightful and encouraging comments at that early stage. Patricio Abinales prompted some of the panelists to think about publication, and assisted in recruiting additional authors. We are grateful to him for his continued intellectual involvement, questions, and challenges, which have sharpened our arguments and broadened our conception of this project. Walter LaFeber also has been a constant source of encouragement and assistance. He read all the essays at an early stage and had helpful suggestions for the editors. We thank Emily Rosenberg for her enthusiasm about the project from its earliest conceptions to its final product.

Perhaps our most heartfelt thank yous should go to Valerie Milholland and Miriam Angress at Duke University Press, who have patiently guided us through the process and continue to provide wonderful support. The anonymous reviewers for Duke University Press were all that authors could hope, in that they read carefully and sympathetically but helped all the authors see ways to improve their essays.

Julian Go especially thanks the Harvard University Academy of International and Area Studies and the Department of Sociology at the University of Illinois at Urbana-Champaign for assistance in the final stages of the project. He also thanks Emily Barman for her consistent encouragement and toleration. Anne Foster thanks her colleagues in the Department of History at Saint Anselm College for their willingness to listen and encourage and Linda Bradley and Deanna Rossetti of Saint Anselm College for their invaluable assistance with manuscript preparation. Walter LaFeber, Frank Costigliola, and Bill Walker have been willing listeners and readers for Anne over many years, for which she thanks them. The International Affairs Research Center at the New Hampshire Institute of Politics, Saint Anselm College, provided financial support and release time from teaching for Anne Foster's work on this project, for which she is grateful. She also thanks Naomi and Geoffrey Brown, whose support makes it all possible.

JULIAN GO

Introduction: Global Perspectives on
the U.S. Colonial State in the Philippines

A new government is being created from the ground up, piece being added to piece as the days and weeks go by. It is an interesting phenomenon, this thing of building a modern commonwealth on a foundation of medievalism—the giving to this country at one fell swoop all the innovations and discoveries which have marked centuries of Anglo-Saxon push and energy. I doubt if in the world's history anything similar has been attempted; that is, the transplanting so rapidly of the ideas and improvements of one civilization upon another. The whole fabric is being made over.—Daniel Williams, Secretary of the Philippine Commission, 1 October 1901

It should not be surprising that Daniel Williams begins this journal entry by referencing the task of building "a new government . . . from the ground up."[1] Just a few years earlier, the United States had officially purchased the Philippines from Spain and had accordingly declared sovereignty over the islands.[2] At the time of Williams's journal entry, the U.S. government had to make its declaration real and palpable on the ground. It had to create a political apparatus by which it could maintain its proclaimed power over the inhabitants and territory of the Philippine archipelago. Williams and his colleagues of the Philippine Commission had been sent to the Philippines to do just that. Agents of an emerging overseas colonial empire, they had been sent to construct and maintain a colonial state: a "new government," indeed.

It should not be surprising, either, that in referring to the process of colonial state-building Williams doubts that "anything similar has been attempted." This doubtfulness scripts U.S. colonial rule as unique and particular, something special. Williams thus articulates a paradigm that was common among American imperialists of the time: the exceptionalist paradigm. In the purview of exceptionalism, the United States was not quite an empire. If it was an empire at all, it was a special one. For unlike European empires, the U.S. enterprise was an exercise in effective benevolence, bringing to those whom it touched the benefits of Anglo-American civilization.[3] Williams merely extends such exceptionalist thinking to the site of U.S. colonialism in the Philippines. To wit, U.S. colonial rule in the Philippines was not exploitative or tyrannical. It was aimed at "transplanting the ideas and improvements of one civilization on another." It was benign, a civilizing mission rather than one of the missions of conquest that ostensibly characterize the "world's history" of imperialism.

What *is* noteworthy about Williams's journal entry, however, is that it starkly discloses how the paradigm of exceptionalism necessarily works. In suggesting that the U.S. colonial state is unique, Williams first situates it within a broader framework. He puts it within the "world's history" of imperialism, thereby placing it inside something else, something larger. It is imperative that Williams make this move. To make the exceptionalist claim at all, Williams has to contextualize. He has to track U.S. colonial rule in relation to other kinds of colonial rule; he has to locate it within a global imperial field. Williams's claim about the supposedly exceptional character of U.S. colonial state building thus demands a widening of the perceptual lens. It demands a global—rather than merely a local—perspective. An exception presupposes a rule. However, in putting U.S. colonial rule within a global field, he then has to put that field outside. He has to render it something from which U.S. rule is excluded, something against which it stands as special and unique: "I doubt if in the world's history anything similar has been attempted." Ultimately, then, the larger history of imperialism and colonialism is rendered marginal and exterior, even as it serves as the very condition for Williams's noteworthy doubtfulness.[4]

Williams's journal entry opens the space for the organizing theme of this collection. The essays here pay attention to the U.S. colonial state in the Philippines, but they do so from a global perspective. The theme is twofold. First, all of the essays critically interrogate the complex processes involved in constructing and maintaining a "new government . . . from the ground up." They discuss the policies, projects, and programs of the U.S. colonial state in the Philippines; the attendant discourses of race, state, and empire; the logics of capital accumulation and revenue extraction necessary for building a state; and the practices of political collaboration and conflict that the colonial state faced or otherwise fostered. All of the essays, then, examine processes of U.S. colonial state building and governance in the Philippine archipelago. Second, the essays situate the U.S. colonial state within a global context. Although each examines processes of U.S. colonial state building and governance, all recognize that those processes were unfolding within a larger field of colonial empires, a field that spanned the global map. Some of the essays compare U.S. colonial policies in the Philippines with contemporaneous policies in other colonies, such as Japanese Taiwan and British Malaya. Other essays situate processes of U.S. colonial state building and governance within larger circuits of inter-imperial exchange and imitation, conversation and contest, or they conduct intra-imperial comparisons and processes. But whatever their particular focus, they all explicitly analyze the U.S. colonial state in the Philippines from a global perspective. This is our organizing theme.

The point of analyzing the U.S. colonial state in the Philippines from a global perspective is neither to affirm nor to "test" the well-worn discourse of exceptionalism. The point, rather, is to appropriate critically the global perspective that exceptionalist reasoning necessarily entails. Such a lens may indeed serve as a way to test the exceptionalist paradigm, but the underlying goal of the collection is to offer a novel analytic lens that examines processes of U.S. colonial state building and governance in the Philippines while always maintaining a global frame of reference. In doing so, the essays here shed new light on old questions about the U.S. colonial state in the Philippines, even as they open new lines of inquiry. Later in this introduction, I will elaborate more precisely how a global perspective enables this. But to specify better the particular intervention of our collection, it is useful to begin where Williams's entry begins—that is, with the problematic of the U.S. colonial state in the Philippines.

THE COLONIAL STATE AND THE FORM
OF IMPERIALISM IN THE PHILIPPINES

For Williams, the U.S. colonial state in the Philippines was a "new government . . . created from the ground up." Of course, this claim is somewhat exaggerated. The Spanish had already constructed a colonial state in the Philippines before the United States arrived in 1898. But in relation to the history of U.S. imperialism, the claim has a measure of truth. To be sure, U.S. imperialism in the Philippines took a specific form as opposed to other forms of U.S. imperialism. Specifically, it took a colonial form. In this sense, the acquisition of the Philippine archipelago from Spain in 1898 initiated a new phase in the career of U.S. imperialism—one that marked the emergence of the United States as an overseas colonial empire and that likewise carried with it the need for the United States to engage in constructing an overseas colonial state.

Certainly, the United States had long been an empire. By the 1890s, it had already expanded into the Western frontier, and it had begun to meddle in the affairs of Latin American republics. Still, U.S. imperialism in the Philippines is analytically irreducible to these other forms of imperialism. Two distinctions are useful here. The first is between *informal* and *formal* imperialism.[5] Briefly, informal imperialism refers to the exercise of control by one sovereign state over other nominally sovereign states through various diplomatic, economic, or blatantly coercive strategies. U.S. intervention in most of Latin America was of this sort. It involved embargoes, sporadic military intervention, tinkering in national politics from afar, control by Washington over local markets and economies, and the export of American capital and goods (not to mention the extraction of local resources). U.S. imperialism in the Philippines was fundamentally different. Foremost, it involved sustained, direct control over the territory and its peoples. By the Treaty of Paris with Spain in 1898, the Philippine archipelago was ceded directly to the United States, and the islands subsequently became the "property" of the United States, to be dealt with as Congress wished.[6] This was formal imperialism. Unlike the targets of U.S. imperialism in Latin America (Puerto Rico aside), the Philippines was not a sovereign state; the United States claimed complete sovereignty. Secretary of War Elihu Root, assigned by President McKinley to formulate colonial policy for the Philippines, made this clear in his annual report for 1899:

> I assume, for I do not think that it can be successfully disputed, that all acquisition of territory under [the Treaty of Paris] was the exercise of a power which belonged to the United States . . . and that the United States has all the powers in respect of the territory which it has thus acquired, and the inhabitants of that territory, which any nation

in the world has in respect of territory it has acquired; that as between the people of the ceded islands and the United States the former are subject to the complete sovereignty of the latter.[7]

In this sense, U.S. imperialism in the Philippines should be characterized more precisely as *colonialism*, a distinct form of imperialism that involves the explicit and often legally codified establishment of direct political domination over a foreign territory and peoples.[8] In fact, American scholars and administrators at the time did not completely eschew the term *colonialism* when referring to the Philippines. Although some shied away from it, others, such as William Willoughby (a Johns Hopkins economist, treasurer of Puerto Rico, and one of the preeminent scholars of U.S. colonial policy), stated matter-of-factly that the acquisition of the Philippines marked the emergence of the United States as a colonial power. According to Willoughby, the acquisition meant that the United States had "definitely entered the class of nations holding and governing over-sea colonial possessions."[9]

That U.S. imperialism in the Philippines took a colonial form did not only mean that the United States became an overseas colonial empire. It also meant that the U.S. government had to construct a special apparatus of rule in the Philippines. The direct political domination of the islands necessitated a central organization that could monopolize the means of coercion, contain other forms of social power, and thereby fulfill the function of governing the alien inhabitants of the territory. If the U.S. government was at all to maintain its sovereignty over the archipelago, it had to construct a colonial state—a political institution that was geographically distant and juridically distinct from, but subordinate to, the metropolitan government.[10] Informal imperialism in Latin America did not need such a political apparatus of rule. All imperial interventions were carried out by the U.S. government in Washington, D.C., which enacted strategies and employed manipulative mechanisms of control from afar. Formal imperialism in the Philippines could proceed only through the efforts of colonial agents, agencies, and bureaucracies inserted directly into the acquired territory and claiming sovereignty over it. It demanded a colonial state that would have to maintain its own policing mechanisms, taxation agencies, and set of policies.[11]

This distinction does not overlook the fact that, even before it acquired the Philippines, the United States had declared sovereignty over contiguous territories in the Western frontier stretching from Louisiana to New Mexico. These territories also demanded a political apparatus of rule. But here a second distinction is worth making—in this case, between types of colonialism. Scholarly attempts to construct a typology of overseas European colonialism intimate a distinction between *settler* colonialism and *administrative* colonialism. The distinction moves across a historical shift in the meaning of the term *colonialism* itself. On the one hand, the term *colonialism* denotes the permanent settlement of a foreign place by emigrants. In Europe, the term had long been synonymous with *plantation*, as in the plantation of peoples to new territory.[12] This notion of colonialism coincides with the earliest colonial empires that ran until the early nineteenth century. But after the establishment of those early colonial empires, the term *colonialism* began to acquire a different accent. Rather than referring to settlement, it came to refer to one society's political domination of another—that is, "the establishment and maintenance, for an extended time, of rule over alien people that is separate from and subordinate to the ruling power."[13] This type of colonialism involves the transplanting of political power and sovereignty to a new territory and not merely, if at all, the transplanting of metropolitan populations. It is primarily a matter of administering new territories and alien peoples.

The distinction between settler and administrative colonies can be roughly applied to the difference between U.S. rule over contiguous lands in the Western frontier and colonial rule in the Philippines. The expansion of U.S. sovereignty into places such as Louisiana and New Mexico, for example, typically involved the movement of settlers who expropriated all of the land for themselves, a process that meant the expulsion or near-annihilation of native populations. As Jack Erickson Eblen summarizes: "Anglo-Americans expropriated, segregated, and relentlessly strove to exterminate the American Indians, occupied their lands in ever-growing numbers and, under the direction of the federal government, formed the true colonies ordinarily referred to, in euphemistic terms, as 'territories.'"[14] Moreover, this pattern of expansion into the Western frontier typically implied the full integration of the newly settled territories into the existing U.S. federal system. This was premised on the Northwest Ordinance, which declared that newly ceded lands should be "settled and formed into distinct republican States, which shall then become members of the Federal Union and have the same rights of sovereignty, freedom, and independence, as the other States."[15] As territories of the Western frontier were acquired, the U.S. federal government established forms of local government designed to pave the way toward statehood. These territories were therefore known as "incorporated" territories.[16]

Colonial rule in the Philippines was notably different on these counts. First, it did not involve settlement and the expropriation of land or the expulsion of native inhabitants. Instead, the population was kept intact in its prior condition, and there was a notorious absence of the multitude of settlers that had populated the Western frontier.[17] Supreme Court Justice Henry Billings Brown pointed out the difference between the Philippines and the contiguous territory of the West by stressing that the latter was "inhabited only by people of the same race [i.e., settlers], or by scattered bodies of native Indians," whereas the Philippines represented "differences of race, habits, laws and customs," as well as "differences of soil, climate and production."[18] Second, and by the same token, the situation in the Philippines demanded unique legislation from Congress. The Northwest Ordinance, which had been applicable to the Western frontier, did not apply in whole to the Philippines. Instead, through a series of contentious congressional debates and Supreme Court decisions in 1901, precedents were set to classify the Philippines as an "unincorporated territory." This meant, among other things, that the Philippines would not necessarily became a full-fledged state in the union. The U.S. government would exercise full sovereignty, and the question of future political status would be deferred.[19] Given such sovereign power, the U.S. Congress established the Organic Act of 1902 that set up civil government in the Philippines, a government that in form was inspired by the Northwest Ordinance but was not at all an unproblematic extension. For example, the Organic Law called for a legal and economic system that would be discontinuous with the U.S. federal system. The Philippines' courts would not be part of the federal court system; U.S. legal statutes would not apply. The Philippines was designated a foreign port, giving Congress the right to establish tariff duties and customs, and it had a local monetary system based on the Philippine peso rather than the dollar.[20] Finally, because of the "unincorporated" status of the Philippines declared by the Supreme Court, the inhabitants of islands would not enjoy full citizenship or all constitutional rights. They would instead be treated as wards of the U.S. government. "Th' supreme court has decided," stated the popular cartoon character Mr. Dooley, "th' constitution don't folow th' flag."[21]

Willoughby summarized the Philippines' novel situation in his book *The Territories and Dependencies of the United States* (1905). U.S. expansion before the acquisition of the Philippines had been marked by the "settlement by emigrants from the old territory and the consequent extension . . . of American institutions, political or otherwise"; the acquisition of former Spanish colonies, by contrast, was completely novel, "filled with events of great importance—events marking the development of an entirely new phase in the expansion of the United States and to a certain extent representing a direct breaking with precedent."[22] Willoughby elaborates:

> In all prior acquisitions [on the North American frontier] . . . the essential principle upon which the acquisitions were based was that of the incorporation of the new territory into the Union upon full equality with the other States. . . . The ultimate result always in view was that of a single union of commonwealths all enjoying the same general form of government, possessing the same political rights and privileges, and together embracing all territory in any manner under the sovereignty of the United States. By the acquisition . . . of the Philippine Islands, the United States was for the first time confronted with the possibility, if not the certainty, that for an indefinite time to come the territory under its sovereignty would have to be divided into two classes having a different political status; the one constituting the United States proper and enjoying full political rights and privileges, and the other dependent territory in subordination to the former and having its form of government and the rights of its inhabitants determined for it."[23]

U.S. colonial rule in the Philippines, of course, had some precedents on the home front that Willoughby here neglects. As intimated already, the U.S. government's previous experience in ruling Native American populations—not to mention freed slaves in the South, women, and immigrant groups in the cities—offered some material with which imperialists and colonial administrators could work. The first U.S. military governors in the Philippines (Wesley Merritt, Elwell S. Otis, Arthur MacArthur, and Adna Chafee) had had considerable experience in administering Indian policy, and the Philippine–American War was often scripted as but another "Indian war." The War Department, which initially supervised the Philippine colonial state, had previously created the Bureau of Freedmen, Refugees, and Abandoned Lands for the Southern states. Furthermore, congressmen, pro-imperialists, and organizations such as the Friends of the Indian society (which met annually at Lake Mohonk in New York) typically collapsed Native Americans and Filipinos into the same category, arguing that rule of the latter was not unlike rule of the former.[24] These continuities and precedents cannot be overlooked, and in the extant historiography they have not been overlooked. But then, the discontinuities and novelties cannot be overlooked, either. For one thing, as noted already, the legal status of the Philippines that underpinned the colonial state was indeed different from that of territories in the Western frontier where reservations for Native Americans were created. Acquisition of the Philippines demanded the new category of "unincorporation," which demanded a novel set of economic, administrative, and juridical boundaries between the U.S. home government and the colonial apparatus overseas.[25] Furthermore, unlike the Native American reservation system, which depended fully on Congress and, hence, the U.S. government for all of its financing, the Philippines had to be internally financed, thereby establishing one of the crucial requirements for analytic designation as a separate state. Unlike their counterparts on the reservation system at home, administrators in the Philippines had to legislate for taxes in the Philippine territory and create autonomous agencies to collect those taxes, and all the while concern themselves with regulating the economy to help meet the state's financial imperatives.[26] It is perhaps for these reasons, among many others, that administrators in the Philippines rejected the administration of Native American populations as a model for the administration of the Philippines, even as some demagogues in the U.S. Congress and the military made ideological equations between Filipinos and Native Americans, and even as some American colonial administrators themselves initially made those equations.[27]

In short, although it incorporated various discursive and practical elements from previous and contemporaneous imperial experience, U.S. colonial rule of the Philippines is irreducible not only to informal imperialism but also to settler colonialism in the Western frontier and internal colonialism at home. In the case of the Philippines, a handful of

U.S. agents had to travel overseas and administer more than seven million people, speaking various languages and dialects, spread across some seven thousand islands. And they had to construct and administer a political, juridical, and economic system separate from the metropolitan state. Simply put, U.S. colonial rule of the Philippines demanded something that the Americans had not yet perfected in their prior experience: an overseas colonial state. Two interrelated processes thus had to unfold in the Philippines: colonial state building and colonial governance. First, American administrators had to attend to the task of state building, instituting basic structures to meet imperatives of formal political control. They needed to create a police force to maintain order and set up agencies and assign personnel for revenue collection. They needed to codify a legal system, build administrative structures, and set up storehouses of knowledge such as the census. The Spanish had already built some of these systems during their period of rule (which spanned three centuries), but the U.S. administrators, not content with Spanish ways, began to modify them.[28] In many areas of the archipelago, the Americans had to start their state-building efforts from scratch, as some regions in which so-called semi-savage or uncivilized tribes lived had barely been penetrated by the Spaniards.

Second, administrators had to attend to the task of government. State building entails the construction of a political apparatus; governing entails its implementation. Government is about administration, the "conduct of conduct," the activity "aiming to shape, guide or affect the conduct [of the colonized]."[29] The administrators had to enact various projects aimed at reconfiguring or otherwise regulating the social, political, and economic spaces in accordance with their particular visions of rule.[30] Not surprisingly, soon after acquisition, scholars and statesmen on the home front began to write tracts and treatises on the particular problem of colonial governance—how best to carry it out, the principles on which it should be based, the goals and problems involved in ruling foreign peoples. The American Academy of Social and Political Science published series under the titles "Colonial Government" and "Notes on Colonies."[31] Scholars such as Alpheus Snow and Horace Fisher wrote books and pamphlets on America's new task of colonial governance. One academic by the name of Alleyne Ireland even taught courses at Cornell and Chicago universities on themes such as "Control and Development of Tropical Colonies."[32] The U.S. colonial state in the Philippines had emerged as a reality on the ground and as an abstraction at home.

But how did U.S. colonial state building and governance play out in the Philippines? How exactly did the United States maintain its sovereignty over the Philippine archipelago? By what particular policies, projects, and programs did it do so, and on what conditions (social, political, economic, discursive) did they depend? What tensions and troubles, for colonizer and colonized alike, did state building and governance foster? And how were colonial agents and colonized peoples, metropole and colony, connected or disjointed, made or re-made in the process? These questions cut to the heart of U.S. imperialism in its colonial-administrative form. They form the problematic that the essays in this collection take up.

THE "STATE" OF EXISTING HISTORIOGRAPHY

Any attempt to address questions of state building and governance must contend with the exceptionalist paradigm. This is due in part to the very character of the historical record. To be sure, the archives of U.S. colonial rule reveal all manner of exceptionalist rhetoric. While anti-imperialist forces rallied against America's imperial power, various politicians and statesmen at home—not to mention colonial officials on the ground— insisted that U.S. rule in the Philippines was to be unique, a benign matter of civilizing Filipinos rather than tyrannizing them, an exercise in benevolent transformation rather than political power and domination. Hence, as we have already seen, administrator Williams scripted colonial state building and governance as an effort toward "transplanting so rapidly the ideas and improvements of one civilization on another." But Williams was not alone in this view. Senator Albert J. Beveridge, who wielded a heavy hand in Congressional legislation for the Philippines, argued that the primary "mission" of the United States in the Philippines was to engage in "civilizing work." President William McKinley contended similarly that "the Philippines are not ours to exploit, but to develop, to civilize, to educate."[33] Elihu Root claimed that "it is our unquestioned duty to make the interests of the [Filipino] people over whom we assert sovereignty the first and controlling consideration in all legislation and administration . . . and to give them, to the greatest possible extent, individual freedom, self-government in accordance with their capacity, just and equal laws, and opportunity for education, for profitable industry, and for development in civilization."[34] The first civil governor of the Philippines, William Howard Taft, reiterated that "the national policy is to govern the Philippine Islands for the benefit and welfare and uplifting of the people of the Islands."[35]

The exceptionalist discourse in the archival record would be easy to dismiss if it were only rhetoric. The hitch is that policymakers and administrators indeed attempted—at least, on some registers—to "transplant" American civilization and thereby transform Philippine society. Of course, U.S. rule in the Philippines did not begin as benignly as the discourse of exceptionalism projected. To the contrary, it began with a war of conquest. After the United States signed the Treaty of Paris and declared sovereignty over the archipelago, many Filipino nationalists resisted. Not content with facing foreign colonial rule, and having already begun to rebel against Spain, wealthy landowners joined peasants and the urban middle classes to obtain national independence. The American military, already occupying Manila as a result of the Spanish–American War, then violently quelled the movement. The result was the Philippine–American War, which entailed the deployment of some 126,000 American troops and the loss of thousands of lives on both sides.[36] Still, both during the war and in its aftermath, the Americans tried to prove their benevolence, to match rhetoric with reality and ultimately win Filipino hearts and minds. When Congress legislated civil government for the islands, and as the transition from military to civil rule ensued, administrators quickly initiated a pattern of state building and governance aimed at "civilizing," "developing," and otherwise "tutoring" colonial spaces and subjects. They built new roads and communications infrastructure; they set up health programs and an extensive educational system for the illiterate populace. They tried to liberalize the economy and initiated programs intended to redistribute land to pioneering peasants. They opened the doors of the colonial bureaucracy to Filipinos, instituted regular elections with a restricted suffrage (later to be expanded), and offered local offices and governments modeled after Tocquevillan ideals. In 1907, they even inaugurated a national legislative assembly to be staffed by Filipinos as part of a larger program of "political education" and democratic tutelage. The stated goal was to offer Filipinos some participation in government and instill in them democratic values so that one day the Philippines might become an independent nation.

Such is the sort of evidence of exceptionalism with which any analysis of U.S. colonial state building and governance in the Philippines has to deal, the present volume included.

A small circle of scholars of the Philippines and U.S.–Philippine relations have in fact already grappled with the exceptionalist thesis—at times more implicitly than explicitly, though. Working under the institutional rubrics of "Philippine studies" and "Philippine–American relations," these scholars have produced studies of U.S. colonial rule that together offer various ways of looking beyond the putative benevolence of U.S. state-building efforts. Broadly speaking, the literature can be divided into two schools. One school has offered studies that question the effects of the Americans' so-called civilizing measures. Rather than denying the sincerity or efforts of the American administrators, this literature has shown that America's "developmental benevolence" was little but an exercise in "myopic arrogance" that ultimately did not meet its grand goals.[37] Glenn May's *Social Engineering in the Philippines* (1980) is most indicative. Restricting his analysis to the period of U.S. rule known as the Taft period (c. 1900–1913), May interrogates the implementation and effects of three of the major programs initiated by the Americans: public education, developmental economic programs, and democratic tutelage. These three programs are exemplary of the exceptionalist narrative; each was designed to transform Philippine society and develop it into a modern, Anglo-style civilization. But May shows convincingly that, for a variety of reasons, the Americans failed to realize their goals in all three of these areas. The administrators' efforts did not transform Philippine society; rather, they had a minimal social and political effect on pre-existing social, economic, and political structures. Thus, the "entire U.S. colonial period . . . was only a brief 'deviation' in the course of Philippine history."[38] Transformative pretensions of U.S. colonialism did not match the realities of rule.

Related studies have extended this critique by showing that the Americans' attempt to introduce democratic institutions was ultimately compromised by patron–client relations between the existing Filipino elite and American administrators. The Americans constructed a system of elections, local offices, and a national legislature in the hope that such a system would teach Filipinos how to conduct a democratic government properly. But as *Philippine Colonial Democracy* (1988), edited by Ruby Paredes, shows, the American administrators undermined the tutelary program, often unintentionally. Inspired by Ronald Robinson's claim that imperialism necessarily involved "mutual collaboration" between native elements and colonizing actors, these studies reveal that, although American agents constructed a quasi-democratic system, they "did not wait for the system to produce natural leaders."[39] Instead, to meet the exigencies of colonial control, they leaned on the very Filipino "oligarchs" and "caciques" whom they had initially derided. They restricted suffrage to the wealthy and educated while cultivating patron–client relations with them. Thus, instead of imparting democratic values to the Filipinos, the Americans kept the existing Filipino elite in control, unwittingly taught them "tactics of guile and manipulation [over the colonial apparatus]," and, in the end, perpetuated pre-existing sociopolitical hierarchies.[40] In this way, U.S. colonial rule contributed to a corrupted democracy categorized by Benedict Anderson as "cacique democracy," the marks of which remain in the Philippine polity to this day.[41]

These studies amend the exceptionalist paradigm by questioning the effects of the Americans' programs. Another school of research, still nascent, offers a somewhat different approach. This literature spends less time on calculating the effects of the Americans' ostensibly benevolent projects than on disclosing how those projects were exercises in power in the first place. American efforts to civilize, democratize, and develop the Philippines not only failed; they were replete from the outset with subtle forms of domination. The very policies and programs praised by contemporaries as exceptions to imperialist power involved the deployment of a certain form of imperialist power—a governmental power based on multiple techniques and technologies of state. For example, in a rich analysis underwritten by Michel Foucault's concept of governmentality, Vicente Rafael has analyzed the "grammar of classification" codified in the Americans' first colonial census. Rafael shows that the census discursively divided the Philippine population into a set of categories (e.g., the "civilized" versus "non-civilized tribes"), which hardened distinctions among the populace or otherwise (re)invented them wholesale. He then suggests that the system of classification in the census was not a neutral instrument; rather, it served for the Americans as a technology to survey populations and construct them as targets for discipline. Hence, the attempt to "civilize" Filipinos, however benign, was "predicated on white supremacy enforced through practices of discipline and maintained by a network of surveillance."[42]

The work of Rey Ileto has also demonstrated that the Americans' efforts were but subtle exercises in power. The early American campaigns against cholera, carried out in the wake of the Philippine–American War, were heralded at the time as examples of benign "heroism" and "medico-sanitary skill" on the Americans' part. But Ileto reveals that the sanitation campaigns depended on practices of discipline and containment. "Native dwellings" were targeted for medical intervention; populations had to be moved around, then confined; lines had to be drawn around social spaces; and local medical practices deemed superstitious and backward by American officials had to be marginalized or uprooted altogether. Ileto thereby suggests that the Americans' concerns over Filipinos' health were logical and practical extensions of the Philippine–American War. The blatant deployment of force by the American military forces was merely transmuted into tactics of discipline and order.[43] Warwick Anderson, who extends Ileto's study to examine the Americans' medical efforts more generally, thus contends that medical knowledge served "to naturalize the power of foreign bodies [so that the United States could] appropriate and command the Islands."[44]

This literature has also uncovered local resistance to the technology of power. Discipline and surveillance may have underwritten U.S. rule in the Philippines, but these were not received passively by Filipinos. Ileto, for example, has produced seminal work on the repressed history of peasant rebellion to American rule. He has also shown how the Filipino elite participated in such rebellion by appealing to the millenarian visions of the Filipino masses in their campaign speeches during American rule, often beyond the surveying eye of the American administrative apparatus.[45] Likewise, Rafael has shown how working-class groups in Manila, through their so-called seditious plays, articulated alternative imaginings to the classificatory schemes of the census. The census's grammar of classification was imposed from without, but it was not necessarily internalized within.[46]

In sum, at least two schools of research offer qualifications to the exceptionalist paradigm. One school problematizes the effects of U.S. colonial rule on Philippine society: Rather than assuming the effects of state building efforts on Philippine society, this school shows how exceptionalist rhetoric and projects were not matched by historical processes of colonial state formation.[47] The second school discloses exceptionalist rhetoric and projects as constituting modes of power in the first place while also attending to the fissures and tensions inherent in colonial governance. Rather than assuming that the benevolent tone of the Americans' projects imply an absence of colonial power, this school shows how "benevolence" itself was constituted as a regime of colonial power. Together, these two schools of research pave the way for the essays in this collection. Indeed, the essays here elaborate on many of the themes raised by both schools. The multiple projects of the U.S. colonial state; how such projects were subverted by historical contingencies and the play of local structures; the nexus of benevolence, colonial knowledge, and power; the patterns of resistance to colonial rule both subtle and direct—all these matters and more are addressed by the essays. This volume thereby marks the first systematic attempt to take stock of these moves away from the exceptionalist narrative and toward critical studies of the colonial state and colonial governance.

Although the essays in this volume take up extant lines of research, however, they do so from a particular angle. Unlike the two existing schools of research, the essays in this collection situate colonial state building and colonial government in a larger context. While tracking the limited effects of U.S. colonial projects and disclosing the modes of power involved in those projects, the essays adopt a global perspective. Herein lies our main intervention.

THE GLOBAL FIELD OF EMPIRES

The term *global* has taken on a number of contested meanings in scholarly discourse, especially as it is typically associated with a similarly contested term: *globalization*. Although the essays in this volume may have something to say about the historical processes involved in the making of our current round of globalization, we use the term *global* in a sense that admittedly is more crude.[48] We employ it to denote the larger field of action and interaction in which the U.S. colonial state in the Philippines was embedded, a field that exceeded the geographical and administrative boundaries of what is taken to be "the Philippines." This was a trans-imperial and trans-colonial field, a terrain characterized by colonial states dotting the world map and by complex dynamics of intra- and inter-imperial competition, contest, and exchange. In this field, the U.S. colonial state in the Philippines occupied but one position.

To be sure, the U.S. acquisition of the Philippines did not mark only the emergence of the United States as an overseas colonial power. It was also contemporaneous with a much larger phenomenon: the emergence and consolidation of the modern empires. After all, the late nineteenth century was the moment of "high imperialism." Existing imperial powers such as England, Portugal, and France acquired new colonies at unprecedented degrees and rates; at the same time, rising powers such as Germany, Italy, Japan, Russia, and Belgium were making their entrance onto the colonial stage. All of these nations, then, were stretching their imperial arms around the world. Eventually they came to occupy regions of Africa, Asia, and the Pacific that had been previously untapped. The novelty of this period cannot be underestimated. Between 1878 and 1914, some 8.653 million square miles of colonies were added to existing colonial claims. Net colonization reached its historical peak in 1921 at 168 colonies.[49] No doubt, this was a global phenomenon. By the end of this wave of colonization, colonies and former colonies covered 84 percent of the world's land surface. By 1939, only a handful of countries enjoyed the distinction of never having been subjected to colonial rule.[50] As Michael Adas summarizes:

> Between roughly 1870 and the outbreak of World War I in 1914, global history took on a new meaning as contacts and exchanges between the world's cultural areas and diverse environments multiplied dramatically. The final burst of centuries of European overseas expansion, which had begun as far back as the Middle Ages, culminated in the extension of European formal colonization at the annual rate of territories equal to the size of metropolitan France or of informal control to virtually all of the globe. . . . Thus the five decades before World War I formed a period of unprecedented closure for the human community and consequently all of the life and lands of the earth.[51]

World-systems analysis might point out that this unprecedented expansion and consolidation of the modern empires brought but a slight rearrangement of the world economy. It was a momentary phase in longer *duree* of global accumulation (only that this particular phase eventually pushed the British out of their hegemonic position).[52] Still, there are a number of political and cultural dimensions to the global-imperial field that are only partially enclosed by traditional categories of world-systems analysis. Foremost, the emergence of the modern empires at the turn of the century meant a proliferation of colonial states spanning the globe, and the formulation and exercise of colonial power by these states was crisscrossed by dynamics of inter- and intra-imperial interaction.

As imperial powers acquired more and more territory, they had to construct and maintain apparatuses of political control. In each territory they had to construct new colonial states. These colonial states were notably distinct from the settler-oriented states and their mercantilist counterparts of prior centuries. Obviously, the territorial scope of these colonial states was historically novel. Colonial states now controlled extensive territory in the interiors of Africa, Asia, and Oceania. But at the same time, their substantive content was relatively distinct from prior modes of rule. For one thing, they were rationalized in a way that prior colonial states were not. As Crawford Young suggests in his analysis of the historical genesis of the colonial state, the new colonial states reflected the professionalization and specialization of state apparatuses in the metropolitan site—that is, rationalized administration that relied on professionals rather than on company placemen or creole subordinates typical of the ancien régime. As Young explains, "The professionalization and specialization of its formal apparatus was far advanced. [The new colonial state] had a scope of action and capacity of control . . . which vastly exceeded that of its early imperial ancestor. Instilled within its structures and agents of rule were conscious notions of the legal–rational order that Weberian reflection identified as the essence of the state, and purposive expansion of the 'capabilities' for regulation, extraction, integration, and penetration of civil society."[53] Further, to match the increased rationalization and specialization, doctrines of legitimation and state jurisprudence became more elaborate. On the one hand, the acquisition and rule of new territory in this period brought with it complex legal differentials between colonial subjects and metropolitan agents. These differentials were far more subtle than those articulated in, say, the debates by Spanish imperialists about whether Indians were human beings or not.[54] On the other hand, ruling new territory demanded new ideologies for justifying overseas conquests to domestic populations—populations that increasingly had come to play a hand in overseas affairs. As Young puts it, the "legitimation imperative of the colonizer" now included "a requirement of justification of colonial conquest to a much larger audience than simply the merchant interests, clerics, and restless aristocrats who had been interested partners in an earlier age." This brought "formidable juridical conceptualization of the prerogatives of domination."[55]

In addition, all of the colonial states of the modern empires employed new strategies for governing native populations. In the long run, these strategies replaced the previous Christianizing efforts of the Spanish conquerors and mercantilist logics of extraction characteristic of the British and Dutch trading companies. The new strategies varied remarkably, but in the broad scope they formed an ideal—typical continuum of rule. At one end was the strategy that came to be known as indirect rule. This strategy, notoriously employed in many British colonies and theorized by Lord F. D. Lugard, meant preserving native "customs" and traditional authority even while manipulating them to maintain political rule and economic accumulation. At the other end was a policy of assimilation. This policy is best exemplified by the French, who sought to "civilize" the "inferior races" and discipline colonial peoples into modern European subjectivities. Certainly, the lines between these two strategies were never clear. Elements combined in various ways in particular sites to create administrative hybrids. Moreover, elements of the two strategies were already evident in the early part of the nineteenth century. The French policy of assimilation, for example, resonated to some degree with the previous efforts of the Spanish in the New World. The French policy merely took the Spaniards' policy of religious assimilation to a secular-civic register. Still, to meet the demands of the new colonial empires, the strategies of indirect rule and assimilation were elaborated on and codified in an unprecedented manner during the late nineteenth and early twentieth centuries. Lugard was High Commissioner of Northern Nigeria from 1900 to 1906, not long after he published *The Dual Mandate* (1965), which sought to legitimate indirect rule to a wide public.[56] The French debated and refined their theory of assimilation during a series of conferences in the 1890s; by 1910, it had become pragmatically revalued into a theory of "association" that resonated throughout the French empire.[57]

Finally, these new strategies of rule articulated particular imaginings of the social race and custom, progress and development. They therefore necessitated the employment of novel governmental technologies and tactics. Preserving native "customs" and traditional political authority, for example, demanded extensive and detailed knowledge of local societies and "administrative ethnography" that mapped out local political relations. Governmental tactics of indirect rule involved attempts to regulate these discursively codified "native" social spaces, employing surveillance mechanisms such as the census and new sanitation policies.[58] In a similar vein, civilizing missions and attempts to assimilate native peoples entailed theories of historico-cultural development, new schemas for indexing that development, and new educational regimes for interpellating the colonized elite. Hence, throughout the colonial world, novel governmentalities were in formation.[59] In fact, many of them were experimental, arguably transferring, transmuting, and sometimes setting the precedent for policies toward domestic populations in the metropole.[60]

The proliferation of colonial states is one noteworthy dimension to the global imperial field. The other has to do with the multiple inter- and intra-imperial dynamics that proliferation set off. One set of dynamics—perhaps the most obvious—comprised inter-imperial rivalry. As colonizing nations attempted to expand their reach, inter-imperial competition and conflict ensued—hence, the "scramble" for Africa and Oceania that caused anxiety for the Australians. Such competition and conflict, of course, form the major site of analysis for diplomatic history and studies of "international relations." But international rivalry and subsequent armed conflict is not the entire story. The rise of the modern empires also brought with it inter- and intra-imperial dynamics that were more subtle than violence—specifically, new circuits of exchange and movement, constituted by the flow of goods, people, and ideas within and among imperial domains. These are the kinds of circuits of exchange and movement that world-systems theory might restrict to relations between "core" and "periphery," but the circuits traversed core and periphery alike.

On the one hand, intra-imperial circuits were critical for the formation and operation of colonial states. In each colony, one could find settlers, military men, native labor forces, and various policy ideas articulated and institutionalized by administrators. But these did not always stay put. They circulated throughout the imperial field. Colonial officials, for instance, were often trained in the same elite schools at home and, after serving in the colonies for some time, were often transferred from one colony to another.[61] Colonized populations moved around, as well. The French constructed a military regiment composed of West

Africans who were then deployed in almost every corner of the French empire, and the British sent Indian soldiers to Africa and indentured laborers to sugar plantations in Fiji.[62] Similar movements can be seen at the register of institutional ideals and ideas. The model of indirect rule laid out in Lugard's *The Dual Mandate* was initially institutionalized in Nigeria, but it soon resonated in other parts of the British Empire. Eventually, it was applied by British administrators throughout Africa. The French originally refashioned their theory of assimilation into one of "association" in Indochina, but the theory was then applied in other parts of the empire, including North Africa. Add to this the fact that governmental technology and tactics used in the colony were often exports from home (though never in a simplistic one-to-one manner) and the larger point becomes clear: The development of each colonial state was tied to multiple circuits that traversed the empire.

Besides intra-imperial circuits, basic forms of rule and policy ideas flowed among (not only within) empires, thereby contributing to processes of inter-imperial imitation and debate, exchange and contest. Policy ideas and administrative forms were especially subject to these trans-imperial processes. The Dutch "culture system" in Java was seriously considered and partially tried by the French in Indochina, by the British in some of their Pacific territories, and by Belgium's Leopold II in Africa.[63] The models of rule employed by the British and French were experimented with by the Belgians and the Portuguese as they began constructing their respective colonial states in Africa, while French colonial advisers in Indochina were inspired in their policy toward the *métis* population by policies toward Indo-Europeans enacted by the Dutch.[64] Therefore, it is not simply that colonial policies and state forms were formulated in the metropole and then transferred, revalued, or transformed abroad; nor is it simply the other way around. There was, too, a horizontal set of circuits, as colonial policymakers and administrators drew from frameworks offered by colonial neighbors and imperial competitors. Inter-imperial conferences beginning in the 1890s contributed to such inter-imperial isomorphism in ideology and institutional form. The 1890 conference in Brussels, the 1906 conference in Algeciras, the League of Nations meeting in 1919—at these, among many other, conferences, the imperial powers tried to define global standards of colonial conduct and morality.[65] As Frederick Cooper and Ann Laura Stoler point out, "Through these circuits moved generations of families, tools of analysis, social policy, military doctrine, and architectural plans. Whole bodies of administrative strategy, ethnographic classification, and scientific knowledge were shared and compared in a consolidating imperial world. . . . Colonial questions had resonance across a wide imperial field. What happened in one place had repercussions elsewhere."[66]

The other side of the coin is that such inter-imperial flows and exchanges also presented possible points of tensions and contest. Imperial powers may have borrowed from one another, but at the same time they tried to differentiate themselves and their own colonial efforts. They borrowed, reformulated, or otherwise rejected others' models; all the while, they engaged in particularistic self-fashioning. Indeed, national-cum-imperial identities were solidified in new ways during this period of high imperialism. Each imperial state claimed to be the "greatest empire the world has ever seen." New discursive categories, from "Greater Britain" to "La Plus Grande France" and "Grossere Deutschland," were articulated, and Anglo-European nations proudly displayed their colonial subjects, spaces, and policies at world expositions.[67] Hence, even as cross-colonial isomorphism and exchange became increasingly common, colonial empires found themselves in constant competition and attempts at differentiation.

A new and expanded imperial field was therefore forged beginning in the late nineteenth century. It was a field that consisted of multiple colonial states and complex intra- and inter-imperial dynamics. This means that, as the United States was building its colonial state in the Philippines, other imperial powers were doing the same in their territories. And as the United States forged an overseas colonial empire through its acquisition of the Philippines, it became part and parcel of new intra-imperial and inter-imperial dynamics. The U.S. colonial state in the Philippines was not alone in the world—a point that, remarkably, was not lost even on U.S. scholars, statesmen, or administrators in the Philippines. To be sure, they were well aware of the larger imperial field, consistently referring to it (or denouncing it) as they debated, formulated, and carried out colonial policy for the Philippines and as they engaged in their state-building efforts. In *The Administration of Dependencies* (1902), the scholar Alpheus Snow urged that America's role as an "Imperial State" could be specified and perfected only by studying other imperial states. His book, which stands as one of many such studies produced at the time, thus detailed the legitimating ideologies and policies of rule preferred by European empires. Similarly, as U.S. congressmen faced the task of legislating government for the Philippines, Henry Cabot Lodge of the Senate Committee on the Philippines requested a bibliography from the Library of Congress on the general history of colonization. The result was not only the publication of a bibliography but a massive review of European colonial rule throughout the world, ostensibly to serve as the basis for policymaking.[68] Likewise, the academic courses proposed by Alleyne Ireland were intended to give aspiring colonial administrators of the U.S. empire knowledge of other colonial administrations. Apparently, Ireland firmly believed that American imperialists could learn well from the experience of other imperial powers.[69]

It is not that U.S. agents copied the policies of other imperial powers wholesale, if at all. It is that, at the very least, the global-imperial field was something that they could not ignore as they formulated, fashioned, and carried out their colonial effort in the Philippines. Hence, when the Philippine administrator Cameron Forbes wrote a review in the 1920s of the first decades of U.S. rule in the Philippines, he did not conclude by comparing U.S. rule in the Philippines with the previous history of U.S. expansion. Rather, he concluded with a chapter implicitly contrasting American benevolence with the supposedly "exploitative" nature of European colonialism.[70] This therefore reiterates the point made in the beginning of this introduction: The exceptionalist paradigm is possible only through comparison and contrast between the United States and other imperial powers or processes. The larger imperial field was the condition of existence for the paradigm that has for so long dominated thinking on U.S. imperialism and colonialism.

BEYOND THE LONE "STATE"

A handful of scholars of European colonialism and imperialism have come to recognize the complexity of dynamics in the global field of empires. Some have even contended that the processes in one colony cannot be grasped fully without taking this larger imperial field into account. They have therefore made concerted moves to integrate its dynamics into their more localized studies.[71] One strategy, for example (though still only partly evident in the literature), has been to trace

cross-colonial, inter-imperial, or intra-imperial isomorphisms, connections, and conflicts. This means analyzing the ways in which the flow of
ideas and ideologies, institutional forms and institutional connections
affected colonial states on the ground (and vice versa).[72] A second strategy has been to compare processes between colonies and empires to
elucidate better the particularities of each case or clarify causal processes.
Scholars of British and French colonial administration, for example,
have long discussed the differences between "direct" and "indirect" rule.
Bruce Berman and John Lonsdale, as well as Mahmood Mamdani, have
tracked different processes of colonial-state formation in Africa. Crawford Young, for his part, has made larger comparisons of the colonial
states across different empires.

Whereas the literature on European empires and colonialism has
attempted to take the global-imperial field into account, existing studies
of U.S. colonial rule in the Philippines have not. One searches in vain for
sustained comparative investigations or studies of cross-colonial links,
imitative logics, and inter-imperial debates. Certainly, there are hints
and allusions in the existing literature. The literature on collaboration
and clientelism, for example, draws from Robinson's model of collaboration, which was induced from European colonial rule. May's *Social
Engineering in the Philippines* alludes to the fact that U.S. policymakers
sometimes considered European models of rule when they were fashioning their own, and throughout his work, May makes various comparisons to European colonialisms. Nevertheless, these leads have yet to be
carried through in a systematic or sustained manner. Instead, research
has remained focused on the lone colonial state, tracking—in implicit or
explicit criticism of the exceptionalist paradigm—the limited effects of
its policies on Philippine society or its tactics and technologies of rule.[73]

To be fair, the elision of the global-imperial field is not restricted to
studies of U.S. colonial rule. The historiography of the United States as a
whole can be faulted for its lack of comparative and transnational perspectives, as can the literature on U.S. imperialism more generally.[74]
Certainly, in regard to the latter, the revisionist historians who examine
the causes of U.S. imperial expansion at the turn of the century have
always claimed that inter-imperial rivalry played a role in that expansion. This is an important recognition of the larger field of empires in
which the United States was embedded. Still, revisionist history has been
concerned with the causes of empire: how inter-imperial competition

and global military-strategic concerns compelled the United States to intervene abroad. This concern about causes, and its subsequent analysis, does not speak to complex processes that were involved in the maintenance of U.S. empire over time or to the processes of colonial rule on the ground. More important, as Daniel Rodgers suggests, this literature explains American empire as "a projection of uniquely American forces and values." Thus, even as this literature was aimed at critiquing exceptionalism, it slips exceptionalism in through the back door.[75]

Similarly, the literature on U.S. empire has not yet made sustained attempts to compare American overseas colonial rule with European colonialisms, even though they were occurring contemporaneously. Explicitly comparative studies of U.S. empire have been carried out, but all of them neglect to use the U.S. colonial empire as the basis for comparison, focusing instead on U.S. informal imperialism. Tony Smith's *The Pattern of Imperialism* (1981) is most indicative here. Smith claims to compare "U.S. imperialism" with "British imperialism," but his comparison completely forgets America's colonial interventions. Smith compares the British colonial empire before World War II with American imperialism after World War II, the latter taking the form of informal imperialism. Such an analysis neglects the more obvious comparison between the British colonial empire and the contemporaneous U.S. colonial empire, which included not only the Philippines but also Puerto Rico, Guam, Samoa, and the U.S. Virgin Islands, among others.[76]

A global perspective on U.S. colonial rule in the Philippines serves as an exciting and fruitful approach for understanding colonial state building and governance in the Philippines. It opens novel lines of inquiry overlooked by existing studies and sheds new light on old questions. For example, a global perspective enables scholars to track how interimperial or cross-colonial connections shaped the efforts and self-fashionings of U.S. colonial agents. U.S. policymakers and administrators may have scripted colonial rule as exceptional but, as intimated earlier, they nevertheless paid attention to the policies of other imperial powers. One therefore wonders how their supposedly unique attempt to "transplant" American civilization may have been drawn from the "civilizing missions" of, say, the French colonialists—or if they were not, how proponents of exceptionalism reconciled their claims with similar claims of the French. Surely, the Americans were not the only ones who contended that colonial rule was a civilizing matter.[77] To take another example, an examination of inter-imperial or cross-colonial connections would enable a more nuanced analysis of technologies of power, such as the classificatory schemes embedded in the census or in medical documents. These were certainly crucial for surveillance and discipline, but they were hardly forged out of thin air. Not only did the American constructors carry with them racialized categories already forged in the metropole; they also had various other frameworks and models available to them. The Spanish had already begun the work of classification for their censuses, and in nearby Indonesia and Malaysia, the Dutch and the British were engaging in similar classificatory endeavors. How, then, did the Americans use or disavow these possible models? How did they negotiate, rework, or appropriate them?

Further, an analysis of inter-imperial dynamics allows a more holistic understanding of tensions or complications that the U.S. regime of power in the Philippines confronted. Colonial administrators not only had to deal with the colonial subjects within their official jurisdiction; they also had to confront inter-imperial and intra-imperial politics. Attempts to develop the Philippine economy necessitated negotiations with, or restrictions on, capitalists at home and capitalists of other empires. Policing Philippine borders to regulate the flow of goods and people meant enlisting the efforts of neighboring colonial regimes. The establishment of a military base in the Philippines implied giving diplomatic assurances to competing imperial powers, and so on. Hence, dealing with local territory and populations meant dealing with a range of trans-colonial actors, forces, and structures. Tracking these negotiations might put the tensions of tutelary rule in new light.

Finally, a global perspective enables sustained comparative study. Comparison raises questions that otherwise might not be brought to the fore. It can also highlight the specificity or generality of U.S. colonial-state formation in the Philippines. On this count, consider the literature on collaboration and clientelism. Some works have suggested that the fact of the Philippine–American War was the crucial condition for subsequent processes of collaboration between American administrators and Filipino elites. To wit: American agents had to concede power to local elites to hasten the end of the war. Others, however, have suggested that the nature of colonial rule itself led to the collaborative patterns. Colonial rule, categorically antithetical to democracy and leaving little room for popular participation in the government, necessitated patron–

client relations among elite segments.[78] These arguments are certainly plausible, but even a cursory consideration of other colonial experiences suggests that they are hardly sufficient. Violent war between colonizer and colonized has not been unique to the Philippines, and all forms of colonial rule were antithetical to democracy. This would imply that collaborative and clientelistic relations in the Philippines were replicated throughout the colonial world, but it cannot be assumed that they were reproduced in exactly the same way across all colonies. The British and French oscillated between forms of indirect and direct rule, and only the former seems similar to the collaborative and clientelistic patterns in the Philippines. An explicit comparative analysis would therefore provide a better understanding of the conditions, as well as the particularities and generalities, of collaborative-clientelistic political practices in colonial Philippines.[79]

These are just some of the lines of research opened by a global perspective. This collection represents the first attempt to pursue them systematically. Each essay examines colonial state building and government while also situating its analysis within a global frame. Some essays adopt a sustained comparative strategy, tracking similarities and differences between patterns of U.S. colonial rule in the Philippines with patterns of rule elsewhere, even in the metropolitan state itself. Others trace how American agents themselves employed comparative strategies to fashion their projects, and how they rejected, adopted, or modified the ideologies, policies, and practices of other colonial powers. Some of the essays actually use a combination of these analytical strategies. But each in its own way adopts a global perspective.

THE ESSAYS IN THIS VOLUME

Of course, it is impossible in this introduction to capture all of the insights gained from the global perspectives taken by the essays in this volume. Nor is it possible to discuss all of the subtle substantive differences among the essays. It is hoped that readers will make their own observations—and, perhaps, criticisms. Still, it is worth highlighting some of the main points in each of the essays and outlining their basic methodological differences and similarities. As will be seen, many of their substantive insights address the issues outlined earlier.

Paul A. Kramer's "Empires, Exceptions, and Anglo-Saxons" begins the exploration by tracking U.S. colonial state-building in the Philippines within the context of inter-imperial dialogue. Kramer shows that the acquisition of the archipelago, as well as the initial stages of U.S. colonial-state building, were animated by a racial rapprochement between Americans and Britons. In this, Kramer joins extant studies of U.S. diplomacy and foreign policy that discuss "Anglo-Saxonism." But unlike these studies, Kramer's also tracks a certain dynamism to, and revaluation of, the existing racial discourse. He does this by situating the formation of trans-imperial Anglo-Saxonism in relation to colonial-state building on the ground. Kramer shows that, as American imperialists and colonialists initially fashioned their overseas venture, they drew on an available racial discourse that connected "Anglo-Saxons" across the Atlantic. They thereby linked at the discursive register their colonial endeavor in the Philippines with contemporary and past endeavors by the British. In a sense, the ideology of Anglo-Saxonism enabled Americans and Britons to forge common ground. At the same time, as colonial-state building proceeded in the Philippines, this racial rapprochement and its projection of a conjoined imperial project were subtly severed. British imperialists, proud of their putatively special imperial civil service and skeptical of American pronouncements to provide eventual self-government to the Filipinos, began criticizing U.S. policy and practice. By implication, then, they criticized the Americans' self-proclaimed status as good Anglo-Saxons. American colonialists, not to be left as passive targets, responded in due measure, employing a rhetoric of distinction to clarify and defend their endeavor. U.S. officials constructed Americans as not merely Anglo-Saxons but as special, privileged ones. And they offered up the American colonial state in the Philippines as proof.

One of Kramer's distinctive contributions is to reveal how the now familiar rhetoric of exceptionalism was constructed historically. He details how it was forged through practices of colonial-state building on the ground and inter-imperial dialogue—or, rather, inter-imperial diatribe—on high. Americans fashioned themselves, their imperial project, and their colonial state in the Philippines through constant engagement with forces outside themselves. His concluding remarks thus note a certain irony: Even though American colonialists offered up state building in the Philippines as proof of exceptionalism, they did not hesitate to turn to regional models of governance as they pursued their state-building projects.

Kramer merely alludes to this practice, but it forms one of the major themes in Anne L. Foster's essay on opium regulation, "Models for Governing." Foster notes that the Americans' policy of opium regulation underwent a critical shift during the course of U.S. colonial-state building. If initially American colonial-state builders such as Taft showed a relative indifference to opium use in the archipelago, they soon constructed it as a pressing problem that called for a new approach. Eventually, they replaced their existing policy, which had put high tariffs on opium imports, with a new policy of suppression. In illuminating detail, Foster locates this shift not in an increased sense of benevolence among U.S. administrators but, rather, in intra-imperial and trans-imperial processes. The colonial administrators' initial indifference evoked the concern, if not the ire, of missionaries not only in the Philippines but also in China and in the United States. In turn, these missionaries pressured politicians and bureaucrats in the metropole for change. At the same time, other colonial states in the region had developed an increasing concern about opium use in their territories, building a regionwide sense of paternalistic benevolence and, with it, new approaches to opium regulation. The Japanese colonialists in Formosa, the British in India and the Straits Settlement, the French in Indochina, and the Dutch in Java all had begun to experiment with new ways to manage opium use. The U.S. colonial administrators in the Philippines were caught up in this trans-imperial and intra-imperial reformist zeal. In fact, this zeal pushed them into their new concern over opium. But again, as things proceeded, distinction became the Americans' rule. Even as U.S. officials examined the new opium policies of other empires, and even as they borrowed from them, they eventually constructed a policy of suppression fashioned as unique, one that they believed other colonial powers should follow.

Taken together, Foster's and Kramer's essays disclose the inter-imperial dialogues and appropriations through which U.S. rule in the Philippines proceeded. They thereby show how the narrative of exceptionalism was dependent on, if not inspired by, the very field of empires against which it claimed its status. But they also suggest that practically, and not just rhetorically, colonial-state building and governmental programs in the Philippines were always embedded in complex inter-imperial dynamics.

Donna J. Amoroso's "Inheriting the 'Moro Problem'" is similar for the way in which it tracks inter-imperial dynamics. The essay attends more specifically, though, to U.S. rule and its handling of the "Moro problem" in relation to pre-existing Spanish frameworks of knowledge and to British rule in Malaya. Amoroso shows that, in establishing their presence among the inhabitants of Mindanao (a region in the southern portion of the archipelago), the Americans initially drew on Spanish knowledge to render them sensible. Like the Spaniards before them, U.S. officials and military officers made an essentializing distinction between the "Moros" and the "Christianized Filipinos." But even though the Americans initially drew from Spanish frameworks, they also over-turned them, eventually adopting a more scientific and secular view of the population. Exemplified in the discourse of the new Bureau of Non-Christian Tribes, this classification served to render comparable the Moros of the Philippines and the Muslim population of nearby British Malaya. At the same time, it rejected parallels with Native American populations in the United States. In this sense, the Americans were quicker to turn to the British for models of rule than to Spain or to their own prior experience at home. However, the matter did not end there. In the Americans' eyes, Moros and Malays showed some similarities, but the former group was ostensibly peculiar: No "natural," or hereditary, group of rulers had emerged among the Moro population. This made the British model of indirect rule an impossibility, and American offi-cials subsequently constructed a form of direct rule that gave little for-mal recognition to conventional structures of power or legality. The Moros were Muslims, but more important, they were a "minority" pop-ulation to be integrated eventually (though not immediately) into the larger Philippine body politic. The comparative point is clear: If the British in Malaya invented tradition to rule, the Americans in Minda-nao, where they found it all, hoped to transcend it.

The chapter by Patricio N. Abinales also discusses U.S. rule in Minda-nao (and in other "special provinces" of the archipelago). But Abinales takes us in a somewhat different analytic direction. "Progressive–Machine Conflict" traces intra-imperial rather than inter-imperial pro-cesses. Abinales first stresses a point made in Amoroso's analysis: that the Americans, in acquiring and ruling the Philippines, made critical distinc-tions among the populations and areas of the archipelago. Abinales argues, in fact, that these distinctions meant that the U.S. constructed not one colonial state but two: one for ruling the more "civilized," Christian

Filipinos; the other for ruling the supposedly "semi-savage," "uncivilized" Muslim populations of the south and the various "tribes" in the highlands throughout the islands. Based on this observation, Abinales compares politics and state building in the two different colonial states before they were integrated into the single state later. This is already a fruitful comparison, but the further innovation in Abinales's analysis is to link politics and state building in the two Philippine "states" to politics and state building in the metropole. In the metropole, during the same period that the United States was consolidating its rule over the Philippines, two political forces were locked in contention. Machine politicians who had been defending sectoral and localized interests found themselves in battle with progressive ideologues who called for a stronger centralized state that was to act through non-politicized, professional agencies. Eventually, the interplay of these two political forces led to the creation of a "patchworked" state in the United States. Abinales suggests that this patchworked state had resonance with the practices in, and eventual integration of, the two colonial states in the Philippines. As the administrators carried to the archipelago ideological baggage and political repertoires packed at home, and as they unpacked their baggage and activated their repertoires to engage in the task of colonial-state building, they created in the Philippines a patchworked complex, as well.[80]

Abinales's intra-imperial analysis reveals some of the parallels and resonances between metropolitan and colonial state-formation. One of his critical insights, then, is to show how the patron–client practices discussed in extant studies of U.S. rule were in part shaped and sustained by the administrators' experiences with "boss" politics at home. Julian Go's essay "The Chains of Empire" resonates on both these counts. He pursues intra-imperial comparison and, in the process, sheds light on patron–clientelism in the Philippines. The difference is that he compares state formation in the Philippines with state formation in Puerto Rico, the other major "unincorporated" colony of the United States at the time. Go shows that, in both colonies, administrators initially had similar designs, not least of which was the so-called project in political education by which Puerto Rican and Filipino elites would be incorporated into the colonial state and be given increasing measures of self-government over time. As Go shows, this project had similar beginnings in the two colonies. Nevertheless, the similarities soon gave way to radical differences. In the end, Puerto Rico saw a more restrictive and concentrated version of political education, while the Philippines saw a more lax and loose form of it—one that ended up sustaining widespread practices of patrimonial-type collaboration between U.S. officials and the Filipino elite. Go traces this divergence to the uneven impact of political forces in the metropole. As state building in the two colonies proceeded, various domestic groups—from labor unions to anti-imperialists—pressured Congress to enact different economic policies in relation to the two colonies. Ultimately, these policies shaped the political strategies that administrators pursued on the ground, leading to the tightened form of political education in Puerto Rico and its decidedly looser form in the Philippines.

Go's overarching contribution is to show that the different practices of political education in Puerto Rico and the Philippines cannot be traced to processes internal to the colonies. Rather, they must be seen as arising from tensions spanning the whole U.S. empire. Puerto Rico and the Philippines were pulled in different directions by America's complex "chain of empire." Thus, although both Go and Abinales focus on inter-imperial processes, they show different ways in which metropole and colonies were connected. Abinales shows that the ideologies and political repertoire of colonial administrators, forged at home, were transferred abroad. Go shows institutional links, or "chains," that directly connected metropolitan and colonial states.

The final set of essays returns to inter-imperial comparison. Paul Barclay's " 'They Have for the Coast Dwellers a Traditional Hatred' " compares American rule over the Igorots in Luzon's Cordillera with Japanese rule over aborigines in Taiwan. He shows that the head-hunting practices of these two populations, and their relative insulation from lowlanders and earlier imperial powers, rendered them comparable in the eyes of contemporaries. Indeed, as the Americans and Japanese sought to make these populations "legible" to the state—transforming "non-state spaces" into state spaces—they deployed somewhat similar rhetorical themes and practices (not least of which was violence). But Barclay shows that the otherwise parallel state-building trajectories in the two territories eventually diverged. Japanese incursions were tense and intense, a costly affair marked by high levels of violence that led to the loss of precious lives on both sides. Conversely, in the Cordillera, the Americans were able to maintain their political presence through a relatively low level of hostility and seemingly amicable relations with local leaders. The irony is noteworthy: Japan's relationship with the Taiwanese highlanders, with its large amounts of bloodshed and intensity of territorial occupation, ended up looking much more like the Americans' relationship with Native Americans than did the Americans' incursions into the Cordillera. Although some contemporaries and subsequent scholarly observers have explained this irony in terms of Western benevolence and local recognition of that benevolence, Barclay's comparative analysis discloses the historical conditions that actually made such congeniality possible: the timidity of foreign capital and the lack of incentives for the Cordillera's resources and revenue, among other things.[81]

Vince Boudreau's "Methods of Domination and Modes of Resistance" also employs inter-imperial comparison, this time to examine anticolonial resistance and protest in Southeast Asia. It is fitting that the volume closes with this essay, for any anthology on the colonial state must attend—at least, in part—to the resistance of the colonized. After all, it was partly through anticolonial resistance that colonial states around the world were hastened toward dissolution. Still, Boudreau hesitates to romanticize the matter; instead, he seeks to locate the sociopolitical conditions under which certain modes and patterns of resistance emerge or do not emerge during colonial rule. He does this by situating resistance in the Philippines within "world-time" and comparing it to counterparts in other colonies of Southeast Asia: French Indochina, British Burma, and Dutch Indonesia. He notes a certain peculiarity to resistance in the Philippines after the Philippine–American War. Elsewhere in the region, nationalist student activists led sustained protest movements on a mass scale; local intellectuals and peasants formed durable anticolonial coalitions; and indigenous bureaucrats pressed for national independence. The Philippines saw little of this kind of activity. Instead, resistance took on a more localized, sporadic, and limited form, typically calling for reform within existing political structures. Collective action in the Philippines thus did not seek to displace the colonial state so much as it aimed for more comfortable accommodation in it.[82] Although it would be tempting to read this peculiarity as rooted in the ostensibly benign character of U.S. rule, Boudreau reveals the dangers in making such an argument. Through his detailed cross-colonial comparison, he shows that although policies regarding education and the economy, the swiftness by which the United States constructed representative institutions, and the Americans' promise of eventual independence indeed contributed to the peculiar mode of protest activity in the Philippines, these factors interacted with local structures and pre-existing conditions in the archipelago. This interaction between historical legacy and American intervention produced sociopolitical processes and cleavages in the Philippines that were not reproduced elsewhere in the region or in other colonies. In this sense, Boudreau suggests a crucial point: If U.S. rule in the Philippines was at all peculiar to Southeast Asia, that peculiarity had as much, if not more, to do with historical conditions preceding U.S. rule than it did with any exceptional character to U.S. rule itself.

All of the essays address different themes and adopt different approaches, but they each take into account the larger global field typically elided in extant studies. By referring to inter-imperial, intra-imperial, or cross-colonial processes and employing comparison and contrast across regions, states, or empires, they bring into clearer view the global field that exceptionalist thought renders marginal and exterior but on which it ultimately depends. Certainly, the essays do not exhaust all of the possibilities of global analysis; they do not cover all the possible ground. Nevertheless, they offer a useful point of departure, moving us in a new direction for analyzing the U.S. colonial state in the Philippines—and, perhaps, for studying U.S. empire more generally.

Amy Kaplan has offered a provocative critique of the exceptionalist paradigm as it applies to U.S. imperialism, suggesting that exceptionalist thought leaves us "alone with America." That is, exceptionalist thought leaves us to assume that the United States was fundamentally unlike European powers; that it did not have an empire, or, if it did, its empire was unique.[83] Such exceptionalist thought, as we have seen, underlies Daniel Williams's journal entry: "I doubt if anything similar in the world's history has been attempted." By taking a global perspective, the essays in this volume put a new twist on Kaplan's theme. They forcefully remind us that, indeed, the United States was not alone. The United States, as an overseas colonial empire, was embedded in a larger global field of imperial interaction that offers the analyst opportunities for critical comparative analyses and studies of intra- and inter-imperial dynamics. The essays in this volume seize the opportunity, hoping that other studies of U.S. imperialism and colonialism will do the same.

For critical comments, helpful suggestions, and general encouragement, the author thanks Anne Foster, the contributors to this volume, Adam McKeown, Ian Tyrrell, and the reviewers at Duke University Press. Not all of their comments were incorporated; the author claims full responsibility for the arguments here.

1. Daniel R. Williams, *The Odyssey of the Philippine Commission* (Chicago: A. C. McClurg, 1913), 320–21.

2. The United States "purchased" the Philippine archipelago from Spain with the Treaty of Paris, which ended the Spanish–American War. I bracket the age-old questions of why the United States acquired the Philippines, but see a review of the historiography in Ephraim K. Smith, "William McKinley's Enduring Legacy: The Historiographical Debate on the Taking of the Philippine Islands," in *Crucible of Empire: The Spanish–American War and Its Aftermath*, ed. James C. Bradford (Annapolis, Md.: Naval Institute Press, 1993), 205–49.

3. The exceptionalism paradigm is well known to historians of U.S. empire. It has been rehashed and criticized in countless forms. For recent reviews and critiques of exceptionalist historiography in relation to U.S. empire, see Akira Iriye, "Exceptionalism Revisited," *Reviews in American History* (June 1988): 291–97, and Amy Kaplan, "Left Alone in America," in *Cultures of United States Imperialism*, ed. Amy Kaplan and Donald E. Pease (Durham, N.C.: Duke University Press, 1993), 3–21.

4. My thinking on the logic of the exception more generally has been informed partly by Agamben's theory of modern governance and "sovereign power." See Giorgio Agamben, *Homo Sacer: Sovereign Power and Bare Life* (Stanford, Calif.: Stanford University Press, 1998).

5. The distinction between formal and informal imperialism that I am using follows the one offered by Michael W. Doyle, *Empires* (Ithaca, N.Y.: Cornell University Press, 1986), 36–38. Initial formulations of informal imperialism are in Ronald Robinson and John Gallagher, "The Imperialism of Free Trade," *Economic History Review* 6 (1953): 1–15. For succinct overviews of the concept of imperialism as it has been used in the social sciences, see David L. Sills, ed., *International Encyclopedia of the Social Sciences* (New York: Macmillan, 1968), s.v. "Imperialism" (Hans Daalder), 101–9. For a recent overview of theories of imperialism more generally, see Patrick Wolfe, "History and Imperialism: A Century of Theory, from Marx to Postcolonialism," *American Historical Review* (1997): 388–420.

6. See the analysis of the Treaty of Paris and the Philippines' legal status in Charles Magoon, "Report of the Legal Status of the Territory and Inhabitants of the Islands Acquired by the United States during the War with Spain, Considered with Reference to the Territorial Boundaries, the Constitution, and Laws of the United States," 55th Cong., 1st sess., Senate Doc. 234 (1900).

7. Report of Elihu Root, Secretary of War, in U.S. War Department, *Annual Reports of the War Department for the Fiscal Year Ended June 30, 1899. Report of the Secretary of War. Miscellaneous Reports* (Washington, D.C.: Government Printing Office, 1899), 24.

8. This notion of formal imperialism as colonialism comes from various but rare scholarly attempts to define the term *colonialism*. See Sills, *International Encyclopedia*, s.v.

"Colonialism" (D. K. Fieldhouse and Rupert Emerson), 1–12; Ronald J. Horvath, "A Definition of Colonialism," *Current Anthropology* 13 (1972): 45–51; A. P. Thorton, "Colonialism," *International Journal* 17 (1962): 341. A more recent attempt to define and theorize colonialism can be found in Jean Comaroff and John Comaroff, *Of Revelation and Revolution: The Dialectics of Modernity on a South African Frontier*, vol. 2 (Chicago: University of Chicago Press, 1997), 19–29.

9. William F. Willoughby, *Territories and Dependencies of the United States* (New York: Century Company, 1905), 7.

10. The colonial state is remarkably undertheorized, but a small body of literature has begun to take it up as a central object of study. See Bruce Berman and John Lonsdale, *Unhappy Valley: Conflict in Kenya and Africa, Book One* (London: James Currey, 1992); Timothy Mitchell, *Colonising Egypt* (Berkeley: University of California Press, 1991); George Steinmetz, "Precoloniality: Ethnographic Discourse and Colonial Practice in German Overseas Imperialism, 1780s–1914" (unpublished ms., Department of Sociology, University of Michigan, Ann Arbor, 1999); Joan Vincent, "Sovereignty, Legitimacy, and Power: Prologomena to the Study of the Colonial State," in *State Formation and Political Legitimacy*, ed. Ronald Cohen and Judith D. Toland (New Brunswick, N.J.: Transaction Books, 1988), 137–54; and Crawford Young, *The African Colonial State in Comparative Perspective* (New Haven, Conn.: Yale University Press, 1994).

11. This is not to say that the colonial state was the only agent involved in colonial rule. Missionaries and medicine men, corporations and capitalists all played a part. See John Comaroff, "Images of Empire, Contests of Conscience: Models of Colonial Domination in Africa," in *Tensions of Empire: Colonial Cultures in a Bourgeois World*, ed. Frederick Cooper and Ann Laura Stoler (Berkeley: University of California Press, 1997), 163–97. It is merely to say that, when speaking of colonialism, one necessarily has to confront the colonial state.

12. M. I. Finley, "Colonies: An Attempt at a Typology," *Transactions of the Royal Historical Society* 26 (1976): 170.

13. Fieldhouse, "Colonialism," 1. See also Herbert Lüthy, "Colonization and the Making of Mankind," *Journal of Economic History [Supplement]* 21 (1964): 483–95, who laments the semantic shift. Fieldhouse suggests that the latter type of colonialism, as opposed to early European colonialism in the Americas, was characteristic of modern European interventions in various parts of Africa, Asia, and the Pacific beginning in the late nineteenth century. See D. K. Fieldhouse, *The Colonial Empires: A Comparative Survey from the Eighteenth Century*, 2d ed. (London: Macmillan, 1982), 372.

14. Jack Erickson Eblen, *The First and Second United States Empires* (Pittsburgh: University of Pittsburgh Press, 1968), 3. See also Lanny Thompson, "The Imperial Republic: Origins of the Unincorporated Territories," paper presented at the 10th Anniversary Conference of the Journal of Policy History, Saint Louis, Mo., 27–30 May 1999 (forthcoming in *Pacific Historical Review*).

15. As quoted in Whitney T. Perkins, *Denial of Empire: The United States and Its Dependencies* (Leyden: A. W. Sythoff, 1962), 14.

16. Ibid, 28–29. Even Hawai'i and Alaska fit into this pattern, as both were declared incorporated territories.

17. In fact, one persistent theme in the discourse of the Philippines by congressmen, colonial-policy makers, and administrators was the lack of opportunities for settlers from the United States. Thompson, "Imperial Republic."

18. As quoted in ibid., 12.

19. For comprehensive studies of these Supreme Court cases, see James Edward Kerr, *The Insular Cases: The Role of the Judiciary in American Expansionism* (Port Washington, N.Y.: Kennikat Press, 1982), and Efrén Rivera, "The Legal Construction of American Colonialism: The Insular Cases (1901–1922)," *Revista Jurídica Universidad de Puerto Rico* 65 (1996): 225–328. For contemporary discussions, see John W. Burgess, "The Decisions of the Supreme Court in the Insular Cases," *Political Science Quarterly* 16 (1901); Abbot Lowell, "The Status of Our New Possessions," *Harvard Law Review* 13 (1899): 155–76; Magoon, *Report of the Legal Status of the Territory and Inhabitants.*

20. "An Act Temporarily to Provide for the Administration of the Affairs of Civil Government in the Philippine Islands," *U.S. Statutes at Large*, 32. Puerto Rico, although an unincorporated territory, was economically integrated into the United States: see Thompson, "Imperial Republic," 20–21, and Julian Go's chapter in this volume.

21. As quoted in Kerr, *Insular Cases*, 3.

22. Willoughby, *Territories and Dependencies*, 7.

23. Ibid., 7–8.

24. On such precedents and continuities, see Gail Bederman, *Manliness and Civilization: A Cultural History of Gender and Race in the United States, 1880–1917* (Chicago: University of Chicago Press, 1995); Roger Bresnahan, " 'Our Little Proteges': Models of American Colonial Rule," *Philippine Social Science and Humanities Review* 43 (1979): 161–71; Matthew Frye Jacobson, *Barbarian Virtues: The United States Encounters Foreign Peoples at Home and Abroad* (New York: Hill and Wang, 2000); Richard Slotkin, *Gunfighter Nation: The Myth of the Frontier in Twentieth-Century America* (New York: Atheneum, 1992); Walter Williams, "United States Indian Policy and the Debate over Philippine Annexation: Implications for the Origins of American Imperialism," *Journal of American History* 66 (1980): 810–31.

25. Although the legal notion of unincorporation versus incorporation has its roots in Western expansion on the North American continent, the application to overseas colonial dependencies such as the Philippines was entirely novel. See Thompson, "Imperial Republic," 11–13.

26. For an overview of U.S. Indian policy, along with its financial issues, see William T. Hagan, "United States Indian Policies, 1860–1900," in *History of Indian–White Relations*, ed. Wilcomb E. Washburn (Washington, D.C.: Smithsonian Institution, 1988), 51–65. On internal revenue as one of the crucial foundations for statehood, see Young, *African Colonial State*, 38. For problems of taxation in the Philippines, see Julian Go's chapter in this volume.

27. See, for example, the report of David Barrows in *Annual Report of the Secretary of War for the Fiscal Year Ended June 30, 1902: Report of the Philippine Commission*, 57th Cong., 2d Sess., House of Representatives (1903), House Doc. 2, vol. 10, pt. 1. The administrators in the Philippines saw Indian policy as better serving as a precedent for the so-called uncivilized tribes of the highlands and Moro populations in the southern parts of the archipelago, but even then, the matter concerned not simple transposition of policy but re-evaluation of and innovation in policy. For preliminary insights into this, see Donna J. Amoroso's chapter in this volume; Thompson, "Imperial Republic"; and Peter G. Gowing, "Moros and Indians: Commonalities of Purpose, Policy and Practice in American Government of Two Hostile Subject Peoples," *Philippine Quarterly of Culture and Society* 8 (1980): 125–49.

28. Unfortunately, a full analysis of the legal changes in the Philippines has yet to be done, but for a preliminary comparative analysis, see Katharine Bjork, "When Empires Change Hands: Transformations in Law in Puerto Rico, the Philippines and Cuba under U.S. Colonial Rule," paper presented at the World History Association Meetings, Boston, 22–25 June 2000.

29. Colin Gordon, "Governmental Rationality: An Introduction," in *The Foucualt Effect: Studies in Governmentality*, ed. Graham Burchell, Colin Gordon, and Peter Miller (Chicago: University of Chicago Press, 1991), 2.

30. For a conceptualization of colonial projects that seeks to integrate ideal-discursive and practical streams of action, see Nicholas Thomas, *Colonialism's Culture: Anthropology, Travel, Government* (Princeton, N.J.: Princeton University Press, 1994), 105–7.

31. See, for example, the pieces in *Annals of the American Academy of Political and Social Science* 14 (January–May 1902).

32. Horace Fisher, *Principles of Colonial Government Adapted to the Present Needs of Cuba and Porto Rico, and of the Philippines* (Boston: L. C. Page, 1899); Alleyne Ireland, *The Far Eastern Tropics* (Boston: Houghton Mifflin, 1905); Bernard Moses, "Control of Dependencies Inhabited by the Less Developed Races," *University of California Chronicle* 7 (1905): 3–18; Alpheus Snow, *The Administration of Dependencies: A Study of the Evolution of the Federal Empire, with Special Reference to American Colonial Problems* (New York: G. P. Putnam's Sons, 1902); Willoughby, *Territories and Dependencies.*

33. Albert J. Beveridge, "The Annual Address: The Development of a Colonial Policy for the United States," *Annals of the American Academy of Political and Social Science* 30 (1907): 3; President McKinley's instructions to the Philippine Commission, reprinted in Cameron W. Forbes, *The Philippine Islands*, 2 vols. (Boston: Houghton Mifflin, 1928), 2:436–45.

34. United States Insular Commission, *Report to the Secretary of War on Investigations into the Civil Affairs of Puerto Rico* (Washington, D.C.: Government Printing Office, 1899), 24.

35. William H. Taft, *Special Report of Wm. H. Taft Secretary of War to the President on the Philippines* (Washington, D.C.: Government Printing Office, 1908), 7. Discourse of exceptionalism persists to this day. Stanley Karnow, an American journalist, rehashed the exceptionalist narrative in his book on U.S.–Philippine relations, *In Our Image* (New York: Ballantine Books, 1989). That book was awarded a Pulitzer Prize. A trenchant critique of the exceptionalist thesis in Karnow's work, although different from the one proposed in this volume, can be found in Michael Salman, "In Our Orientalist Imagination: Historiography and the Culture of Colonialism in the United States," *Radical History Review* 50 (1991): 221–32.

36. Brian Linn, "The White Man's Burden: The U.S. Military in the Philippines, 1898–

1902," in *1898: Enfoques y perspectivas. Simposio internacional de historiadores en torno al 1898*, ed. Luis E. González Vales (San Juan: First Book Publishing, 1997), 115.

37. Peter Stanley, ed., *Reappraising an Empire: New Perspectives on Philippine–American History* (Cambridge, Mass.: Harvard University Press, 1984), 7. For representatives of this literature, see the essays in Norman G. Owen, ed., *Compadre Colonialism: Studies in the Philippines under American Rule*, Michigan Papers on South and Southeast Asia, no. 3 (Ann Arbor, Mich., 1971); Ruby R. Paredes, ed., *Philippine Colonial Democracy*, Southeast Asia Studies Monograph Series, no. 32 (New Haven, Conn.: Yale Southeast Asian Studies Center, 1988); Stanley, *Reappraising an Empire*.

38. Glenn A. May, *Social Engineering in the Philippines* (Westport, Conn.: Greenwood Press, 1980), 183.

39. Ruby R. Paredes, "Introduction: The Paradox of Philippine Colonial Democracy," in Paredes, *Philippine Colonial Democracy*, 8. On the theory of collaboration, see Ronald Robinson's influential essay, "Non-European Foundations of European Imperialism: Sketch for a Theory of Collaboration," in *Studies in the Theory of Imperialism*, ed. Roger Owen and Bob Sutcliffe (London: Longman Group, 1972), 117–40.

40. Paredes, "Introduction: The Paradox of Philippine Colonial Democracy," 6.

41. Benedict Anderson, "Cacique Democracy in the Philippines," in *Discrepant Histories: Translocal Essays on Filipino Cultures*, ed. Vicente L. Rafael (Philadelphia: Temple University Press, 1995), 3–47. See also the essays in Alfred W. McCoy, ed., *An Anarchy of Families: State and Family in the Philippines* (Madison: University of Wisconsin Press, 1993).

42. Vicente Rafael, "White Love: Surveillance and Nationalist Resistance in the U.S. Colonization of the Philippines," in Kaplan and Pease, *Cultures of United States Imperialism*, 195. A related approach to photography during the early years of U.S. colonial rule is found in Benito M. Vergara Jr., *Displaying Filipinos: Photography and Colonialism in Early 20th Century Philippines* (Quezon City: University of the Philippines Press, 1995).

43. Reynaldo Ileto, "Cholera and the Origins of the American Sanitary Order in the Philippines," in *Imperial Medicine and Indigenous Societies*, ed. David Arnold (Manchester: Manchester University Press, 1988), 125–48.

44. Warwick Anderson, " 'Where Every Prospect Pleases and Only Man Is Vile': Laboratory Medicine as Colonial Discourse," in *Discrepant Histories*, ed. Vicente L. Rafael, 84. See also Warwick Anderson, "Excremental Colonialism: Public Health and the Poetics of Pollution," *Critical Inquiry* 21 (1995): 640–69.

45. Reynaldo C. Ileto, *Payson and Revolution: Popular Movements in the Philippines* (Quezon City: Ateneo de Manila University Press, 1979); idem, "Orators and the Crowd: Philippine Independence Politics, 1910–1914," in Stanley, *Reappraising an Empire*, 85–113.

46. Rafael, "White Love," 204–15.

47. In this sense, the literature matches Berman and Lonsdale's distinction between colonial-state building and colonial-state formation. The former refers to "a conscious effort at creating an apparatus of control," while the latter refers to a "historical process whose outcome is a largely unconscious and contradictory process of conflicts, negotiations and compromises": Berman and Lonsdale, *Unhappy Valley*, 5.

48. For critical issues in the conceptualization of *global* and *local*, see Arif Dirlick, "The

Global in the Local," in *Global/Local: Cultural Production and the Transnational Imaginary*, ed. Rob Wilson and Wimal Dissanayake (Durham, N.C.: Duke University Press, 1996), 21–45. See also Mike Featherstone, "Localism, Globalism, and Cultural Identity," in Wilson and Dissanayake, *Global/Local*, 46–77. Our use of the term *global* is pitched at a more basic level than these and other highly theorized approaches.

49. Terry Boswell, "Colonial Empires and the Capitalist World-Economy: A Time Series Analysis of Colonization, 1640–1960," *American Sociological Review* 54 (1989): 186; Fieldhouse, *Colonial Empires*, 178.

50. Fieldhouse, *Colonial Empires*, 373.

51. Michael Adas, ed., *Islamic and European Expansion: The Forging of a Global Order* (Philadelphia: Temple University Press, 1993), 311.

52. Giovanni Arrighi, *The Long Twentieth Century* (London: Verso, 1994). For a world-systems analysis explaining the timing of this wave of colonization, see Boswell, "Colonial Empires." For a review of the literature on U.S. trade relations within this world system in the late nineteenth century, see Joseph A. Fry, "From Open Door to World Systems: Economic Interpretations of Late Nineteenth Century American Foreign Relations," *Pacific Historical Review* 65 (1996): 277–303.

53. Young, *African Colonial State*, 73–74.

54. Thomas, *Colonialism's Culture*, 66–104; Young, *African Colonial State*, 74.

55. Young, *African Colonial State*, 74.

56. Frederick John Dealty Lugard, *The Dual Mandate in British Tropical Africa* (London: Frank Cass, 1965).

57. The literature on "indirect rule" is massive, but an informative analysis of indirect rule and its effects in Africa can be found in Mahmood Mamdani, *Citizen and Subject: Contemporary Africa and the Legacy of Late Colonialism* (Princeton, N.J.: Princeton University Press, 1996). On the civilizing mission in France, see Alice L. Conklin, *A Mission to Civilize: The Republican Idea of Empire in France and West Africa, 1895–1930* (Stanford, Calif.: Stanford University Press, 1998), and Martin Deming Lewis, "One Hundred Million Frenchmen: The 'Assimilation Theory in French Colonial Policy,'" *Comparative Studies in Society and History* 4 (1962): 129–53. A brief historical overview of the formulation of these two modes of rule is found in Fieldhouse, *Colonial Empires*, chaps. 12–13. On the dangers of valorizing the distinction between indirect and direct rule, see Berman and Lonsdale, *Unhappy Valley*, 160–61.

58. For an analysis of administrative ethnography in British Tanganyika, see Peter Pels, "The Pidginization of Luguru Politics: Administrative Ethnography and the Paradoxes of Indirect Rule," *American Ethnologist* 23 (1996): 738–61. For a Foucauldian-informed study of state surveillance and sanitation in British Fiji, see Nicholas Thomas, "Sanitation and Seeing: The Creation of State Power in Early Colonial Fiji," *Comparative Studies in Society and History* 32 (1990): 149–70.

59. See, for instance, the study of the relationship among emerging anthropology, notions of culture, and colonial endeavors in Talal Asad, ed., *Anthropology and the Colonial Encounter* (London: Ithaca Press, 1973). For a historical periodization of colonial governmental tactics derived from Foucault's theory of governmentality, see David Scott, "Colonial Governmentality," *Social Text* 43 (1995): 191–220.

60. Mitchell, *Colonizing Egypt,* suggests the exportation of modern disciplinary modes to Egypt, while Paul Rabinow, *French Modern: Norms and Forms of the Social Environment* (Cambridge, Mass.: MIT Press, 1989), examines colonial architecture.

61. Fieldhouse, *Colonial Empires,* 299; Vincent, "Sovereignty, Legitimacy, and Power," 149–51.

62. Myron Echenberg, *Colonial Conscripts: The Tirailleurs Sénégalais in French West Africa, 1857–1960* (Portsmouth, N.H.: Heinemann, 1991); John D. Kelly, " 'Coolie' as a Labour Commodity: Race, Sex, and European Dignity in Colonial Fiji," *Journal of Peasant Studies* 19 (1992): 246–67.

63. Raymond F. Betts, *The False Dawn: European Imperialism in the Nineteenth Century* (Minneapolis: University of Minnesota Press, 1975), 227.

64. Young, *African Colonial State,* 149–53; Frederick Cooper and Ann Laura Stoler, "Between Metropole and Colony," in Cooper and Stoler, *Tensions of Empire,* 28.

65. Fieldhouse, *Colonial Empires,* 378; Gerrit W. Gong, *The Standard of "Civilization" in International Society* (Oxford: Clarendon Press, 1984).

66. Cooper and Stoler, "Between Metropole and Colony," 28, 32; Michael Adas, " 'High Imperialism' and the 'New' History," in Adas, *Islamic and European Expansion,* 323–25.

67. Betts, *False Dawn,* 10–11, chap. 3. Seminal theoretical works on empire and world expositions include Tony Bennett, "The Exhibitionary Complex," *New Formations* 4 (1988), and Timothy Mitchell, "The World as Exhibition," *Comparative Studies in Society and History* 31 (1989): 217–36. For the U.S. empire and expositions, see Robert W. Rydell, *All the World's a Fair: Visions of Empire at American International Expositions, 1876–1916* (Chicago: University of Chicago Press, 1984).

68. U.S. Treasury Department Bureau of Statistics, *Colonial Administration, 1800–1900* (Washington, D.C.: Government Printing Office, 1903).

69. On Ireland, see Franklin Chew Lun Ng, "Governance of American Empire: American Colonial Administration and Attitudes, 1898–1917" (Ph.D. thesis, Department of History, University of Chicago, 1975).

70. Forbes, *Philippine Islands.* See also Moses, "Control of Dependencies," for a related comparative discussion by a colonial administrator.

71. Vincent's typically overlooked piece on the colonial state, "Sovereignty, Legitimacy, and Power," is most indicative.

72. Cooper and Stoler, "Between Metropole and Colony," 29–33, intimates this approach.

73. One study that can be seen as an exception is Theodore Friend's fascinating analysis of how the Filipinos were embroiled in conflicts between the United States and Japan in the late period of U.S. colonial rule. See Theodore Friend, *Between Two Empires: The Ordeal of the Philippines, 1926–1946* (New Haven, Conn.: Yale University Press, 1965). Of course, the lack of comparative studies in the literature on the Philippines makes perfect sense, considering the highly influential and much needed focus on local histories—for example, Glenn May, *Battle for Batangas: A Philippine Province at War* (New Haven, Conn.: Yale University Press, 1991); Alfred McCoy and Ed. C. de Jesus, eds., *Philippine Social History: Global Trade and Local Transformations* (Quezon City: Ateneo de Manila University Press, 1982). These studies demand painstaking research in provincial archives. A global perspective would not be antithetical to such research; rather, it would be complementary and supplementary.

74. For critiques of American historiography's relative lack of comparative and transnational studies, see Raymond Grew, "The Comparative Weakness of American History," *Journal of Interdisciplinary History* 16 (1985): 87–101; and Ian Tyrrell, "American Exceptionalism in an Age of International History," *American Historical Review* 96 (October 1991): 1031–55. Tyrrell's essay is especially informative for the way in which it seeks to transcend exceptionalist historiography through transnational study, not merely comparative study; the latter still runs the risk of being nation-centric. The essay can be faulted, though, for paying scant attention to U.S. empire, despite its "transnational" agenda.

75. Daniel Rodgers, "Exceptionalism," in *Imagined Histories: American Historians Interpret the Past*, ed. Anthony Molho and Gordon S. Wood (Princeton, N.J.: Princeton University Press, 1998), 29.

76. Darby's *Three Faces of Imperialism* suffers from the very same elision: Phillip Darby, *Three Faces of Imperialism: British and American Approaches to Asia and Africa, 1870–1970* (New Haven, Conn.: Yale University Press, 1987).

77. Conklin, *Mission to Civilize.*

78. See, for example, the essays in Paredes, *Philippine Colonial Democracy*, and Stanley, *Reappraising an Empire.*

79. Studies of European colonial rule in Africa have been especially fruitful in detailing variations in collaborative patterns. See Mamdani, *Citizen and Subject*, and Berman and Lonsdale, *Unhappy Valley.*

80. I borrow the term *ideological baggage* from Comaroff and Comaroff, *Of Revelation and Revolution.*

81. In this sense, Barclay's analysis converges with Go's, as both implicitly offer qualifications of crude versions of Marxist theories of the colonial state wherein the colonial state always appears beholden to the interests of domestic capital.

82. It would be informative to read Boudreau's findings alongside Ileto's work on elite politics. Ileto suggests that Filipino elite nationalism had two sides: on one side, a nationalism that was congenial to the Americans' colonial project, and on the other, a nationalism articulated to and through the peasantry. The latter was more radical than the former. Boudreau's analysis can be read as explaining why these two nationalisms were separated in elite practice. See Ileto, "Orators and the Crowd."

83. Kaplan, "Left Alone with America."

PAUL A. KRAMER

Empires, Exceptions, and Anglo-

Saxons: Race and Rule between the

British and U.S. Empires, 1880–1910

Setting out to address *The Problem of Asia and Its Effect upon International Policies* in 1900, the year of the joint expedition against the Boxers
and one year into the Philippine–American War, the American navalist
Alfred Thayer Mahan observed that "it would be an interesting study . . .
to trace the genesis and evolution in the American people of the impulse
towards expansion which has recently taken so decisive a stride." That
study, he warned, "would be very imperfect if it failed clearly to recognize . . . that it is but one phase of a sentiment that has swept over the
whole civilized European world within the last few decades."[1] Other
builders of the U.S. empire would have agreed. Along different time
lines, pursuing varied agendas, and mobilizing diverse discourses to
defend them, Americans from varied political backgrounds came to
recognize that the United States' new colonial empire—part of its much
vaster commercial, territorial, and military empires—operated within a
larger network of imperial thought and practice.

The factors that encouraged the overlap of empires were similar to
those linking together the contemporary "Atlantic crossings" of welfare-
state ideas and institutions recently described by Daniel T. Rodgers.
Foremost was the growing productive and geographic scale of industrial
capitalism in the Atlantic world and its imperial outposts. Intensifying
transportation technologies did not simply make possible the aggressive
military expansion of European and U.S. power in the late nineteenth
and early twentieth centuries. They also made the consolidating colonial
regimes in Africa and Asia stages for interacting and overlapping em-

pires of commerce and evangelism, which drew "inter-imperial" communities together around both common and competitive projects.[2] But even within the formal limits of imperial state building, colonial empires penetrated one another. Despite multiple pressures that forced empires apart conceptually, inter-imperial crossings played a central role in state building throughout the colonial world. In organization, policymaking, and legitimation, the architects of colonial rule often turned to rival powers as allies, foils, mirrors, models, and exceptions.[3]

Whereas many U.S. empire builders would have endorsed Mahan's anti-exceptionalism, most of that empire's historians have not. To be sure, there is enough that is truly different—if not exceptional—in the history of the United States to warrant contrasts between the U.S. empire and the British, French, Dutch, and German empires of the late nineteenth and early twentieth centuries. First and foremost, there was the first U.S. empire, the long and contested incorporation of continental territory based on settlement colonialism. There was the commercial–industrial dominion that began with that first empire and, on its resources, projected itself as an informal empire of capital and goods throughout the world, especially in Europe, Latin America, the Pacific Islands, and East Asia. In land, population, and trade—if not in military and strategic terms—the U.S. overseas colonial empire would remain small, an annex to the informal empire.[4]

* * *

But actual differences between the U.S. and European colonial empires do not explain the complete denial of U.S. colonialism in American culture or Americans' understanding of the United States not only as a non-empire, but as an anti-empire.[5] Those actual differences inspired exceptionalist enthusiasms that were virtually absolute, erasing what the empires had in common, including the exchanges in which they engaged.[6]

Some of the erasures are byproducts of the structure of historiography. Emerging from diplomatic history, the historiography of the U.S. empire has been notably state-centered and nation-bounded, its inter-imperial history exploring the interactions between bounded states but not the ideas and practices they circulated, borrowed, and shared.[7] New historiographies have added methodological breadth, especially toward social and cultural history, and widened the range of actors recognized as engaged in U.S. "foreign relations." Recent works have done much to bring empire toward the center of U.S. history, providing rich and novel accounts of U.S. imperialism.[8] But most nevertheless remain locked in metropole–colony dyads that neglect inter-imperial dynamics and connections. Ironically, while the emerging study of U.S. colonialism draws on theoretical insights developed in the critical study of other empires—notably postcolonial theory and history—the field has not yet explored the interconnections among empires.[9]

This essay is an effort to chart one of the most significant inter-colonial connections: the complex invocations of the British Empire and of racial "Anglo-Saxonism" in the effort to legitimate U.S. colonialism during and after 1898. It takes as its focus debates regarding the Philippines—their annexation, conquest, and administration—partly because the British exerted influence in the Philippines and the surrounding region and partly because the Philippine annexation sparked debates over U.S. colonialism in which the British Empire was most commonly invoked. The first section argues that "Anglo-Saxon" racism developed as a self-conscious bond connecting Britons and Americans in the late nineteenth century, forged on their violent imperial frontiers and solidifying at points of elite Anglo-American social and intellectual contact. During and after 1898, American and British advocates of U.S. overseas colonialism enlisted Anglo-Saxonism as a racial-exceptionalist argument, leveled against claims of national exceptionalism. The second section explores the tensions within, and challenges to, Anglo-Saxonist racial exceptionalism emerging in the United States among national-exceptionalist "anti-imperialist" critics of the Philippine-American war, who opposed acquisition of overseas colonies but not all other forms of empire. Those tensions were exposed most sharply during the Anglo-Boer War, when many Americans came to identify with the enemies of their would-be Anglo-Saxon racial kin. The third section discusses the decline of the Anglo-Saxonist argument for colonialism and the triumph of a national-exceptionalist colonialism more suited to changing geopolitics, the increasing "racial" diversity of the United States, and the political realities of the postwar Philippines. It also describes the simultaneous development of inter-colonial policy dialogues that ran counter to the national-exceptionalist discourse.[10]

This story is only part of the broader story of Anglo-American connections, along with rapprochement, geopolitical rivalry, economic nationalism, wartime alliances, and decolonization. Aspects of this essay, for example, were well explored by Stuart Anderson in *Race and Rapprochement* (1981), which foregrounds the role of Anglo-Saxonist racial ideology in organizing Anglo-American diplomatic and military cooperation at the turn of the century. Anderson's goal was to revisit diplomatic-historical questions with the tools of intellectual and cultural history, to show that ideas such as Anglo-Saxonism mattered in American geopolitics.[11]

This essay draws on the literature of Anglo-American connections but approaches its themes from two different angles. First, it centers on the problem of empire rather than that of rapprochement and looks at how Anglo-Saxonism legitimated U.S. overseas colonialism rather than how it consolidated Anglo-American ties. The enlistment of race in turn-of-the-century Anglo-American geopolitics, I argue, involved not only recognizing racial identity and fashioning diplomatic cooperation from it but also debating the boundaries and characteristics of racial identities in relation to empire.

Second, this essay revisits the role of racial ideology in the history of U.S. foreign policy with an eye to its historical dynamism, contextual dependence, political contingency, and internal tensions. In traditional accounts of race and rapprochement, for example, racial systems such as Anglo-Saxonism are stable, coherent, and consensual tools of foreign policy. This essay, by contrast, explores tensions within Anglo-Saxonist ideology and its dynamic construction and reconstruction in light of specifically colonial politics. If race mattered for empire, empire also mattered for race. Although empire is often represented as a mere outlet for metropolitan racial tensions, a screen onto which prior, homegrown racial anxieties are projected, a well-defined crucible in which domestic racial identities are forged, none of those representations can fully account for the imperial dynamics of race making. This essay argues that both U.S. debates over empire and forces at work in colonial settings had a decisive impact on American racial ideology itself. More broadly, it argues that histories of U.S. race making, like histories of the United States in general, belong in a transnational frame from which they have long been isolated.[12]

RACE, PATRIOTISM, AND EMPIRE

"England has suddenly become a guiding star to many of the American people," the anti-imperialist J. W. Martin noted with dismay in 1900.

"Conquest, extension of territory, subjugation of semi-barbarous peoples, establishment of a Roman peace—all these have been common in the British experience. But to the United States they are fresh problems, perplexing and irritating, and already bringing battles in their train." The British Empire was not the only European empire that Americans imagined in seeking their place in the world in the late nineteenth century. Its predominance in American thinking was determined both by common language and deep and long-standing social and intellectual connections and by the vast, world-spanning scope of British commercial, naval, and colonial power. An empire with the sun perpetually over its shoulder could cast a long shadow across the imperial borders of its rivals. Even the architects of empires with a far longer history of anti-British antagonism and far fewer ties of language and culture to Britain than the U.S. empire had (such as the Spanish) set out in pursuit of the secrets of British imperial might.[13]

But American enthusiasm for the British Empire often took a racial, Anglo-Saxon form that lent the weight of racial history and destiny to the controversial U.S. annexation of the Philippines. Anglo-Saxonism was, of course, far from the only type of racism to develop in the context of empire building. For the liberal English parliamentarian and political observer James Bryce, the aggressive, competitive racisms of the fin de siècle were themselves the product of geopolitical rivalries. Bryce wrote about "the race consciousness which the rivalry of other great races has produced, that . . . pride in the occupation and development of the earth's surface which has grown with the keener competition of recent years." Others similarly identified dynamic, reciprocal connections between race making and empire. John Fleming had noted in 1891 that Anglo-Saxonism was merely the self-serving attempt by Great Britain to guarantee its hold on a fabricated "cousin" of increasing international power. "In proportion as the North American republic grows powerful and overshadowing," he wrote, "grows the anxiety of Englishmen to have it understood that this potent factor in the world's affairs is what they term Anglo-Saxon . . . in race, feeling, and literature."[14]

Anglo-Saxonism would reach the height of its explanatory power in foreign-policy arenas in the years immediately after 1898, when it helped to cement an Anglo-American accord and provide a historical and political rationale for a U.S. overseas colonial empire in the Philippines and the Caribbean Sea. The Anglo-Saxonist defense of U.S. overseas colonialism emerged from both England and the United States. Sir Edward Grey, the Liberal Party politician and future secretary of state for foreign affairs, confirmed Bryce's connections between empire building and race making when he hailed the Spanish–Cuban–American War: "the struggle in which the United States is engaged must be one to stir up our blood, and makes unconscious of the ties of language, origin, and race." With the aid of British Anglo-Saxonists such as Grey, American colonialists folded the controversial annexations into deep structures of history and destiny. "The entry of our country upon what appears to be a new policy of foreign conquest and colonization," wrote Frederick Chapman, "must evidently impart a doubled impetus to that active extension of Anglo-Saxon civilization for which the mother country alone has been in modern times so conspicuous."[15]

As a discourse, Anglo-Saxonism was an echoing cavern of banalities out of which even a well-lit historian might never emerge. By the late nineteenth century, it was a racism built against a multitude of opponents on innumerable violent frontiers. British Anglo-Saxons had contended with Normans, colonized Celts, enslaved Africans, conquered Indians, and challenged Latins for world dominance. American Anglo-Saxons had defended African slavery, conquered Native Americans, confronted Latin empires, wrenched land away from Mexicans, and struggled to fend off waves of immigrants. Having begun as a British defense of the superiority of the Anglican church and having early confronted Catholic "others"—the "Celtic" race in Ireland and the "Latin" in Spain—Anglo-Saxonism was closely allied to Protestantism and was often said to share its virtues.[16]

Anglo-Saxonism was a nested or branching racism: Anglo-Saxons were frequently depicted as having split off from older racial groups, usually "Teutons"; Teutons themselves were sometimes traced back to a still larger and more ancient group of "Aryans." Anglo-Saxonism was also directional, its historical development moving in space. Its rise in England was identified as only one stage in a relentless Western movement that had begun in India, had stretched into the German forests, and was playing itself out in the United States and in the British Empire's settlement colonies. While Anglo-Saxonism hailed ancient Aryan ancestors, its rhetorical age was youthful and vigorous; while women could claim its virtues, its gender was often distinctly masculine, tied to tasks of struggle and conquest. While used as a shorthand for racial purity,

Anglo-Saxonism featured a contained hybridity. No other late-nineteenth-century racism wore so prominent a hyphen. Anglo-Saxonism represented the alloy of superior but distinct racial elements. Although it was sharply delimited, that hybridity—and the theoretical possibility of future assimilations—lent porousness to Anglo-Saxonism's boundaries in race, culture, and destiny.

But if, as Alexander Saxton observed, racism is a theory of history, it is also a theory of politics.[17] Anglo-Saxons were said to be the possessors and progenitors of unique, "free" political values and institutions. At their most inward-looking, Anglo-Saxons were a consistently liberated people, although the sources of oppression that had bound them varied; when they looked outward, Anglo-Saxons often liberated others. Throughout much of its history, Anglo-Saxon freedom radiated from racial diaspora itself: Only Anglo-Saxon bodies could carry the germs of liberty across space and time. But especially from the mid-nineteenth century onward—with the Mexican War and the mid-century British imperial crises in India and Jamaica—Anglo-Saxons were also described in a language of order, force, and power. Uniquely adept at extending and sustaining vast empires, they efficiently exploited the lands they overtook, inevitably extirpated the weaker races with whom they came into contact, or administered them with stern but evenhanded law. Even here, however, the language of liberty flourished, with lands freed from neglect, trade emancipated from tariff barriers, and conquered peoples liberated from ignorance and savagery. Wherever and however they conquered, Anglo-Saxons were racially destined to spread empires of liberty.

Much of Anglo-Saxonism resonated powerfully with American republican, destinarian nationalism. Like Anglo-Saxons, Americans had a special mission in the world to transform and redeem other nations, especially through the example of their republican institutions. American destiny, like Anglo-Saxon history, was unfolding westward in space. Those defined as outside the sacred realm of Anglo-Saxon dominion or American republican virtue were equally subject to just war. Anglo-Saxonism and U.S. nationalism were congruent enough that, in mid-nineteenth-century discussions of the white conquest of Native Americans and Mexicans, Anglo-Saxons were proclaimed the racial embodiments and shock troops of American Manifest Destiny. But there were tensions here. If Anglo-Saxons carried freedom with them and imposed it on others, it was not necessarily American republican freedom. And how special and separate could the American mission be if Anglo-Saxonism connected it backward in racial time to Britain, to Germany's forests, and ultimately to Aryan ancestors? Anglo-Saxon racial exceptionalism and U.S. national exceptionalism might lend each other rhetorical momentum, but they could rarely be identical.[18]

There was also division on whether Anglo-Saxonism was a matter of blood or of culture. Anglo-Saxons had always been known by their language, laws, religion, and institutions. Some Americans and Britons (including Theodore Roosevelt) referred to the "English-speaking peoples" rather than the "Anglo-Saxon race." Emphasis on culture or language did not negate race; linguistic racialism had a long history, and the traits of the English-speaking people were often seen as expressed by and traveling with Anglo-Saxon blood. But some authors sought to separate blood and culture and to redefine Anglo-Saxonism by the latter.[19] The immediate impulse behind such disembodiment of Anglo-Saxonism was to preserve its viability in an Anglo-American world being transformed by immigration. Frederick Chapman noted that the racial diversification of Anglo-Saxonism was a byproduct of British imperialism itself. "The accelerating extension of the British empire beyond the seas to all quarters of the globe, over its continents and islands, its civilizations old and wilds newly broken to human habitation, its varied populations,—Aryan, Semitic, Mongolian, white, brown, black—has had its undoubted reflex action upon the ethnic character of the conquerors."

This "shifting and interchange of population" had been "facilitated by modern methods of conveyance . . . toward the seat of empire, from whence the streams of conquest have gone forth, tend ever-returning currents, representative of all its outlying tributaries." As increasingly wide-ranging groups were brought under Anglo-Saxon dominion, "the term 'Anglo-Saxon' practically ceases to be a race designation. . . . It stands rather for a civilization; for ideals and institutions, originating indeed with a certain ethnic type of mankind, but no longer its exclusive property." Chapman had met people "bearing unquestionably English names and English (using the term in its broadest sense) in their language, their ideas, ideals and general mental culture" whose "swarthy complexion, raven hair, deep dark irides and general aquilinity of physiognomy" suggested "Italian, Levantine or Oriental blood." Such people illustrated how cultural Anglo-Saxonism had become. "Any rational being brought up under the dominance of these ideals and identified therewith," he wrote, "whatever his ancestral life currents,—Teutonic, Celtic, Semitic, Mongolian, Malay or African—is an Anglo-Saxon."[20]

As Anglo-Saxonism was becoming less embodied, assertive immigrants were gradually and partially "de-Saxonizing" U.S. nationalism. In 1891, John Fleming noted that Anglo-Saxonism was "an idea received with enthusiasm by some here in America, with indifference by others, but by a large section of our people with dislike, because it is false and because it is offensive." He cited the Irish, who were forced to "tacitly admit the Anglo-Saxon to be something like a proprietor of these United States and representative of a race aristocracy." He wrote, "What about the descendants of Frenchmen, of Germans, of Slavs, and of Scandinavians, who do not admit Anglo-Saxon superiority? When, overpowered by his emotions, the average Fourth-of-July orator eulogizes the Anglo-Saxon, he does not pause to consider that the Celts and Germans among his audience may inquire of one another if there is any room on this continent for them." Such a speaker might be indulging in the vanity that his entire audience was "allied in blood to the Anglo-Saxon on the other side of the Atlantic who rules so mighty an empire," or "he may imagine that every white man is an Anglo-Saxon." Either way, Americans should reject Anglo-Saxonism and instead "be content with our Caucasian origin and American citizenship," affirming "a type developing itself which is destined to pass into the future as essentially American, as different from Celtic as from Latin, as different from Anglo-Saxon as from either." But as early as 1891, the imperial destiny of that American type was clear. The American, rather than the Anglo-Saxon, would "so spread . . . as to render impossible a Cossack or Chinese destruction of the world's civilization."[21]

Despite such challenges, the virtues attributed to racial Anglo-Saxonism—extraordinary purity and continuity, raging outward movement, and transformative power over land and people—made it a persuasive form of racial exceptionalism. Analytically, it cut deeply across the boundaries of national politics, pride, and history, calling forth visions of a heroic racial diaspora that snaked through the borders of states and broke fearlessly through frontiers. Its chief British ethnographer, whose work set the template for later accounts in both Britain and the United States, was the parliamentarian Charles Dilke, who in 1866–1867 made a racial grand tour through "English-speaking or . . . English-governed lands," a territory Dilke called "Greater Britain." The trip centered on the United States, Australia, and India. To his great satisfaction, Dilke found that, although "climate, soil, manners of life, that mixture with other people had modified the blood, . . . in essentials the race was always one." Even in the United States, where "the peoples of the world are being fused together," they were being "run into an English mould." Indeed, the United States was a kind of British megaphone. "Through America," he wrote famously, "England is speaking to the world."[22]

One of the most articulate racial exceptionalists on the other side of the Atlantic Ocean was the historian Theodore Roosevelt who, in his best Dilkean style, began his 1889 epic, *The Winning of the West*, with a chapter titled "The Spread of the English-Speaking Peoples." For Roosevelt, the spread of the "English-speaking race" across "the world's waste spaces" over the previous three centuries was "the most striking feature in the world's history." That race, into which he easily folded Americans, was unique among many dimensions in a world of clashing races. There was the sheer scope of its diaspora. Many other races "had their great periods of race expansion—as distinguished from mere conquest," he wrote, "but there has never been another whose expansion has been either so broad or so rapid." Furthermore, the race had not blended its racial stock with that of the conquered. Most European countries, he wrote, "derive portions of their governmental system and general policy from one race, most of their blood from another, and their language, law, and culture from a third." The "English race, on the contrary, has a perfectly continuous history," taking "neither creed nor custom, neither law nor speech, from their beaten foes." That purity had relevance for the "average English, American, or Australian of to-day who wishes to recall the feats of power with which his race should be credited in the shadowy dawn of its history." Having introduced its racial protagonists, the book set them in motion. "In obedience to the instincts working half blindly within their breasts," Roosevelt wrote, "they made in the wilderness homes for their children, and by so doing wrought out the destinies of a continental nation."[23]

For some Britons, this vision of the Anglo-Saxon colonization of North America held important lessons for imperial Britain itself. Facing external and internal threats—from continental rivalries to working-class revolt and colonial nationalist movements—British imperialists in the late nineteenth century sought to give the empire greater efficiency, coherence, and stability. Many called for a federation in which the white settlement colonies would receive tariff protection and broader self-government in exchange for continued loyalty and colonial troops for Britain's imperial wars. Federation schemes and societies proliferated in the 1880s and 1890s on both sides of the Atlantic; one of the most influential plans was that of Sir John Seeley at Oxford University, who in his 1882 book, *The Expansion of England*, articulated what he, following Dilke, called "Greater Britain." For Seeley, the problem was how to unify the far-flung "English-speaking" settlement colonies, "how to give moral unity to vast countries separated from each other by half the globe, even when they are inhabited in the main by one nation." Telegraphs and steamships would help, but Seeley also called for the abandonment of non-white colonies and greater centralization of what remained, making Greater Britain less an empire than "a vast English nation." In search of an exemplary "English nation" on which to remodel the empire, Seeley turned confidently to North America. "Instead of comparing [Greater Britain] to that which it resembles in no degree, some Turkish or Persian congeries of nations forced together by a conquering horde," Seeley wrote, "let us compare it to the United States." The United States, he observed, had sent migrants out beyond existing settlements, colonized territory with them, and consolidated a racially homogeneous state. (Neither sectionalism nor the Civil War applied much brake to his enthusiasm.) The American past might be the British future. Once Britons learned to "contemplate the whole Empire together and call it England," he wrote, "we shall see that here too is a United States . . . a great homogeneous people, one in blood, language, religion and laws, but dispersed over a boundless space."[24]

The similarity of the accounts of Dilke, Seeley, and Roosevelt suggests the density of Anglo-American connections in the late nineteenth century. Indeed, the success of Anglo-Saxonism as a racial-exceptionalist bridge between the United States and the British Empire was due in part to the social, familial, intellectual, and literary networks that tied elite Americans and Britons together. Such complex and long-standing exchanges widened and deepened as accelerating travel and communication enabled greater contacts between the British and American upper classes; middle-class tourists; business, professional, and academic elites; and abolitionist, temperance, civil-service, and Progressive reformers.[25] Anglo-American dialogue and Anglo-Saxonist racism were also given life by a publishing revolution in the 1890s. Many of Anglo-Saxonism's chief literary exponents published through transatlantic houses with joint centers in New York and London. Genteel Anglo-American literary-political magazines—*Atlantic Monthly, North American Review, Scribner's, Century Magazine, Fortnightly Review, Nineteenth Century*— burdened late-Victorian tabletops on both sides of the Atlantic. The new publishing circuits helped create an "imagined community" of literate, English-speaking Americans and Britons with common affiliations and reference points, even among the less traveled. The title of one short-lived publication, the *Anglo-Saxon Review*, suggests the role of journals in establishing self-consciously racist solidarities.[26]

*   *   *

Anglo-Saxonism was also employed to describe proliferating strategic marriages between American and British elites, often between American heiresses and British diplomats, military officers, or imperial officials. Through the unions and their offspring, a language of Anglo-Saxon blood and cultural "kinship" crystallized around actual genealogy. One editor foresaw "a day when a considerable proportion of the head men in England will be the sons of American mothers." Anglo-American alliance itself was frequently figured as a harmonious marriage. The Wall Street lawyer and writer John R. Dos Passos (father of the novelist) stated in his 1903 book, *The Anglo-Saxon Century and the Unification of the English-Speaking People*, that an alliance between England and the United States would be "as natural as marriage between man and woman" because it "consummates the purposes of the creation of the race." The British journalist W. T. Stead asked, "What would be the net effect upon India if America and Britain amalgamated their forces, and bore the White Man's burden in Asia between them?" Without an actual imperial alliance to examine, Stead turned to the marriage of Mary Leiter, a Chicago heiress, to George Nathaniel Curzon, who would go on to become viceroy of India. The union suggested promising joint imperial ventures: "It may be that in the marriage which made a Chicago girl Vice-Empress of India we see a foreshadowing of things to come, when Britain and America, happily united in the permanent ties of a race alliance, may pool their resources and devote their united energies to the work of the ameliora-tion of the lot of the impoverished myriads of Asia."[27]

But if Anglo-Saxonism was sparked and recognized at moments of

Atlantic Anglo-American convergence, it was reinforced by the more and more frequent rendezvous between Americans and Britons in the colonial world. As late-nineteenth-century American merchants, missionaries, tourists, naval officers, and writers widened their geographic reach, they found themselves on imperial pathways already charted and inhabited by the English. It was unsurprising that Anglo-Saxons came to recognize one another where their empires coincided and cooperated. Take Anglo-Saxonism's chief origin myth, frequently recounted in clubs and social gatherings on both sides of the Atlantic in the late nineteenth century. In 1858, an American naval vessel under Commodore Josiah Tattnall, traveling the Pei-ho River near Peking, encountered a British ship under Chinese attack. As the New York editor Whitelaw Reid told the story in a toast to Queen Victoria at her 1897 Diamond Jubilee in London, on seeing the English sailors "entrapped and slaughtered on an Asiatic sea," Tattnall had "without any possible warrant rushed to the rescue with the sole excuse: 'I can't stand that; blood is thicker than water!' " This latter phrase—Dilke expressed in liquids—was resonant enough to become a central metaphor of racial nationalism, leaving its specific Anglo-American origins in obscurity.[28]

Anglo-American imperial contacts often took the shape of inter-imperial subcontracting, as American actors directed the colossal industrial force of the United States toward British colonial projects. On the one hand, this was inter-imperial competition, with U.S. companies beating out British ones for imperial state contracts. But on the other, it fostered intensive contacts between Americans and Britons throughout the colonial world. Bridge building between Americans and the British Empire became literal in 1898 when the Pennsylvania Steel Company received a contract from the Indian government for the construction of a 2,260-foot-long railway viaduct across the Gokteik Gorge in the Shan Hills of Burma, apparently the longest such construction in the world, "about as high as the towers of the new Brooklyn Bridge." For the editors of the *World's Work*, the bridge signified a new era of U.S. industrial power and Anglo-American cooperation: "Ten years ago an American bridge in India would have seemed an impossibility; today the globe-trotter can stand on the rocks at the bottom of the Gokteik Gorge and see the Mandalay-Kunlon train shoot by eight hundred and twenty feet above him, drawn by an American locomotive across an American bridge."[29]

Anglo-American solidarity still had to meet the tests of economic interest and imperial protectionism. In the Gokteik case, the American company had won the contract by underbidding British competitors on both time and cost, "much to the chagrin of their rivals, whose patriotism rallied vociferously around the flag at this stab through the pocket." Later, at the construction site, the American team was visited by a few subordinate [British] engineers disgruntled at seeing foreigners encroaching on their formerly exclusive ground. But the project allowed American engineers to observe the empire up close from the vantage point of their British partners. The chief engineer on the project, John C. Turk, traveled to the site with his wife via London, Marseilles, and Rangoon, enjoying the "delightful Anglo-Indian hospitality" of the Burma Railways' general manager. En route he noted admiringly that, although the region had been part of the Indian empire for only fifteen years, "the country has already been reduced to systematic order," with collaborating Burmese soldiers "now building better roads than I have ever seen in my native State in New England."[30]

Turk also seems to have embraced British imperial custom as part of a growing Anglo-American solidarity. Arriving at the site with British overseers, Turk watched as indigenous laborers dropped their picks and shovels to genuflect before the party. "At first it gave me a shock of surprise," he noted, but "later I became used to such performances." Turk noted that the government and railway officials who frequently visited "impressed [him] strongly with their splendid training and great ability, their friendliness to our undertaking, and their amicable attitude toward the United States." By the end of 1901, the company boasted of having completed the one entirely American piece of the British imperial edifice: a bridge designed by Americans, all its parts manufactured in Pennsylvania mills by American workmen, shipped to Burma, hauled 150 miles inland to the site by Burmese laborers, and assembled under American overseers. The technological means to an empire in the American West were equally needed in the British East. "It is an intensely dramatic bit of modern business enterprise," said one writer about the Gokteik Gorge viaduct, "typical to the last degree of the true 'American expansion.'"[31]

On other occasions, Americans found themselves a minority community in Britain's informal empire. Take the future U.S. colony in the Philippines, where Americans were the smallest foreign merchant community, declining to just a few dozen in the 1890s. According to Joseph Earle Stevens, representative of the only remaining U.S. hemp firm, "These fair islands are no place for the permanent residence of an American. We seem to be like fish out of water here in the Far East, and as few in numbers. The Englishmen and the Germans are everywhere." Stevens's Philippines was a strikingly British place. Within short shipping, telegraph, and naval distance of some of the British Empire's most important Asian possessions, the Philippines were encircled by Anglo-Saxonism, with roughly 70 percent of their foreign trade in British hands. Economically, by 1898 the British had dominated the Philippines for twenty years, running the islands' three major banks, investing in large-scale infrastructure projects, and commanding export commerce and much internal commerce via Chinese intermediaries. Hong Kong, which Stevens called an "interesting stronghold of Old England in the Far East," was most Americans' gateway to Asia.[32]

Isolated Americans such as Stevens found solace in joining the British merchant community on Anglo-Saxon terms. After a hectic first morning in Manila purchasing white cotton suits, Stevens "was introduced to the members of the English Club and began to feel more at home stretched out in one of the long chairs in the cool library." When space became available, he moved into a guest room there. In the racially exclusive and homosocial hallways of "the little foreign colony of Anglo-Saxons," trade figures, news, and gossip circulated freely, while "small serving boys in bare feet rushed hither and thither with meat and drink." In mid-1898, this node in Britain's informal empire would give way to a formal American one, with curious English clubmen watching the battle between the Spanish and American navies at Cavite from the clubhouse roof.[33]

The Anglo-Saxonism that emerged from points of Anglo-American contact was pressed vigorously into use in the American defense of overseas colonialism during and after 1898. Advocates of overseas colonialism found in Anglo-Saxon racial exceptionalism a formidable argument against national-exceptionalist anti-imperialists. Both the 1898 war and the U.S. annexation of the Philippines could be read as expressions of Anglo-Saxonism: Through England, it seemed, America was speaking to the world.

The Anglo-Saxonist argument for overseas colonialism operated on two principal levels. The first, meant to answer the charge that colonial annexations were contrary to U.S. political traditions, was historical. Anti-imperialists had claimed that overseas colonies would violate and undermine American republican traditions and had distinguished between the annexation of the Philippines and the conquest of the continental West, which for most represented the legitimate unfolding of republican institutions across space and time. Colonialists answered this national-exceptional challenge with a racial-exceptional one, arguing that overseas colonies represented the very essence of Anglo-Saxon politics. "The people of our blood never pause midway in the syllogism of events, but go on to its conclusion," wrote Senator Albert Beveridge of Indiana. "And so in our present and future colonial expansion, we shall only be working out the logic of history."[34]

Connecting Philippine annexation to the "logic of history" meant, in turn, making the process the furthest extension of Anglo-Saxonist westward expansion. In his preface to the 1900 edition of *The Winning of the West*, Theodore Roosevelt attached the controversial Caribbean and Pacific annexations to the long history of continental conquest by the "English-speaking race." "In the year 1898," he began, "the United States finished the work begun over a century before by the backwoodsman, and drove the Spaniard outright from the western world." Roosevelt specifically addressed anti-imperialist critics in connecting the ultimately futile opposition movements sparked by different stages of expansion. Opposition to "expansion" had been "fundamentally the same, whether these wars were campaigns in the old West against the Shawnees and the Miamis, in the new West against the Sioux and the Apaches, or [in] Luzon against the Tagals." Similarly, the Spanish–Cuban–American War and the Philippine–American War had been natural outgrowths of American continental conquest, historically indisputable expressions of Anglo-Saxon power. "At bottom," he wrote, "the question of expansion in 1898 was but a variant of the problem we had to solve at every stage of the great western movement."[35]

The first level of Anglo-Saxonist colonial argument was historical. Its second level was political, relating Anglo-Saxons' peculiar political and moral talents to Philippine annexation. Evidence of Anglo-Saxon virtue was often found in the American conduct of the Spanish–Cuban–American War itself. If the war had technically been won by Americans, had not the victors demonstrated qualities said to characterize Anglo-Saxons? The decisiveness of the land battles and the crushing superiority of the U.S. Navy had demonstrated America's Anglo-Saxon vigor and manhood, particularly when contrasted with the decadent, feminized, Latin, Spanish empire against which so much British Anglo-Saxonism had been forged. The Caribbean campaign scrambled the Anglo-Saxon compass, but the battle of Manila Bay had given the war a decisive, westerly orientation. The war had also been waged in the name of liberty, which Anglo-Saxons were known to spread. All those features—manly vigor, a westward thrust, crusading battles for liberty—would also be made to characterize the Philippine–American War to come.

But often Anglo-Saxonist political claims were aimed beyond war toward successful colonial-state building. Political Anglo-Saxonism explained how the United States might successfully construct a functioning overseas colonial state without any prior history in doing so and might avoid exporting its weak, inefficient, and corruptible state of courts and parties. Here again the British Empire was rhetorically invoked, its impressive organizational capacities infused into the United States by racial blood. "The sovereign tendencies of our race are organization and government," wrote Beveridge. "We organize by instinct. Under the flag of England our race builds an empire out of the ends of the earth. In Australia it is to-day erecting a nation out of fragments. In America it wove out of segregated settlements that complex and wonderful organization called the American Republic." The Spanish had lost their colonies because they were, as Beveridge put it, "no longer a successful administrative race as the English are, or the Germans, or as the American people are coming to be," citing, in the latter case, the "amazing and honest managements of some of our mighty corporations." A vote against annexation, he thundered from the Senate, would deny "that ours is the blood of government; ours the heart of dominion; ours the brain and genius of administration." Beveridge offered those who raised a constitutional protest against colonialism a racial substructure for American institutions. "Let them study the history, purposes and instincts of our race," he wrote, "and then read again the Constitution, which is but an expression of the development of that race."[36]

American colonialist voices gained legitimacy from their resonance with the ringing racial endorsements of many prominent British interlocutors, arguably the primary arbiters of Anglo-Saxon standing. British diplomatic support for the United States against Spain had forestalled continental European engagement and provided the most immediate political grounds for Anglo-Saxon enthusiasm by prominent Britons. In a widely reported 13 May 1898 address at Birmingham, Colonial Secretary Joseph Chamberlain explicitly defended U.S. actions in the Caribbean and employed Anglo-Saxonist terms to call for an Anglo-American alliance. "Our first duty is to draw all parts of the empire into close unity," he stated, "and our next to maintain the bonds of permanent unity with our kinsmen across the Atlantic." The United States was a "powerful and generous nation, speaking our language, bred of our race, and having interests identical with ours." Chamberlain's speech and other Anglo-Saxonist salutations from England were broadly and favorably received in the United States. The *Chicago Tribune* interpreted the speech as a signal that "the two great branches of the Anglo-Saxon race are drawing nearer and nearer together for cooperation in peace, and, in logical sequence, in war as well." By July, parallel Anglo-American Leagues made up of British and American political, business, civic, and religious leaders had formed in London and New York to exchange greetings and vague hopes for, as the American league put it, "an intimate and enduring friendship between these kindred peoples."[37]

The Anglo-Saxon defense of U.S. imperialism culminated in imaginings of a joint Anglo-American empire, especially directed against the "Slavic" threat of Russian expansion in Asia. This meant surrendering English and U.S. nationalism for a deeper "patriotism of race" that cut across them. Such dreams had been indulged in as early as the midnineteenth century, but in the wake of the Spanish–Cuban–American War, "race patriots" on both sides of the Atlantic argued that the United States and Britain should learn the lessons of Dilke's, Seeley's, and Roosevelt's settlers and turn races into imaginary countries. "Let us pool the resources of the Empire and the Republic," proposed Stead, "and regard them with all their fleets, armies, and industrial resources as a political, or, if you like, an Imperial unit." Some Anglo-Saxonists mapped their Anglo-American race patriotism as a maritime rather than a territorial empire. The Social Gospel leader Josiah Strong, who had been beating the drum for Anglo-Saxonism since the 1880s, read in the U.S. rush into the Pacific and annexation of the Philippines divine providence and the fulfillment of an Anglo-Saxon duty to the world at large. "To abandon them," he wrote, "would be treason to ourselves, to the Anglo-Saxon race, to humanity, and to Western civilization." As Strong observed, four out of the six "Anglo-Saxon families—the United States, Canada, Australia, and New Zealand—rimmed the Pacific Ocean," while "scattered over its broad surface at strategic points are many hundreds of islands under the British or American flag." Here, indeed, was an "Anglo-Saxon Sea," destined in the twentieth century to be "the center of the world's population and the seat of its power."[38]

BETWEEN BOER AND BRITON

The success of Anglo-Saxon racial exceptionalism as a conceptual frame encompassing the British and U.S. empires was vividly illustrated by the seemingly unlikely entanglement of the Anglo-Boer War and the Philippine-American War. Ironically, what the newly connected Anglo-Saxon imperial powers had most in common by 1899 was colonial revolt. To be sure, the two conflicts differed wildly in their structures and causes. The former was a defense of English mining interests and an attempt to anchor the southern end of an emerging British African empire. The latter was the first territorial push of a long-growing commercial Pacific empire and an outgrowth of the Spanish–Cuban–American War and the first Philippine revolution.[39]

Yet in testament to the emerging inter-imperial dialogue, numerous commentators on both sides of each conflict turned simultaneity into identity, observing between the two, in the words of an October 1899 *London Times* report, "a curious resemblance." Hugh Clifford, the former official British resident of Pahang in Malaya, observed that, "unless the Filipinos are convinced, as the Boers are now convinced, that the idol of Independence is never to be set up in their midst, no finality can be hoped for in those troubled islands." In a justificatory essay entitled "The Transvaal and the Philippines," Mahan claimed that the British Empire and the United States had the right to remove the territories in question from inhabitants equally "incapable of statehood." "The annexation of the Boer republics was a measure forced upon Great Britain," he wrote elsewhere, "as the annexation of the Philippines has been upon ourselves." Mahan assured a friend that "a short experience of the comforts of peace and good government," along with "vivid recollection of the miseries of being ever on the run," would make "both Boers and Filipinos careful about quarreling."[40]

For some, the wars were comparable enough to be traded literally and imaginatively. On the literal end, the British lieutenant G. J. Younghusband, sent from Singapore to the Philippines to report on conditions during the Philippine–American War, met a U.S. Army private who revealed privately that he was in fact English, an Oxford University man who, after fighting in South Africa, had "pocketed [his] nationality," traveled to New York as a ship's cook, and eventually enlisted in a Montana infantry unit to fight in the Philippines. More figuratively, an American editor noted that "we have listened to impromptu debate . . . as to how the English would have managed the Philippine problem had it been theirs, and how we Americans would have managed the Boer War had it been ours." Speculating on this interchange of "responsibility," he concluded that each imperial power would have handled the other's colonial uprising with greater finesse: After initial defeats, the American military might have pushed back the Boers, although the United States probably would not have gone to war with the Boers in the first place. The British would have won the hypothetical Anglo-Philippine War, not by force, but by prowess. The editor claimed to have overheard an American say:

> The Philippines? Why if the English had had our contract, the place by this time would have been a little Egypt. There wouldn't be any war at all. Just a beautiful, holy peace. Aguinaldo would be Governor of Something-or-Other, with a K.C.B. after his name. All the rest of his gang would have offices and good salaries, and it would look as though they were running everything in sight; while . . . if you looked into the thing you'd see that England owned the whole bag of tricks.[41]

In the wartime Philippines, Americans and Britons compared the two wars. News from South Africa was easily had there. During the fighting, both the pro-American *Manila Times* and the pro-Filipino *La Independencia* published regular war news from South Africa, the American paper nearly always above war reports from the Philippine archipelago itself. As a result, trading wars may have become something of an Anglo-American conversational pastime. In his memoir of the Philippine–American War, Captain Jacob Isselhard, an American officer, noted that the tendency to "make comparisons of the relative qualities of their countries and people, between Americans and Englishmen," was "proverbial." Isselhard (himself of Dutch ancestry) had overheard a dialogue "typical of its kind" on the island of Cebu between a "Lieut. D" in the U.S. Signal Corps who was supervising the construction of a telephone line and "Mr. W.," a "typical Englishman" and manager of a highland plantation. "W. being one of the few white men encountered in that region," Isselhard recalled, "and furthermore, speaking the same language, it was an easy matter to strike an acquaintance, or better to say, the most natural thing for humans to do under such conditions." W. noted that "if England had been warring with the Filipinos for two years" as the Americans had, "the insurrection in the Islands would have been completely quelled." D. rejoined "somewhat sarcastically, 'I suppose it is due to this inferred superiority of your English soldiers that 200,000 of them have been fighting a handful of Boers for months without getting as much as the first kopje; or whatever they call their hills over there.'"[42]

But even as many were comparing, fusing, and trading the U.S. and British colonial empires, a vocal anti-imperialist movement arose to combat U.S. colonial annexation. Opponents of U.S. colonialism, some of whom organized the Anti-Imperialist League, were drawn from diverse and otherwise conflicting political factions, from New England Mugwumps to Southern white supremacists. Their arguments ranged from the fear of domestic corruption through imperial tyranny to terror at the racial implications of colonial immigration to, in far fewer cases, a sense that Filipinos had the right and capacity to govern themselves. What nearly all shared was a commitment to U.S. national exceptionalism. Their name itself—"anti-imperialist"—was a declaration of virtuous distance from a homogenized imperial Europe. In diplomatic terms, they argued, by acquiring colonies the United States would become involved in European power politics; in historical terms, it would become more like Europe, surrendering its republican mission.[43]

Among the ideological weapons in the arsenal of anti-imperial national exceptionalism, few were more venerable than anglophobia. The fear of British imperial tyranny was older than the United States and still audible at any Fourth of July address in the late nineteenth century. American suspicion of England rose and fell with the issues to which it was attached. In the 1890s, diplomatic tensions supplied some of the driest tinder, as U.S. military and economic ambitions ranged over the Caribbean and the U.S. Navy struck up against British spheres of influence. The Venezuela boundary dispute of 1895–1896 had raised American anglophobia to fever pitch, almost to war. By the late nineteenth century, the United States also had growing immigrant constituencies that were willing and able to drive wedges between the United States and Britain, especially among the Irish—many of them fiercely anti-British—and Germans, whose suspicions of Britain were extensions of geopolitical rivalry.[44]

For the anti-imperialists, therefore, the invocation of British methods to condemn American imperial actions proved irresistible.[45] The most common strategy was to draw unfavorable analogies between U.S. imperialism and the abuses of the late-eighteenth-century British Empire that had sparked the American Revolution. The United States, in this telling, had been born as—and ought to remain—the British Empire's essential opposite. But American fears of British imperialism also drew on more recent history. Rudyard Kipling, after attending a Fourth of July banquet in San Francisco in 1889, noted sardonically that the after-dinner speakers "hurled defiance at 'our natural enemy' (England, so please you!) 'with her chain of fortresses across the world.'" The American anglophile George Herbert Adams decried Americans' "belief in the domineering and monopolizing character of England's policy everywhere in the world." Senator Augustus Bacon of Georgia, an anti-imperialist, while noting proudly that "all the blood that I have in me comes from English ancestry," had grown up with a vision of the British Empire as unspeakably cruel and violent. "I was a school-boy at the time [of the Sepoy revolt]," he recalled,

> and I shall never forget the impression made upon me in looking at the pictorial newspapers, *Harper's Weekly* I recollect particularly, with the pictures of these boys bound to the mouths of cannon and blown to pieces. And, if we are to maintain dominion over these millions of people in the Philippine Islands, nothing but the strong hand, nothing but cruelty, nothing but the iron rule will enable us to maintain that dominion. I do not want any such transactions under the American flag.[46]

Like Bacon, other critics of U.S. overseas colonialism on both sides of the Atlantic made concerted efforts to peel apart Anglo-Saxon racial solidarity and colonial empire, themes that their opponents had successfully fused. Critics such as James Bryce and Carl Schurz took advantage of the cultural Anglo-Saxonism described earlier, holding up the superiority of Anglo-Saxon institutions even as they cautioned against war and colonialism as racial imperatives and as the only methods for extending them. Common geopolitical interests, including imperial projects, they maintained, did not flow directly from shared Anglo-Saxon blood or cultural heritage. Schurz acknowledged Anglo-American kinship in "language, literature, and principles of government" but believed Anglo-Saxonists "touch[ed] doubtful ground" in their invocation of "common interests in many parts of the world." Might not the Anglo-Saxon mission of the United States be separate from Britain's? "We are in the habit of speaking of the Americans and the English as two branches of the Anglo-Saxon stock," he wrote. "But . . . , it does not follow that . . . they have exactly the same kind of work to do in and for the world; that in order to fulfill her duty, the American republic must imitate the example of England."[47]

Most forcefully, anti-imperialists identified America's work in providential, republican terms: In radical distinction to the British, Americans had been chosen to spread republican institutions across the globe. Acquiring overseas colonies meant tumbling into a corrupt world from which the United States had heretofore removed itself. In an 1899 address, "America's Mission," William Jennings Bryan acknowledged the momentum of racial-exceptionalist argument in defense of colonialism even as he sought to assert the national-exceptionalist virtues of anti-imperialism. "Much has been said of late about Anglo-Saxon civilization," he stated. Bryan did not wish "to detract from the service rendered to the world by the sturdy race whose language we speak," but he employed Anglo-Saxonism's contained hybridity and nested structure to depict the United States as a fusion of great civilizations, only one of them Anglo-Saxon:

> The union of the Angle and the Saxon formed a new and valuable type, but the process of race evolution was not completed when the Angle and the Saxon met. A still later type has appeared which is superior to any which has existed heretofore; and with this new type will come a higher civilization than any which has preceded it. Great has been the Greek, the Latin, the Slav, the Celt, the Teuton and the Anglo-Saxon, but greater than any of these is the American, in whom are blended the virtues of them all.[48]

Against the outward similarities between Anglo-Saxonism and Americanism, Bryan proceeded with a catechism of political contrast, pitting Anglo-Saxon racial exceptionalism against U.S. national exceptionalism.

Anglo-Saxons built colonial empires, while Americans did not. Anglo-Saxonism had "by force of arms, applied the art of government to other races for the benefit of Anglo-Saxons"; Americanism would, "by the influence of example, excite in other races a desire for self-government and a determination to secure it." Anglo-Saxon civilization had "carried its flag to every clime and defended it with forts and garrisons"; American civilization would imprint its flag upon the hearts of all who long for freedom. For Bryan and many other anti-imperialists, Anglo-Saxonism and U.S. republican nationalism were not racial, historical, or political extensions of each other, but complete antitheses.[49]

The sometimes fierce debate over the boundary between Anglo-Saxonism and Americanism and its meaning for overseas colonialism hinged, ironically, on a point of consensus: the legitimacy of the U.S. colonization of the West. The question was whether the new island annexations were extensions of the West or not. While some anti-imperialists included criticisms of the treatment of Indians in their warnings against overseas colonial rule over additional "backward races," for most the conquest of the West represented the peaceful and natural outpouring of "civilization," the pushing back of the frontier of liberty. Some were willing to credit continental conquest to Anglo-Saxon instincts and to reserve criticism for overseas colonialism. But because the racial exceptionalists had used Anglo-Saxonism to identify the United States with the British Empire as a whole—including its crown colonies without large white settlements—anti-imperialists tended to make the West an "American," rather than an explicitly "Anglo-Saxon," accomplishment, something that set the United States apart from Britain. They also identified a sharp discontinuity between continental and overseas colonialism. "Those who advocate the annexation of the Philippines call themselves expansionists but they are really imperialists," wrote Bryan. "The word expansion would describe the acquisition of territory to be populated by homogeneous people and to be carved into states like those now in existence. An empire suggests variety in race and diversity in government."[50]

Tensions between racial and national exceptionalism and between settlement and administrative colonialism became clear in U.S. responses to the Anglo-Boer War. Early in the conflict, many Americans assumed that the United States would support the British imperial cause, not least because of British backing in the Spanish–Cuban–American

War. American interests in South Africa were long-standing, with approximately a thousand Americans among the white non-Boer, or Outlander, population, and American mining engineers—contracting with British interests, as Turk had done in Burma—had been a powerful lobby for a British conquest since the 1880s.[51] American banks and exporters stood to profit from wartime loans and trade with Britain; the Republican Party in power was stocked with influential East Coast Anglo-Americans; and the United States was looking for powerful allies in its own drawn-out imperial war in the Philippines. Throughout the fighting, the McKinley and Roosevelt administrations pursued a policy of formal neutrality that favored British goals in the interest of U.S. investment. U.S. economic interests and geopolitical considerations appeared to line up with the emerging logic of Anglo-Saxon destiny and inter-imperial solidarity.

But in the wake of stunning Boer victories, American opinion began to shift, and pro-Boers were able to seize much of the traditional idiom of American Anglo-Saxonism from the British Empire. The Boers seemed every bit as Anglo-Saxon as Roosevelt's settler colonialists who had conquered North America. They had trekked north (rather than west) in search of liberty from British colonial rule; they had extirpated inferior races they had encountered and manfully challenged the imperial tyrannies that stood in their path. One American journalist's rhapsodic account of the Boers could almost have described the Anglo-Saxon diasporas of Dilke, Seeley, and Roosevelt. "These sturdy colonists went out in the wilds of Africa," he wrote, and began "small political communities which represented everything they desired—freedom, isolation, independence, and a life of rural simplicity." Like the United States' own founders, the Boers had flaunted their "defiance of the British Empire." Britain's initial failures, reliance on massive reinforcements, and a strutting arrogance among its politicians and in its press dredged up volatile American anglophobia. The British were not the exemplars of Anglo-Saxon civilization, it seemed, but "a bully among nations, speaking softly to the powerful and browbeating with intolerable insolence the weak and helpless." Not surprisingly, this also challenged their racial integrity. The Outlanders, for example, were nothing more than "sleek Jews and dapper diamond gamblers."[52]

The Boers' cause found a political home in the U.S. Democratic Party, which became a strange mirror of the Boer campaign. The Boers' struggle against the British drew the party's anglophobic Irish and German immigrants; its Southern and Western agrarian wings were attracted to a hazy vision of Boer yeoman culture, squeezed between bankers and blacks, in which they saw their own fates reflected. Although the war was not a significant issue in the 1900 presidential campaign, state platforms often included pro-Boer planks; Democrats brought Boer envoys to Washington to try to mediate a settlement, although they were snubbed by the Republican administration. Implicit links between American and Boer settler colonialism were made explicit when, after the failed negotiations, some American pro-Boers suggested relocating "these God-fearing, liberty-loving descendants of Old Holland" on unoccupied lands in the South or West. Some Americans even adopted the Boers as racial kin against the grain of Anglo-Saxonism, stating that "they are people of our own stock; they are a small people; their cause is just." In frank admiration for Boer tenacity, Roosevelt noted that, like Americans and the English, they were "Teutons," but one branch further back on the racial family tree.[53]

The tensions between Anglo-Saxonism and Americanism and between settler and administrative colonialism were explored in a 1900 boys' novel by the American writer Edward Stratemeyer titled, *Between Boer and Briton; or, Two Boys' Adventures in South Africa*. The story centers on two young Anglo-Saxon cousins scattered in a Dilkean diaspora: Dave Nelson is the son of a Texas rancher; Will Nelson is the son of a South African Outlander farmer and mine owner. Dave and his father lose their ranch and join their relatives in South Africa. Stratemeyer writes: "Surely, though he was American and they were English, blood was a good deal thicker than water." Arriving at the Pretoria train platform on the eve of the Anglo-Boer War, Dave meets his cousin Will with an embrace, "and in less than five minutes the two cousins felt as though they had known each other for years." When Dave expresses surprise at his South African uncle's use of American rather than English mining equipment, the uncle chuckles: "You know better than that, Dave. . . . Time was when both Americans and Englishmen were very much prejudiced in favor of their own country. But that time is passing away swiftly, and I think that now each great branch of the Anglo-Saxon race thinks a good deal of its brother across the ocean."[54]

Dave and Will's Anglo-Saxon friendship develops on a manly big-game hunting expedition, where they are aided by Roko, the obligatory

"Kafir" servant. But (inevitably) they become dangerously tangled in world events when war erupts and Dave finds himself "between Boer and Briton." Will's blood is stirred by the British call to arms; Dave's, by Boer aspirations for liberty. Tensions subside when the boys are captured by the Boers and thrown into a filthy prison, where they force several Hottentots to stay on the other side of the cell. But once free, the boys again divide in their loyalties. Dave argues that the Boers "are fighting for what they consider their natural right—Liberty. You must remember that we Americans fought for the same thing during the Revolution." Will, by contrast, follows his "blood." "In a person of real backbone blood will always tell," writes Stratemeyer, "and to him England was his country." But in a vaguely sketched surprise finish, blood does not tell. Dave's solidly Anglo-Saxon father is found recovering in a Boer hospital, having fought briefly on the Boer side in an effort to find his son. "The Boers are not as bad as some folks make them out to be," he concludes.[55]

Anglo-Saxon racial exceptionalism had framed the U.S. and British empires so persuasively that their respective colonial wars in the Philippines and South Africa had been compared, fused, and exchanged. But the Anglo-Boer War pitted the Anglo-Saxons' two principal historical tasks—white settlement and colonial administration—directly against each other. For many Americans, the former task trumped racial Anglo-Saxonism. Blood may have been thicker than water, but republicanism was thicker than both, especially when brewed with American anglophobia. That outcome suggested that, although Anglo-Saxonism had served its function in making continental and insular expansion continuous historically and politically, it remained fragile along multiple axes.

REMAKING EXCEPTIONS

Although it was decisive during and immediately after 1898, the racial-exceptionalist argument for U.S. colonialism lost momentum in the first years of the twentieth century, and national-exceptionalist claims became dominant in American colonial discourse. This retreat of Anglo-Saxonism in the Pacific context was finalized by the outcome of the Russo-Japanese War, but also anticipated it. By 1900, one of the most important geopolitical forges of Anglo-Saxonism had been the "Slavic threat" of Russian expansion in eastern Asia. Russian incursions into northern China had been perceived as a fundamental threat to U.S. and British commercial interests, and both Americans and Britons eager to defend the Open Door had proposed Anglo-Saxon military cooperation against the Slavic menace. After 1904–1905, however, that threat imploded with the defeat of the Russians by Japan, which subsequently emerged as the chief imagined obstacle to U.S. interests in Asia. The fact of a British alliance with Japan since 1902, however, made the notion of the Pacific as an "Anglo-Saxon sea" increasingly problematic.[56]

More important, perhaps, was the de-Saxonization of U.S. colonialism, in both the metropole and the Philippine colony. To be sure, Anglo-Saxonism had a long and insidious career ahead in diverse cultural and political arenas in the United States. But by 1900, the constituencies for and stakeholders in U.S. colonialism had become far more diverse than a tight circle of self-conscious Anglo-Americans. Although appeals to Anglo-Saxonism had been employed to connect apparently novel actions to racially justified histories, they were retracted when confronted with increasingly vocal immigrants. One could see glimmers of de-Saxonization even during the exchange of resolutions by the Anglo-American Leagues at the Anglo-Saxonist fever point of 1898. The British league had emphasized that Britons and Americans were "closely allied by blood"; the American league (with several prominent non-Saxons among its officers) de-emphasized blood ties, reciprocating with claims about common language and institutions. Although some immigrants had opposed Anglo-Saxon imperialism on anglophobic grounds, as Matthew Frye Jacobson has shown, at least some immigrant editors supported the Philippine–American War, giving U.S. colonialism a far more diverse, cosmopolitan flavor.[57]

More significant still was the de-Saxonization of colonialism in the Philippines. If immigrants contributed to the debate on colonialism in the United States, they also figured among the soldiers who fought in the Philippines and remained there as adventurers, entrepreneurs, or colonial officials. It seems likely that such immigrants—perhaps especially the Irish—had little investment in an Anglo-Saxon sense of self and mission. Filipinos, who filled the lower ranks of the bureaucracy, had an even smaller stake in Anglo-Saxonism. Although many among the urban ilustrado elites had ties to Britain through trade, travel, and study—either in England itself or in Hong Kong—their own struggles within the American colonial state flew in the face of a racially Anglo-Saxon government.

The racial formation of the colonial bureaucracy traded in a language of childhood, evolution, tutelage, and eventual self-government, but the formal rhetoric of Anglo-Saxonism was notably absent: It was difficult to imagine simultaneously having Sir Edward Grey as an "Anglo-Saxon cousin" and Emilio Aguinaldo as a "little brown brother." The tension between metropolitan and colonial discourses on race and the limited Philippine relevance of Anglo-Saxonism manifested themselves in a ceremony described by Mrs. Campbell Dauncey, a caustic British travel writer. A U.S. senator visiting the Philippines had delivered a speech invoking the contained hybridity of the Anglo-Saxon as an argument against "race-distinction" in the Philippines. Dauncey found the analogy discordant: "An old Senator with a venerable beard was making a long speech [to Filipinos] on the subject of freedom and the folly of race-distinction. In defence of the latter theory, he rather rashly quoted Tennyson, repeating the lines about 'Saxon and Norman and Dane are we,' which could not be applied in the remotest way to either Americans or Filipinos and came out pure gibberish."[58] The turn from Anglo-Saxonism was also influenced by colonial sociology on the spot. Although British merchants remained the dominant economic power in the islands until after World War I, the center of political and social gravity between Britons and Americans shifted after 1898. British merchants and other residents were folded into a rapidly expanding American official, military, and commercial community, some receiving positions in the new colonial state. Colonial Americans quickly organized racially exclusionist social institutions as a bulwark against the ambitious Filipino elite, but Anglo-Saxonism was not their organizing principle. Both the American immigrants and the existing European expatriate community were too diverse. While smaller cities such as Iloilo saw the emergence of such associations as the Anglo-American Society, a more typical racial invention was the awkward novelty "American–European" attached to the segregated Manila Young Men's Christian Association (YMCA) inaugurated in 1909. But the American side of the hyphen was far heavier than it had been in Stevens's Manila. The still powerful British investors would seek licenses, contracts, patronage, and equal tariffs from the American newcomers, and British importers and merchants would jockey with American rivals. Manila's English Club would remain, but it would compete for membership and prestige with the Americans' Army–Navy Club and University Club.[59]

Tensions loosened connections between racial Anglo-Saxonism, Americanism, and overseas colonialism. The breakdown of imperialist racial exceptionalism, however, was triggered by debates over the Philippine colonial service and the Americans' insecure status as an "administrative race." As we have seen, Anglo-Saxons were supposed to have a unique capacity for establishing efficient, orderly, and just governments. That particular political feature was most likely relatively new to Anglo-Saxonism, probably tied to the expansion of the British imperial state and the reform of the civil service in the late nineteenth century. By 1900, the virtues of the British imperial civil service were among the touchstones of elite British manhood and national and imperial identity. It was little surprise, then, that Anglo-Saxons were redefined as the race of bureaucracy.

Although the Americans had demonstrated their Anglo-Saxonism through the conquest of the continent, that status was seriously undermined by the way they governed it. The critique of American democracy was a British intellectual cottage industry by the last decades of the nineteenth century. Even to the United States' sincerest British admirers, such as Bryce, the organization and execution of government, especially in U.S. cities, appeared to be a scandalous failure. As the English writer George Boxall commented in 1902, "The people of America believe in the necessity for the existence of their rings and bosses almost as religiously as the English believe in the necessity for their princes, dukes, and lords." But where political capacity and racial identity were inseparable, this political failing had inevitable racial implications. The attribution of "corruption" to immigrant voters and proposals for disfranchisement were the principal and predictable results. But another was doubt about the racial capacities of "Americans" themselves. Boxall determined that the United States was not so Anglo-Saxon, but was deeply inflected with a "Latin" political mode, its polar opposite. Anglo-Saxons ruled in the name of reason, fairness, and the public good; Latins ruled through passion, intolerance, and private gain. "The American boss appears to me to be the modern representative of the class which founded the Latin aristocracy," he wrote, representing "the Latin spirit among us in its worst form—that of the greedy self-seeker for wealth and power."[60]

The annexation of colonies after 1898 raised the problem of administration with special urgency. For many Americans and Britons, the

"Philippine question" was almost a corollary to debates on American corruption and administration. Would colonies contribute to domestic reform, or would they merely be a new, open, and less supervised field for the sinister entanglement of public and private interest? Annexationists held that colonial-state building, by "reflex action," would lead to reform at home, citing the British example. But many Americans and Britons, even among the defenders of U.S. colonialism, were pessimistic. "If the U.S. were to acquire an empire," Julian Hawthorne had lamented in 1897, "a pack of ward-heelers and other political hucksters and hangers-on would be sent out to administer them, instead of the good blood, honest hearts, and clear brains of the country." Archibald Colquhoun, one of the Philippine regime's most strident British critics, observed in his book-length critique *Greater America* (its title, the author noted, "challenges comparison with a far more important, studied, and weighty work") that the spoils system was "the cornerstone of governmental power in the United States" and prophesied that in the new colonies, "the whole internal government of each dependency, as well as the policy of the federal power toward *it*, will take its color from party conflicts."[61]

In the eyes of many Britons, Americans definitively proved that they were insufficient Anglo-Saxons by their promise of eventual self-government and rapid and extensive employment of Filipinos in the colonial bureaucracy. British criticism of U.S. colonial-state building in the Philippines flooded Anglo-American journals, dialogue, and correspondence. "Englishmen have been very free with advice and criticism about the Filipinos since 1898," complained James LeRoy, secretary of the Philippine Commission, in 1905. Not the least of these was Kipling himself, whose cautionary February 1899 poem, "The White Man's Burden," was addressed and dedicated not to the British Empire, but to the U.S. struggle in the Philippines. Looking back from 1914, the American journalist Carl Crow noted that early "mistakes and failures" in colonial rule had "proved vastly amusing to our English cousins, especially those connected with the British Colonial Service, who offered advice with that patronizing air which the professional reserves for the amateur. Many well-meaning persons kindly pointed out how much better things were being done in Java and the Federated Malay States and other nearby places."[62]

Some Britons mistakenly criticized Americans for insufficiently harsh, hierarchical, or public racism against Filipinos, revealing tin ears for the dark subtleties of American colonial paternalism. Dauncey filled her Philippine travelogue with tirades against the racially leveling rhetoric of the American regime. "I am told that the United States does not pose as either 'white' or 'ruling' in these islands," she remarked, "preferring, instead, to proclaim Equality, which seems a very strange way to treat Malays." Hugh Clifford, eager to lend advice derived from his own colonial service in Malaya, cautioned that "those Englishmen who know the East intimately, and are most anxious to see the Americans succeed in the task which they have undertaken," read of emerging American colonial policy "with great misgivings." Filipinos must, "in common with other brown peoples . . . be ruled by a paternal government for their own good, not led to cherish a vain hope that the power they would only misuse will some day be placed in their hands." Even as he urged the Americans toward reform, Clifford cautioned them that their very Anglo-Saxonism was at stake:

> The Americans have failed conspicuously in a field of activity which their fellow Anglo-Saxons have made their especial province. Are they prepared to accept failure as final? Are they ready to confess to all the world that, in spite of all the fine talk with which they have inundated us during the past decade, they are incapable of doing their share of the white man's work in Asia, and of lifting onto their broad shoulders their proper portion of the white man's heavy burden?[63]

Americans tended to respond against the British Empire, rather than through it. The most significant factor in undermining imperial racial exceptionalism was the consolidation of an American colonial state. American colonialists had invoked the British Empire between 1898 and 1902 in part because they had no colonial state of their own to point to. The glories of the British imperial past and present had to stand in for a hypothetical American colonial future to which it was connected by Anglo-Saxon racial destiny. But after the war, the promotional and informational machinery of the American colonial state made possible arguments based not on Anglo-Saxon empire in the abstract, but on actually existing American colonialism. American civil engineers were busy deepening Manila's harbor; botanists and mineralogists were classifying the islands' exploitable resources; anthropologists were studying the islands' peoples; constabulary patrols were eyeing their neighborhoods. Colonial departments and bureaus advertised their success and rights to expanded appropriations in the annual report of the Philippine Commission, published and distributed annually by the Bureau of Insular Affairs. A new class of American colonial experts stepped forward to engage the press and public.[64]

Those American colonial experts and their metropolitan allies responded to British skeptics with outrage and data. "The whole tribe of British critics gets little patience from me," wrote the colonial educator David Barrows. In short order, they actively displaced the English-language authorities of the pre-1898 era. For example, an 1890 travelogue by John Foreman, a British agent of a machinery company and a long-time Philippine resident, had been the principal English-language account of islands in circulation in 1898. Like Clifford and Dauncey, Foreman had roundly criticized the American regime for its inexperience and naive assumptions about self-government, earning the ire of American colonial officials in the process. Barrows privately attacked Foreman's "intense jealousy of anything that does not conform to the precise British colonial pattern." Barrows's friend and confidant James LeRoy attacked Foreman's book, reissued with a critical preface in 1904, in a review in the *Boston Evening Transcript* entitled, "A Disputed 'Authority.'" The book was "Malicious and Untrustworthy," motivated by pettiness, greed, and economic frustration. "The most reckless critics of the present administration," LeRoy wrote, were British merchants angered at the end of their profiteering. LeRoy did not condemn British critics wholesale; he praised Colquhoun as "a very good spokesman." But, in general, he declared, "one would not go to the English Club of Manila for broad-minded or well-informed views about the Philippine situation." The transition from Joseph Earle Stevens, an American eager for membership in that club just ten years earlier, was complete.[65]

American colonialists answered British authorities in explicitly national-exceptionalist terms. It was the consolidation of a colonial state that made possible such terms, suited less to British sympathizers than to Filipino nationalist and American anti-imperialist oppositions. The standards held up by British critics, it was claimed, simply did not apply to the American colonial Philippines. The United States was attempting something entirely new to human history—not empire but "expansive republicanism"; not colonial rule but "tutelage in self-government"; not oppression but "benevolent assimilation." Reviewing critical British books in 1905, LeRoy wrote that "it is entirely impracticable and undesirable to set up the British colonial civil service as a pattern for the Philippines." William S. Washburn, chairman of the Philippine Civil Service Board, dramatically agreed:

> In their criticisms of American methods in the Orient both Mr. Ireland and Mr. Colquhoun fail to realize that they have no standard by which to judge fairly of the success or the failure of the American system of government in the Philippines, from the fact that never before has there been instituted a scheme of colonial government so beneficent and humanitarian. . . . There is no precedent in history to which they can point as an example.[66]

U.S. colonialists sometimes accommodated Anglo-Saxonism even as they articulated national exceptionalism. Senator Beveridge, for example, nested national within racial exceptionalism, calling the United States "the most merciful of the world's great race of administrators." But a recast providential republicanism often carried the day. It was not so much that Americans had a unique anticolonial mission to the world, as the anti-imperialists had maintained. Rather, Americans had a mission to teach the world how to govern "dependencies" on the basis of unprecedented selflessness, uplift, benevolence, assimilation, and the promise of eventual self-government. British critics noted the tendency toward U.S. national exceptionalism with both bemusement and alarm. Colquhoun wrote that Americans were attempting to bring "good government" and democracy to the Philippines "without following any precedent laid down by other nations." Dauncey charged that "America with this funny little possession of hers is like a mother with her first child . . . and thinks her own bantling something without parallel or precedent."[67]

National-exceptionalist depictions of American colonialism did not, however, prevent Americans from scouring the European colonies of Southeast Asia in search of practical models of colonial-state building. Both Anglo-Saxonism and U.S. national exceptionalism were historical and political abstractions. If they did not know it beforehand, American colonialists soon realized that neither brain knots of Anglo-Saxon imperial expertise nor U.S. republican genius could tell them what Islam was, how high to set the sugar tariff, or how much rubber could be planted on a hectare of Southeast Asian lowland. Soon enough, American colonial officials took their place in a network of imperial policy tours and exchanges with colonial officials from the American Philippines, Dutch

Java and the East Indies, and the British Straits Settlements and Federated Malay States. On such tours, officials discussed regime organization, schooling, public health, plantation agriculture, and opium and vice control, among other immediate problems. Transits of this kind were aided by developments in commercial steamship travel in the region. In 1899, a voyage between Manila and Hong Kong lasted just under three days; one between Singapore and Batavia lasted about two days. By the middle of that year, the British India Steam Navigation Company was advertising in U.S. military newspapers regular circuits between Manila and Calcutta every three weeks that called at Singapore, Peking, and Rangoon on every voyage.[68]

Crossings among Southeast Asian colonies began even before the declared end of the Philippine–American War. The Philippine commissioner Jacob Gould Schurman made an inspection tour of Sandakan in British North Borneo on the U.S.S. *Bennington* just five months into the Philippine–American War. The tour was conducted, according to a Hong Kong newspaper, "with the object of studying the manner in which our Government proceeds in governing so many races." Schurman had been able to interview "three of our commissioners and obtained extremely good and valuable information," and came away "expressing his admiration for the form of government England provided for administering no small territory with so few official personnel." The warm feeling had been mutual, with Schurman leaving behind him "an agreeable impression on the officialdom of the colony."[69]

These exchanges appear to have been densest where questions of science, technology, agriculture, and trade were concerned. In 1900, for example, American botanists in the insular government's new Bureau of Science picked up correspondence and plant-sample exchanges with the British Empire's Royal Botanical Gardens at Kew more or less where their Spanish equivalents had left off. In mid-August 1910, the U.S. consul in Singapore invited Agricultural Secretary A. W. Prautch to display Philippine abaca, maguey, pineapple, and piña and jusi cloth and wood samples at an agricultural exposition in the British colony. On arrival, Prautch was given a tour of the interior, where he observed British colonial systems of production and labor in the colony's rubber and tapioca plantations. The report he filed on his return to the Philippines suggested that both crops could be profitably exploited there.[70]

Such intercolonial exchanges suggest a world of inter-imperial contacts, dialogues, and exchanges that is still largely unexplored by historians. During a crucial period in the metropolitan debate over annexation, Anglo-Saxon racial exceptionalism had been an essential argument for American colonialists and their British supporters, constructing a racial history for U.S. overseas colonialism where no other was available. But Anglo-Saxonism had not been entirely functional to their cause. It was not entirely clear whether Americans were Anglo-Saxons; whether one measured Anglo-Saxonism by blood or culture; whether Anglo-Saxons were inherently empire builders; or whether settler colonialism and administrative state building were equally legitimate Anglo-Saxon missions. Anti-imperialists had forced national-exceptionalist terms into these points of vulnerability, arguing that Americans, even if they were Anglo-Saxons, did not necessarily share Britain's imperial destiny; the special mission of the United States was to serve as a republican and "anti-imperial" beacon to the world. Ironically, perhaps, anti-imperialists lost their battle at the turn of the century but won the rhetorical war, as their national exceptionalism came to dominate representations of U.S. colonialism, especially those generated by the colonial state. In those accounts, Americans were again building an empire of liberty that was both Anglo-Saxon and scarcely an empire at all. Through both racial exceptionalism and its nationalist undermining, the United States remained the empire on which the sun never shone.

NOTES

This essay originally appeared in the *Journal of American History* (spring 2002). Earlier drafts of this paper were presented at the Anthropology Colloquium of Johns Hopkins University in March 1999; the joint Johns Hopkins–University of Maryland Departmental Seminar in April 1999; the Organization of American Historians meeting in April 2000; the Pairing Empires conference at Johns Hopkins University in November 2000; and the Atlantic Seminar at the University of Pittsburgh in December 2000.

I thank Dirk Bönker, Thomas Borstelmann, Antoinette Burton, Kristin Hoganson, Joanne Meyerowitz, Daniel Rodgers, David Roediger, Emily Rosenberg, Dorothy Ross, Wigan Salazar, Ian Tyrrell, and Judith Walkowitz for their careful readings, comments, and support; Susan Armeny for her energetic copyediting; and the anonymous readers at the *Journal of American History* for their helpful criticism. My thanks also to the Newberry Library, the Fulbright program, and the Philippine–American Educational Foundation for travel and research grants that made research for this essay possible. Finally, my thanks go to Julian Go and Anne Foster for their assistance in preparing the essay for this volume. Any errors are my own.

1. Alfred Thayer Mahan, *The Problem of Asia and Its Effect upon International Policy* (Boston: Little, Brown and Co., 1900), 4.

2. Daniel T. Rodgers, *Atlantic Crossings: Social Politics in a Progressive Age* (Cambridge, Mass., 1998). For a framework useful for discussing global integration, see Michael Geyer and Charles Bright, "World History in a Global Age," *American Historical Review* 100 (October 1995): 1034–60.

3. On the need to integrate metropolitan and colonial historiography, in part through analysis of inter-imperial connections, see Ann Laura Stoler and Frederick Cooper, "Between Metropole and Colony: Rethinking a Research Agenda," in *Tensions of Empire: Colonial Cultures in a Bourgeois World*, ed. Ann Laura Stoler and Frederick Cooper (Berkeley: University of California Press, 1997), 1–56.

4. On the informal U.S. empire in the late nineteenth century, see Walter LaFeber, *The New Empire: An Interpretation of American Expansionism, 1860–1898* (Ithaca: Cornell University Press, 1963). For the twentieth century, see Emily Rosenberg, *Spreading the American Dream: American Economic and Cultural Expansion, 1890–1945* (Toronto: Hill and Wang, 1982); and idem, *Financial Missionaries to the World: The Politics and Culture of Dollar Diplomacy, 1900–1930* (Cambridge, Mass.: Harvard University Press, 1999).

5. Amy Kaplan, " 'Left Alone with America': The Absence of Empire in the Study of American Culture," in *Cultures of United States Imperialism*, ed. Amy Kaplan and Donald E. Pease (Durham, N.C.: Duke University Press, 1993), 3–21; Robin Winks, "The American Struggle with 'Imperialism': How Words Frighten," in *The American Identity: Fusion and Fragmentation*, ed. Rob Kroes (Amsterdam: Amerika Instituut, Universiteit van Amsterdam, 1980), 143–77; Louis Perez Jr., *The War of 1898: The United States and Cuba in History and Historiography* (Chapel Hill: University of North Carolina Press, 1998).

6. On the historiography of exceptionalism, see Daniel T. Rodgers, "Exceptionalism," in *Imagined Histories: American Historians Interpret the Past*, ed. Anthony Molho and Gordon S. Wood (Princeton, N.J.: Princeton University Press, 1998), 21–40; George M. Fredrickson, "From Exceptionalism to Variability: Recent Developments in Cross-National Comparative History," *Journal of American History* 82 (September 1995): 587–604; Mary Nolan, "Against Exceptionalisms," *American Historical Review* 102 (June 1997): 769–74; Michael Adas, "From Settler Colony to Global Hegemon: Integrating the Exceptionalist Narrative of the American Experience into World History," *American Historical Review* 106, no. 5 (December 2001): 1692–1720; and Serge Ricard, "The Exceptionalist Syndrome in U.S. Continental and Overseas Expansionism," in *Reflections on American Exceptionalism*, ed. David K. Adams and Cornelis A. van Minnen (Staffordshire: Ryburn Publishing, 1994), 73–82. On the intellectual roots of U.S. national exceptionalism, see Dorothy Ross, *The Origins of American Social Science* (Cambridge: Cambridge University Press, 1991). On the relationship between transnational history and exceptionalism, see Ian R. Tyrrell, "American Exceptionalism in an Age of International History," *American Historical Review* 96 (October 1991): 1031–55; Michael McGerr, "The Price of the 'New Transnational History,' " *American Historical Review* 96 (October 1991): 1056–67; Ian R. Tyrrell, "Ian Tyrell Responds," *American Historical Review* 96 (October 1991): 1068–72; and Robert Gregg, *Inside Out, Outside In: Essays in Comparative History* (New York: St. Martin's Press, 1999), 1–26.

7. On the historiography of U.S. foreign relations in this period, see Edward P. Crapol, "Coming to Terms with Empire: The Historiography of Late Nineteenth-Century American Foreign Relations," *Diplomatic History* 16 (fall 1992): 573–97; and Robert Beisner, *From the Old Diplomacy to the New, 1865–1900* (Arlington Heights, Ill.: Harlan Davidson, 1986).

8. Mary A. Renda, *Taking Haiti: Military Occupation and the Culture of U.S. Imperialism, 1915–1940* (Chapel Hill: University of North Carolina Press, 2001); Eileen Findlay, *Imposing Decency: The Politics of Sexuality and Race in Puerto Rico, 1870–1920* (Durham, N.C.: Duke University Press, 1999); Kristin Hoganson, *Fighting for American Manhood: How Gender Politics Provoked the Spanish–American and Philippine–American Wars* (New Haven, Conn.: Yale University Press, 1998); Vicente L. Rafael, *White Love and Other Events in Filipino History* (Durham, N.C.: Duke University Press, 2000); Gilbert M. Joseph, Catherine C. LeGrand, and Ricardo D. Salvatore, eds., *Close Encounters of Empire: Writing the History of U.S.–Latin American Relations* (Durham, N.C: Duke University Press, 1998); Michael Salman, *The Embarrassment of Slavery: Controversies over Bondage and Nationalism in the American Colonial Philippines* (Berkeley: University of California Press, 2001); Kelvin A. Santiago-Valles, *"Subject People" and Colonial Discourses: Economic Transformation and Social Disorder in Puerto Rico, 1898–1947* (Albany, N.Y.: State University of New York Press, 1994); Laura Wexler, *Tender Violence: Domestic Visions in an Age of U.S. Imperialism* (Chapel Hill: University of North Carolina Press, 2000); Eileen Scully, "Taking the Low Road to Sino-U.S. Relations: 'Open Door' Expansionists and the Two China Markers," *Journal of American History* 82 (June 1995): 62–83; Gervasio Luis Garcia, "I Am the Other: Puerto Rico in the Eyes of North Americans, 1898," *Journal of American History* 87 (June 2000): 39–64.

9. On ways to integrate U.S. history into colonial studies, see the recent *Journal of American History* roundtable "Empires and Intimacies: Lessons from (Post)Colonial Studies," *Journal of American History* 88 (December 2001): 829–87. For inter-imperial histories, see Ian R. Tyrrell, *Woman's World/Woman's Empire: The Woman's Christian Temperance Union in International Perspective, 1880–1930* (Chapel Hill: University of North Carolina Press, 1991); Dirk Bönker, "Admiration, Enmity, and Cooperation: U.S. Navalism and the British and German Empires before the Great War," *Journal of Colonialism and Colonial History* 2 (spring 2001); Catherine Candy, "The Inscrutable Irish–Indian Feminist Management of Anglo-American Hegemony, 1917–1947," *Journal of Colonialism and Colonial History* 2 (spring 2001); and Anne MacPherson, "Colonial Reform, Colonial Hegemony: Gender and Labor in Belize and Puerto Rico, 1932–1945," paper presented at the conference "Pairing Empires: Britain and the United States, 1857–1947," Johns Hopkins University, November 2000 (in the author's possession). For early attempts to situate U.S. imperialism in an international context, see Ernest R. May, *American Imperialism: A Speculative Essay* (New York: Atheneum, 1968), esp. chaps. 6–8; and Robin Winks, "American Imperialism in Comparative Perspective," in *The Comparative Approach to American History*, ed. C. Vann Woodward (New York: Basic Books, 1968), 253–70. For a comparison within the U.S. empire, see Julian Go, "Chains of Empire, Projects of State: Political Education and U.S. Colonial Rule in Puerto Rico and the Philippines," *Comparative Studies in Society and History* 42 (April 2000): 333–62. On

transnational U.S. historiography, see David Thelen, "The Nation and Beyond: Transnational Perspectives on United States History," *Journal of American History* 86 (December 1999): 965–75.

10. For related accounts of Anglo-Saxonism and U.S. imperialism, see Anna Maria Martellone, "In the Name of Anglo-Saxondom, for Empire and for Democracy: The Anglo-American Discourse, 1880–1920," in Adams and van Minnen, *Reflections on American Exceptionalism*, 83–96. See also Thomas F. Gossett, *Race: The History of an Idea in America* (Dallas: Southern Methodist University Press, 1963), 310–38. For an early attempt to describe American perceptions of the British Empire, see Peter Henry King, "The White Man's Burden: British Imperialism and Its Lessons for America as Seen by American Publicists, from the Venezuela Crisis to the Boer War" (Ph.D. diss., University of California, Los Angeles, 1959). On the need to connect the history of the U.S. colonial state in the Philippines with global and inter-imperial history, see Julian Go's chapter in this volume; and Michael Adas, "Improving on the Civilizing Mission? Assumptions of United States Exceptionalism in the Colonisation of the Philippines," *Itinerario* 22, no. 4 (1998): 44–66. On inter-imperial policy exchanges, see Paul A. Kramer, "The World's Work: The Uses of European Colonialism in the American Colonial Philippines," paper presented at the European Southeast Asian Studies Conference, School of Oriental and African Studies, University of London, September 2001 (in the author's possession).

11. On Anglo-American diplomatic rapprochement, see Bradford Perkins, *The Great Rapprochement: England and the United States, 1895–1914* (New York: Atheneum, 1968); R. G. Neale, *Great Britain and United States Expansion, 1898–1900* (East Lansing: Michigan State University Press, 1966); Alexander E. Campbell, *Great Britain and the United States, 1895–1903* (London: Longmans, 1960); Charles S. Campbell Jr., *Anglo-American Understanding, 1898–1903* (Baltimore: Johns Hopkins University Press, 1957); and Richard Heathcote Heindel, *The American Impact on Great Britain, 1898–1914* (Philadelphia: University of Pennsylvania Press, 1940), esp. chaps. 4–5. On economic rivalry and the limits of rapprochement, see Edward P. Crapol, *America for Americans: Economic Nationalism and Anglophobia in the Late Nineteenth Century* (Westport, Conn.: Greenwood Press, 1973); and idem, "From Anglophobia to Fragile Rapprochement: Anglo-American Relations in the Early Twentieth Century," in *Confrontation and Cooperation: Germany and the United States in the Era of World War I, 1900–1924*, ed. Hans-Jürgen Schröder (Providence: Berg Publishers, 1993), 13–32. See also Stuart Anderson, *Race and Rapprochement: Anglo-Saxonism and Anglo-American Relations, 1895–1904* (Rutherford, N.J.: Fairleigh Dickinson University Press, 1981).

12. On racial ideology and the making of U.S. foreign policy, see Michael Hunt, *Ideology and U.S. Foreign Policy* (New Haven, Conn.: Yale University Press, 1987); Hazel M. McFerson, *The Racial Dimensions of American Overseas Colonial Policy* (Westport, Conn.: Greenwood Press, 1997); and Rubin Francis Weston, *Racism in U.S. Imperialism: The Influence of Racial Assumptions on American Foreign Policy, 1893–1946* (Columbia, S.C.: University of South Carolina Press, 1972). On empire, race, and popular culture, see Robert Rydell, *All the World's a Fair: Visions of Empire at American International Expositions, 1876–1916* (Chicago: University of Chicago Press, 1984). On the political dynamism of race, see Michael Omi and Howard Winant, *Racial Formation in the United States from* the 1960s to the 1990s (New York: Routledge, 1994), esp. chaps. 1–5; Thomas C. Holt, "Marking: Race, Race-Making, and the Writing of History," *American Historical Review* 100 (February 1995): 1–20; Barbara J. Fields, "Ideology and Race in American History," in *Region, Race, and Reconstruction: Essays in Honor of C. Vann Woodward*, ed. J. Morgan Kousser and James M. McPherson (New York: Oxford University Press, 1982), 143–78; Ann Laura Stoler, "Racial Histories and Their Regimes of Truth," *Political Power and Social Theory* 11 (1997): 183–206; Virginia R. Dominguez, "Implications: A Commentary on Stoler," *Political Power and Social Theory* 11 (1997): 207–16; David Roediger, "A Response to Stoler," *Political Power and Social Theory* 11 (1997): 217–18; Loïc J. D. Wacquant, "For an Analytic of Racial Domination," *Political Power and Social Theory* 11 (1997): 221–34; Uday Singh Mehta, "The Essential Ambiguities of Race and Racism," *Political Power and Social Theory* 11 (1997): 235–46; and Ann Laura Stoler, "On the Politics of Epistemologies," *Political Power and Social Theory* 11 (1997): 247–55. On the imperial dynamics of race making, see Nicholas Thomas, *Colonialism's Culture: Anthropology, Travel, and Government* (Princeton, N.J.: Princeton University Press, 1994). On the tensions of race within U.S. foreign policy and empire building, see Gerald Home, "Race from Power: U.S. Foreign Policy and the General Crisis of 'White Supremacy,'" *Diplomatic History* 23 (summer 1999): 437–61; Harvey Neptune, "White Lies: Race and Sexuality in Occupied Trinidad," *Journal of Colonialism and Colonial History* 2 (spring 2001); Paul Kramer, "Making Concessions: Race and Empire Revisited at the Philippine Exposition, St. Louis, 1901–5," *Radical History Review* 73 (winter 1999): 74–114. For transnational histories of race, see, for example, Virginia Dominguez, "Exporting U.S. Concepts of Race: Are There Limits to the U.S. Model?" *Social Research* 65 (summer 1998): 369–99; Martha Hodes, "Mutable Racial Identities in the 19th-Century U.S. and British Caribbean," paper presented at "Pairing Empires" conference; Carl Nightingale, "The World Travels of Racial Urbanism (Or, Some New Ways of Asking Whether American Ghettos Are Colonies)," paper presented at "Pairing Empires" conference. See also Paul A. Kramer, *The Blood of Government: Racial Politics in the American Colonial Philippines* (forthcoming).

13. J. W. Martin, *English Lessons on Territorial Expansion* (New York: League for Political Education, 1902), 3; Josep Fradera, "Els principios generales del arte de la colonización segons Joaquin Maldonado Macanaz: Idees victorianes en un context Hispánic" (The general principles of the art of colonization according to Joaquin Maldonado Macanaz: Victorian ideas in a Hispanic context), *Illes Imperis* (Barcelona), no. 3 (spring 2000), 61–86.

14. For James Bryce's statement, see Philip Kennedy, "Race, Strategy, and American Imperialism in the Pacific, 1895–1905," *Duquesne Review* 15, no. 2 (1970): 259. John Fleming, "Are We Anglo-Saxons?" *North American Review* 153 (August 1891): 253.

15. Edward Grey, as quoted in Heindel, *American Impact on Great Britain*, 70; Frederick William Chapman, "The Changed Significance of 'Anglo-Saxon,'" *Education* 20 (February 1900): 364.

16. On the history of Anglo-Saxonism through the mid-nineteenth century, see Reginald Horsman, *Race and Manifest Destiny: The Origins of American Racial Anglo-Saxonism* (Cambridge, Mass.: Harvard University Press, 1981); and J. R. Hall, "Mid-Nineteenth-Century American Anglo-Saxonism: The Question of Language," in *Anglo-Saxonism and* the *Construction of Social Identity*, ed. Allen J. Frantzen and John D. Niles (Gainesville: University of Florida Press, 1997). Anglo-Saxonism was a variant of British and U.S. "whiteness." On American "whiteness," see David R. Roediger, *The Wages of Whiteness: Race and the Making of the American Working Class* (London: Verso, 1991); Matthew Frye Jacobson, *Whiteness of a Different Color: European Immigrants and the Alchemy of Race* (Cambridge, Mass.: Harvard University Press, 1998); Grace Elizabeth Hale, *Making Whiteness: The Culture of Segregation in the South, 1890–1940* (New York: Pantheon Books, 1998); Alexander Saxton, *The Rise and Fall of the White Republic: Class Politics and Mass Culture in Nineteenth-Century America* (London: Verso, 1990); and Noel Ignatiev, *How the Irish Became White* (New York: Routledge, 1995). Anglo-Saxonism was not shaped entirely within Britain and the United States. It was also shaped by its critics, opponents, and rivals elsewhere. See, for example, Alan Pitt, "A Changing Anglo-Saxon Myth: Its Development and Function in French Political Thought, 1860–1914," *French History* 14 (June 2000): 150–73. On British racial ideology, especially regarding slavery, abolition, and colonialism, see Thomas C. Holt, *The Problem of Freedom: Race, Labor, and Politics in Jamaica and Britain, 1832–1938* (Baltimore: Johns Hopkins University Press, 1992); Antoinette Burton, *Burdens of History: British Feminists, Indian Women, and Imperial Culture, 1865–1915* (Chapel Hill: University of North Carolina Press, 1994); Catherine Hall, Keith McClelland, and Jane Rendall, eds., *Defining the Victorian Nation: Class, Race, Gender, and the Reform Act of 1867* (Cambridge: Cambridge University Press, 2000); Shearer West, ed., *The Victorians and Race* (Brookfield, Vt.: Ashgate Publishing Co., 1996); and D. A. Lorimer, *Colour, Class, and the Victorians: English Attitudes to the Negro in the Mid-Nineteenth Century* (Leicester: Leicester University Press, 1978). On the making of British identity in dialogue with imperial "others," see Linda Colley, "British-ness and Otherness: An Argument," *Journal of British Studies* 31 (October 1992): 309–29. On Anglo-Saxonism directed against the Irish in Britain and the United States, see L. P. Curtis Jr., *Anglo-Saxons and Celts: A Study of Anti-Irish Prejudice in Victorian England* (Bridgeport, Conn.: Conference on British Studies at the University of Bridgeport, 1968). On colonial racism and immigration, see R. A. Huttenback, *Racism and Empire: White Settlers and Colored Immigrants in British Self-Governing Colonies, 1830–1910* (Ithaca, N.Y.: Cornell University Press, 1976). On late-nineteenth-century and early-twentieth-century U.S. racial ideologies, see, for example, John Higham, *Strangers in the Land: Patterns of American Nativism, 1860–1925* (New Brunswick, N.J.: Rutgers University Press, 1955); and Matthew Frye Jacobson, *Barbarian Virtues: The United States Encounters Foreign Peoples at Home and Abroad 1876–1917* (New York: Hill and Wang, 2000); Gail Bederman, *Manliness and Civilization: A Cultural History of Gender and Race in the United States, 1880–1917* (Chicago: University of Chicago Press, 1995); George M. Frederickson, *The Black Image in the White Mind: The Debate on Afro-American Character and Destiny, 1817– 1914* (New York: Harper and Row, 1971); Brian Dippie, *The Vanishing Indian: White Attitudes and U.S. Indian Policy* (Middletown, Conn.: Wesleyan University Press, 1982); Ronald T. Takaki, *Iron Cages: Race and Culture in Nineteenth-Century America* (New York: Oxford University Press, 1990); Richard Drinnon, *Facing West: The Metaphysics of Indian-Hating and Empire Building* (Minneapolis: University of Minnesota Press, 1980); Hors-man, *Race and Manifest Destiny*; and Gossett, *Race*.

17. Saxton, *Rise and Fall of the White Republic*, 14.

18. On U.S. millennial nationalism and national exceptionalism, see Ernest Lee Tuveson, *Redeemer Nation: The Idea of America's Millennial Role* (Chicago: University of Chicago Press, 1968). On the intersections of destinarianism and empire, see Anders Stefanson, *Manifest Destiny: American Expansion and the Empire of Right* (New York: Hill and Wang, 1996); Frederick Merk, *Manifest Destiny and Mission in American History: A Reinterpretation* (New York: Knopf, 1963); Horsman, *Race and Manifest Destiny*, chaps. 10–12; Albert K. Weinberg, *Manifest Destiny: A Study of Nationalist Expansion in American History* (Baltimore: Johns Hopkins University Press 1935).

19. See Thomas G. Dyer, *Theodore Roosevelt and the Idea of Race* (Baton Rouge: Louisiana State University Press, 1980); and Frank Ninkovich, "Theodore Roosevelt: Civilization as Ideology," *Diplomatic History* 10 (summer 1986): 221–45. On linguistically oriented Anglo-Saxonism, for example, see C. J. W. Parker, "The Failure of Liberal Racialism: The Racial Ideas of E. A. Freeman," *Historical Journal* 24 (December 1981): 825–46. On Mugwump anti-imperialists as cosmopolitan liberals, see Leslie Butler, "New World, Old Empire: The Response of Anglo-American Liberals to 1890s Imperialism," paper presented at "Pairing Empires" conference.

20. Chapman, "Changed Significance of 'Anglo-Saxon,'" 367–69.

21. On the transformation of "whiteness" under pressure from European immigration in the nineteenth and early twentieth centuries, see Jacobson, *Whiteness of a Different Color*; Fleming, "Are We Anglo-Saxons?" 253–54, 256.

22. Charles Dilke, *Greater Britain: A Record of Travel in English-Speaking Countries* (London: Macmillan, 1869), vii–viii, xvii.

23. Theodore Roosevelt, *The Winning of the West*, vol. 1 (New York: G.P. Putnam's Son, 1900), 3–4, 6–7, 25.

24. On the British imperial federation movement, see Carl Adolf Bodelsen, *Studies in Mid-Victorian Imperialism* (Copenhagen: Gyldendalske boghandel Nordisk forlag, 1924). For the work of the most prominent imperial federationist intellectual other than John Robert Seeley and Charles Dilke, see James Anthony Froude, *Oceana; or, England and Her Colonies* (New York: Scribner's, 1886). John Robert Seeley, *The Expansion of England: Two Courses of Lectures* (Boston: Roberts Brothers, 1883), 62–63, 141, 236. See also Deborah Wormell, *Sir John Seeley and the Uses of History* (Cambridge: Cambridge University Press, 1980); and Raymond F. Betts, "Immense Dimensions: The Impact of the American West on Late Nineteenth-Century European Thought about Expansion," *Western Historical Quarterly* 10, no. 2 (1979): 149–66. On triangulations among British, German, and American historians of imperial frontiers, see Benedikt Stuchtey, "'Westward the Course of Empire Takes Its Way': Imperialism and the Frontier in British and German Historical Writing around 1900," in *British and German Historiography, 1750–1950: Traditions, Perceptions, and Transfers*, ed. Benedikt Stuchtey and Peter Wende (Oxford: Oxford University Press, 2000), 289–334.

25. On Anglo-American political exchanges in the nineteenth century, see Robert Kelley, *The Transatlantic Persuasion: The Liberal-Democratic Mind in the Age of Gladstone* (New York: Alfred A. Knopf, 1969). On Anglo-American liberalism and civil-service reform, see John G. Sproat, *The Best Men: Liberal Reformers in the Gilded Age* (New York: Oxford

University Press, 1968). On Anglo-American Progressive links, see Rodgers, *Atlantic Crossings*; and Kenneth O. Morgan, "The Future at Work: Anglo-American Progressivism, 1890–1917," in *Contrast and Connection: Bicentennial Essays in Anglo-American History*, ed. H. C. Allen and Roger Thompson (Athens, Ohio: Ohio University Press, 1976), 245–71. On the role of travel in U.S. foreign relations, see Christopher Endy, "Travel and World Power: Americans in Europe, 1890–1917," *Diplomatic History* 22 (fall 1998): 565–94. On Theodore Roosevelt's Anglo-American social and intellectual connections, see H. A. Tulloch, "Theodore Roosevelt and His English Correspondents: The Intellectual Roots of the Anglo-American Alliance," *Mid-America* 53, no. 1 (1971): 12–34. See also idem, "Changing British Attitudes toward the United States in the 1880s," *Historical Journal* 20 (December 1977): 825–40.

26. On the "magazine revolution" of the turn of the twentieth century, see Frank Luther Mott, "The Magazine Revolution and Popular Ideas in the Nineties," *Proceedings of the American Antiquarian Society* 64 (April 1954): 195–214. On Anglo-American literary connections through new magazines, see idem, *A History of American Magazines, Vol. 4: 1885–1905* (Cambridge, Mass.: Belknap Press of Harvard University, 1957), 131–34, 225–30. *Anglo-Saxon Review* 1–10 (June 1899–September 1901). Anglo-Saxonism was enough of an intellectual growth industry during the early twentieth century to result in the commission of a Library of Congress bibliography: A. P. C. Griffin, *Select List of References on Anglo-Saxon Interests* (Washington, D.C.: Government Printing Office, 1903). For a similar racialization of post offices and telegraph lines, see Katie-Louise Thomas, "Racial Alliance and Postal Networks in Conan Doyle's 'A Study in Scarlet,'" *Journal of Colonialism and Colonial History* 2 (Spring 2001).

27. "A Futile Resolution," *Harper's Weekly*, 11 May 1895, 433. John Dos Passos, as quoted in Gossett, *Race*, 326. W. T. Stead, *The Americanization of the World, or, the Trend of the Twentieth Century* (New York: H. Markley, 1902), 213.

28. Whitelaw Reid, *Two Speeches at the Queen's Jubilee, London, 1897* (New York: De-Vinne Press, 1897), 9.

29. J. C. Turk, "Building an American Bridge in Burma," *World's Work* 2 (September 1901): 1148. Such technological innovations both justified and enforced imperial power. See Michael Adas, *Machines as the Measure of Men: Science, Technology and Ideologies of Western Dominance* (Ithaca, N.Y.: Cornell University Press, 1989); and Daniel R. Headrick, *The Tools of Empire: Technology and European Imperialism in the Nineteenth Century* (New York: Oxford University Press, 1981).

30. Turk, "Building an American Bridge in Burma," 1148–49, 1152, 1166.

31. Ibid., 1148, 1153, 1166–67.

32. See Rhoda Hackler, "The United States Presence in the Northern Philippines prior to 1898, Part I," *Bulletin of the American Historical Collection* 27 (October–December 1989): 22–49; idem, "The United States Presence in the Northern Philippines prior to 1898, Part II," *Bulletin of the American Historical Collection* 28 (January–March 1990): 49–72; Joseph Earle Stevens, *Yesterdays in the Philippines* (New York: Scribner's, 1898), 219. On the British in the Philippines, see a series of five articles in *Bulletin of the American Historical Collection* by Ifor B. Powell: "The Nineteenth Century and the Years of Transition: The Origins of the Firms" (vol. 9, no. 2 [1981]: 7–25); "The Banks" (vol. 9, no. 3

[1981]: 39–52); "The Brokers" (vol. 10, no. 1 [1982]: 60–81); "Non-Business Britishers: Government Servants" (vol. 10, no. 2 [1982]: 43–59); and "The Social Round" (vol. 10, no. 3 [1982]: 36–62). On Germans in the Philippines, see Wigan Salazar, "German Economic Involvement in the Philippines, 1871–1918" (Ph.D. diss., School of Oriental and African Studies, University of London, 2000). On British, German, and Spanish commercial competition in this period, see Maria Dolores Elizalde Pérez-Grueso, "De Nación a imperio: La expansión de los EEUU por el Pacifico durante la Guerra Hispano–Norteamericana del 1898" (From nation to empire: The U.S. expansion in the Pacific during the Spanish–American War), *Hispania* (Madrid) 57 (May–August 1997): 551–88; idem, "Valor internacional de Filipinas en 1898: La perspectiva norteamericana" (The international value of the Philippines in 1898: The North American perspective), in *La nación soñada: Cuba, Puerto Rico, y Filipinas ante el 98: Actas del congreso internacional celebrada en Aranjuez del 24 al 28 de abril de 1995* (The dreamed nation: Cuba, Puerto Rico, and the Philippines: Proceedings of the international congress convened in Aranjuez, 24–28 April 1995), ed. Consuelo Naranjo Orovio, Miguel Angel Puig-Samper, and Luis Miguel García Mora (Aranjuez: Doce Calles, 1996), 767–84; Wigan Salazar, "British and German Passivity in the Face of Spanish Neo-Mercantilist Resurgence in the Philippines, c. 1883–1898," *Itinerario* 21, no. 2 (1997): 125–53; Stevens, *Yesterdays in the Philippines*, 5, 16.

33. See Angus L. Campbell, *The Manila Club: A Social History of the British in Manila* (Manila: St. Paul's Press, 1993); Joseph Earle Stevens, "Life of Manila," *New York Evening Post*, 21 May 21 1898; Stevens, *Yesterdays in the Philippines*, 16, 20; G. J. Younghusband, *The Philippines and Round About* (New York: Macmillan, 1899), 64. On British reactions to the Philippine revolution, see Nicholas P. Cushner, "British Consular Dispatches and the Philippine Independence Movement, 1872–1901," *Philippine Studies* 16 (July 1968): 501–34.

34. Anti-imperialist arguments were aided by the assumption that whites degenerated in racial, medical, and moral terms in the tropics, where they confronted harsh physical climates and "densely settled" populations. See Warwick Anderson, "Immunities of Empire: Race, Disease, and the New Tropical Medicine, 1900–1920," *Bulletin of the History of Medicine* 70 (spring 1996): 94–118; Albert Beveridge, "The Development of a Colonial Policy for the United States," *Supplement to the Annals of the American Academy of Political and Social Science* (May 1899): 5.

35. Roosevelt, *Winning of the West*, I:vii. See Walter Williams, "United States Indian Policy and the Debate over Philippine Annexation: Implications for the Origins of American Imperialism," *Journal of American History* 66 (March 1980): 810–31.

36. On the transformation of the weak state of courts and parties into an administrative state, see Stephen Skowronek, *Building a New American State: The Expansion of National Administrative Capacities, 1877–1920* (Cambridge: Cambridge University Press, 1982); Albert Beveridge, *For the Greater Republic Not for Imperialism, An Address at Union League of Philadelphia, February 15, 1899* (Philadelphia, 1899), 5, 12; Beveridge, "Development of a Colonial Policy for the United States," 9; Beveridge, as quoted in Weston, *Racism in U.S. Imperialism*, 46.

37. Chamberlain, as quoted in Gossett, *Race*, 324. See Wolfgang Mock, "The Function of

'Race' in Imperialist Ideologies: The Example of Joseph Chamberlain," in *Nationalist and Racialist Movements in Britain and Germany before 1914*, ed. Paul Kennedy and Anthony Nicholls (London: Macmillan, 1981), 190–203; *Chicago Tribune*, as quoted in Mock, "The Function of 'Race,' " 325. For the English petition and its American answer, see Anglo-American Committee, *An American Response to Expressions of English Sympathy* (New York: Anglo-American Committee, 1899).

38. Stead, *Americanization of the World*, 6; Josiah Strong, *Expansion under New World-Conditions* (New York: The Baker and Taylor Company, 1900), 204–5.

39. See Stuart Creighton Miller, *"Benevolent Assimilation": The American Conquest of the Philippines, 1899–1903* (New Haven, Conn.: Yale University Press, 1982); Brian M. Linn, *The Philippine War, 1899–1902* (Lawrence: University of Kansas Press, 2000); Angel Velasco Shaw and Luis Francia, eds., *Vestiges of War: The Philippine–American War and the Aftermath of an Imperial Dream, 1899–1999* (New York: New York University Press, 2000); Paul A. Kramer, "Invincible Ignorance: Knowledge and the Philippine–American War, 1899–1902," paper presented at the Philippine Social Science Council Conference, Quezon City, July 2000.

40. For the *London Times* report, see Heindel, *American Impact on Great Britain*, 89. See Keith Wilson, ed., *The International Impact of the Boer War* (New York: Palgrave, 2001); Hugh Charles Clifford, "The Destiny of the Philippines," *Macmillan's Magazine*, vol. 87 (1902), 154. On Clifford, see Kathryn Tidrick, *Empire and the English Character* (London: J.B. Tauris, 1990), chap. 3; Alfred Thayer Mahan, "The Transvaal and the Philippine Islands," *Independent*, vol. 52 (February 1900), 289–91; Mahan, *Problem of Asia*, 190; Alfred Thayer Mahan to Bouverie F. Clark, 3 May 1901, in *Letters and Papers of Alfred Thayer Mahan, Vol. II: 1890–1901*, ed. Robert Seager II and Doris D. Maguire (Annapolis: Naval Institute Press, 1975), 721–22.

41. Younghusband, *Philippines and Round About*, 115; "British Irony and the Spanish–American War," *Bookman* 11 (March 1900): 10. A tendency to switch the wars appeared in boys' fiction. In Elbridge Streeter Brooks, *With Lawton and Roberts: A Boy's Adventure in the Philippines and the Transvaal* (Boston: Lothrop Publishing Company, 1900), the American boy protagonist begins as a volunteer in the Philippine–American War and finishes fighting for the British in South Africa.

42. The Spanish–Cuban–American War had also been reported upon in South Africa. See M. Boucher, "Imperialism, the Transvaal Press, and the Spanish–American War of 1898," *Kleio* 5, no. 2 (1973): 1–32; Jacob Isselhard, *The Filipino in Everyday Life: An Interesting and Instructive Narrative of the Personal Observations of an American Soldier during the Late Philippine Insurrection* (Chicago, 1904), 116–17.

43. On U.S. "anti-imperialism," see Richard E. Welch Jr., *Response to Imperialism: The United States and the Philippine–American War, 1899–1902* (Chapel Hill: University of North Carolina Press, 1979); Daniel Schirmer, *Republic or Empire: American Resistance to the Philippine War* (Cambridge, Mass.: Schenkman Publishing Co., 1972); Robert L. Beisner, *Twelve against Empire: The Anti-Imperialists, 1898–1900* (New York: McGraw Hill Book Co., 1968); Jim Zwick, ed., *Sentenaryo/Cenennial*, Web site, available from http://www.boondocksnet.com/centennial/index.html (17 December 2001); E. Berkeley Thompkins, *Anti-Imperialism in the United States: The Great Debate, 1890–1920* (Philadelphia: University of Pennsylvania Press, 1970); Jim Zwick, "The Anti-Imperialist League and the Origins of Filipino-American Oppositional Solidarity," *Amerasia Journal* 24 (summer 1998): 64–85; and James A. Zimmerman, "Who Were the Anti-Imperialists and the Expansionists of 1898 and 1899? A Chicago Perspective," *Pacific Historical Review* 46 (November 1977): 589–601. On the anti-imperialist sense of history, including national-exceptionalism, see Fabian Filfrich, "Falling Back into History: Conflicting Visions of National Decline and Destruction in the Imperialism Debate around the Turn of the Century," in *The American Nation, National Identity, Nationalism*, ed. Knud Krakau (Münster: LIT, 1997), 149–66. On gender and anti-imperialism, see Hoganson, *Fighting for American Manhood*. On the importance of anti-imperialism to twentieth-century foreign policy, see Frank Ninkovich, *The United States and Imperialism* (Malden, Mass.: Blackwell Publishers, 2001). For anti-imperialist arguments, see Philip Foner and Richard C. Winchester, *The Anti-Imperialist Reader: A Documentary History of Anti-Imperialism in the United States* (New York, 1984); Roger Bresnahan, ed., *In Time of Hesitation: American Anti-Imperialists and the Philippine–American War* (Quezon City: New Day Publishers, 1981); and Zwick, *Sentenaryo/Centennial*. On racist anti-imperialism, see Christopher Lasch, "The Anti-Imperialists, the Philippines, and the Inequality of Man," *Journal of Southern History* 24 (August 1958): 319–31; and Eric Tyrone Lowery Love, "Race over Empire: Racism and United States Imperialism, 1865–1900" (Ph.D. diss., Princeton University, Princeton, N.J., 1997).

44. William C. Reuter, "The Anatomy of Political Anglophobia in the United States, 1865–1900," *Mid-America* 61 (April–July 1979): 117–32. On anglophobia and tariff politics, see Crapol, *America for Americans*. On early-nineteenth-century American fears of British imperial expansion, see Kinley Brauer, "The United States and British Imperial Expansion, 1815–1860," *Diplomatic History* 12 (winter 1988): 19–37.

45. Although they directed their arguments primarily against U.S. colonialism, U.S. anti-imperialists also criticized the British Empire. See Alan Raucher, "American Anti-Imperialists and the Pro-India Movement, 1900–1932," *Pacific Historical Review* 43, no. 1 (1974): 83–110.

46. Rudyard Kipling, as quoted in Gossett, *Race*, 322; George Herbert Adams, *Why Americans Dislike England* (Philadelphia: Henry Altemus, 1896), 17; Augustus O. Bacon, "Independence for the Philippines," in William Jennings Bryan, *Republic or Empire: The Philippine Question* (Chicago: The Independence Co., 1899), 545.

47. Carl Schurz, "The Anglo-American Friendship," *Atlantic Monthly*, vol. 82 (October 1898), 437–38.

48. William Jennings Bryan, "America's Mission," in Bryan et al., *Republic or Empire*, 37–38.

49. Ibid., 38–39.

50. On debates about the closing of the continental frontier and its relationship to U.S. national exceptionalism, see David Wrobel, *The End of American Exceptionalism: Frontier Anxiety from the Old West to the New Deal* (Lawrence: University Press of Kansas, 1993). William Jennings Bryan, "Imperialism, Not Expansion," in Chicago Record, *Debate on "Our Duty to the Philippines"* (Chicago 1901), Ayer Collection, Newberry Library, Chicago.

51. On U.S. interests and the development of U.S. South African policy, see Thomas J.

Noer, *Briton, Boer, and Yankee: The United States and South Africa, 1870–1914* (Kent, Ohio: Kent State University Press, 1978); and Stuart E. Knee, "Anglo-American Understanding and the Boer War," *Australian Journal of Politics and History* 30, no. 2 (1984): 196–208.

52. On Richard Harding Davis's shift from English to Boer sympathies, for example, see Todd Uhlman, "Dispatching Anglo-Saxonism: Richard Harding Davis Reports from South Africa," paper presented at "Pairing Empires" conference. Harry Thurston Peck, "American Opinion on the South African War," *Bookman* (vol. 10, 1900), 530, 531.

53. On the global dimensions of Progressive Era racism in the U.S. South, as illustrated by Boer–white supremacist solidarity, see Jack Temple Kirby, *Darkness at the Dawning: Race and Reform in the Progressive South* (Philadelphia: Lippincott, 1972), chap. 6. African American critics argued against U.S.–Boer solidarity. See Willard Gatewood Jr., "Black Americans and the Boer War, 1899–1902," *South Atlantic Quarterly* 75 (spring 1976): 226–44; *New York World*, as quoted in *Literary Digest*, 6 June 1900), 716; Peck, "American Opinion on the South African War," 531–32.

54. Edward Stratemeyer, *Between Boer and Briton; or Two Boys' Adventures in South Africa* (Boston: Lee and Shepard Publishers, 1900), 50–51, 104–5, 134. Stratemeyer's Old Glory series opportunistically took place in the land and sea campaigns of the new colonial empire of the United States. He wrote and profited from the syndicate production of children's series, including the Bobbsey Twins (1904), Tom Swift (1910), the Hardy Boys (1927), and Nancy Drew (1930). See Carol Billman, *The Secret of the Stratemeyer Syndicate: Nancy Drew, the Hardy Boys and the Million Dollar Fiction Factory* (New York: Ungar, 1986). On the gender of imperial popular fiction in the 1890s, see Amy Kaplan, "Romancing the Empire: The Embodiment of American Masculinity in the Popular Historical Novel of the 1890s," *American Literary History* 2, no. 4 (1990): 659–90.

55. Stratemeyer, *Between Boer and Briton*, 140, 292–93, 330, 352.

56. Anderson, *Race and Rapprochement*, chap. 8.

57. Jacobson, *Whiteness of a Different Color*, chap. 6.

58. On Filipino–American collaboration politics within the U.S. colonial state, see Ruby Paredes, ed., *Philippine Colonial Democracy* (Manila: Ateneo de Manila Press, 1989); Paul Hutchcroft, "Colonial Masters, National Politicos, and Provincial Lords: Central Authority and Local Autonomy in the American Philippines, 1900–1913," *Journal of Asian Studies* 59 (May 2000): 277–306; Julian Go, "Colonial Reception and Cultural Reproduction: Filipino Elites and United States Tutelary Rule," *Journal of Historical Sociology* 12 (December 1999): 337–68; Norman C. Owen, ed., *Compadre Colonialism: Studies on the Philippines under American Rule* (Ann Arbor: Center for South and Southeast Asian Studies, University of Michigan, 1971); and Bonifacio Salamanca, *The Filipino Reaction to American Rule, 1901–1913* (Hamden: Shoestring Press, 1968). Filipinos traveling and studying in European capitals in the late nineteenth century and advocating colonial reform in the Propaganda Movement sometimes praised the British Empire over the Spanish, arguing for its superior economic development and political liberalism, a critique sharpened by Hong Kong's status as a political refuge. Arguments of this kind frequently appeared in the Filipino journal *La Solidaridad* (1889–96). For example, José Ramos distributed secret pamphlet literature from his Manila-based store, La Gran

Bretaña, after he studied business in London. E. Arsenio Manuel, ed., *Dictionary of Philippine Biography* (Quezon City: Filipiniana Publications, 1955–70), s. v. "Ramos, José," 353–61. See John Schumacher, *The Propaganda Movement, 1880–1895* (Manila: Solidaridad Publishing House, 1973). On Manuel Quezon's use of the British Empire as a nationalist lever, see Nicholas Tarling, "Quezon and the British Commonwealth," *Australian Journal of Politics and History* 23, no. 2 (1977): 182–206. On Filipino connections to Australia, see Reynaldo Ileto and Rodney J. Sullivan, eds., *Discovering Australasia: Essays on Philippine–Australian Interactions* (Townsville: Department of History and Politics, James Cook University, 1993); Mrs. Campbell Dauncey, *An Englishwoman in the Philippines* (London: J. Murray, 1906), 333.

59. By 1916, for example, the Iloilo American–British Community was roughly equally divided between Britons (mostly merchants, commercial agents, and bank officials) and Americans (nearly all local government functionaries). That March, the society gave a farewell party for two British members leaving the Philippines "to join the British Army" and an American member, a constabulary officer, "who was leaving to join the Standard Oil Co. in India." Photo caption, folder, "Iloilo American–British Community (1916)," Events and Features file, American Historical Collection, Rizal Library, Ateneo de Manila University, Quezon City. The photo itself apparently no longer exists. On American colonial social and institutional life in Manila, including club life, see Lewis Gleeck, *Manila Americans, 1901–1965* (Manila: Carmelo and Bauermann Inc., 1977); and idem, *Over Seventy-Five Years of Philippine–American History: The Army–Navy Club* (Manila: Carmelo and Bauermann, Inc., 1976).

60. George Boxall, *The Anglo-Saxon: A Study in Evolution* (London: G. Richards, 1902), 220–21.

61. On the intersections between colonialism and Progressive reform movements in the United States, an area that requires further study and elaboration, see Patricio N. Abinales's chapter in this volume; and Paul A. Kramer, "Reflex Actions: Toward a Transnational History of U.S. Imperial Progressivism," paper presented at the University of Bielefeld, Germany, July 2001 (in the author's possession). Julian Hawthorne, "A Side Issue of Expansion," *Forum* 27 (June 1899): 443; Archibald Colquhoun, *Greater America* (New York: Harper and Brothers, 1904), iii, 277.

62. James LeRoy, "A Disputed Authority,'" *Boston Evening Transcript*, 22 October 1904. On British opinion of U.S. foreign policy between 1898 and 1902, see Geoffrey Seed, "British Views of American Policy in the Philippines Reflected in Journals of Opinion, 1898–1907," *Journal of American Studies* 2, no. 1 (1968): 49–64; and idem, "British Reactions to American Imperialism Reflected in Journals of Opinion, 1898–1900," *Political Science Quarterly* 73 (June 1958): 254–72. On "The White Man's Burden" and its reception, see Jim Zwick, "'The White Man's Burden' and Its Critics," http://www.boondocksnet.com/kipling/, in *Anti-Imperialism in the United States, 1898–1935*, ed. Jim Zwick, http://www.boondocksnet.com/ai1198–35.html (17 December 2001). Carl Crow, *America and the Philippines* (Garden City, N.Y.: Doubleday, Page and Co., 1914), 65.

63. Dauncey, *Englishwoman in the Philippines*, 13; Clifford, "Destiny of the Philippines," 155, 159; Hugh Charles Clifford, "America's Problem in the Philippines," *Living Age* 251 (1906): 80.

64. On the projects of the early U.S. colonial state in the Philippines, see Glenn May, *Social Engineering in the Philippines: The Aims, Execution, and Impact of American Colonial Policy, 1900–1913* (Westport, Conn.: Greenwood Press, 1980); and Vicente L. Rafael, "White Love: Surveillance and Nationalist Resistance in the U.S. Colonization of the Philippines," in Kaplan and Pease, *Cultures of United States Imperialism*, 185–218. On urban planning, see Thomas Hines, "The Imperial Facade: Daniel H. Burnham and American Architectural Planning in the Philippines," *Pacific Historical Review* 41, no. 1 (1972): 33–53. On the medical state, see Reynaldo Ileto, "Cholera and the Origins of the American Sanitary Order in the Philippines," in *Imperial Medicine and Indigenous Societies*, ed. David Arnold (Manchester, U.K.: Manchester University Press, 1992), 125–48; Ken De Bevoise, *Agents of Apocalypse: Epidemic Disease in the Colonial Philippines* (Princeton, N.J.: Princeton University Press, 1995); and Warwick Anderson, " 'Where Every Prospect Pleases and Only Man Is Vile': Laboratory Medicine as Colonial Discourse," *Critical Inquiry* 18 (spring 1992): 502–29. On the Bureau of Insular Affairs, see Romeo Victorino Cruz, *America's Colonial Desk and the Philippines, 1898–1934* (Quezon City: University of the Philippines Press, 1974).

65. David P Barrows to James LeRoy, 10 December 1904, "Jan[uary]–Dec[ember] 1904" folder, David P. Barrows Papers, Bancroft Library, University of California, Berkeley; LeRoy, "Disputed 'Authority.' "

66. James LeRoy, "The Philippines and the Filipinos," *Bulletin of the American Historical Collection* 26 (July–September 1998): 10; William S. Washburn, "Civil Service Reform and the Evolution of Good Government," in "Exhibit D: 5th Annual Report of the Philippine Civil Service Board," *Report of the Philippine Commission to the Secretary of War for 1905*, 1906, 1:711. Alleyne Ireland was a British subject and critic of the American colonial state in the Philippines in works that included *Tropical Colonization: An Introduction to the Study of the Subject* (New York: Macmillan, 1899) and *The Far Eastern Tropics: Studies in the Administration of Tropical Dependencies* (Boston: Houghton, Mifflin and Co., 1905).

67. Beveridge, *For the Greater Republic*, 14; Colquhoun, *Greater America*, 68; Dauncey, *Englishwoman in the Philippines*, 134.

68. See *Report of the Philippine Commission to the Secretary of War, 1901–16*; Younghusband, *Philippines and Round About*, 217–22; advertisement for the British India Steam Navigation Company, *Manila Times*, 13 June 1899, 1, Lopez Memorial Museum, Manila.

69. "El Comisionado Schurman en Borneo" (Commissioner Schurman in Borneo), *La Independencia* (Malabon), 11 August 1899. Translation from Spanish by the author. The original article was in the *Hong-Kong Telegraph*, 15 July 1899.

70. Spanish botanists in the Philippines had exchanged specimens and publications with British botanists in the 1870s and 1880s. "Kew Gardens Memos and Correspondence about the Philippines," microfilm 1936, Filipiniana Collections, University of the Philippines, Manila; "La exhibición de productos agrículos en Singapore" (The exhibition of agricultural products in Singapore), *El Renacimiento Filipino* (Manila), 14 October 1910, 10.

ANNE L. FOSTER

Models for Governing:
Opium and Colonial Policies
in Southeast Asia, 1898–1910

This article builds on two absences, both of them near-total. The first is beginning to be filled, as the other essays in this collection demonstrate, and that is the absence of a comparative perspective for the study of U.S. colonialism. Washington officials often did present the American colonial project in exceptionalistic terms familiar to all who study the history of the United States. They—and even more so, their counterparts in the Philippine islands—also carefully studied the experiences of other colonial powers in Asia and compared their policy choices to known successes and failures elsewhere. Scholars subsequently have paid more attention to the rhetoric of difference than to the practice of comparison.

The second absence at the center of this article is the U.S. policy toward opium use in the Philippines. The classic studies of Philippine history from 1898 to 1946 contain almost no references to opium; nor do most of the memoirs of officials making or implementing colonial policy, such as Elihu Root and Dean Worcester. This absence is also striking. Opium had provided a major revenue source during Spanish rule. The U.S. decision to prohibit opium smoking could easily have been portrayed by involved officials as proof of the United States' benevolent intentions and by later scholars as coercive, intrusive policy. Yet they chose not to discuss it at all. Perhaps the officials avoided the topic because prohibition was only partially successful. Attention to the role of opium in the creation and maintenance of Southeast Asian colonial states by scholars is relatively recent, even for those colonies whose budgets depended on opium revenues.

These two absences, as one might suspect, are related. In a simple way, they are related because U.S. officials, in attempting to determine what policy to adopt regarding opium, studied and even visited several Asian colonies to learn what had and had not worked. Their relationship extends, however, to helping reveal how the colonial project was, and continues to be, imagined by Americans. The timing, method, and goals of American colonialism seemed self-evidently to set the U.S. colonial endeavor apart. Whether it was set apart for praise or condemnation has not changed its exceptionalistic nature. The absence of comparison has allowed this assumption to remain relatively unchallenged.[1] In the culture of prohibition—which was strong and growing in the United States by 1898, too—there was no room to imagine any opium policy for a U.S. colony other than eradication. The logic is simple: Opium smoking is unhealthy and immoral; the United States wanted to improve the lives of Filipinos; U.S. policy must have opposed opium smoking from the beginning.

From the beginning, however, U.S. officials in the Philippines tended to accept, and even approve of, continued legal and taxed sale of opium. Their questioning of that policy grew out of criticism from officials in Washington, D.C., and missionaries, and their doubts were confirmed by what they learned from other colonial officials. After the United States became the first regional power to prohibit opium consumption, these officials did not cease to view their actions in a regional context. Rather, they began a quest, in which the United States is still engaged, to create an effective prohibitionist regime for the region.

OPIUM IN THE UNITED STATES

There is a certain irony in U.S. leadership of the regional prohibition policy, because opium remained a legal commodity in the United States throughout most of the period 1898–1910. Although Progressives and many religious activists agitated against opium in both the United States and the Philippines, consumption of the drug was an integral part of American life and not easily eradicated. Before 1909, opium was imported, subject only, in most years, to an import tax. In 1909, in preparation for the Shanghai Opium Commission meeting, the U.S. Congress passed the Smoking Opium Exclusion Law. This law restricted access only to opium prepared for smoking, the method used more often by immigrant Chinese than other Americans. But it began the trend that by 1914 had led to the Harrison Narcotic Act, which set up a prohibitionist regime for the United States. This law also was passed immediately before a major international conference on opium regulation, to ensure that the United States, the rhetorical leader in the field, had laws restricting opium that were at least as stringent as those of the other participants.

Histories of this prohibition trend in the United States have focused on the changing nature of the addict in the United States. In a careful, compelling study, David Courtwright has noted that, in the nineteenth century, most addicts were middle-class, white women and, to a lesser extent, Civil War veterans. The former took—not smoked—opium as a more discreet and socially acceptable way than alcohol to deal with the cares of the world. The latter consumed opium to alleviate pain from old war wounds. Most of these addicts took opium in tonic or powdered form rather than smoked it, the most common means of consumption among ethnic Chinese the world over. Courtwright argues that, as addiction spread to different ethnic groups, including African Americans and ethnic Chinese; to the lower classes; and to the opium derivative heroin, the prohibition campaign grew stronger out of fear that these new addicts would commit crimes and generally disrupt society in the service of their addiction. This image of the addict is the now familiar one.[2]

The chronology of prohibition in the United States and the Philippines suggests that there is another strand in the web of explanation for opium prohibition, however. Prohibition advocates found opium a threat not merely because addicts might commit crimes, but also because they believed opium users were less committed to creating a model society of industrious, thrifty citizens. Here the connection to the role of opium in the Philippines is clear. Few indigenous Filipinos smoked opium, in part because they had been forbidden to purchase it under Spanish law and in part, as the historian Carl Trocki notes, because of their "poverty."[3] By continuing to prevent indigenous Filipinos from smoking opium, American colonial officials were demonstrating their benevolent intentions to improve the colony. There is a complication here, however, that also suggests problems with Courtwright's argument. In the Philippines, the primary consumers of opium, the ethnic Chinese, were also the most powerful and wealthy businessmen, not the lower classes likely to commit violent crime. Yet the same reformers who worked to prohibit opium in the United States, especially people such as Hamilton Wright, were active in the anti-opium campaign for the Philippines. The ethnic Chinese opium smoker was no threat, but he was an outsider in the minds of many U.S. officials. From the few mentions of ethnic Chinese in the debates about whether to restrict opium in the Philippines, it seems that U.S. officials hoped that prohibition might help make the whole ethnic Chinese problem, as they saw it, literally go away. Then U.S. officials could concentrate on reforming the indigenous inhabitants.

FROM OPIUM FARM TO HIGH TARIFF

Under Spanish rule, opium had been legal, and regulated through the opium farm. During the nineteenth century, opium farms had become the most common way for colonial governments in Southeast Asia to tax opium sales. The opium farms were state-granted monopolies for the sale of opium in a particular region. Opium farmers bid for the rights to this monopoly and purchased their stocks of opium from the colonial government, which remained the sole legal importer. Colonial governments found this system lucrative, because they received revenue for granting the monopoly and for selling the opium, but they were able to leave policing of the system up to the opium farmer.[4] The opium contract for 1896–1897 yielded 576,000 pesos for the Spanish government. One unusual aspect of the opium farms in the Philippines is that they were allowed to sell only to ethnic Chinese residents. Filipinos were not allowed to smoke.[5]

The U.S. military government in the Philippines did not award an opium contract; rather, it believed that instituting a high tariff on opium imports would be simpler. During 1899, legal imports of opium amounted to approximately 120,000 pounds, with a value of $328,713, on which a duty of $111,469, or about 33 percent, was paid. For the next two years, opium imports increased by approximately 100,000 pounds each year, but dropped back briefly to only 137,000 pounds in 1902, when the tariff increased to approximately 45 percent. The tax rate remained the same in 1903, but imports again went up, to 255,000 pounds.[6]

U.S. officials in the Philippines found this revenue situation perfectly acceptable: The quantity of opium legally imported was not dramatically higher than during the Spanish era, and although the U.S. revenue was also lower, it was easy to collect. In addition, opium was still legal in the United States at the turn of the century, so its consumption in the Philippines, while not encouraged, was accepted. Lieutenant-Colonel William F. Spurgin, Collector of Customs in Manila, explained that "all of the Colonial possessions in the Orient except Java and the French possessions" had a contract system for opium sales, which he believed was best because it "relieved the Government from maintaining an expensive revenue service to prevent the smuggling of opium." In the Philippines, he continued, "opium is only used by the Chinese residents," who he claimed were "expert smugglers." Setting a tariff too high "would be a failure," therefore, especially because of the "peculiarities and extent of the Coast line of the Philippines." He proposed viewing opium sales as a "business proposition," in which case the contract system would be adopted as providing the most revenue.[7]

Military officials were not the only ones to demonstrate a lack of concern about the sanction the U.S. government was lending to the sale of opium through its taxation policies. Preparation for full civilian government began in 1900 with the arrival of the Second Philippine Commission, led by William H. Taft. The commission's first task was to study the "conditions and immediate wants of the Philippine Islands." This study concluded that opium was "a very legitimate and lucrative subject of taxation," although it also noted that any decrease in consumption of opium would be "a clear gain to the well-being of the community, which will more than offset the loss of revenue." The Philippine Commission's conclusion was highly pragmatic. Its authors agreed that it was better not to smoke opium, but they believed that prohibition could "hardly be enforced," and that high import duties would encourage "extensive smuggling." They recommended creating "some other form of tax . . . to make opium return its proper contribution to the revenue."[8] These statements constitute the whole of the discussion of opium in the Philippine Commission report for 1900 and suggest that its authors did not find opium consumption a hindrance to the civilizing policy they believed the United States would pursue in the islands.

DEBATE OVER OPIUM POLICY

Both military and civil colonial officials agreed that legal opium sales would and should continue and that the U.S. government should merely decide how it wanted to tax such sales. American missionaries in Asia, long-time opponents of opium, believed that the new U.S. responsibility offered an opportunity to promote severe restrictions on opium. Reverend H. C. DuBose, an American missionary in China, wrote in 1899 to Senator John McLaurin to note "responsibility of [the] U.S." for the opium trade, because the United States profited from it. DuBose argued that opium had "no judicious use . . . save as administered by a physician," and therefore the U.S. government should limit, if not stop, "sale of this poison to a semi-civilized people."[9] The internal memoranda circulated in the Departments of State and War in response to DuBose's assertion establish the terms of the debate that would continue until 1908. One group was represented by Lieutenant-Colonel Spurgin, who sought to make regulation of the opium trade profitable and as simple as possible for the U.S. government. He saw no problem in copying policies that the British and Dutch had implemented successfully and recommended a contract system for the Philippines.[10]

Washington officials worried more than Spurgin about the ability to justify U.S. policy to skeptics at home. They likewise sought a cost-effective and easily implemented opium policy, but one that was also as consistent as possible with existing U.S. law. So while they made little comment on the proposal to reinstate the contract system, they had even less to say about DuBose's proposal to prohibit opium sales. The issue was referred, as a revenue issue, to the Department of the Treasury, and Lyman Gage, Secretary of the Treasury, wrote to the Secretary of War that opium was a legal and dutiable product according to U.S. law and that "the contract or farming system . . . is foreign to our administration of the revenue." He recommended maintaining the existing high-tariff policy, a policy similar to that in effect in the United States at the time. The chief of the Division of Customs and Insular Affairs in the Department of War concurred and instructed E. S. Otis, military governor of the Philippines, to make no change "in the existing system of controlling the opium traffic" of the Philippines.[11]

During 1901–1902, the policy remained in effect. In 1902, the ban on Chinese citizens' importing opium into the Philippines, which stemmed from a treaty between the United States and China regarding imports of opium in those two countries, was lifted. Paying the steep import tax, which amounted to about 45 percent of the value of the opium by 1902, was the only means of restriction. As more problems of colonial government began to be resolved, the Philippine Commission turned its attention again to the opium issue in 1903 and discovered that the high-tariff policy had undesirable effects. The quantity of opium imported into the Philippines appeared to be increasing steadily, which had not been the intended outcome of the high tariff, and the habit of smoking opium was spreading from ethnic Chinese to the Filipino population. In addition, the high level of the tariff seemed to be encouraging opium smuggling. Members of the Philippine Commission decided to reconsider the high-tariff policy in 1903.[12]

The initial proposal, as Commissioner Henry C. Ide explained in response to a request from Secretary of State John Hay, was to establish an opium-farm system like that in other countries in Asia. The opium farmer would be "under heavy bond" and therefore have great incentive to comply with all laws. Ide anticipated that an opium concession would not "increase or diminish the sale of opium but . . . regulate it in such a manner that the whole operations of the system can be known to the Government" and result in "a large revenue from a source not now available." Ide's attitude was as pragmatic as the Philippine Commission's had been in 1900: He believed that the farm system was the "most effective method of dealing with this vice, if opium smoking among orientals is to be considered a vice."[13] The Philippine Commission proposed a bill to establish an opium-farm system for the Philippines in 1903. This bill met many of the growing concerns, with a provision that only "a Chinese person of the full blood over the age of twenty-one years" could smoke, import, prepare, or sell opium. It also stated that the opium concession would be granted to one person and that opium could be imported only through Manila. Careful records were to be kept of the quantities of opium sold, and to whom. Other provisions attempted to address problems experienced in other colonies with opium farms, particularly those regarding the amount of opium the farmer could import during the last few weeks of the concession.[14]

In June 1903, the debate over the proposed opium bill heated up. In 1900, the protesting missionaries had been in China and were presumed to be ill informed about conditions in the Philippines. By 1903, the number and prominence of American missionaries in the Philippines had increased dramatically, and they organized to express their opposition to this bill. Initially led by Reverend Homer C. Stuntz of the Methodist Episcopal mission, the anti-opium forces soon used the resources of the Evangelical Union, the umbrella organization for most of the Protestant mission groups in the islands, to promote their cause. The Evangelical Union sent a telegram to President Theodore Roosevelt, and Stuntz told the Philippine Commission that the union, and its "constituency not less than thirty millions strong in the United States alone," would not rest until they saw defeat of the opium-concession bill.[15] Stuntz only slightly overestimated the response in the United States. Thousands of Americans sent letters, cables, and preprinted cards to Washington to protest the proposed opium concession. The editor of the Missionary Society of the Methodist Episcopal church, Charles H. Fahs, was a prominent but typical example. He echoed the widespread concern in other letters with the duty of the U.S. government to the "native peoples" of the Philippines as a reason for prohibiting opium traffic altogether, and he deplored the idea that the United States might "duplicate the disgraceful record of Great Britain in toying with this awful curse."[16]

This anti-opium campaign may have hit its target, because the proposed opium bill of 1903 received more concerted attention than had the 1900 proposals. Officials in the Bureau of Insular Affairs learned of the proposed bill from a request for more information about it from the Department of State, on behalf of the Chinese Legation. Philippine Commissioner Ide happened to be in Washington at the time and hastily prepared an explanation of the provisions of, and rationale for, the proposed opium concession. Ide stressed that the government would receive increased revenue without any increase in opium consumption and compared the proposed policy not only to that in effect in other Asian colonies, but also to commonly used methods for "the regulation of the sale of intoxicating liquors."[17] Further communication waited until the draft copy of the bill arrived in Washington.

After it did, Secretary of War Elihu Root cabled the Philippine governor, General Taft, that U.S. policy should not "either in substance or appearance . . . promote such traffic." Root's caution stemmed from his belief that Americans had always disapproved of "England's course in China" in trading opium and would "condemn any regulation" that did not have the goal of reducing opium traffic. Taft's cabled reply referred to public opinion in the Philippines and asserted that only those "in favor of prohibition of liquor" opposed the bill. Taft implied that opium and alcohol were substances of similar danger levels—slight, but manageable with regulation. He hoped in this way to get Root to acknowledge that local officials had greater expertise for judging the local situation.[18]

It did not work. The Bureau of Insular Affairs cabled immediately that the proposed bill would have to be approved by President Roosevelt and suggested sending it "before final passage instead of passing it with the possibility of disapproval."[19] This same cable asked for more complete explanation than Ide had been able to give in May and for regulations regarding the opium trade in Japan and Burma.[20] Root, when first appointed Secretary of War during the Spanish–American War, had immediately turned to his collection of books on British colonial rule for guidance; on the opium issue he did the same, initially, despite his disapproval of British opium sales to China.[21] U.S. officials in 1903 also looked to what other colonial powers in Asia were doing for guidance on the opium issue. Root asked Taft whether a policy of "absolute prohibition" or "qualified prohibition following Japanese example" might not be possible for the Philippines. In a later telegram, Root acknowledged that he was growing "more reluctant" to endorse the opium-farm system for the Philippines, because he worried that "the revenue to the government," one of the positive points from the perspective of the Philippine Commission, "would be a continual barrier against government efforts to decrease the business as it has been in India."[22]

Taft mounted a spirited, and confidential, defense of the opium-farm system, which, he noted, reflected the "full views of the Philippine Commission." Most important, the proposed bill would not allow Filipinos to smoke, only Chinese, of whom, he claimed, half of those resident in the Philippines were already addicts. The increased value of opium concessions in British colonies, he continued, stemmed from the rise in price that accompanied the award of an opium monopoly rather than from an increase in the percentage of the population smoking opium. Finally, he argued that the opium farmer had "personal knowledge and strongest motive . . . to suppress almost all smuggling and violations of the law." Although the possibility that government would become "dependent" on opium revenues was a danger, Taft claimed that U.S. officials had learned from the example of India and devised the Philippine system for the purpose of decreasing usage, with "revenue only an incident to secure rise in price."[23]

Taft's argument rested on the expertise of local officials, whose knowledge of conditions in the Philippines and in Asian colonies enabled them to predict better what was both feasible and beneficial for the U.S. colony. Taft's career goals were oriented toward Washington, not Manila, however, so he also carefully noted that the "success of the government here" required it to "retain confidence of the large body of right minded people in America." He proposed viewing the opium policy as an experiment and recommended, before any final decisions were taken, that a study commission be sent to Japan, Burma, Formosa, and Java to investigate the various policies of those countries, particularly the "reported failure" of prohibition in Formosa and the "experience in changing systems in Java."[24] Root, after a discussion with President Roosevelt, cabled the administration's inclination to favor a "high license" system like that used for alcohol sales in the United States but also welcomed the chance to have a more scientific basis for U.S. opium policy, which would result from the "commission of inquiry."[25] Taft appointed E. C. Carter, commissioner of health in the Philippines; Charles H. Brent, the Episcopal bishop for the Philippines; and José Albert, a physician from Manila, to this committee, which investigated opium policies of the French, Dutch, British, and Japanese in their colonies.

FROM OPIUM FARMS TO GOVERNMENT MONOPOLIES

Taft, like other U.S. officials in the Philippines, had advocated the opium-contract system largely because he believed opium use was intractable and that European colonial governments had had great success in regulating opium through the contract system. Subsequent investigations, however, found that in all the other colonies of Asia, the farm system was under scrutiny. Critics were questioning the incentives to smuggle opium and create new addicts, the impact on the welfare of indigenous peoples, the amazing profits earned by ethnic Chinese opium farmers, and the apparent incompatibility of legalized opium and the civilizing mission that all colonial governments were beginning to claim.

By the 1890s, other Asian colonies had instigated debates about the proper role of opium in colonial society and economy similar to the debates that occurred in the Philippines and Washington after 1898. Although anti-opium sentiments had been expressed in both Britain and the Netherlands by the early nineteenth century, the anti-opium forces did not become organized or politically potent until well into the second half of the nineteenth century. In Britain, the debate took on new urgency in 1893, when the Liberal Party took control in Parliament partly on the basis of anti-opium pledges during the campaign. The Society for the Suppression of the Opium Trade did not get the investigation it wanted into how opium should be suppressed, but it did get a Royal Commission on Opium to study "whether" opium should be suppressed and the financial consequences of doing so. The resulting seven-volume study also focused almost exclusively on use in India and the India–China trade. The total pages devoted to the Straits Settlements, for example, numbered only thirty-eight. Most British officials in the Straits breathed a sigh of relief at this slight. Opium farms provided as much as half the colony's revenue, and they did not welcome criticism of the most steady revenue source the free port colony had, especially as several massive internal improvements were planned.[26]

Straits officials were better able to stave off critical inquiry than many colonial officials elsewhere, partly because opium provided so much of the government's revenue, and partly because Singapore did not have the same issues of indigenous welfare to deal with, because almost no one was indigenous to the island. These officials only delayed the inevitable. Medical doctors and some prominent ethnic Chinese continued to press the issue on both physical and moral grounds. The Straits government began administering the monopoly for import and retail sale of opium itself, rather than contracting it out, only in 1910, more as a consequence of developments in other colonies than as a result of any internal debate.

The government monopoly, which Singapore finally adopted, had by then become the choice of all other colonies except the Philippines. French, Dutch, British, and Japanese officials all gave similar reasons for having adopted the government-monopoly system during the 1880s and 1890s. Each colony had at least one group for whom opium smoking was deemed acceptable (ethnic Chinese) and at least one group for whom opium smoking was deemed dangerous (usually the indigenous people or peoples). Most advocates of the government monopoly argued that the government and its agents would have less incentive to increase the potential market for opium by reaching out to new customers, because the government was not motivated by the desire to increase profits. In Burma, for example, officials required all opium addicts to register as of

1893. After that date, Burmese could not register as opium addicts, and unregistered Burmese had thereafter no legal means of purchasing opium. The owners of the retail stores where opium was sold had to keep detailed records of the name, registration, and amount of opium purchased for all transactions and faced heavy fines for incomplete records or sales to non-registered Burmese.[27] The Dutch Opium Regie had even more stringent controls. By the early twentieth century, all people who sold opium were civil servants, salaried employees of the Dutch colonial government, with no financial interest at all in the quantity of opium sold. These civil servants were supposed to be motivated to administer the opium laws scrupulously to ensure continued employment and promotion.[28] The Opium Regie was designed to prevent indigenous peoples of the Netherlands Indies from smoking opium, while guaranteeing that all financial benefits of indulgence by ethnic Chinese would go to the colonial government. U.S. officials in the Philippines saw the issue similarly. They perceived little physical or moral harm to Chinese opium smokers but believed the drug would lead to degeneracy among Filipinos.[29]

The regionwide concern about the spread of opium smoking was one component of rhetoric in all the colonies about the European civilizing mission. William McKinley's oft-quoted desire to "educate . . . , and uplift and Christianize them"[30] sounds more like an echo than a new cry for what he surely believed to be a wilderness. The French, in their new colony in Cochinchina, grappled with the problem. One French official, A. Dussutour, argued in the government's official newspaper that France, "a government at the head of European civilization, and with a providential mission in these countries [of Indochina], should not provide also the poisonous executioner of these peoples" by selling them opium.[31] The Dutch were struggling not with new policies for a new colony but, rather, with growing criticism of long-standing colonial policies. The Ethical Policy would not be named until 1901, but the "reformist spirit," as one historian has called it, was growing by the 1880s.[32] Indigenous peoples of the Indies were "younger brothers" who needed care and education. Promoting opium use by one's wards, even indirectly, did not seem to these reformists to be a consistent policy. During the 1880s, two popular novels by Dutch authors revealed the horrors and corruption that affected everyone—Javanese, Chinese, or Dutch—involved with opium. Both were modeled on the widely influential *Max Havelaar* in hopes that they would evoke a similar moral outrage. The Dutch government was increasingly concerned, as well, and ordered a thorough investigation, which appeared in 1888.[33] In French Indochina and the Netherlands Indies, the strongest anti-opium activists, including missionaries in the latter, often couched their criticisms in the language of uplift and civilizing missions. When U.S. officials began investigating regional policies, they heard these appealing and familiar goals most often in conjunction with anti-opium sentiment.

Growing attention to a civilizing mission was not the only concern common to colonies with opium farms in the 1880s and 1890s, however. One of the great advantages of the opium farm had been that it provided revenue, sometimes in very large sums, with minimal governmental involvement. For decades, both of these characteristics had appealed to colonial administrators, but by the late nineteenth century, colonial governments had begun to extend their control in the colonies. A concern with setting and defending boundaries among countries was one aspect of this control.[34] Colonial officials also wanted better control over local government, economic activity, and even what we might now call lifestyle choices.[35] It is telling that Dutch critics of the opium-farm system were particularly concerned, according to the historian James Rush, because farms "defied effective supervision" and "represented an *imperium in imperio*."[36]

Officials expressed their concern about control by complaining that the opium-farm system generated a great deal of money—evident in the fees paid by farmers and in the profits farmers must have been making to want to pay those fees—but that colonial administrators did not know how much money or from where it came. Some wondered why the government was allowing all that profit to go to the opium farmers when it could be going to the colonial government. Others believed that opium farmers could be making a profit only if they were also smuggling in cheaper opium.[37] As colonial officials began to investigate the opium-farm system in the 1880s and 1890s, their suspicions on these two fronts were confirmed. Better government meant both more cost-effective government and a government better able to protect the people. In the area of opium control, these two goals seemed best achieved by more government involvement in the sale of opium.

France was the first colony in the region to adopt a government-monopoly system, for Cochinchina. Once it acquired the colony in 1858, the French administration initially attempted to use the farm system, with the twist that the farmers were Frenchmen. Those farmers had insufficient experience, however; inefficiency and corruption plagued those contracts. The French returned to traditional-style farms, headed by ethnic Chinese, but remained dissatisfied. The revenue from the farms varied dramatically, because farmers often overbid and then were unable to meet their obligations. By 1881, the French government had begun to administer the importing of opium, to take over its preparation, and to issues licenses for the retail sale of opium in Cochinchina. During the 1890s, the system spread through French Indochina.[38]

Critics of the farm system in the Netherlands Indies watched the French experiment carefully, especially as the government-sponsored investigations of the 1880s began to expose the shortcomings of the Dutch system. In 1890, W. P. Groenveldt, a member of the Indies Council, traveled to French Indochina, on instruction from Dutch Colonial Minister L. W. C. Keuchenis, to study the French system and determine whether a monopoly might work for the Indies. Groenveldt was impressed by the workings of the French system. He reported that the French had devised a monopoly system that they believed corrected the worst abuses of the farms, and put the revenue on a more predictable footing. Groenveldt strongly recommended that the Dutch institute an opium monopoly, as well, with an even greater degree of control than the French exerted. After observing, in his opinion, that the greatest weaknesses of the French system stemmed from continued smuggling and lax control over retail sale, Groenveldt stressed the need for "a powerful opium police, on water as well as land." He also stipulated that the government should centralize and control the preparation of smoking opium; that opium should be packed in clearly identifiable containers with only the amounts people smoked at a sitting; that opium should be sold only by civil servants, preferably European; and that prices should be carefully maintained to keep them low enough to discourage smuggling but high enough to discourage new smokers.[39]

Both anti-opium activists and officials who believed opium provided an important revenue source praised Groenveldt's report, and by 1893 the Dutch government had approved an experimental Opium Regie for the island of Madura, off the coast of Java. The French-inspired Opium Regie was effective enough to spread through Java by 1897, and to the rest of the Indies by World War I.[40] Opium monopolies spread through the region, too. In Burma, all opium was imported by the government, and opium retail shops had to be licensed. Japan, after acquiring Formosa in 1895, worried about Japanese officials' succumbing to the bad example provided by Chinese addicts there. After studying what other colonial powers had done in their colonies, the director of the Civil Affairs Bureau in the colony, Mizuno Jun, recommended "a government monopoly over opium with the goal of gradually suppressing its use." This option allowed the Japanese government to prevent Japanese on the island from acquiring the opium habit, because a doctor's examination and a registration certificate were required to buy opium from the licensed opium retailers.[41] The stated goal of Japan's monopoly was to end opium consumption. To that end, no addicts were supposed to be added to the rolls after the initial registration period, which ended in 1900. Japan's rhetoric of gradual suppression appealed to many American observers at the turn of the century.

By the 1890s, the opium-farm system, which some U.S. officials initially advocated for the Philippines, was being superseded in many other colonies in the region by a government-monopoly system that allowed colonial officials to extend mechanisms of control into the economic and social life of the colonies. Advocates hoped that the monopoly system would meet the twin, apparently contradictory, goals of limiting the number of indigenous smokers and maximizing the efficiency of revenue collection. The concerns that prompted the shift were shared by officials of all the region's colonies, including the Americans, who had recently arrived in the Philippines. As these U.S. officials began to consider their opium-policy options, they were greatly influenced by the experiences of other colonies with opium farms and opium monopolies.

STUDYING REGIONAL POLICIES

By 1903, then, when the Philippine Commission faced the task of devising a more permanent opium policy for the islands, most other colonies had moved away from the farm system. When Governor Taft appointed the three-member Opium Committee to travel in the region to investigate the operation of opium laws, he had already begun to move away from supporting the contract system, as well. In his instructions to the committee he asked for a report to help the Philippine Commission "in determining the best kind of law to be passed in these islands for reducing and restraining the use of opium by its inhabitants."[42] His greatest concern had been ease of administration and possible revenue; by August 1903, he was more concerned about decreasing the amount of opium consumed. By appointing Reverend Brent, who in July 1903 had written a strong letter opposing the proposed contract system, Taft ensured that the final report would have at least some strongly moralistic, anti-opium sentiment.[43]

The Opium Committee traveled to Japan, Formosa, China (Shanghai), Hong Kong, Singapore, Saigon, Burma, and Java to collect reports and laws and interview officials, physicians, merchants, and missionaries. The committee also corresponded with prominent Filipinos in many parts of the Philippine Islands and gathered reports on conditions in several provinces. David E. Owen, a student of the opium issue before the 1930s, praised the Philippine Opium Committee report as better than the 1895 British report because it was done more carefully, with time taken to "assimilate the evidence as it was received."[44] Carter, Brent, and Albert visited Japan and Formosa first and were most impressed with the policy and the goals there. They found the policy that they termed "progressive prohibition" to be "unique among all the laws that came under the observation of the Committee," and they recommended Formosa's system as "humane and apt."[45] Formosa would provide the model for their recommendations almost six months later, but policies elsewhere were earnestly studied, as well.

The committee found "no special measure to discourage or limit the use of opium" in Shanghai, and they spent little time in China. Hong Kong, which still had a full-fledged opium-farm system, had laws that were "models of clearness, definiteness [sic] and accuracy," but opium brought a "considerable part of the income of the colony," and its use was widespread and increasing. The laws in French Indochina likewise were praised for being "clear, definite, comprehensive and full" but also solely for the purpose of revenue, as there appeared "to be no effort to diminish or prevent the use of opium by the natives or Chinese." In both the Straits Settlements and Burma, the committee noted, the laws were supposed to prevent the spread of the opium habit, respectively, to Malays and Burmese. In neither colony, however, were the laws effective because there were numerous simple ways to evade ethnic restrictions.[46]

The committee's members cited two lessons they had learned from the Burmese example about what to avoid when writing an opium law.

First, the people engaged in the retail sale of opium should not benefit financially from it. Second, if two groups lived "in juxtaposition" to each other, it was impossible to permit one to smoke and deny it, with any hope of effectiveness, to the other.[47] Java struck the committee as a society with many characteristics similar to that in the Philippines. That, and the recentness of the switch from farm to government monopoly on Java, increased the committee's curiosity. Its members found that the Dutch were making a conscientious and concerted effort; that the laws were well thought out; and that perhaps consumption was steady or slightly diminished under the monopoly. As with Burma, they noted some specific lessons, although more positive ones. First, "education and religion," particularly Christianity, seemed to help the Javanese resist opium use. Second, although Javanese "are held to be the most submissive to law among all the colonies of the world," prohibition had failed in Java. Third, the opium-farm system led only to increased numbers of smokers and corruption of officials. Finally, the "system of absolute government control" had proved its "superiority" over all other systems.[48]

The committee's findings have been worth summarizing at some length because their recommendations so clearly drew on the experiences of several of the colonies. Although Brent initially had desired prohibition sooner rather than later, for example, he agreed in the report with Carter and Albert that "immediate enforcement of a prohibition law" would work only in those places in the world where no one yet smoked opium. The committee recommended an immediate government monopoly in order to gain all the benefits of the system that they had observed on Java, particularly the salaried sales agents. They also recommended that all current addicts, Chinese or Filipino, be allowed to register as such, although the law had traditionally forbidden opium to Filipinos. They believed that "the interests of equity and justice are thus best subserved."[49]

Finally, they recommended that the "progressive-prohibition" policy of Japan on Formosa could be sped up in the Philippines, with total non-medical prohibition three years after instigation of the government monopoly. Their optimism on this point stemmed from the small percentage of the population who smoked. They claimed only one-third of 1 percent of the entire population, and one-eighth of 1 percent of Filipinos smoked opium. That distinction hints at the unspoken reason for optimism. The committee members, like many U.S. officials, believed opium smoking to be a problem primarily among China-born Chinese and noted that the continuance of the "present Chinese exclusion act" would prevent a new "influx of opium smokers." The committee perhaps hoped that, as had happened in Japan, Chinese addicts would leave the Philippines when prohibition began. They certainly hoped that addicts would get treatment to cure their addiction, because they also stipulated "gratuitous treatment" in hospitals for all who wished to "free themselves from the opium vice."[50]

Far from seeing themselves as unique in their approach to colonial rule, those Americans involved in the formulation of opium policy took every opportunity to learn from the successes and failures in neighboring colonies. The recommendations of the Opium Committee drew heavily on specific laws and procedures from elsewhere, and their justifications differed only in eschewing any revenue, as they recognized that all governments find abandoning existing revenue sources difficult. The rhetoric in the committee's report did not present the United States as a trendsetter even for opium policy in the region. The committee's recommendations were not, however, adopted wholesale. The government monopoly was never instigated, although prohibition did follow almost as quickly as suggested. After 1903, in addition, U.S. officials did begin to present themselves as the regional leaders on opium policy and began pushing other colonial officials to adopt first the rhetoric, and later the policy, of opium prohibition, with unforeseen consequences for the opium trade.

PROHIBITION FOR ALL

The Opium Committee returned to Manila on 5 February 1904 but took several months to prepare its report. Attention seemed to have shifted elsewhere, because in early January 1905, prompting came from the Secretary of War in the form of a cable to Governor Luke E. Wright "to approve the report of the opium committee and to adopt an act enforcing it and this at once."[51] Wright's reply stressed a few logistical difficulties. First, because the tariff for the Philippines was set by the U.S. Congress and opium was a legal, duty-paying import, Wright was not sure the Philippine Commission had legal authority to prohibit opium imports. Second, the government monopoly might be legal, but Wright believed that hiring the "considerable number of government agents" [necessary to] "prevent suffering and smuggling" would be expensive. Wright proposed a "high license" system and registration of smokers for the three years until prohibition took effect. He argued that there was "no difference between monopoly and license."[52]

The tactics of delay in Manila prompted action in Washington, and on 3 March 1905, Congress passed a law prohibiting import of opium into the Philippines after 1 March 1908. The Philippine Commission then merely had to decide how best to regulate opium for the intervening three years; in March 1906, it passed a law requiring the licensing of all opium smokers on payment of five pesos, the restriction of such licenses to the Chinese, and payment of a tax of 200 pesos by retail dealers in opium or 1,000 pesos by wholesalers. In addition, import taxes of five to ten pesos per kilo of opium were levied. Some of the proceeds from these taxes were designated to pay the hospital expenses of addicts seeking treatment.[53] The increased taxes for import and consumption seemed to work in 1906: Only 150,292 pounds of opium were imported that year. In 1907, however, in anticipation of the total ban beginning in 1908, legal opium imports had hit an all-time high since the beginning of U.S. rule, totaling 728, 530 pounds.[54]

Brent, a member of the 1903 Opium Committee, recognized that prohibition in one country probably would not work. In July 1906, he wrote to President Roosevelt proposing that the United States build on its "manifestly high" approach to the opium issue by promoting a regional solution. Brent believed that an international "investigation" of existing conditions in the region would encourage other countries to follow the U.S. lead. He then noted the benefits of a "common aim" among the "nations that are oriental either by nature or through the possession of dependencies in the Orient"; by the latter, he meant the European colonial powers.[55] Taft, the Secretary of War in 1906, advised Roosevelt that an international investigation of the opium situation was "worth trying." Taft saw little hope of British cooperation, however, because he wondered "what the British government would do for income if it gave up the opium business" in India, Hong Kong, and Singapore.[56] Charles Denby of the Department of State also argued that the United States was fully justified "in approaching the other powers for our mutual benefit." Roosevelt was swayed, and by late September 1906, invitations had gone out to Britain, France, the Netherlands, Germany, China, and Japan to join in a "general and impartial investigation of the scientific and material conditions of the opium trade and the opium habit in the Far East."[57]

The turn of the century saw many similar international conferences convened in attempts to study—and, it was hoped, solve—social ills. The International Sanitary Convention of 1892, for example, was signed in the wake of a cholera epidemic; it led to several conferences and, a few years later, to an International Office of Health in Paris. Concern about the "white slave traffic," usually conducted to acquire women and children for prostitution, led to the creation in 1899 of an international bureau for the suppression of this activity and to several conferences in Europe during the first decade of the twentieth century. Slave trading in general, long an object of international reform efforts, was declared a criminal offense at an 1890 conference in Brussels, including by three countries—Turkey, Iran, and Zanzibar—that still had legal slavery. All of these international reform efforts, opium regulation included, would receive more systematic attention under the League of Nations.[58]

Two and a half years passed before the international meeting regarding opium trade and use took place in Shanghai, with Reverend Brent presiding as chair. By early 1909, when the meeting took place, it was becoming clear that 1906, as the historian Carl Trocki has argued, had been "the key year for the turn of the tide against the opium trade." Trocki's claim rests primarily on the agreements between India and China to link opium eradication in China with cuts in exports of opium from India to China, and on passage of a resolution in the British Parliament calling the opium trade "morally indefensible."[59]

The U.S. decision to prohibit opium imports after 1906 was equally important as a turning point.[60] As Brent suspected, and as other U.S. officials gradually discovered after March 1908, it was impossible to succeed in prohibiting opium use in one country of Asia while opium was still legal and widely used in nearby countries.[61] Effective implementation of the prohibition law in the Philippines depended in part on encouraging regional colonial powers to move toward greater restriction, and eventually prohibition, in their own colonies. The U.S. representatives at the 1909 Shanghai meeting attempted to turn attention to problems of opium regulation in Asian colonies, but they had only limited success. In two areas, however, they did persuade the delegates to endorse resolutions that would provide the basis for future developments along the lines the United States wanted.[62]

One resolution was designed to meet the immediate problem of increased smuggling of opium. During the Shanghai meeting, James F. Smith, governor-general of the Philippines, cabled Brent to ask for the "aid" of regional powers in enforcing prohibition in the Philippines, because the "large quantities of opium" smuggled were undermining the law. Brent did report to the other delegates that "a constant supply of contraband opium" entered the Philippines from Hong Kong, Singapore, and North Borneo.[63] The other delegates made no public statements of support; rather, they reiterated the superior control that their government monopolies provided. Nevertheless, the end of the opium-farm system in the Philippines, the Netherlands Indies, and, after 1910, the Straits Settlements left a large network of suddenly unemployed former opium farmers with the expertise and capital to run smuggling operations. The Shanghai commission passed a resolution calling on all signatories to "adopt reasonable measures to prevent" shipment of opium from any country to "any country which prohibits the entry of opium."[64] Ostensibly designed to help China resist unwanted opium imports, this resolution also marked the beginning of cooperation among the colonial powers to prevent smuggling.

The second resolution had almost no immediate impact, but it allowed U.S. officials to set the tone for all discussions of opium use through the 1930s. Initially, the U.S. resolution proposed that participating countries "at once or in the near future confine the use of opium . . . to legitimate medical practice." British delegates objected that medical practice and opium habits varied widely, and a compromise was reached on the phrase "gradual suppression" of opium use.[65] With no timetable set, British delegates seem to have equated "gradual" with indefinite future. The U.S. delegates were pleased merely to have endorsement from an international body of the goal, even if far in the future, of total prohibition. At all future international meetings on opium, U.S. delegates skillfully and persistently reminded other countries of this universally proclaimed goal.

By 1909, Americans comfortably employed the rhetoric of moral superiority of U.S. rule in the Philippines when compared with other colonial powers, not least because the United States was the only power to give up the lucrative opium revenue voluntarily. U.S. officials by then may have seen themselves standing above other colonial officials, but they never saw themselves as standing alone. Opium policy in the Philippines drew on lessons learned from success and failure elsewhere in the region. The U.S. decision for prohibition was unique but presented as something that other colonial powers were attempting to put themselves in a position to do, as well. Prohibition also provided greater incentive for smuggling in the region and required ever closer cooperation between Philippine authorities and those of other colonial powers in hopes of effective enforcement.

NOTES

1. Theodore Friend's *The Blue-Eyed Enemy: Japan against the West in Java and Luzon, 1942–1945* (Princeton, N.J.: Princeton University Press, 1998) is a noteworthy exception, and should have prompted more research along similar lines suggested than it has.

2. David T. Courtwright, *Dark Paradise: A History of Opiate Addiction in America* (Cambridge, Mass.: Harvard University Press, 2001), chaps. 1–2, explain the extent and nature of opium addiction before prohibition.

3. Carl A. Trocki, *Opium, Empire and the Global Political Economy: A Study of the Asian Opium Trade, 1750–1950* (London: Routledge, 1999), 89.

4. The system is explained well in James Rush, *Opium to Java: Revenue Farming and Chinese Enterprise in Colonial Indonesia, 1860–1910* (Ithaca, N.Y.: Cornell University Press, 1990), chap. 3; and Carl A. Trocki, *Opium and Empire: Chinese Society in Colonial Singapore, 1800–1910* (Ithaca, N.Y.: Cornell University Press, 1990), 70–81.

5. U.S. Department of War, *Reports of the Taft Philippine Commission* (Washington, D.C.: Government Printing Office, 1901), 104 (hereafter, *Taft Philippine Report*). After the Americans took over, the peso was stabilized at two pesos to one U.S. dollar. This report does not specify the value of the peso in 1896–1897.

6. Philippine Commission Opium Committee, *Report of the Committee Appointed by the Philippine Commission to Investigate the Use of Opium and Traffic Therein* (Washington, D.C.: U.S. War Department, Bureau of Insular Affairs, 1905), 165 (hereafter, *Philippine Opium Report*). It is difficult to find statistics from the Spanish era. In 1873, opium imports from India totaled 17,163 kilograms. The quantity imported surely increased over the next twenty-five years, because the bids for the opium contracts quadrupled during those years. See the discussion in Edgar Wickberg, *The Chinese in Philippine Life, 1850–1898* (New Haven., Conn.: Yale University Press, 1965), 113–19.

7. William F. Spurgin, U.S. Collector of Customs, Manila, to Secretary of War, 21 December 1899, file 1023, entry 5, Record Group (RG) 350, Records of the Bureau of Insular Affairs, U.S. National Archives (NA), College Park, Md.

8. *Taft Philippine Report*, 104. "Conditions and Immediate Wants" is part of the report's subtitle.

9. Reverend H. C. DuBose to Senator John McLaurin, extracted in memorandum, 23 September 1899, file 1023–1, entry 5, RG 350, NA.

10. Spurgin to Secretary of War.

11. Lyman Gage, Secretary of the Treasury, to Elihu Root, Secretary of War, 2 April 1900, file 1023–3, entry 5, RG 350, NA. For a discussion of changing legal policies about opium in the United States, see Courtwright, *Dark Paradise*, 78–83.

12. Lieutenant-Colonel O. J. Sweet, Military Governor of Jolo, to William H. Taft, president, U.S. Philippine Civil Commission, 24 April 1901, file 1023–83; Kieng Hwo Lau, ethnic Chinese merchant in the Philippines, to William H. Taft, Governor General of the Philippines, 15 September 1902, file 1023–61; Customs Administrative Circular no. 129, "Chinese Persons May Import Opium into the Philippine Islands," 13 December 1902, file 1023–4, all in entry 5, RG 350, NA; "Smuggling in the Philippines," 29 December 1902, file C-1418, entry 8, RG 350, NA.

13. John Hay, Secretary of State, to Elihu Root, Secretary of War, 5 May 1903; U.S. Philippine Commissioner Henry C. Ide, memorandum, 15 May 1903. Both in file 1023–5, entry 5, RG 350, NA.

14. Draft of "An Act to Suppress the Sale of Opium to the Filipino People, to Confine Its Use to People of the Chinese Race, and to Restrict and Reduce Its Consumption by Chinese within the Philippine Islands," 1903, file 1023–13, entry 5, RG 350, NA.

15. Frank C. Laubach, *The Peoples of the Philippines: Their Religious Progress and Preparation for Spiritual Leadership in the Far East* (New York: George H. Doran Co., 1925), 212. See also Reverend Homer C. Stuntz to Wilbur Crafts, 2 May 1903, file 1023–17, entry 5, RG 350, NA. Kenton J. Clymer provides an informative discussion of missionary influence in *Protestant Missionaries in the Philippines, 1898–1916: An Inquiry into American Colonial Mentality* (Urbana: University of Illinois Press, 1986).

16. Charles H. Fahs to President Theodore Roosevelt, 9 June 1903, file 1023–28, entry 5, RG 350, NA.

17. Ide, memorandum.

18. Root to Taft; William H. Taft to Elihu Root (confidential), 13 July 1903, file 1023–25, entry 5, RG 350, NA. Many of the cables on the proposed bill were retyped in this file for release to the press.

19. Presidential approval was required for all grants of economic concessions during these years of transition from military to civilian rule, but it was a rare intervention. See Garel A. Grunder, *The Philippines and the United States* (Norman: University of Oklahoma Press, 1951), 74–81; and Philip C. Jessup, *Elihu Root, Vol. 1: 1845–1909* (New York: Dodd, Mead and Co., 1938), 359.

20. Clarence Edwards, chief, Bureau of Insular Affairs, to William H. Taft, 9 June 1903, file 1023–5, entry 5, RG 350, NA.

21. Jessup, *Elihu Root*, 1:345.

22. Elihu Root to William Taft, 17 June 1903; Elihu Root to William H. Taft, 10 July 1903. Both in file 1023–25, entry 5, RG 350, NA.

23. Taft's language echoes eerily an editorial from the *Straits Times* of 24 October 1863, which stated: "If our thus adding to the expense of the vice, at the same time adds to our revenue, it should be a matter of congratulation with us, and not of superstitious aversion." *Straits Times*, as Quoted in Trocki, *Opium and Empire*, 205.

24. Root to Taft (10 July 1903).

25. Root to Taft (14 July 1903).

26. Trocki, *Opium and Empire*, 206–9. See also Cheng U Wen, "Opium in the Straits Settlements, 1867–1910," *Journal of Southeast Asian History* 2, no. 1 (March 1961): 52–60.

27. *Philippine Opium Report*, 30–31.

28. Rush, *Opium to Java*, 220–23. The system did not function as hoped, partly because the Opium Regie did not lead to good promotions and career development. It therefore did not attract the best people.

29. Taft, for example, noted that the "real cause" of the proposal for opium farms in 1903 was "increase of [opium] use among Filipinos," which was to be avoided: Taft to Root (13 July 1903).

30. As quoted in Grunder, *The Philippines and the United States*, 37.

31. As quoted in Chantal Descours-Gatin, *Quand l'opium finançait la colonisation en Indochine* (Paris: L'Harmattan, 1992), 39. The quote is from 1869.

32. Rush, *Opium to Java*, 199, 218. The Ethical Policy is the name given to reformers' attempts around the turn of the century to do well by doing good. They wanted to improve the standard of living of Indonesians both because they believed it was their duty and because the Indonesians could then become better laborers.

33. Ibid., 201–3. The novel *Max Havelaar*, written by Edward Douwes Dekker under the pen name Multatuli, was designed to expose to the Dutch people the horrors and degradations of the Dutch colonial system of the 1850s, much as Harriet Beecher Stowe exposed the slave system in *Uncle Tom's Cabin*.

34. This issue is gaining increasing attention. One important study is Thongchai Wini-chakul, *Siam Mapped: A History of the Geo-Body of a Nation* (Honolulu: University of Hawai'i Press, 1994).

35. The intimate connections between the expansion of control and the notion of a civilizing mission seem increasingly clear. The chapter by Patricio N. Abinales in this collection is particularly helpful for understanding the domestic sources of both for U.S. officials.

36. Rush, *Opium to Java*, 198. Groenveldt reported that French officials also had worried that the monthly reports from the opium farmers in Indochina "never corresponded, as far as they could tell, with the truth." W. P. Groenveldt, *Rapport over het Opium-Monopolie in Fransch Indo-China* (Batavia: Landsdrukkerij, 1899), 23–24.

37. Concern about this issue was one motivation for the French to change their system. See Groenveldt, *Rapport*, 26–31. The British had similar worries in the Straits Settlements, as discussed in Margaret Julia Beng Chu Lim, "Control of the Opium Trade in Malaya, 1900–1912" (master's thesis, London School of Economics, London, 1965), 70–80.

38. Descours-Gatin, *Quand l'opium*, 91–95.

39. Groenveldt, *Rapport*, 128–37; Rush, *Opium to Java*, 209–10.

40. Rush, *Opium to Java*, 214.

41. John M. Jennings, *The Opium Empire: Japanese Imperialism and Drug Trafficking in Asia, 1895–1945* (Westport, Conn.: Praeger, 1997), 20.

42. *Philippine Opium Report*, 53.

43. Charles H. Brent, Bishop, Episcopal Mission in the Philippines, to James F. Smith, U.S. Commissioner of Education, 6 July 1903, file 1023–68, entry 5, RG 350, NA. Governor Taft personally selected Brent for the Opium Committee. See cable from C. Magoon, Law Officer, Bureau of Insular Affairs, to Elihu Root, 25 July 1903, file 1023–52, entry 5, RG 350, NA.

44. David Edward Owen, *British Opium Policy in China and India* (New Haven: Yale University Press, 1934), 327.

45. *Philippine Opium Report*, 18, 20.

46. Ibid., 23, 28–29.

47. Ibid., 37.

48. Ibid., 40.

49. Ibid., 40, 46–47.

50. Ibid., 14, 20, 45, 48.

51. Delay may have resulted in part from the change in personnel after Governor Taft left to become Secretary of War in December 1903. The quote is from an 8 January 1905 copy of a telegram from William H. Taft, Secretary of War, to Luke E. Wright, Governor-General of the Philippines, 6 January 1905, file 1023–110; the reference to the original date is in Luke E. Wright to William H. Taft, 8 January 1905, file 1023–111. Both are in entry 5, RG 350, NA.

52. Wright to Taft (8 January 1905).

53. Referred to in "An Act for the Purpose of Restricting the Sale and Suppressing the Evil Resulting from the Sale and Use of Opium," 8 March 1906, file 1023–44, entry 5, RG 350, NA.

54. *Report on International Opium Commission*, Senate doc. 377, 61st Cong., 2d sess. (1910), 27–28; Elihu Root, Secretary of State, to President Theodore Roosevelt, 7 May 1908, in *Foreign Relations of the United States* (Washington, D.C.: Government Printing Office, 1908), 88 (hereafter, *FRUS*).

55. Charles H. Brent to Theodore Roosevelt, 24 July 1906, in *FRUS 1906*, 1:360–61.

56. William H. Taft, Secretary of War, to President Theodore Roosevelt, 1 September 1906, roll 104, microcopy 862, RG 59, Records of the Department of State, NA.

57. Charles Denby, Department of State, to Robert Bacon (Assistant Secretary of State), 7 September 1906, roll 104, microcopy 862, RG 59, NA; invitation by Alvey A. Adee, Acting Secretary of State, to Whitelaw Reid, U.S. Ambassador to Britain, 27 September 1906, in *FRUS 1906*, 1:361–62.

58. James Avery Joyce, *Broken Star: The Story of the League of Nations (1919–1939)* (Swansea: C. Davies, 1978), 69; F. S. Northedge, *The League of Nations: Its Life and Times 1920–1946* (New York: Holmes and Meier, 1986), 182–86.

59. Trocki, *Opium to Empire*, 210.

60. Trocki does mention this decision as part of the 1906 turning point, saying that prohibition began that year. The law was passed in Congress in 1905, and prohibition did not begin until 1908. The 1906 Philippine law did, however, make preparations for the coming total prohibition.

61. The Opium Committee had made a similar claim about the impossibility of allowing some groups within a country to smoke opium and forbidding it to others.

62. For discussion of the regional consequences of developments after the 1909 meeting, see Anne L. Foster, "Prohibition as Superiority: Policing Opium in South-East Asia, 1898–1925," *International History Review* 22, no. 2 (June 2000): 253–73.

63. James F. Smith, Governor-General of the Philippines, to U.S. Consul-General at Shanghai, 19 February 1909, entry 33, RG 43 Records of International Conferences, Commissions, and Expositions, NA; International Opium Commission, *Report of the International Opium Commission, Shanghai, China, February 1 to February 26, 1909, Vol. 1: Report of the Proceedings, Vol. 2: Reports of the Delegations* (Shanghai: North-China Daily News and Herald, 1909), 20 (hereafter, *Proceedings*).

64. *Proceedings*, 47, 51.

65. Ibid., 84. Initially, the U.S. delegates were not happy with the compromise. Hamilton Wright was especially upset. See his complaints in Elihu Root, Secretary of State, report by the American Delegation to the International Opium Commission (confidential), 1 March 1909, entry 47, RG 43, NA.

DONNA J. AMOROSO

Inheriting the "Moro Problem":

Muslim Authority and Colonial Rule

in British Malaya and the Philippines

In 1904, George Langhorne, a captain in the Eleventh Cavalry and secretary of the Philippines' Moro Province, made a survey of neighboring colonial possessions. Langhorne visited and reported on Dutch and British rule in Java, Sarawak, Singapore, and the Federated Malay States. Langhorne, an admirer of European imperialism, was following up an earlier idea. He wrote in his report that, "in 1899, en route to the Philippines for the first time, I passed through London and went to the colonial office there, and . . . asked the officials if they had any colony where the people were similar to those of these islands. They then told me of the Malay States and gave me a number of blue books, reports, etc. . . . They were of much use in the associations I had with the Filipinos during my first tour in Luzon."[1]

Langhorne's report reflects an emergent colonial power orienting itself to its new role and offers us entry into two related aspects of that process. First is the notion of comparability. The remarkable image of Langhorne stopping by the British Colonial Office reminds us that, although Americans were initially profoundly ignorant about their new possession, they perceived a similarity of peoples in the region and in the task of colonial government itself. These perceived similarities, along with Langhorne's reference to "these islands," should caution us about how Americans thought of their new possessions at the turn of the century. Rather than take for granted "the Philippines" as a singular geographical body, we should remember that "the Philippine islands" were often referred to in the plural, reflecting both their social diversity and Spain's minimal control of the southern part of the archipelago. The first decade of American policy in the south especially hinged on this absence of a definitive "Philippines": The contested process of integrating Muslim Mindanao into the whole—juridically, administratively, legislatively, and fiscally—did not begin until 1913. In the context of exploring comparative and alternative approaches to colonial rule in Mindanao, this suggests that we seek comparisons not only, or even primarily, within the Philippines. The integration and definition of the Philippines was precisely what was at hand, but within a wider frame of reference.

Related to comparison, and at the heart of America's orientation to empire, was classification. The success of colonial government was understood to depend in part on selecting methods of government suited to the characteristics of the colonized people. When officials pursued comparisons with British Malaya, the Netherlands Indies, or Native American reservations in the American West, this pragmatic purpose was never far from mind. Because Langhorne knew something about Malays, he reasoned, he was successful in dealing with Filipinos. But a contending frame of reference inherited from the Spanish also possessed considerable explanatory power. This view, while accepting historical regional links, put much more emphasis on a contemporary duality between Muslims—the incompletely conquered "Moros," cousins to the Muslim Malays under British rule—and the numerically dominant Hispanized Christian Filipinos. Tension between the two frameworks was complicated by the relative standing of Britain and Spain as imperial powers and by the desire of U.S. officials to distinguish American colonial outcomes from both.

In contrast to the alleged tyranny and decadence of Spanish imperialism, the supremacy of Anglo-Saxon civilization and self-proclaimed British governing genius were accepted at face value.[2] When the first Philippine Commission proposed a plan for the American government of the Philippines, it critiqued the Spanish system of government and used British Malaya as a basic model for some aspects of the colonial relationship.[3] The projected number of American officials—one per 250,000 natives—was based on the idea that five British officials set up governments in three Malay states in 1874. And the system of indirect rule, in which British "advice must be asked and acted upon" by indigenous rulers, was praised; it was thought that Filipinos might benefit from a system used in "the political education of their brother Malayans."[4]

But the commission rejected in principle an American protectorate modeled on Britain's indirect rule of the Federated Malay States, where British officials governed in the name of Malay sultans.[5] There were found to be "two fundamental differences between the conditions and circumstances of the Malayans and Filipinos." First, while the United States was in possession of sovereignty over the Philippine Islands, British intervention in Malaya had come through "voluntary engagement" with sovereign chiefs. That is, due to anarchic conditions resulting in erratic revenues, Malay rulers had invited, or had been induced to invite, British advice and influence to restore order and profitability. Second, in Malaya "there was in each state an established sovereign to whom the people owed and recognized allegiance." In the Philippines, Spanish rule had eradicated such a hereditary leadership, and "now that Spanish sovereignty is gone there are no constituted authorities, no natural leaders, who can speak for the inhabitants of the archipelago." The idea that Emilio Aguinaldo was such a leader was dismissed; apparently, even the Tagalogs "never entertained for their parvenu dictator that universal, deep, and life-long loyalty which binds the Malayan to his hereditary sultan."[6]

In these interpretations of Philippine status and leadership the commission distinguished between the Christians of Luzon and the Visayas, on the one hand, and the Muslims of the Sulu archipelago, Mindanao, and Palawan, on the other. Because the Moro areas had never come under effective Spanish control, the sovereignty over them that the United States had inherited from Spain was only "a nominal suzerainty." This made the Moros more analogous to the Malays, particularly with regard to the "undiminished vigor" of their indigenous institutions of leadership—the sultans and *datus*, or chiefs. Therefore, it was suggested that the British model of indirect rule might be appropriate there but nowhere else in the Philippines. This report established the similarity of Malays to Moros while dismissing the link between Malays and Christian Filipinos that Langhorne had assumed. It also opened a debate about the proper method of governing what were described as "semi-civilized and barbarous people," a debate to which two institutions, the Bureau of Non-Christian Tribes and the U.S. Army, would make decisive contributions.

This essay examines the contending comparative frameworks for classifying the Muslims of Sulu and Mindanao and the contending philosophies of their governance in the first decade of colonial rule. The inherited Spanish framework of knowledge, though largely replaced as Americans accumulated their own experience, imprinted on American policy makers the assumption that the Muslims, by virtue of their religion, culture, and independence from Spain, were something of a "nonstandard" version of the Filipino, a minority to be integrated into the Christian majority. In the ethnographic vision pieced together by the Bureau of Non-Christian Tribes, the Philippines was pictured not as a nation but as a collection of racial and tribal subgroups in need of integration. Along with the pagans, the Muslims represented the extreme case of non-integration and were labeled "wild" in contrast to "civilized" Christians.

This initial understanding of the place of Muslims in the Philippines had important implications for developing the purpose and methods of governance, the direct responsibility of the U.S. Army. Conceiving of the Muslims as a hostile minority culture gave army rule its raison d'être—to civilize and integrate them. Thus, no matter how much similarity was acknowledged between the Muslims under American and British control, there would be a strong disinclination to validate or reinforce Muslim structures of authority, even if only nominally. But army rule was also imbued with institutional practices and ideological premises that undercut its integrating mission: paternalistic distrust of democracy, neutrality toward evangelism, antipathy toward Hispanized Filipinos, and a wish to populate the new "frontier" that fed recurrent dreams of Mindanao separatism.[7] These tendencies meant that the army often construed its responsibility to the Muslims in a wholly opposite light—to protect them from the "debased" majority until they could be integrated without being overwhelmed. These contradictory impulses were never resolved but continued to inform evolving notions of Moro Mindanao.

THE SPANISH INHERITANCE

Initial American impressions of the Philippines were heavily filtered through the writings of Spaniards and other Europeans. This filter can be seen in the ethnographic survey in the first *Report of the Philippine Commission*, a compilation and translation of Jesuit scholarship that discusses the peopling of the Philippine islands through waves of migration from other parts of Asia.[8] In understanding Mindanao and Sulu,

Americans were particularly dependent on the Spanish Jesuits, who had established a missionary presence there in the second half of the nineteenth century and who viewed the population through a religious lens.[9] The Muslims, who are characterized by linguistic and political diversity, were grouped together as "Moros," a name derived from the "Moors" Spain had fought closer to home. As Muslims, these Moros, too, were an enemy: "The Moro tribe ought to be cited among the peoples which have most deeply impressed their characteristics in these islands. In an evil hour a death-bearing plague of them invaded many regions of India and the archipelago of Oceania."[10] Their refusal to yield to the Jesuits and become Christian rendered the Muslims a minority and thus a problem in the mostly Christian Philippines. Spanish Jesuits and American colonizers shared the idea that civilization was bound up with Christianity. The stubbornly Muslim Moros were thus not civilized and showed no interest in becoming so. This was the Moro Problem.

All other aspects of Moro life were seen to flow from this problem: their "warlike and hostile spirit," hostility to outside authority, "tendency toward robbery and piracy," attacks on Christian towns, ignorance and cruelty, pride and laziness, and immoral attachment to the vices of polygamy and slavery. The Moros were even criticized for being bad Muslims, because most of them could not read the Quran and were superstitious.[11]

The most influential Spanish account of the Moros was not simply incorporated into American writings but reproduced in official government publications at least twice. Reverend Pio Pi, Superior of the Jesuit Order, wrote a thirty-one–page monograph, "The Moros of the Philippines," in 1901 for the consideration of American policymakers. It was appended in its entirety to the 1903 report of General George Davis, then commanding the Division of the Philippines, and in an abridged version to the first census of the Philippines in 1905.[12] Pi first addressed himself to proving that the Moros would always constitute an impediment to the "reduction [i.e., conversion], colonization and civilization of Mindanao"—in other words, that they were indeed a problem.[13] He cited their haughtiness, their sense of superiority to other peoples, their consideration of themselves as the "true lords of Mindanao and Jolo," and their fanatical conviction that only their religion was true. With evident exasperation, he described how Moro resistance to Spain had been "constant and tenacious" for more than three centuries and how every submission to Spanish authority ended with "treacherous" rebellion. He attributed their zeal to love of wealth, love of their territory, and love of independence. Pi explicitly connected the Moros' cultural identity and political organization to their control over their territory and the pagan peoples who lived there with them. Thus, conversion and civilization would destroy the Moros' ability "to preserve their possessions and advantageous positions." Pi asserted that Moros were well aware of this connection and that it stiffened their resistance: "It is . . . certain that the day in which the reduction becomes a fact, all their autonomy and their political, military and religious organization must cease to exist. . . . Well they know that this would be the loss of the interior constitution of their people, the end of their nationality still sustained in those islands, and above all, in their disappearance from the country as a distinct race."[14]

That which the Moro feared, the Jesuit desired. But how could that end be attained?

Pi recommended a four-pronged approach. First, he asserted that some Moros were less hostile than others and called for the so-called "submissive Moros" to be assimilated and gradually treated like other Filipinos. What he desired was the separation of Moro society from the sultans and datus, whom he blamed for perpetuating the evil characteristics of the race and for tyrannizing and reducing to slavery most of their fellow Moros. Second, he would emancipate all pagan slaves held by Moros, pointing out that their labor would be necessary to the development of Mindanao. Third, Pi recommended the use of force against Moros who would not submit: "The Government ought to . . . proceed to the reduction of Moroism as it exists in the Philippines, to a perfect assimilation with the remaining population under a common law and this under the penalty of driving it out from the territory by means of war."[15] To this end, Pi urged a frequent and vigilant presence by the army and navy at forts and outposts, ports and rivers. He also envisioned the posting of police who would protect Moros from abuse by their sultans and datus, as well as by whites and one another. Finally, Pi would have the government protect Catholic missionaries, arguing that this would not violate the principle of religious liberty so long as none were converted by force; furthermore, a converted Moro was likely to be a loyal subject of the state.

Pi's approach was typical of the Spanish framework: the Moro-qua-Moro was a timeless enemy, always capable of treachery; the hereditary leadership was the repository of Moro evil and should not be dealt with; race could disappear through conversion, which was synonymous with civilizing. To the Jesuit, the "aim was to accomplish the perfect assimilation of the Moros into the other races."[16] The only good Moro was an assimilated Moro—that is, no Moro at all. Many of these assumptions would be long-lived, but as the U.S. Army gained experience, others were challenged.

The first thing Americans discovered was that Moros were not unremittingly hostile and that good results could come from sending officers among them unarmed. According to Brigadier-General W. A. Kobbe, commander of the Military District of Mindanao and Jolo (1900–1901), "This policy was so much in contrast with the policy of the Spaniards, who never permitted their officers to leave the town except under a strong guard of armed soldiers, that it never failed to take the Moros by surprise, and it proved that not only was our confidence not misplaced, but that the Moro is not all bad, as some Spanish historians would lead us to believe." Kobbe also found it easy to make alliances with "wealthy and powerful datos" in Mindanao who had an interest in the establishment of stable government. This led him to arrive at a more nuanced assessment of Muslim leadership: "The government of each dato is paternal and, while arbitrary, is by no means oppressive, and the result has been that certain datos are becoming more powerful and rich at the expense of poorer rivals, because the followers and retainers of the latter leave them and seek the distinction, protection, and comforts which the former offer."[17]

In general, American exposure to Moro society during the establishment of military government (1899–1903) led to a rejection of Spanish assessments and methods. In some cases, qualities the Spanish fathers had condemned, such as "personal pride and dignity," were admired by the Americans and even credited with the often good relations obtaining between Moros and Americans. The army's method of governing was also contrasted with Spanish practice and accorded credit: "American officers . . . unlike the Spaniards, have treated him as an equal with an intuition born of [his] own free institutions." Some of the received wisdom was rejected outright: "They are in no wise prejudiced against the religion of others, but may be converted into bitter enemies by the slightest interference with their own. . . . They are not lazy, in spite of assertions to the contrary, but have something of the warrior's contempt for labor. . . . They are universally addicted to gambling and chew betel, but as a race are neither liars nor thieves."[18]

Neither were army officers interested in conversion. Expediency as well as principle dictated that the U.S. Army would not interfere with Muslim religious practice; it was the easiest way to avoid conflict with the Moros. Removing conversion as the primary goal of colonization led to some blurring of the official categories that had been established according to religion. Moros were officially classified as "wild," but Americans tended to reserve that term for the pagans, referring to the Moros as barbarous, semi-civilized, and semi-savage.[19] Then, too, as Americans increasingly measured the Moros against the standard of "Anglo-Saxon civilization," they further rejected Spanish religious categories for evolving racialist ones.[20]

Army officers had a precedent for constructing a new, secular framework for understanding the Moros—their role fighting and governing Native Americans in the United States.[21] Able to draw from their own experience rather than the increasingly suspect Spanish sources, officers often compared the Moros to the Native Americans. To a friendly observer such as Kobbe, the Moros compared favorably: "The Moros of Mindanao are very like the best North American Indians—as the Nez Perce and Northern Cheyenne—in features and manners, in their love of independence, and in personal dignity and pride."[22] Others were not so positive, judging the Native Americans to be more skillful and innovative fighters.[23] However, the important change is that the categories were secular, based on observation of physical characteristics, customs, and political institutions. In short, a scientific view was being developed.

The Bureau of Non-Christian Tribes exemplified the professional secularism of this evolving American framework, banishing the religious for the ethnographic. The Philippine Commission had accepted the Spanish division of *civilized* and *uncivilized* and had concentrated on policy for the civilized. The bureau was established in 1901 to remedy this neglect of the uncivilized, "to investigate the actual conditions of these pagan and Mohammedan tribes, . . . to recommend legislation for their civil government, and . . . to conduct scientific investigations in the ethnology of the Philippines."[24] From the start, the focus shifted from conversion to "correct understanding and scientific grasp" in order to govern effectively and "rear a new standard of relationship between the white man and the Malay."[25] Not only the Spanish but all European encounters with "the mind of the Malay" (here referring broadly to the people of insular Southeast Asia) were judged a failure; the science of ethnology being developed in American universities would lay the basis for a better future.[26] To pursue these ends, the bureau conducted field-work throughout the Philippines, published ethnographic studies, and started a small museum.

In his first report, the bureau's chief, David P. Barrows, singled out the work of the Austrian Ferdinand Blumentritt as the "starting point for future research." Blumentritt was a wave-migration theorist; grounding the bureau's work in this theory brought all Filipinos into the eth-nographic universe of Southeast Asia, diluting the Spanish division be-tween Christian and Muslim but laying the basis for multiple tribal or racial distinctions. The Negritos, for example, were judged "almost cer-tain" to be identical with the Sakai of the Malay Peninsula, the Ifugao to be "mixed Negrito–Malayans." The Visayans "represent a Malayan mi-gratory wave" that "felt the contact of the Hindu civilization" of Java and the Malay Peninsula, and the Muslim Malays "arrived in the Sulu Archi-pelago probably between 1300 and 1400 A.D."[27] Aside from culture and language, the judgment rested most basically on physical characteristics: "Dwarf," "tall in stature," "dark color," "wavy hair," and "frizzy hair" were phrases used to distinguish one tribe from another. To be sure, this classification into distinct subgroups was a hard fit. At times, the reports leave off their careful delineations in frustration: "There is a confused mass of tribes in Davao and vicinity, about which very little that is authentic is known."[28] This approach did, however, lead the Americans to recognize the diversity obscured by the designation "Moro": "Contrary to the general idea, the term Moro covers not one people with common customs and a common language, but a number of tribes of Mindanao and the neighboring islands, who differ in customs and in language but have the common tie of the religion of Mohammed."[29] Thus situated ethnographically, the Moro was no longer demonized and did not stand alone as the one factor preventing the civilization of Mindanao.

But the Moros, like other non-Christians, were still construed as a "minority." With racial distinctions overlaying the obvious religious dif-ference, this construction had probably been hardened. Minority status was reflected in the continuing division of policy and jurisdiction be-tween Christians and non-Christians. Although the bureau was respon-sible for cataloguing all the racial and tribal sub-groups it perceived in the Philippines, it had a special responsibility, as its name suggests, for non-Christians. And the military continued to administer those areas where non-Christians predominated, as other areas of the Philippines were "pacified" and shifted to civilian control. Although accommodation with Christian Filipino elites was settled on quite early, the best way to rule Muslims would be the subject of debate for several years.

Like army officers, Barrows had occasion to compare the people under his jurisdiction with Native Americans. When first appointed to his post, Barrows was instructed to investigate Native American reservations and schools for models that could be used in the Philippines. His conclusions were entirely negative. He particularly condemned the impoverishing reservation system, the violations of "solemn promises" about land rights, and the large boarding schools. Barrows found that by teaching Native Americans as if they were city dwellers, the schools were "nearly useless to the Indian." His critique of Native American education is instructive for how it resonates with British thinking about education for colonial subjects. Like most British administrators, Barrows concluded that education "among these races should be of an exceedingly practical character—being largely industrial." Unlike the British, however, Barrows and other Americans believed that everyone should be taught English.[30] The reason for the difference went to the heart of the colonial project—in the American case, integration with the majority, which was also being taught English to serve the larger goal of Americanization.

Barrows's commentary pointed to a further difference between British and American colonization efforts. He noted that Native Americans were "clothed" with authority to keep the peace and bring offenders to trial under the supervision of U.S. agents. This worked well, he argued, because Native American leadership was neither oppressive nor hereditary, their society "thoroughly democratic." In contrast, he described "Malayan society, as we find it in the Philippines" to be "oppressively aristocratic." His conclusion is worth quoting in its entirety: "The power of the man of wealth, position, or inheritance is inordinate. He is not only able to commit abuses, but is morally blinded to their enormity. Beneath him the man of poverty and unenlightened mind takes rank with the animals that till the soil. I believe that this characterization is true of *both Christian and non-Christian communities*. The intrusting of authority, then, especially police and judicial authority, should be safeguarded and restricted in every possible way."[31]

This passage represents a dissent from the American accommodation with the "enlightened" Philippine elite, which was to enjoy precisely this kind of authority. But while no one read Barrows's report for advice on the Christian Filipinos, the condemnation of Muslim authority—especially the aristocratic nature of the sultans and datus—did become common among the military officers stationed in Moro Province. Although secularization and ethnographic classification had established the comparability of Moros and Malays, American and British attitudes toward those societies would be at odds.

THE BRITISH MODEL OF INDIRECT RULE

When Americans looked at the Federated Malay States, they saw a system of indirect rule that preserved indigenous structures of authority while securing strict British control over revenues and expenditures. To the Philippine Commission, British Malaya was a "veiled crown colony" in which "the Sultan has only the semblance of power, the British authorities having absolute control, even to the point of exercising such acts of dominion as the deposition of the Sultan, the settlement of his succession, and a general manumission of slaves."[32] But the continued and highly visible presence of the aristocratic element was significant in determining American attitudes toward indirect rule. What should be the relationship between a "civilizing" colonial power and a hereditary indigenous elite?

Established in the last quarter of the nineteenth century, British rule in the Malay states transformed the economic, demographic, and political foundations of the peninsula, yet the British also sought to preserve Malay society in traditional form—overwhelmingly rural, politically docile, and deferential to traditional aristocracies and royalties. This would have been a surprising outcome to any Briton resident in the area in the early- to mid-nineteenth century. At that time, British power was based in the Straits Settlements, especially Singapore, from whence its influence radiated to the peninsula. British opinion, then, was very hostile to Malay culture. In pursuit of raw materials, investment opportunities, and free trade, the British demanded within their sphere of influence what they called good government, or civilization. This was characterized by the rule of law, the creation of wealth through capitalism, and free labor. In contrast, Malay culture was condemned as offering mainly piracy, civil war, and slavery.

Malay politics before colonial rule consisted of control of manpower embedded in a spiritual system of leadership. Malay rulers represented "the organizing principle in the Malay world," and their success was measured by graceful demeanor and the spiritual rewards they bestowed as much as by their military achievements.[33] Successful rulers maintained large retinues of followers and slaves. Their ability to command obeisance of more or less autonomous regional chiefs ebbed and flowed. Where the role of wealth was to further politico-spiritual power, rulers did their best to monopolize trade and appropriate surplus, although this meant that no one became very wealthy. British demands over the course of the century for protection of property, free labor, and the safe movement of capital were demands the Malay system simply could not meet. They were not part of the Malay world on the eve of colonial rule, as they were not in Mindanao and Sulu in 1899.

The moral condemnation heaped on the Malays was thus quite similar to American criticism of the Moros: arbitrary justice, extortion by the chiefs, no civil service—in short, no civilization. It was argued by expansionists in the 1850s and 1860s that the extension of British control over the states of the peninsula would be justified by the imposition of British values and the consequent progress the Malays would make toward civilization.

Yet by the early 1880s, as the British extended their control to the peninsula, a new attitude was ascendant: As an Oriental people, the Malays were deemed incapable of achieving the same heights of civilization as the British and probably would never be able to govern themselves well.[34] This shift in attitude, from the Enlightenment belief in the perfectibility of man to the idea of inherent racial inferiority, was no doubt encouraged by the very fact of foreign rule. Once in control of the peninsula, the colonial power no longer relied on the triumph of liberal ideas among the Malays. The British would provide the legal and economic structure necessary for the territory to develop, regardless of the progress made by the Malays themselves. Within this legal structure, backed by military power, those aspects of nineteenth-century Malay society that hindered capitalism were gradually eliminated: slavery, piracy, Malay control over revenue collection and justice. The new economic structure—ports, railways, land-tenure system—facilitated an influx of capital, followed by large numbers of Chinese laborers, who would eventually outnumber the Malay population on the west coast.[35] In essence, British control would render the Malays first harmless, then superfluous to the project of expanding capital.

But Malays had not been blind to the opportunities offered by a changing economy. Backed by investors in the Straits Settlements, Malay chiefs on the west coast had been teaming up with Chinese miners to make money from the booming demand for tin, as well as the sale of spirits and opium to the Chinese laborers who mined it. This had given chiefs who were lucky enough to be sitting on tin an enhanced ability to move beyond the reach of their rulers, leading, in turn, to increased political rivalry and instability. In Malay terms, this was a swing of the pendulum in the historical tension between rulers and chiefs, even if the new elements of foreign capital and labor made the swing extreme. To the British, it was a loss of power by "central governments"—a sign of "decay" in Malay culture and further justification for intervention.[36]

As British control was consolidated in the 1880s and 1890s, then, Malay culture became less and less a hindrance to capitalism. But at the same time, because changing that culture was no longer a priority, its supposed "decay" became a cause for concern. If the Malays could no longer aspire to be civilized like the British, they must certainly remain recognizably Malay, lest they fall into the despised category of imperfectly Westernized Oriental. Hence, the British became nostalgic about the Malays, obsessive in their search for the "true Malay" and determined to restore and preserve Malay culture.

But what was Malay culture? In a view that served colonial interests, Malay culture was distilled into two components: an agrarian economic base and a feudal class structure. Nineteenth-century British maritime power and the suppression of piracy had forced Malay power to shift from the sea to the land, resulting in a sharp drop in strength and resources. Then, beginning in the late nineteenth century, the arrival of immigrant labor at plantations and mines made Malaya a rice-deficient area. Forced to import rice from other parts of the empire, the colonial government increasingly urged higher levels of Malay rice production. The evolving needs of the export-oriented economy thus dovetailed with what was construed as the natural or traditional occupation of the Malays. Finally, the British mechanism for extending control over the

Malay states, as the commission had noted, acknowledged their sovereignty. Protectorate treaties, rather than direct rule, necessitated the retention of a reformed and subordinate ruling elite.

Malay rulers and chiefs used this shift in emphasis from civilization to preservation to survive the surge of British power that had at first threatened to sweep them away. With British encouragement and on their own initiative, rulers and chiefs quickly invoked tradition to safeguard a position in the new colonial order. It was a selective tradition, to be sure: The opium-smoking ruler and the chief with multiple *krises* (curved daggers) tucked into the waist of his *sarung* faded away. It was often an invented tradition: State council meetings attended by British, Malays, and Chinese required new royal ceremonial to legitimize the innovative gathering of colonial officialdom, hereditary privilege, and foreign capital. It was a standardized tradition: Most Malay rulers now took the title "sultan," in the style of proper Muslim royalty. And it was a hybrid tradition: Imported foreign elements such as the honor guard of Sikh soldiers, the seventeen-gun salute, the oath of office, and the loyal toast to Queen Victoria located Malay ritual firmly within the greater glory of the British Empire.[37]

Finally, it was a tradition that heavily favored rulers over chiefs. To correct the imbalance they perceived, the British reduced the number of chiefs eligible for pensions, while the alien requirements of good government meant that few of the first generation under colonial rule made suitable magistrates. The one area of administration reserved to Malays under the terms of the treaties—Malay religion and custom—became the avenue of further royal power. No longer governing all of Malay life as before colonial rule, religious courts concentrated on marriage, divorce, inheritance, and religious observance. In some states, *kathis* (religious officials) advised British law officers on Malay custom in matters of civil law. In all cases, kathis became officers of the state whose appointment, powers, and salary were acknowledged to be the ruler's area of responsibility. British oversight eliminated practices that offended liberal sensibilities—fines replaced flogging as punishment—but Muslim law was a visible feature of traditional authority that the colonial power committed itself to maintaining. In time, this commitment would result in large religious establishments that bolstered the political power of the Malay rulers.

The most visible feature of updated Malay tradition was the rulers' public role. As their positions became stabilized politically and through regular salaries, Malay rulers pursued the development of a new, highly public manner of living that was greatly influenced by European models of royalty. Their clothes and residences, only recently much like those of Malay peasants, now consumed tens of thousands of dollars a year. Rulers dressed in Western suits with a modified Malay sarung; residences were built to look like Moorish palaces; trips were taken to Singapore, Penang, and London; travel was by steamship, yacht, and horse-drawn carriage. It was above all the public nature of this transformation that was significant. The visibility of the Malay ruler was proof that his state was still a Malayo-Muslim sultanate. It cemented his place within his own society—for none could challenge his British backers—while shielding from view his state's subordination to the British Empire. This was the model of Muslim authority under indirect rule, as seen from Manila.

It was also the model as seen from Jolo. Sultan Jamal-ul-Kiram, whose Sulu sultanate had extensive trading relationships in China and Southeast Asia, spent part of each year in Singapore and had his own Sikh guard.[38] Sulu also had connections with the British through North Borneo. In 1878, the nascent British North Borneo Company had acquired the right to administer territories in northeastern Borneo from Sulu for an annual rent of $5,000.[39] This move eclipsed the company's American and British competitors, and in 1885 Spain also renounced claims of sovereignty over North Borneo. Since 1851, however, the Spanish had claimed sovereignty over Sulu itself, an overlordship that was conceded by the defeated sultan in that year and again in 1878. Nevertheless, Spain was seldom able to exercise more than nominal control over the Sulu archipelago, and the British North Borneo Company never recognized Spanish sovereignty there. Insistence that the sultan was an independent ruler had the effect of legitimizing the North Borneo cession, where the sultan was always accorded an honor guard and twenty-one–gun salute when he visited.[40]

In 1897, as Spain's position began to seem terminal, the sultan entered into correspondence with the acting governor of the Straits Settlements, hinting at his desire for British protection. He stopped at North Borneo on his way to Mecca late that year and at Singapore on his way home. Although the sultan received some encouragement from private quarters, the official British position was to wait and see what U.S. intentions were. Some speculated that the United States might not want to administer areas that Spain had not really governed. American rule over Sulu and Mindanao was acceptable to the British, as the United States came into the Pacific with an open-door trade policy. But German rule (which the sultan also apparently feared) was not acceptable, at the very least because of that country's economic protectionism. Once the Americans had signaled their intention to maintain possession of all the territory Spain had claimed, the British advised strongly that they exert control over piracy and slavery in the region. British interests (Colonial Office as well as the British North Borneo Company) were best served by a steady government, even if it was not British, so long as it was not German.[41]

In seeking to strengthen his ties with the British, the sultan was striving to preserve his position in the midst of changing circumstances, just like his counterparts on the Malay Peninsula. With U.S. or German control looming as an unknown prospect, the sultan appealed to the paramount power of the region. It is clear that the British practice of recognizing sovereignty and granting protection in return for control of government was seen by the sultan as the norm. Accepting a British resident whose advice "must be asked and acted upon on all questions other than those touching . . . religion and custom" probably seemed a better deal than the uncertainty surrounding American or German rule.[42] It would almost certainly have raised his standard of living. In the event, the sultan's experience under the Americans would turn out very differently, but that was not immediately apparent because of the signing of the Bates Treaty in 1899.

Brigadier-General John Bates arrived in Jolo in July 1899 in search of an agreement recognizing U.S. sovereignty; the main objective was to keep the Moros from joining the Philippine insurrection.[43] Jacob Schurman, head of the Philippine Commission, had visited the month before and won a verbal agreement from the sultan. But when Bates arrived, the sultan tried to negotiate a treaty with him that resembled an Anglo-Malay treaty, though on much more favorable terms. The sultan would promise to suppress piracy; the Americans would pay him and his principle datus, protect him from outside powers, and otherwise leave him alone. This was unacceptable to Bates only because it did not acknowledge American sovereignty; he was not averse to the payments or to leaving internal Moro affairs to the sultan. The final draft did just this and was, further, a model of vagueness, which operated to Sulu's advantage. Although the sultan recognized the United States as the sovereign power and promised to suppress piracy, the United States promised that the "rights and dignities of His Highness the Sultan and his datos shall be fully respected." Even beyond the question of whether the English and Tausug versions of the treaty conveyed the same sense of "sovereignty," the "rights" of the Moros were left undefined.[44] The draft also appeared to condone slavery, which raised an uproar in the United States. The sultan and the principle datus had clearly made what seemed like a good deal, but they had not actually guaranteed their future.

Complaints about the "agreement" (so called by the United States to deprive it of the international standing of a "treaty") came almost immediately from army officials stationed in Sulu. General Kobbe complained about the seemingly unlimited rights claimed by the sultan, such as those in "the pearl fisheries over vast and undefined areas of water." His other comments are precisely the same critiques heard from the British about the Malays earlier, but the Americans had little recourse to change the situation under the terms of the treaty: "It is known that sultan and datos inflict arbitrary fines and punishments, enrich themselves by these means, and support by them large numbers of idle retainers. It is believed that this destroys all incentive to work and keeps the common Moro and the islands poor." Kobbe was also dissatisfied with the sultan's promised cooperation against piracy: "This cooperation can not be controlled, and is believed to be perfunctory and valueless, because piracy has existed in one form or another for many years and is considered by the average Moro a perfectly fair game."[45]

There was apparently little common understanding between the Joloanos, whose expectations were based on their own experience and the Anglo-Malay model, and the Americans, who thought that the recognition of their sovereignty should carry more significance. For example, a captain stationed in the town of Siassi reported that the datu always complied with requests to arrest criminals in his locality by bringing them in on ships flying the American flag. He interpreted these actions in this way: "We deal with [the Moros] through the datos and uphold the authority of the latter in their respective districts, and *these begin to regard themselves as representing the United States*."[46] Bates also noted with satisfaction that several of the U.S. flags he had distributed as gifts were flown the next day by their recipients. He further reported that "each dato had carefully preserved the letter I had given him saying he was a friend of the United States."[47] What both American officers failed to understood was that the flags and letters increased the power of the recipient without subordinating him to the United States. The sultan and datus were able to use U.S. backing to their own advantage, much as the Malay rulers were doing on a far more profitable scale in Malaya. And because of the terms of the treaty, the United States could demand little in return.

This situation did not last long. The United States, like Britain before, had the advantage in setting the terms of its relationship with Muslim leaders. Once the Philippine insurrection was defeated, the Bates Treaty was doomed. But would the United States continue to concede a place for sultans and datus, even nominally?

THE AMERICAN POLICY OF DIRECT RULE

It was on the question of sovereignty that Americans most quickly distinguished their approach from the British. At the heart of army discontent with the Bates Treaty was the way the Joloanos played with American authority: agreeing to do as the Americans demanded, then doing just the opposite, while always acknowledging the American governor as "father" and "protector." General Davis argued that the treaty made serious and unnecessary concessions by even referring to such a thing as the "Government of the Sultan," and that to settle the question of ultimate authority "the Americans and Jolo Moros must some day come to blows."[48] So whatever similarities may be found in the American and British critiques of Malayo-Muslim society, at base their goals were different. Britain wanted to make Malays behave in a manner consistent with British interests; reluctance to annex territory had necessitated treaties with sovereign sultanates. The U.S. Army, in contrast, wanted the form of sovereignty as well as the substance of power to achieve more ambitious goals of governance.

Consequently, although the Americans noticed the same weakness of the sultans in relation to the chiefs that the British had in Malaya, they had no reason to regard this as a particular problem. Reflecting the historical tension between rulers and chiefs, Haji Butu, a principal minister of the sultan of Sulu, said it was "a Moro custom, though a bad one, [that] even when the Sultan sends for any chief, they take their own time about coming."[49] But the American commander, Brigadier-General Samuel S. Sumner, concluded simply that the sultan of Sulu was only a "nominal" leader with "very little actual control," and that "the more powerful chiefs do about as they please without any regard to his wishes or directions."[50] Davis even thought that "the Sultan's pretensions to sovereignty are often not recognized by some of the local chiefs," and noted the more extreme disintegration of royal power in Cotabato: "There is, or was, a real or pretended Sultan of Mindanao whose seat was in the Rio Grande Valley, but other dattos who are stronger have driven him away from his ancient home, and he has migrated to a remote part of the sultanate."[51] The result of this fragmentation of power was that army commanders initially spent a lot of time dealing with fighting between sultans and datus and among datus, many of whom appealed to the Americans for material assistance in defeating their enemies.[52]

A longer-term result was that, except in the case of the sultan of Sulu, Americans tended not to differentiate between sultans and datus when discussing Muslim authority. This was especially true of the Lanao district, where thirty sultans and hundreds of datus ruled about 70,000 Moros.[53] According to Sumner, the Lake Lanao and Cotabato Moros "have no general form of government, are broken up and divided into numberless tribes and clans, each ruled by a Sultan or Datto. . . . Every Datto and Sultan is a law unto himself." This fragmentation was taken as a given for a "semi-civilized" people and was seen to operate to American advantage. Sumner concluded that "it would perhaps be as well not to inaugurate any methods towards concentration of power and authority."[54]

In this context, it was the continued existence of the sultan of Sulu that appeared to be the anomaly, and arguments were soon heard in favor of a new course: "to abate the sultan nuisance, just as the Moros themselves have done with their own Sultan in Mindanao."[55] But even if the abrogation of the Bates Treaty removed the sultan, the question of how to rule would still be problematic. On the one hand, American aims of integration and civilization brought them into direct conflict with the structures of indigenous authority. Davis wrote that "Americans have come here to teach and convince these people that all men are born free and equal and that there is no such thing as inherited caste or privilege. The working out of this doctrine and the enforcement of it means the upsetting of the whole system of tribal and patriarchal government among the Moros."[56] Sumner also argued that it would be "necessary to eradicate about all the customs that have heretofore governed their habits of life."[57] Nor did the Americans intend to meet the Moros halfway, teaching them the lessons of civilization in their own languages. Where the British withheld English-language education so that Malays would remain Malay, the Americans insisted Moros learn English in order to become Americanized Filipinos.[58] To accomplish these goals, it was felt that "more direct control and supervision" was necessary.[59]

On the other hand, although the sultans could easily be dispensed with, the datus were numerous and significant. Davis therefore recommended that "no sultan or king over all the Moros . . . or over other datos be recognized," but that "hereditary datos be recognized as headmen." He took this position because he felt the Moros should not be moved away from patriarchal despotism too quickly; that it was "all they have and all they are capable of understanding."[60] Others recognized the practical side: that Americans did not have the personnel to supervise the Moro population directly. In fact, cooperative datus had already reduced the need to fight in some areas altogether—Dato Mandi in Zamboanga, for example, and Dato Piang in Cotabato.

Only one voice argued in favor of respecting datu authority for its own sake: Najeeb M. Saleeby, who worked with the Bureau of Non-Christian Tribes compiling the histories of the Moros before becoming superintendent of schools for Moro Province. Saleeby's approach was completely at odds with the military government under which he served. First, he connected the Moros to the civilization of Islam, asserting that they did in fact have a history, which included "laws, an organized government, an alphabet, and a system of education."[61] Second, he used history to explain the Moros' "pitiful state of political disunion," arguing that wars with Spain had weakened the once powerful institution of the sultanate: "Before the campaign of 1878, the sultan ruled with a strong hand, lived in state, was prosperous, and had considerable wealth. . . . [He] had every chief under his control, and held the state intact."[62] Spanish promotion of a pretender encouraged the "dispersion" of the datus. After the passing of this strong sultan, Sulu "was reduced to small, insignificant, and disunited entities" that were easy to conquer but impossible to manage. Now, only "vestiges of the former state" could be seen in some of the titles given to nobility. Saleeby declared this "an abnormal condition of affairs."[63]

He also argued that the United States was following in the disastrous footsteps of Spain, the third area in which his thinking opposed the military consensus. Saleeby wanted the datu to be respected and recognized as a "regular officer of state," because "his dignity is the dignity of his people and his good will is theirs." This was consistent with the British model, in which the dignity of the sultanate was secured, not with the evolving American model, in which indigenous leaders could, at best, represent the authority of the United States.[64]

But Saleeby was not a preservationist in the British Malayan mold. He did not propose restoring sultanates where they had disintegrated, thus endorsing the American focus on the datus. And he wanted to win over the datus to integrate the Moros with the Christian majority in social organization, if not in religion: "We can not instruct the datu unless we employ him, and he can not learn unless he retains his position and exercises his authority. . . . Let the datu's mind rest assured as to what his position and power will be and the questions of slavery, nobility, equality of rights, building public works, constructing public roads, maintaining [a] police force, establishing schools, securing labor, and acquiring homesteads, all can be solved and dispensed with in a very short while." Saleeby wrote that "nobility is actually passing away and wealth is already superseding blood." He would help the process along by establishing "datuship councils." Resembling the "old institutions of Moroland," these councils would dilute the autocratic powers of the datus and eventually approximate the municipal councils of Christian Filipinos.[65]

But Saleeby served under the Moro Province, a government that embodied the military's desire to take more direct control of the Moros, and his views carried little weight in a legislative council in which military votes outnumbered civilian votes and the three successive governors of the province were generals. Conceived as a transition from military to civil rule, the ostensible goal of the province was to bring its people under a "form of control, approximating and finally attaining the method of control exercised among the civilized peoples of the Philippine Islands." It was expected, however, to be "a long time before this object [was] attained."[66] And indeed, in its ten years of direct rule, the U.S. Army neither meaningfully engaged the existing power structure in governance nor introduced alternative, representative structures. Instead, Moro Province, inaugurated in 1903, would perpetuate the Moros' status as an uncivilized minority, only to turn them over to Christian Filipino civilian control in 1913.

Leonard Wood, the first governor of Moro Province (1903–1906), was particularly distrustful of Muslim nobility and British-style rule. Wood also took a tour of the British Empire on his way to the Philippines. He was very impressed with Cairo but less so with Malaya, disapproving of the large number of Chinese laborers and the government's reliance on revenue from opium and gambling.[67] Neither was he as sanguine about the condition of Malay royalty as Captain Langhorne, the provincial secretary, for whom the sultan of Selangor's "large palace at Jugra . . . yellow coach with good Australian horses, [and] well liveried coachmen and footmen"[68] were simply a sign of the country's prosperity. To Wood, these cut against the democratic grain. As he wrote to an English friend: "You are quite content to maintain rajahs and sultans and other species of royalty, but we, with our plain ideas of doing things, find these gentlemen outside of our scheme of government, and so have to start at this kind of proposition a little differently."[69]

Wood had an especially low opinion of the sultan of Sulu and quickly secured the abrogation of the Bates Treaty on the basis of the sultan's inability to fulfill the terms of the agreement. The absence of "good government"; the killing of Christians; the taking of slaves; the "entire failure to give their people reasonable security of life, person, and property"; the theft of U.S. property; and organized hostility to the American government were all "illustrations of the fact that this so-called Sultan and his datos have not sufficient authority to carry out the agreement."[70]

The sultan protested in a letter to the governor-general as a sovereign vassal speaks to an overlord: "The American nation is our power and protection. . . . The American nation told me when they first came to Jolo, that the reason why they came to Jolo was that they would give profit to me and to all my subjects."[71] The sultan asked for retention of his rights to pearls and tortoise shells; agreed to give up slavery ("because we see that it is for the good"), but requested compensation; and asked that the United States guarantee the sultanate "for ever and ever," as well as his line of succession, "because the Sultan is the head of the Muhammedan religion, the representative of Muhammad."

When Wood met with the sultan, he offered him only dignity, recognition of his religious leadership, and a lifetime income (nothing for his heirs).[72] The sultan was invited to stay close to the government but was supposed to give the Americans advice, not the other way around. His temporal power was gone, and without the sovereignty and visibility inherent in the Anglo-Malay model, little else was left.

Once the Bates Treaty had been abrogated, the recognition of Muslim authority expressed by the first Philippine Commission report was rejected. The sultan was deemed "worthless . . . even as a figurehead," and the British model did not, after all, apply: "The English, in dealing with the Malays of the Straits Settlements [*sic*], where the population is practically the same as that inhabiting the Sulu Archipelago and Mindanao, had adopted the . . . method [of ruling indirectly], but there the English had found a few sultans or chiefs whose authority was recognized by the people. The situation in the Moro Province . . . was very different."[73] Langhorne took the British model more seriously, but his admiring gaze saw mostly the image of muscular empire. He was impressed by the paternalism of the European governments, the maintenance of "the supremacy of the white race," and the realization that "the native has his limitations."[74] When, as acting governor in Wood's absence, Langhorne had to decide whether to accept the surrender or pursue to the death the rebel Dato Ali of Kudarangan, he strenuously chose the latter, citing "experience with our own Indians and the English and Dutch in their various colonies."[75]

But like the military commanders who preceded them, the governors of Moro Province suffered a shortage of American personnel and needed the datus to keep the peace. Accordingly, datus were selected to represent U.S. authority to the people they already led.[76] This recognition of leadership was a practical expediency, not a legitimation of indigenous authority. To emphasize this, the datus were given the new, decidedly unexalted title of "tribal ward leader" and joined the government in a structurally inferior position. (The tribal wards were on a lower political level than the fourteen municipalities initially incorporated on the basis of having advanced populations—Chinese, Christian Filipino, etc.) In return for this recognition, tribal ward leaders were to extend American rule into their communities as policemen who would deliver criminals to the American authorities.

In this way, the United States made a start at eliminating the Moro customs that were deemed inconsistent with "good government," especially slavery and the autonomous collection of tax revenue. A special priority was to end inconsistencies between Muslim and Philippine law in the punishment of crime. Murder, for example, was punished only by fine under Moro legal codes, something Wood found particularly offensive. So instead of modifying Muslim laws in accordance with American standards, as Saleeby wished, Wood simply replaced the indigenous legal systems with American laws.[77]

This policy left a whole realm of existing social relations—Muslim marriage law, for example—outside official recognition, although indigenous authorities continued to carry them out. The failure to codify Muslim legal code was a result of the American policy of neutrality on religious matters combined with army hostility to Islam. On the one hand, despite a friendliness toward Protestant missionaries that sometimes resulted in unofficial help, army officials did not risk harming Moro relations by sponsoring missionary activity.[78] On the other hand, neutrality meant that Americans would never seek to strength the position of the indigenous religion, as the British had in Malaya. Seeking to preserve neither traditional culture nor authority, Wood could simply dismiss its relevance: "It is not thought advisable to attempt to codify and put in force, under the name of laws, the customs which have hitherto obtained among these people, as many of them are revolting and but few embody principles which we would wish to perpetuate."[79] In fact, the army may have been particularly hostile to allowing religion any political or administrative place in subject societies at this time: Its own forceful opposition to the messianic Native American Ghost Dance religion had led to the massacre at Wounded Knee in 1890.[80]

THE IMPACT OF DIRECT AND INDIRECT RULE ON MALAYS AND MOROS

One can draw tentative conclusions in three areas about the effects of British and American rule on Muslim communities in Southeast Asia: (1) its impact on the ruling class; (2) its impact on the connection between religion and politics; and (3) its impact on the ascription of minority status.

The British method of indirect rule led to the apotheosis of Malay royalty and the weakening of Malay chiefs—at least, until the turn of the century. In the Philippines, the reverse was true. Sultans in Cotabato and Lanao continued to sink into obscurity, and even the sultan of Sulu was forced in 1915 to renounce his authority in return for a pension and recognition as a religious figure. By age seventy, he could no longer afford ceremonial clothing and would grant an audience to anyone who brought him cigars.[81] Meanwhile, his erstwhile adviser, Haji Butu, was demanding that Americans accord him power and prestige similar to that given the sultans of Johor and Perak by the British.[82] Eventually, even the datus would give up such dreams and instead become assemblymen in a political system dominated by Christian Filipinos.

Religious policy in Malaya and Mindanao manifested itself in both similarities and differences in outcome. Like the British, who left religion alone as a matter of preservationist policy, the Americans did not interfere with the religious practice of Moros. This was despite the avowed aim to integrate Muslims into the Philippines and the fact that it was precisely their religion that had first marked them as different. This forbearance was due to expediency, the principle of separation of church and state, and the secularization of the Spanish framework. In both Malaya and Mindanao, sultans who no longer had temporal political power were still considered guardians of the faith. This meant very little practically in Mindanao, where Muslim law was not codified. But in Malaya, it led to the development of powerful bureaucracies that enforced religious orthodoxy, thus associating early-twentieth-century reformist Islam with movements against the entrenched Malay leadership. In Mindanao, Islam was not used as tool for political mobilization until the 1960s.

Finally, in the matter of ascribing minority status to Muslim communities, the two outcomes are curiously similar and bound up with judgments about the capacity for self-government. The British held two different opinions about the Malays in two different periods of time: The mid-century belief that Malays could become civilized gave way to the late-century belief in their incapacity to govern. This shift occurred as Chinese immigration began to show a way to "open up" the country without Malay participation. By the time the Americans arrived in the Philippines, the British had abandoned the idea of civilizing the Malays, who were were on their way to becoming a minority on the west coast of Malaya.

In contrast, the Americans saw the Moros from the start as a minority to be integrated into the national life of the Philippines. By contrasting them with the more advanced Filipinos, Americans reached the same conclusion the British had about Muslim capacity for self-government. By this time, of course, the populations under British control offered an example of what the Moros might become: "industrious and peaceable and contented," but not self-governing in the foreseeable future.[83] Although political integration with the Philippines did take place, Moros continued to be seen as a religious and cultural minority by Americans, by Filipinos, and by themselves. The long-term result was marginality, dissatisfaction, and ultimately, among many, rejection of the Philippine nation-state.

NOTES

1. "Report of Geo. T. Langhorne, Captain, Eleventh Cavalry," in *Report of the Philippine Commission, 1904* (Washington, D.C.: Government Printing Office, 1904), vol. 2, 694. (Hereafter, the Philippine Commission reports are cited as *RPC*.)

2. See the massive *Colonial Administration, 1800–1900. Methods of Government and Development Adopted by the Principal Colonizing Nations in their Control of Tropical and Other Colonies and Dependencies* (Washington, D.C.: U.S. Treasury Department, Bureau of Statistics, 1901), Record Group (RG) 350, U.S. National Archives (NA).

3. "Plan of Government for the Philippines," *RPC 1900*, 1:97–121.

4. Ibid., 98, 100. In determining that "only a small number of Americans are needed as the organizing and directing brain of the civil administration of the Philippines," the ratio of British officials to population in India and Sri Lanka was also considered. Ibid., 115–16.

5. Ibid., 101. Other British models were also discussed and dismissed: the self-governing colony (exemplified by Canada), because it depended on a "community of blood, race, and language" with the mother country; the crown colony (Hong Kong), because the complete control exercised by the mother country was "inimical to the habit of self-government"; and the colony with representative institutions but not responsible government (British Guiana), because a more perfect method of safeguarding the rights of the sovereign power while encouraging the development of genuine home rule had "developed substantially into the American scheme of Territorial government." The commission sought to avoid the term *"colony,"* which it felt Filipinos would associate with oppression and misrule, and therefore recommended the territorial model developed in the settlement of the American west. Ibid., 103–6.

6. Ibid., 99–102.

7. For the structural effects of U.S. Army rule in Mindanao, which continued until 1913, see Patricio N. Abinales, *Making Mindanao: Cotabato and Davao in the Formation of the Philippine Nation-State* (Manila: Ateneo de Manila University Press, 2000).

8. *RPC 1900*, 3:333–77. For a discussion of how the "wave-migration theory" racialized Philippine cultural history, see Vicente Rafael, "White Love: Surveillance and Nationalist Resistance in the U.S. Colonization of the Philippines," in *Cultures of United States Imperialism*, ed. Amy Kaplan and Donald E. Pease (Durham, N.C.: Duke University Press, 1993), 199–200. For its lingering presence in Philippine education, see Niels Mulder, "Philippine Textbooks and the National Self-Image," *Philippine Studies* 38 (1990): 84–102.

9. The Americans also inherited Spain's allies and enemies when occupying Mindanao and Sulu. See Wayne W. Thompson, "Governors of the Moro Province: Wood, Bliss, and Pershing in the Southern Philippines, 1903–1913" (Ph.D. diss., University of California, San Diego, 1975), 29.

10. *RPC 1900*, 3:338.

11. "Character and Customs of the Moros," in ibid., 370–77.

12. "Annual Report of Major General George W. Davis, from October 1, 1902 to July 26, 1903," in *Annual Report of the War Department 1903* (Washington, D.C.: Government Printing Office, 1903), app. X. (Hereafter, the U.S. War Department reports are cited as *ARWD*.) Davis had been military commander of the Military District of Mindanao and Jolo in 1901–1902.

13. All quotes are from *ARWD 1903*, 117–49.

14. Ibid., 121.

15. Ibid., 133.

16. Ibid., 134. Pi anticipated criticism of his dismissal the datus. He acknowledged that a small number of datus had been faithful allies of the Spanish but characterized them, respectively, as a Spanish mestizo (Datu Mandi), a Tagalog (Pedro Cuevas), and a Chinese mestizo (Datu Piang). Hence, these allies were not really Moros. Ibid., 123–26.

17. "Annual Report of Brig. Gen. W. A. Kobbe, U.S.V., Commanding Department of Mindanao and Sulu," in *ARWD 1900*, 3:259–60.

18. Ibid., 269–70. The positive characteristics were more often attributed to the Moros of Mindanao than to those of Sulu, where the army encountered more resistance.

19. Thompson quotes an officer justifying the free use of ammunition against "semi-savages" (Thompson, "Governors of the Moro Province," 56) and Bliss characterizing Zamboanga as a "mixture of Paganism and barbarism" (ibid., 141). These terms accord roughly with the middle stage of Lewis Henry Morgan's three stages of human development—from savagery, through barbarism, to civilization. See Curtis M. Hinsley Jr., *Savages and Scientists: The Smithsonian Institution and the Development of American Anthropology, 1846–1910* (Washington, D.C.: Smithsonian Institution Press, 1981).

20. "Annual Report of Major General George W. Davis," 36.

21. For a more extensive treatment of this topic, see Peter G. Gowing, "Moros and Indians: Commonalities of Purpose, Policy and Practice in American Government of Two Hostile Subject Peoples," *Philippine Quarterly of Culture and Society* 8 (1980): 125–49.

22. "Annual Report of Brig. Gen. W. A. Kobbe," 269.

23. "Were the Filipinos or American Indians defending the Lanao country we would have on our hands a problem of vastly greater difficulty than the one which now confronts us, for the force would be brave, desperate, resourceful, and elusive, while now we know beforehand exactly where to find the enemy and what will be his general plan of operation": Davis, as quoted in Peter Gordon Gowing, *Mandate in Moroland: The American Government of Muslim Filipinos, 1899–1920* (Quezon City: New Day Publishers, 1983), 94–95.

24. "Report of the Chief of the Bureau of Non-Christian Tribes for the Year Ending August 31, 1902," in *RPC 1902*, 1:679. The bureau's name was changed to the Ethnological Survey in 1903.

25. Ibid., 681.

26. Ibid., 685–86.

27. Ibid., 680–81. The bureau signaled the arrival of American ethnology in Southeast Asia by sending a small exhibit to the Hanoi Exposition in 1903. "The exhibit, which consisted for the most part of photographs of racial types and maps, attracted considerable attention, especially from those interested in scientific work. . . . The best results in the study of Philippine ethnology can be obtained only by a wide comparison of material from Malaysia, Polynesia, and the continent of Asia": *RPC 1903*, 2:775.

28. "Report of the Acting Chief of the Ethnological Survey," in *RPC 1904*, 2:562.

29. Ibid., 569.

30. *RPC 1902*, 1:683–85.

31. Ibid., 685; emphasis added.

32. "Plan of Government for the Philippines," in *RPC 1900*, 1:99.

33. See A. C. Milner, *Kerajaan: Malay Political Culture on the Eve of Colonial Rule* (Tucson: University of Arizona Press, 1982).

34. Hendrik M. J. Maier writes about this shift in the philosophical basis of British rule in *In the Center of Authority: The Malay Hikayat Merong Mahawangsa* (Ithaca, N.Y.: Cornell University Southeast Asia Program, 1988).

35. By 1947, Malays and other "Malaysians" (a category that meant indigenous people of the region, including Indonesians and aborigines) constituted only 43.49 percent of the population of British Malaya. Chinese made up 44.7 percent, and Indians (including Sri Lankans) made up 10.25 percent. Chinese and Indian immigration was connected with the extractive and agricultural industries that grew under colonial rule, mainly tin mining and rubber planting. Although they were considered transients by the British and the Malays, by 1931 one-third of the Chinese and one-fourth of the Indians were locally born.

36. See Khoo Kay Kim, *The Western Malay States 1850–1873: The Effects of Commercial Development on Malay Politics* (Kuala Lumpur: Oxford University Press, 1972); J. M. Gullick, *Indigenous Political Systems of Western Malaya* (London: University of London, Athlone Press, 1958), 127–30; and Barbara Watson Andaya, "The Nature of the State in Eighteenth Century Perak," in *Pre-Colonial State Systems in Southeast Asia*, ed. A. Reid and L. Castles, Malaysian Branch of the Royal Asiatic Society Monograph no. 6 (Kuala Lumpur: Council of the Malaysian Board of the Royal Asiatic Society, 1975), 35.

37. For an example of Malay ceremonies that combined "ancient" and imperial elements, see the account of the installation of Sultan Idris of Perak in 1889 in J. M. Gullick, *Malay Society in the Late Nineteenth Century* (Singapore: Oxford University Press, 1989), 33–34. For entirely new ceremonies bringing together the rulers of the Federated Malay States, see "Report of the Durbar (Federal Council) at Kuala Kangsar, July 13–17, 1897," Colonial Office file 273/229, and "Minutes of the Conference of Chiefs of the Federated Malay States held at Kuala Lumpur, July 20–23, 1903," supp. to Selangor Government Gazette, 2 October 1903, Colonial Office file 469/13 (London: Public Record Office).

38. James Francis Warren, *The Sulu Zone, 1768–1898* (Quezon City: New Day Publishers, 1985); Thompson, "Governors of the Moro Province," 31; "Report on the Situation at Zamboanga and Jolo, Including the Occupation of Siassi and Bongao, Description of

Zamboanga and Cagayan Jolo, Interviews with Natives, Salaries Paid to Sultan of Jolo and his Datos, etc., September 20, 1899, by Brig. Gen. J. C. Bates, U.S.V.," in *ARWD 1900*, 4:419.

39. For the origins of company rule, see K. G. Tregonning, *A History of Modern Sabah, 1881–1963* (Singapore: University of Malaya Press, 1965). For a detailed account of British relations with the sultan of Sulu, see Nicholas Tarling, *Sulu and Sabah: A Study of British Policy towards the Philippines and North Borneo from the Late Eighteenth Century* (Kuala Lumpur: Oxford University Press, 1978).

40. Tarling, *Sulu and Sabah*, 326.

41. Rumors that the United States might give up Muslim areas circulated again in late 1899, provoking British concern. Tarling, *Sulu and Sabah*, 287–99.

42. From the Pangkor Treaty (1874), in which the British recognized Abdullah as sultan of Perak in exchange for his acceptance of a resident on these terms. The treaty became a model for subsequent treaties.

43. This account of the Bates Treaty is based on Gowing, *Mandate in Moroland*, 30–36.

44. See Thompson, "Governors of the Moro Province," 44–46.

45. "Annual Report of Brig. Gen. W. A. Kobbe," 256–57.

46. Ibid., 266; emphasis added.

47. "Report on the Situation at Zamboanga and Jolo," 4:420.

48. *Affairs of the Philippine Islands: Hearing before the Committee on the Philippines of the United States Senate, April 10, 1900* (Washington, D.C.: Government Printing Office, 1902), 2126, 2128.

49. "Report of General Wood as to Abrogation of Bates Treaty," in *RPC 1903*, 1:526.

50. *ARWD 1903*, app. II, 30.

51. *Affairs of the Philippine Islands*, 2124.

52. Ibid., 2145–50, especially the letter from the sultan of Sulu asking for the loan of a ship or one hundred rifles to fight the rebellious datus. See also attachments to "Report of General Wood," 489–542.

53. Thompson, "Governors of the Moro Province," 62.

54. *ARWD 1903*, app. II, 28, 36.

55. *Affairs of the Philippine Islands*, 2129.

56. George W. Davis, "Notes on the Government of the Country Inhabited by Non-Christians in Mindanao and the Neighboring Islands," memorandum, 25 August 1902. This memorandum was later incorporated into *ARWD 1902*.

57. *ARWD 1903*, app. II, 36.

58. See ibid., 29, for a reference to the impossibility of conversing directly with the Moros. The frequency of rotation of army officers in and out of the area was a more practical reason that Americans did not learn local languages. A partial exception to the rule was Captain (later General) John Pershing, who studied Lanao customs and dialects and spent time with the Moros. This did not aid in his pacification efforts, however, which still required punitive expeditions. Gowing, *Mandate in Moroland*, 90–91.

59. *ARWD 1903*, app. II, 30.

60. *Affairs of the Philippine Islands*, 2127–28.

61. Najeeb M. Saleeby, "The Moro Problem. An Academic Discussion of the History and

Solution of the Problem of the Government of the Moros of the Philippine Islands, [1913]," *Dansalan Quarterly* 5, no. 1 (1983): 12.

62. Ibid., 17.

63. Ibid., 17–18, 37.

64. Ibid., 25, 35. See also Thompson, "Governors of the Moro Province," 42–44, for a comparison of Saleeby's views with those being developed in Nigeria.

65. Ibid., 32, 38–40.

66. "Annual Report of the Governor of the Moro Province," in *RPC 1904*, 2:578.

67. Gowing, *Mandate in Moroland*, 109; Thompson, "Governors of the Moro Province," 24–25. Wood later worked to keep big plantations out of Mindanao, in part because of their need for Chinese labor. Thompson, "Governors of the Moro Province," 110. He did admire the British (and Dutch) for their ability to live "very contented and healthy lives" in their tropical colonies and saw it as a sign that Americans could settle in Moro Province. *RPC 1904*, 2:590.

68. "Report of Geo. T. Langhorne," 685.

69. As quoted in Gowing, *Mandate in Moroland*, 115.

70. "Report of General Wood," 1:489–90.

71. The letter is reproduced in Gowing, *Mandate in Moroland*, app. C.

72. Gowing, *Mandate in Moroland*, 118–19.

73. "The Moro Province" (the annual report), in *RPC 1904*, 1:7–8, 12.

74. "Report of Geo. T. Langhorne," 694.

75. As quoted in Gowing, *Mandate in Moroland*, 153.

76. The legislative council of the Moro Province was authorized "to enact laws for the creation of local governments among the Moros and other non-Christian tribes, conforming as nearly as possible to the *lawful customs* of such peoples, and vesting in their local or tribe rulers as nearly as possible the same authority over their people as they now exercise": "The Government of the Moro Province," 77; emphasis added. See also "Act No. 39. An Act Temporarily to Provide for the Government of the Moros and other Non-Christian Tribes," in *RPC 1904*, 2:633–38.

77. Gowing, *Mandate in Moroland*, 129; Thompson, "Governors of the Moro Province," 50; Saleeby, "The Moro Problem," 36–38.

78. Kenton J. Clymer, *Protestant Missionaries in the Philippines, 1898–1916* (Urbana: University of Illinois Press, 1986), 158–62.

79. "Annual Report of the Governor of the Moro Province," 579. See also Gowing, *Mandate in Moroland*, 191–93.

80. Edmund J. Danziger Jr., "Native American Resistance and Accommodation during the Late Nineteenth Century," in *The Gilded Age: Essays on the Origins of Modern America* (Wilmington, Del.: Scholarly Resources, 1996), 179.

81. Carl N. Taylor, *Odyssey of the Islands* (New York: Charles Scribner's and Sons, 1936), 74.

82. Howard T. Fry, "The Bacon Bill of 1926: New Light in an Exercise in Divide-and-Rule," *Philippine Studies* (1978): 260, 267.

83. Davis, "Notes," 11.

PATRICIO N. ABINALES

Progressive–Machine Conflict

in Early-Twentieth-Century

U.S. Politics and Colonial-State

Building in the Philippines

During the first decade of the twentieth century, U.S. domestic politics underwent an intense electoral and institutional struggle, pitting the party machines against disparate groups of reformers associated with the Progressive Movement. The influence that such changes in American domestic politics had on the policies, perceptions, and practices of colonial-state builders—that is, the political and administrative connections between metropole and colony—constitutes an aspect of the American colonial experience in the Philippines that so far has gone unstudied.

Two of the most contentious issues fought by these political forces were the character of American political processes and the future of the American federal government. The machines, which represented sectional interests and dominated Congress and the local states, maintained that politics meant the mobilization of supporters through the astute use of patronage and the spoils system. They strongly opposed strengthening the federal state, which they considered a threat to popular and local state power and an obstacle to patronage politics, particularly when it undertook to make federal administration more efficient and relatively free of the corrupting influence of the spoils system.[1] Opposed to the machines were the Progressives, who regarded machine dominance of domestic politics as having created a system that was profoundly corrupt and needing radical administrative reforms. The Progressives also viewed sectionalism and the machines' bias in favor of local state interests as weakening the ability of various agencies of the federal government to accomplish their functions as effective and professional instruments of the central state.[2]

At the turn of the century, Progressives mounted electoral challenges against the machines and fought for legislative and administrative reforms in Congress, as well as in major cities in the United States.[3] Others sought to strengthen agencies of the federal state (such as the presidency and the military) from within, fighting for reforms not only within the legislature but also in venues such as the court system. Neither of the two protagonists completely prevailed over the other, and the outcome of the battle was a political accommodation that preserved the powers of the machines while conceding the necessity of certain progressive reforms. The institutional manifestation of this compromise was emergence of a "new" national state, which was a patchwork structure that precariously combined the localist, patronage-driven, and compromise-prone interests of the machines with the federalist, "professional," and pro-autonomy reformers of the movement.[4]

This patchworked national state emerged almost simultaneously as the United States began to construct the colonial state in the Philippines. Confronted not by a single territory, but by a "series of societies" that, under the departing Spanish, had yet to cohere into one body politic, the colonial state initially comprised two regimes—one, civilian; the other, military.[5] The civilian regime consisted of the "pacified" provinces where the majority of the population was "Christianized" and where local Filipino elites took over after the Spanish were ousted. Colonial officials began early on to create civilian-dominated regimes with considerable Filipino elite participation. A military regime, however, ruled the so-called "unpacified" provinces, territories that the Spanish had failed to subjugate and that were populated by "non-Christian" tribes. The goal of the military regime was to oversee the "civilizing" process of these "backward tribes." The future of this "civilizing mission" remained unclear as American officials debated whether to integrate, separate, or keep autonomous these provinces from the rest of the Philippines. What was clear, however, was that during the first decade of colonial rule, pace the contention of many Philippine and Filipino scholars, these two regimes made up the colonial state in the Philippines.[6]

The battles within American domestic politics found resonance in these two regimes. Each became a laboratory of sorts for colonial-state builders to introduce and implement features and practices associated with the machine and with Progressive Movement politics.[7] Both also developed Philippine counterparts. The emergence of a more coherent colonial policy in Washington, D.C., and the success of Filipino-American collaboration, however, prevented these regimes from developing separately from each other. Filipinization reintegrated these two regimes, although it did not completely do away with the centrifugal tendencies they spawned. Yet the colonial state was never whole. Instead, it also "mirrored" its continental counterpart: a patchworked apparatus of agencies and offices that mixed patronage, corruption, and compromises with isles of administrative efficiency and autonomy.

In describing these regimes as laboratories, I do not mean to say that they were pure experiments in machine or Progressive administration. As scholars have shown, other ideational and political undercurrents lay behind the U.S. colonial project in the Philippines. The dominant ones were explanations that point to the racism underpinning "benevolent-assimilation" policy, as well as the economic ambitions of a rising U.S. industrial power to partake of the imperial division of China.[8] Yet partly because of their predominance, other perspectives that could enlighten us further about colonial-state building have not been given appropriate consideration. One such explanation was how the intense struggle between the machines and the Progressives, and the resultant new but patchworked American national state, affected the construction of its colonial counterpart in the Philippines.

There is also the problem of the attenuated vista of many American studies to regard Philippine political development as distinct and separate from that of the United States. In his book *Social Engineering in the Philippines: The Aims, Execution, and Impact of American Colonial Policy, 1900–1913* (1984), Glenn May argues, for example, that the first decade of colonial rule "did not constitute an experiment in 'progressive imperialism,' as some writers on U.S. colonial policy seem to think." *Progressivism*, however, is narrowly defined to mean those reformers "who attempted to introduce majoritarian and humanitarian reforms and to check the power of business consolidation."[9] It excludes reformers who favored strengthening national-state formation by modifying and making more efficient the agencies of the central state, some of whom ended up in the Philippines. And because May concludes that no evidence of Progressivism's influence in the Philippines can be found, we have been precluded from exploring meaningful comparisons between two societies that were intimately linked to each other and whose central states were being (re)constructed at almost the same historical juncture.

This paper seeks to reexamine and reinterpret the evidence from a different angle by reconnecting the Philippines to the United States and by arguing that two processes, instead of one process, of state formation took place during the first decade of American rule that had an impact on the subsequent development of the Philippines.

STATE BUILDING IN THE REGULAR PROVINCES

A wave of "local-history" studies from the late 1970s to the present has provided a substantial lode that allows us to view a pattern of colonial-state building in the regular provinces of the Philippines.[10] Filipino-American accommodation may have started in Manila, but the consolidation of this relationship became possible only once it was replicated at the local levels. By 1902, once it became clear to elites that the Americans had gained the upper hand in their battle with Filipino revolutionary forces, they readily switched sides to preserve and expand their local power.[11] The collaboration proved decisive. By mid-1903, with Filipino assistance, the Americans had established more than 1,035 municipal governments and 31 provincial governments throughout the colony.[12]

Filipino elites did not come into the arrangement without prior experience in local politics. The Spanish allowed limited Filipino involvement in colonial governance, particularly at the municipal level. Filipinos could become *gobernadorcillos* ("little governors") by being elected to the post by a select group of people consisting of current and past local officials. The Spanish saw the gobernadorcillo as a means of enhancing colonial control, but Filipino elites regarded it as the means to establish their presence in local politics and, when possible, challenge Spanish hegemony. By the nineteenth century, municipal elections became "a marionette play, where the puppets on the stage performed according to a script and the men behind the scenes pulled the strings."[13] But this was only half of the story. Elections likewise were one of a number of political instruments Filipino elites took advantage of to set up mass bases that were crucial in the 1896–1898 revolution against

Spain, to create provincial support for the Malolos revolutionary government, and to sustain, even for a brief moment, Filipino resistance to American occupation.[14]

With lessons from the Spanish experience as guide, Filipino elites who decided to cooperate with the Americans adapted easily to the ways of the new colonizer. The case of the young politico from Cebu province, Sergio Osmeña, represented this political dexterity: "[In 1900] Osmeña accumulated a large quantity of books, some English, about the United States. Long before most ilustrados had given much thought to learning English, Osmeña began taking lessons in Cebu early on. . . . Although these lessons lasted only a short while and he achieved limited proficiency in the language he made some efforts to communicate in English with the Americans and to familiarize himself with certain aspects of American government."[15] This initiative earned Osmeña the confidence of the Americans, and a few years later, in 1904, he cashed in his political dividends by being appointed acting governor of Cebu Province, and then provincial fiscal (a coveted position one step away from appointment as justice of the court). In 1906, with the backing of Governor-General James F. Smith and Secretary of War William H. Taft, Osmeña ran for and won the governorship of Cebu. With his provincial network consolidated, he proceeded to "legitimately seek national leadership," establishing alliances with "several like-minded fellow governors" to control the vital governors' convention. He became a stalwart of the Nacionalista Party, the party that dominated politics throughout the colonial period. When the Americans created a Philippine Assembly to act as the "lower house" of the Philippine Commission, Osmeña ran as his province's candidate and won handily. He was then chosen "by acclamation" as speaker of the Assembly. In power, he became much closer to the Americans, assuring them that he would control nationalist agitation on the assembly floor. Within the first decade of American rule, Osmeña had become one of the two most powerful Filipino leaders.[16]

Another politician—Manuel L. Quezon—rose to power almost in the same manner, although unlike Osmeña he "require[d] direct intervention from provincial Americans to establish himself as the leading political figure in his province."[17] In 1901, Quezon was an unknown petty bureaucrat from a peripheral municipality of Tayabas Province. Two-and-a-half years later, however, he was provincial governor, and in three more years, the province's representative to the Philippine Assembly.

This phenomenal rise came with the help of the constabulary Colonel Harry Bandholtz and other American "friends."[18] Bandholtz, whose power in Tayabas was described as "a blend of despotism and patron–client politics," twisted the arms of other Filipino leaders and used their official powers to get the "dark horse" Quezon elected.[19] After placing "little Quezon" on top, Bandholtz and friends sped his ascent by connecting him with other provincial leaders and top American players in Manila.[20] Together with Osmeña, Quezon would lord over the Nacionalista Party and the legislature while becoming the spokesman of Filipino interests vis-à-vis the Americans.[21]

Osmeña's and Quezon's political pilgrimage represented the pattern of state building in the "regular provinces." Local elites competed for control over local power via elections, then extended their power beyond the province into the "national" arena, with the aid of American patrons and allies.[22] At the Philippine Assembly, these leaders entrenched themselves further through intricate ties with other local elites. Filipino participation in colonial governance reached a high point in 1913 when the presidential victory of the Democratic Party hastened the Filipinization of the state. A one-party regime dominated by the Nacionalista Party and led by Osmeña and Quezon came into being, which climaxed in the establishment of the Philippine Commonwealth in the 1930s.[23] Americans expressed discomfort with this type of rule but did very little to change it.[24] For despite public declarations by the Filipinos in favor of eventual Philippine independence, the Americans were assured privately that the Filipinos still preferred colonial rule.

It quickly became evident to Americans that Filipino political responses were uncannily familiar. Peter Stanley was only partly correct when he argued that the United States "sacrificed initiative for the sake of accommodation" with the Filipino elite.[25] In fact, such accommodation was accepted by the Americans not because of Filipino pressure, but because the accommodation was somewhat familiar. Colonial officials such as Taft, Forbes, and Bandholtz understood Filipino actions because they were analogous to "the game" that was vintage turn-of-the-century American politics.[26]

Scholars have shown that in this "Gilded Age," party-driven patronage politics and the use of official positions for spoils and expanding political influence were widespread.[27] Unlike in Napoleonic France, the U.S. federal government was a national state structure that was penetrated, influenced, and weakened by the disparate social forces representing what Walter Dean Burnham calls warring "sectional sub-cultures."[28] Their conveyor belts were the political parties, which were not so much organizations fighting for a national purpose as patronage machines that represented the diverse local desires, aspirations, and interests of these social forces.[29] These machines were found throughout the American political landscape and embodied the U.S. party system "in its classic form," establishing "their hegemony by arranging an accommodation among the major political forces" in such places as Philadelphia, New York, St. Louis, Cincinnati, and San Francisco.[30]

It would not be far-fetched, therefore, to suggest that the Americans saw in Osmeña and Quezon replicas of their own politicians—perhaps cruder in their view ("little Quezon"), but definitely familiar. Provincial fiefdoms, patronage, and negotiated politics in Cebu and Tayabas mirrored the famous U.S. party machines: Tammany Hall in New York, Senator Matt Quay and the "Organization" in Philadelphia, and the Irish machine of Boston.[31] Martin Shefter's portrait of the American party could very well apply to the experiences of Quezon, Osmeña, and the Nacionalistas: "The party organizations that Jacksonian politicians built . . . were the means by which a particular political class squeezed out its competitors and came to power in the United States. The construction of a mass-based, geographically-organized, and patronage-fueled party apparatus enabled professional politicians who were drawn from, or had ties to the middle class, to establish their hegemony over the working class."[32]

Although there is very little characterization by scholars of U.S. colonial officials as machine politicians, the hints are there.[33] Taft was one who sought to implement a cohesive colonial policy in the Philippines, addressing foremost political stability and economic development driven by trade and American capital; he was also a "conservative" who looked at the Philippines as a test case for the implanting of American institutions.[34] Missing in these descriptions is Taft's familiarity with machine politics, which dated back to his relationship with the Republican Party's "Old Guard" in Cincinnati. Taft may have despised machine politics, but he "rarely fought the Republican bosses, however corrupt."[35] His connections with machine politicians such as Boss Cox and Governor Joseph Benson Foraker of Ohio continued as he rose to power, and when he became president, his allies in Congress were leaders of the Republican machine.[36] Other officials had similar backgrounds. Philippine Commissioner Henry Clay Ide was active in his state's politics in the 1870s and 1880s, and Francis Burton Harrison, who became governor-general of the Philippines in 1912, represented a Tammany-controlled district in New York City in Congress. His acceptance speech was described as "a fourth of July 'short talk' at Tammany Hall."[37] When Dean C. Worcester described Bandholtz as "first, last, and all the time a politician," the context of this description could not simply be unique to the Philippines.

These Americans' familiarity with party machines found echoes in their associations with Filipino politicians. Although most accounts of the first decade of colonial rule highlight the administrative achievements and failures of Taft as the American consul, Taft's patronage and machine-like dealings with Filipinos were also manifest. Taft complained that *caciquism* had eroded Filipino self-government, yet he acted as patron to the same caciques who formed the pro-assimilationist Federalista Party.[38] As Ruby Paredes points out: "Although they dismissed municipal politicians as *caciques*, or corrupt local autocrats, the Americans nonetheless worked with them to extend the electoral system from the municipality (1901) to the province (1903), and thence to the national legislature (1907)."[39] When the Nacionalistas displaced the Federalistas as the new locus of Filipino power, machine-type relations between Filipinos and Americans deepened. Harrison was a close ally of Quezon and his patron-defender against Americans protesting the Filipinization process.[40]

This portrait of American bureaucrats and their political practices suggests that colonial politics—particularly, accommodation with Philippine elites—was not just a product of convenience and pragmatism. Benedict Anderson's assessment of early American colonization captures the importance of political habit: "The timing of American colonization also had a profound formative influence on the emerging oligarchy and its style of rule. The America of 1900–1930 was the America of Woodrow Wilson's lamented "congressional government." The metropole had no powerful centralized bureaucracy; office was still heavily a matter of political patronage; corrupt urban machines and venal courthouse rural cliques were still pervasive; and the authority of presidents, except in time of war, was still restricted."[41]

Decentralized patronage politics in the Philippines, begun in the late Spanish period and routinized in the American, was thus a first cousin of politics in the United States. As the practitioners faced one another, it was not unlike gazing in a mirror.

However, the machines and "congressional government" were not the only centers of power in American domestic politics. There was also the Progressive Movement, which saw a "corrupt and irrational" American political system "dominated by a party machine" as an obstacle to real political progress.[42] The movement sought to undermine the political bosses, with the goal of changing how politics and economic policies were implemented.[43] Specifically, the movement made an effort to alter what one author calls the "conduct of politics" by demanding that "public servants [be] serious about issues and governance."[44] Movement activists began targeting the electoral process and fighting for administrative reforms to professionalize local and state bureaucracies to free them from the clutches of the machines. They also opened a new political front by advocating a stronger national state that could govern the nation, not just one that kowtowed to the sectional, ethnic, and patronage forces that the parties represented.[45] The Progressives fought to reconstitute the national army by diminishing the power of the local state militias, and pushed for laws designed to improve fiscal and monetary policies, as well as the federal government's ability to regulate business.[46] Thus, the Progressives supported the Interstate Commerce Act and the Sherman Anti-Trust Act, efforts to curb the power of monopolies, because they had the potential to strengthen the capacities of the national state and weaken the machines.

The most important transformation that the movement brought about was the strengthening of the presidency in relation to Congress and the courts. In part because of Progressive efforts, the Office of the President began to change from an executive arm that merely implemented congressional policies into a policy player.[47] The role of the presidency in shaping the legislative agenda was seen as an indication of the mark the Progressive Movement had made on domestic politics. Although the movement's impact ultimately was diffused, and reformers had to compromise with the machines, reformism had become potent enough to cause a major electoral realignment in party politics. Joel Silbey notes that, by the end of the century, the political parties "found themselves less able to resist the reformist onslaught than they had once been. Consequently, the equilibrium between them and their challengers was upset. Political party dominance was never again as it had been once the partisan nation began to unravel."[48]

Nothing in the existing work on American colonialism examines the effect of the Progressive Movement on the colonial state—perhaps because, when it comes to colonial rule, scholars have seen no policy difference between Progressives and their machine opponents. After all, both were avid supporters of imperialism.[49] However, one can detect evidence of reformist influence in a couple of places. Take, for example, the background and attitudes of leading American policymakers toward the "appropriate" manner of governing the Philippines. Many of these officials brought to the colony policies and practices that suggest the influence of progressivism. Taft was a good amalgam of the machine and the Progressive. He acted as patron to the Federalista Party but also devoted much of his time to making the Philippines a laboratory of administrative efficiency and economic development.[50]

Taft's plan included the modernization of Manila, the colonial capital; infrastructure development; and the empowerment of the colonial state's executive agencies. The Philippine Commission was also committed to creating a professional civil service ("open on an equal basis to Filipino and Americans"), a "reformed" tax and judicial system to replace the reactionary Spanish setup, capital investments, and public education.[51] Taft justified many of these programs as a way "to end discrimination against the poor."[52] Such acts of statesmanship were usually cited as evidence of American racial superiority. But they can also be regarded as Progressive demonstrations that the United States' first experiment with colonial-state formation could work.[53]

Certain agencies of the colonial state, especially at the executive level, had Progressivist dispositions. Joseph Ralston Hayden describes the Executive Bureau, an office under the American governor-general, as having established "unity and uniformity to the administration of provincial and municipal government throughout the Islands and to see to it that provincial officials did not exceed or abuse their legal authority."[54] It controlled the use of local finances, conducted regular administrative reviews, and supervised provincial and municipal tax collection, and it tried as much as possible to stay clear of partisan politics.[55] Echoes of Progressivist inclinations for state centralization clearly are evident in the way the Executive Bureau operated. Hayden likewise cited the civil service as an example of successful state centralization and efficiency. He praised the introduction of the service, and his description was all Progressive talk:

> In its major characteristics, the system established was a modified copy of the American civil service as it existed in 1901. It was centralized, in that it embraced within one system, under the administrative control of a single bureau, the classified employees of all divisions and organs of insular, provincial and municipal governments. The bureau of civil service was an independent office under the immediate supervision and control of the Governor-General. It possessed extensive powers over the selection and promotion of classified officials and employees, and performed many of the functions of a central personnel bureau with reference to conditions of work, efficiency records, leaves of absence, transfer, discipline and pay. As in the United States, the examination system was designed primarily to test the ability of the applicant to perform the duties of the particular position to which he aspired. However, general examinations of three grades, were based upon three stages of non-technical positions, and were basic to the tests to determine fitness for particular positions.[56]

And how did it fare at least in the first decade, when the Americans had full control of the colonial state? Hayden was effusive:

> Events confirmed the wisdom of the civil service program thus carried out. Between 1899 and 1913, under American leadership and with indispensable Filipino cooperation, a modern government of remarkable honesty and efficiency was organized in the Philippines. This government was manned by thousands of officials chosen either from the almost wholly unprepared native population or from adventurous Americans not especially trained for public administration, many of whom originally went to the Islands, in the Army or as public school teachers.[57]

This professional—and Progressive character—of the civil service survived Filipinization and the patrimonial takeover by Filipino politicians of the state apparatus, thanks largely to continued American control. When Filipinos took over the leadership of the service in 1920, Hayden noted that their American training ensured that they "did their best to carry on in the old spirit and to meet the added responsibilities which Filipinization had placed upon them."[58] Hayden, who was not entirely convinced of the ability of Filipinos to practice democracy and efficient government, would nevertheless conclude that the civil service was

one of the most successful products of American–Filipino collaboration. This body of permanent public servants, working under conditions such as now exist, is entirely capable of administering the Philippine Government in a manner which will contribute to its future stability and progress. A civil service based upon a rigid application of the merit principle, has been provided for in the Constitution of the Philippines, established by sound, progressive legislation, and brought into being by wise and energetic executive action.[59]

"Politicization" of the state, an issue that preoccupied Progressives, was likewise attacked by these officials.[60] Forbes's predecessor, James F. Smith, complained that municipal governments were spending too much of their resources on "salaries and wages and little or nothing on public works of any kind." In so doing, he expressed a Progressive sentiment that demanded public administration be a professional, efficient, and corruption-free enterprise. Forbes himself took the initiative in fighting actual and potential politicization of colonial offices by Filipinos. Using as pretext complaints that "self-government" was so "bad that it is really an offense to the American government to permit it," Forbes directed the passage of a series of measures designed to expand executive (read, American) control of vital functions and agencies of the colonial state.[61] American officials also attempted to hinder the Filipino elite's attempt to use official positions to amass more wealth. As governor, Smith fought to deter corruption after lands confiscated from delinquent taxpayers drew the attention of Filipino officials who saw an opportunity to purchase them at "distressed prices."[62] Smith also issued executive warnings against "certain employees of the Philippine civil service engaging in private business and lending money at exorbitant rates." When it became apparent that the Filipinization was a foregone conclusion, pro-reform Americans continued to introduce measures to forestall the erosion of administrative efficiency and executive control. The American-dominated Philippine Commission, for example, created the office of the insular auditor, a position that had "no counterpart in American government." The office "was given broad powers over the accounts of the insular government and exclusive jurisdiction in determining the legality of all transactions involving these accounts. The law specified that decisions of the auditor did not fall within the jurisdiction of the insular courts but could be appealed to the head of the executive department involved. *This office became a bulwark of American executive power as legislative authority was gradually transferred to the Filipinos.*"[63]

American bureaucrats tried to systematize revenue collection. Governors Forbes and Luke E. Wright set in motion internal-revenue reforms to make tax collection more efficient. These reforms were opposed by Filipino manufacturers, whose investments had not been fully assessed during the first years of American rule, and by caciques whose lands would be newly subject to taxation.[64] In the end, taxation and revenue collection remained skewed to favor the landed elites while efforts to make the colonial-state bureaucracy professional were undermined by a local version of the spoils system.[65] Yet while the landed elite managed to preserve its wealth, limited taxation did lead to some stable economic growth, especially when combined with revenues from foreign trade.[66] The struggle eventually led to a compromise wherein the Americans allowed Filipino caciques to keep their estates in exchange for land taxes' "remain[ing] a productive source of revenue of major importance to the growth of local government functions and services."[67] An amply subsidized regime was established, although it fell short of the full administrative capacity and political will dreamed by colonial reformists.

The Filipino response to these reformist measures was predictably machine-like. American fine-tuning of the colonial apparatus was met by Filipino resistance in the form of legislative resolutions opposing tax reform and attacking the Philippine Commission's revenue plans and of laws designed to strengthen the Filipino-dominated legislature vis-à-vis the executive and the commission.[68] These "turf wars" resulted in a colonial state that was a patchwork of Progressive practices blended with patronage machines—much like the U.S. federal government. In many places, colonial administrators who regarded themselves as Progressives and serious state builders compromised with Filipino machine politicians to establish what became the general norm of colonial politics.[69]

Giving this patchworked state some permanence was the failure of Washington to match rhetoric with generous financial support. The Philippine government suffered from the same lack of metropolitan interest as its counterparts in British Malaya, the Netherlands East Indies, and French Indochina.[70] The U.S. Congress consistently opposed tariff and revenue-raising proposals from Manila, which eventually forced colonial administrators such as Forbes to evolve a "strategic modification of . . . original plans" that led to "a new pattern of collaboration with local political elites."[71] Filipinos immediately saw in this metropolitan apathy an opportunity to strengthen their positions in the colonial state and combined their patrimonial and machine-like interests with American desires for some semblance of efficient colonial administration.

Progressivism's colonial presence can be measured in another way: Progressives, as noted earlier, were out to destroy the machines and to reinforce the capacities of the federal government to function effectively. To achieve these goals, they fought to make federal agencies autonomous from the local machines and from the U.S. Congress. In the Philippines, this quest for state autonomy was typified by the efforts of military officers to keep the special provinces they governed out of Manila's, and the Filipinos', hands. In these areas, racist goals blended with Progressivist commitment to create regimes that epitomized centralized, efficient, and autonomous governance.[72]

STATE BUILDING IN THE SPECIAL PROVINCES

The special provinces consisted largely of two vast but underpopulated areas in the archipelago—one in the mountainous northern portion of the island of Luzon, which became known as the "Cordillera" region, and the other in the southern portion of Mindanao, the second-largest island after Luzon. The Americans adopted the Spanish administrative classification and manner of ruling, defining each area as a "special province." The Cordillera (later renamed Mountain Province) was placed under the direct control of the Philippine Secretary of Interior, and southern Mindanao was called "Moro Province" and placed under army rule.[73]

American racism clearly was a "motive" behind the paternalistic rhetoric of protecting "wild races."[74] However, more than superiority was at work here. In these areas, autonomous and powerful military administrators pursued the "reasons of state" with the use of their martial-law powers.[75] The justification for these regimes was an early policy that put the "non-Christian tribes" in a category separate from

the Christian population. Moro Province in Muslim southern Mindanao was designed differently from regular provinces. In particular, it
limited "Moro" participation in the conduct of local administrative affairs because these Muslim subjects were considered "backward."[76] In
fact, the military believed that its assignment to civilize the "non-Christians" would be one of long duration.[77]

Army officers also believed that the differences between the "non-
Christians" and the Filipinos were so apparent that southern Mindanao
would be best served by being separated from or substantially independent of Manila.[78] In the Cordillera, each sub-province was placed under
an American lieutenant-governor from the Philippine Constabulary
who had "*ex officio* powers far exceed[ing] those provided by statute."[79]
The justification was cogently stated by Worcester, the architect of the
Cordillera: " 'Personal equation was essential' since highlanders knew
nothing of American laws and policies 'but they understood individuals
uncommonly well. The men in immediate control of them must be
absolutely fearless . . . [and] must make good every promise or threat.' "[80]

Thus, the character of colonial-state formation in the special provinces was closer to the European experience in Africa than to what was
being done in the rest of the Philippines. Crawford Young describes the
colonial state in Africa in these terms: "A basic territorial grid of regional
administration, staffed by Europeans, was indispensable. This required a
coercive underpinning from a military force directly controlled by the
colonial state; however, only a small cadre of European officers was
needed, to train, discipline and command forces whose basic ranks were
filled with locally-recruited (or conscripted) solders. Effective occupation could only be mediated through an array of collaborating indigenous intermediaries."[81] The similarities to how the U.S. Army built the
state in the special provinces are clear: small disciplined cadres of junior
officers wielding enormous and autonomous authority over their subjects and integrating the latter through intermediaries whose power
depended on their army superiors. The difference between army rule in
these provinces and "civilian authority" in the regular province was
significant, given that the former's domain covered about 40 percent of
the Philippine territory.[82]

These agencies governed well. The Cordillera's lieutenant-governors
were not only able to win over local leaders of the different "tribes"
(some by "going native"); they also facilitated provincial unity by creat-

ing a common militia unit (the Cordillera Constabulary) and setting up common activities that brought the "tribes" together.[83] Road-building projects to connect communities in the mountainous region were likewise successful—the result of an ingenious plan that replaced taxation with compulsory labor and encouraged labor competition among the communities to hasten the project as well as improve inter-"tribal" relations.[84]

A parallel situation was developing in Moro Province. The American military had to use more of its brutal firepower to pacify the "warring Moros," but by 1907, General Leonard Wood, who headed the province, could declare with confidence that "there need be no apprehension of a general Moro uprising or of concerted action among them."[85] Although it was less ambitious than that in the Cordilleras, an infrastructure project in Moro Province managed to build a 164-kilometer road network that connected vital towns and military outposts with one another, complemented by telegraph and telephone communications and coastline naval patrols.[86] Government expenditures were kept to a minimum; tax collection was remarkable in the province's first decade of operation; and initial exploitation of commercial agriculture appeared to be succeeding.

The result was remarkable growth in provincial income and unprecedented confidence among U.S. Army officials that economic development in this backwater of the colony was speeding ahead.[87] By 1910, this belief had turned into reality, as exports of rubber, coconut, and hemp generated 3,410,712 pesos, doubling to 6,468,587 pesos in 1913, the eve of the transfer of power to civilian and Filipino rule.[88] These administrative successes showed the ability of a hastily organized army to function as state builder and administration. Again, although racism toward the Muslims and the Cordillera communities and the U.S. Army's distaste for "cacique" rule may have played a dominating role, one cannot ignore that these officers' administrative philosophy and skills derived greatly from the Progressive Movement's outlook toward governance and administration. The impulse was clearly present, albeit couched in the language of paternalist racism, in the reports of Leonard Wood, Tasker Bliss, and John Pershing, all military governors of the province and their subordinates and comrades in the Cordillera.

Another indication of Progressivist influence was these regimes' fierce defense of their autonomy against efforts by the colonial capital to control them. Officials of Mountain Province openly "called for a separate system of government that would provide a buffer from the deleterious influences found in the lowlands."[89] Francis Burton Harrison, the Democrat governor-general who presided over the Filipinization of the colonial state and helped destroy the autonomy of the special provinces, complained that until 1914 "an aggressive effort was made to keep the Filipinos from all interference with or control over these pagans of the mountains, and to accentuate in every possible way the separation of races."[90] These officials saw their rule as a way of "saving the [Cordillera] race from the perils of a spirit-crushing civilization such as the Americans felt they saw among the Hispanized Filipinos."[91]

Military officers who had served in the districts of Moro Province fought every effort by Manila to place the province under its direct control. They even went to the extent of rallying "mass support" among Muslims and American settlers to defend their autonomy. When this coalition began to unravel, the more passionate of these officers openly declared their desire to separate Mindanao and rule it as a protectorate, like Guam.[92] Although these separatist and autonomist aspirations never became a reality, they did persist in the consciousness of the people of these two regions. In the Cordilleras, the most important impact of military rule was the emergence of a "regional consciousness" among the communities of the province that differed from the evolving Filipino "national" identity in the lowlands. Thus, Gerard Finin writes:

> As American officials created the reservation-like Mountain Province to protect "the Igorot" from hispanicized lowlanders, an effort was made to group highlanders "scientifically" according to their "natural" characteristics. New maps with subprovincial boundaries were then derived from these groupings. These maps served as the basis for a unified system of administration that was imposed upon people who previously experienced a significantly greater measure of isolation from each other. *A system of direct American rule based on the new administrative grid began to gradually affect highlanders' thinking both about themselves and about those in the lowlands.* While these initial forms of supra-village activity by no means resulted in instant trust and friendship, it did widen highlander's horizons in a manner that introduced more people to each other, and ushered in more expansive territorial concepts.[93]

When Harrison's administration sought to Filipinize the Cordilleras, the Cordillera communities who saw these new governors as representative of the rapacious and hostile "lowland" communities opposed his new appointments.[94] In Moro Province, martial law preserved Spanish-era enmity between the Muslim communities that dominated southern Mindanao and the disparate "Christian" settlements in central and northern Mindanao. Muslim leaders vehemently opposed the transfer of power from the army to civilian rule in 1912, with some even threatening to break the peace.[95] The fight for autonomy against interference from the colonial capital would nurture anti-Manila sentiments long after the military left.[96]

Scholars tend to view these battles for autonomy as specific to each special province. Still, in the context of the reformist zeal and administrative ardor displayed by their respective military administrators, it is possible to broaden our view of these battles beyond their specific realms. In a sense, the fight to keep the Cordillera and Moro Province out of Manila's control reflected the conflict in the American state between advocates of state (federal) centralization and their localist-oriented machine adversaries, because it was an effort by reformers to endow the central state with the autonomy necessary to accomplish its work with very little or no interference from the latter. As Richard Hofstadter points out, Progressives argued that the "power of the boss . . . was a consequence of the weakness of the political executive and the more general division of authority and impotence in government."[97] Agencies of the federal government that came under Progressive control were defended—often vehemently—when attacked by localist forces in Congress and the party system.[98] In the Philippines, similar pro-autonomy forces could be found in the special provinces.

Administration of the Cordillera and southern Mindanao were likewise notable for becoming laboratories of Progressive-type state-building mind sets and practices. Although the evidence here is indirect, the manner of administering the Cordilleras and Moro Province, and the policies that were implemented, echoed the practices made popular by the movement. Their centralized character, as well as their administrative successes in pacifying, integrating, and taxing communities previously inaccessible to the Spanish colonial state, distinguished both special provinces. The institutionalization of state authority, which included central planning under the supervision of "professional" army bureaucrats, was the same administrative reform for which Progressives in America were fighting. The fierce defense of their autonomy against Filipino intrusions likewise reminds one of the efforts of American reformers to prevent the political parties from "politicizing" military administration. According to Stephen Skowronek, army reformers regarded "the most basic operating standards of the early American state—patronage appointment, pork barrel politics, and a radical devolution of authority—[as] insuperable obstacles to national administrative modernization. The army could be made palatable to political elites only by destroying its organizational integrity and turning it into an extension of inimical political arrangements." Officers such as Wood were clearly influenced by the writings of Emory Upton, who called for "a concentration of power, a centralization of authority, an insulation of army administration from politics, and a penetration of central controls throughout the territory." Like their Progressive mentors, they also tended to despise Filipino political leaders who appeared to epitomize the mainland machines.[99] The manner in which the special provinces were governed was thus regarded as a demonstration of the type of regime Progressive reformers could install if they were only given a free hand and could sanitize the state from "politics."

The background of some of these officers further suggests the extent to which Progressivism must be considered as a possible major ideological–administrative impulse behind their distinctive practice of government. Wood, for example, was identified with a group that included the Progressives Elihu Root, Alfred Thayer Mahan, and Henry Cabot Lodge. This cabal, whom Samuel Huntington has described as "neo-Hamiltonian," was committed to ending America's isolation from the world and establishing a strong national army (and one that was not militia-based). Their views of government emphasized combining military preparedness with "a broader education in citizenship and the ideals of national service." Wood consistently maintained that this broad education would, among other things, help "unite the country, forming a *single national spirit transcending sectional, class, and nationality group differences.*"[100] One could note that the "sectional, class and nationality group differences" that Wood found disagreeable were the very bases on which the machines mobilized their electorates and founded their power.[101]

The reformist inspiration and administrative enthusiasm that Wood and his successors, including Tasker Bliss, felt were reflected in turn in their choice of junior officers charged to govern the "remote districts among the half-civilized peoples" of the Philippines.[102] Both demanded professionalism and experience from their subordinates. Bliss required his subordinates "to acquire the knowledge and experience necessary for local popular government" and to wield power over their tribal wards honestly so that "law and order and individual freedom shall be maintained."[103] The achievement of these junior officers showed strong agreement with their superiors' notions of governance. Two of the more notable district governors, Captain John Finley (Zamboanga district) and Lieutenant Edward Bolton (Davao district), received high praise from superiors for their accomplishments and their commitment, prompting Leonard Wood to refer to them as a "class of men . . . anxious to enter the public service in this part of the world and who are well qualified to do so."[104] Progressives such as Wood had found their critical mass base within the colonial state.

UNIFYING THE TWO REGIMES AND THE
CONSOLIDATION OF THE COLONIAL STATE

By the second decade of American rule, however, this de facto second regime within the colonial state had relinquished control of both special provinces to Manila and the Filipinos. Ironically, it was both the characters of these administrations and their success as state bodies that led to their decline. Their strongest asset—personnel—became their most potent handicap. Part of the reason the Cordillera was governed well was that it needed only a few officers who could govern like autocrats in an extensive area. As governance became more stable, however, responsibilities expanded. The constabulary did not have enough personnel to undertake these tasks. Finin makes the important point that, even as "broad responsibilities for the management of day-to-day affairs was devolved to American subprovincial deputy governors, there were never really enough Americans to staff all of the clerical, administrative and teaching positions created to transform the highlands. Moreover, few of the Americans could speak more than elementary Ilocano [a local language spoken among the lowland communities adjacent to the Cordilleras], and fewer still any of the more localized Cordillera languages."[105]

Stable governance made new positions imperative. The all-around military administrator now had to give way to specialized personnel—

judges, lawyers, accountants, customs officers, assessors, and so on. Although the U.S. Army had qualified candidates for such posts in Moro Province, these bureaucratic demands clashed with structural features inherent in the military. Administrative work took attention away from the army's main concern: fighting. Although Wood and his colleagues had proved that they were as adept as state builders as their civilian politician counterparts in the regular provinces, they were also well aware that their principal responsibility was to wage war, not govern. Moreover, governing not only took considerable energy; it also required holders of these positions to devote adequate time to ensure the long-term success of their administrative plans.[106] This ran counter to the military's system of rotation, promotion, and reassignment, which were decided in Washington, not by the provincial leadership.[107] The ambitious officer regarded his provincial post as transitory; he resisted being kept in his provincial post for a long time, because this was anathema to his advance within the military hierarchy. Many officers and enlisted men, in fact, requested transfers or sought promotion back to the United States, as they saw very few possibilities of advancement within the confines of Moro Province.[108]

The more deleterious effect, however, was felt in the lack of administrative continuity. Military leaders and their allies griped about this organizational weakness. Wood complained in his last year as governor of Moro Province about how detrimental rotation was. He remarked that "officers were constantly undergoing a change of personnel, and if there is anything which should be avoided under conditions such as that existing in the Philippine Islands, it is this constant change of officials."[109] This grand patron of the constabulary rulers of the Cordilleras likewise took exception to the "bad" policy of using army men who could not be "retained [at] a given office long enough to carry a policy through to its logical conclusion and get the results."[110]

Military leaders tried to resolve this personnel problem by recruiting "natives" into the local state structure. This, however, came late in the picture.[111] The earlier insistence on autocratic rule—while helping to create regional identities—had failed to nurture a viable "separatist movement." Simultaneously, colonial goals became better defined: tutelage training of Filipinos in preparation for commonwealth status and, eventually, political independence. As Quezon's and Osmeña's power broadened, their ability to undermine attempts made by army officers and their allies to keep the special provinces autonomous also became stronger. Worcester, who fashioned himself as the main defender of Cordillera administrators, tried to use his considerable political clout to keep Manila (and the Filipinos) from gaining control of "his" non-Christian special provinces, but he failed in the long run.[112] Pershing, the last army governor of Moro Province, did not even pick up where his pro-separatist predecessors left off. Recognizing the Filipinos' newfound power, he accepted the eventuality of civilian and Filipino rule and helped ease the entry of the new regime by wiping out whatever remained of the Muslim "armed threat."[113]

What sealed the fate of these military regimes and their administrative projects was U.S. domestic politics. Political battles in Congress, and between Congress and the executive offices, over the fate of a federal army had a profound impact on military rule. Although army reformers —in alliance with the presidency—were able to institute reforms that would create a cohesive national military, they were unable to win all their battles against the machine-controlled, localist-oriented Congress. The latter wanted the "old-type" of military organization—state militias and the state-based National Guards—to continue even in the imperial era and to reduce the federal army to a token force.[114] Supporters of a strong national army, including Wood, got caught up in these institutional wars, robbing them of time and interest to devote to the future of the provinces they once governed.[115]

In 1914, the military ceded power to the civilians and the Filipinos, ending what could have been two distinct processes of state formation. The "unification" was done under the aegis of the Filipinization program worked out by Quezon, the Filipino leadership, and the newly elected Democratic President Woodrow Wilson. The change in regime in the United States from the Republican Party, whose leadership favored retention of the Philippines as a colony, to the Democrats, who favored eventual independence, coincided with Quezon's and Osmeña's having reached the pinnacle of their power in the Philippine party and legislative systems. Yet, although Quezon and the Nacionalistas were firmly committed to integrating the special provinces, they were also sensitive to the enduring presence of separatist sentiments that history and the rule of the U.S. Army had ingrained among the people in these areas.

Instead of using force, Quezon recognized that these centrifugal tendencies were not entirely opposed to evolving colonial politics. He was well aware that Muslim animosity toward Manila and Filipinos also stemmed from a desire to be left alone. This echoed the interests of many a political leader in a decentralized political setting (Quezon's centralist projects notwithstanding) where different clans and families, as well as up-and-coming colonial strongmen, carved power niches at the provincial and municipal levels. All that was needed was to persuade the Muslim leaders that their own local interests were best preserved under Filipinization; all that was demanded of them was to alter their allegiance and learn the mechanics of this new politics.[116] Thus, Filipino leaders used patronage, elections, and participation in the expanding party system to "make them an integral governing part of the republican government, [thus] reuniting them with Filipinos."[117] Filipino elites preserved communal differences as part of the "nation-building" process, engaging in "ethnic juggling" to frustrate separatist appeals and undermine the influence of the military, as well as to provide access to the state to "friendly" Muslim and Cordillera leaders.[118] By the end of the second decade, these two regions were structurally integrated, and their politics had begun to mirror those of the regular provinces. Although elections remained closely regulated by the state (mainly because the Filipinos shared with the Americans the racist view that the special provinces were still uncivilized and backward areas), these regions' elites were given as much opportunity to experience the advantages of colonial politics.

Muslim and Cordillera leaders initially resisted Filipinization but were eventually resigned to the fact that the comforts of a separate existence under military rule were no longer possible. With no military patrons, with their armed capacities virtually nonexistent, and facing a superior and determined Filipinized colonial state, leaders of these communities sought ways to adjust to the new order.[119] While many surrendered to the new reality out of a sense of helplessness, others saw opportunity in Filipinization. Among the young generation of educated Cordillerans, the chance to take the place of the departed constabulary officers and become the new leaders of the region increased under Filipinization. In fact, most of the region's dominant families today can trace their political beginnings to this administrative substitution.[120]

Among the Muslims, growing appreciation of a new political game with Manila and the Filipinos as the centers of power steadily displaced suspicion toward Filipinization. Muslim leaders took advantage of Quezon's offer to join colonial politics, and many began to declare themselves "spokesmen for the Moros" to win seats in the national assembly. Like many aspiring politicians in the "Christian" provinces, these leaders were quick to learn the long-term political value of education, especially the law. They began sending their children to Manila for "advanced studies," to create a pool of advisers acquainted with the administrative, regulatory, and even ideological facets of colonial politics. This younger generation ensured continuity of political leadership within their communities, and their training prepared them to work with the colonial state.[121]

By the 1930s, a new breed of "minority" leaders was slowly displacing the older generation, and the new leaders regarded their political ambitions as inextricably linked to colonial politics. Although they retained their "ethnic identities," they also took pride in being Filipino and having become involved in Filipino politics.[122] They were especially comfortable with the fact that their "local interests" were preserved and respected by colonial leaders: They continued to be "spokesmen" for their communities in the Philippine Assembly and the political parties, as well as regional leaders to be consulted about state projects in their areas. They were, in short, becoming more and more like machine politicians in the Osmeña and Quezon mold, albeit less experienced and ingenious. As their participation in the Filipinized state deepened, so, too, did their integration. When Quezon presided over the Philippine Commonwealth, the American colonial state had become one.

* * *

The "paired-comparison" method has hitherto been used mainly to ascertain similarities and differences in the political development of regions, countries, or societies. The concern, as Charles Tilly puts it, is on developing "huge comparisons" on "big [social and political] structures" and "large [social and political] processes."[123] Here, I have used the paired-comparison method to investigate two contrasting processes of state building within one colonial territory: the Philippines. Following the examples of scholars who are reconsidering the relationship between India and the British Empire, I have also used this method to explore political and administrative connections between colony and metropole within one imperial state: the United States.[124] The result, I hope, is a more intricate political and administrative development of the U.S. colonial state in the Philippines.

Ideas and practices of American domestic politics influenced the manner in which the United States created its colonial Leviathan in the Philippines as much as economic interests and paternalist racism did. The American colonial adventure in Southeast Asia was distinct for a number of reasons. First, it was an anomaly within the colonial experiences of the period. Although the United States' European rivals had developed "relatively well elaborated notions of how a colonial state should be organized, distilled from four centuries of imperial history," the Americans had to start virtually from scratch.[125] The "Indian campaigns" did not wholly apply, and the Americans did not find the Spanish precedent or the experiences of the neighboring British and Dutch worth emulating.[126]

The nearest comparison was European colonial expansion in the fifteenth century; then, colonial-state building occurred "as a process paralleling the development of the modern [European] state."[127] Both fifteenth-century Europe and the late-nineteenth-century United States "stumbled" their way into colonial domination in part because of the need to adjust to "local conditions," but also because, in their respective metropoles, modern state construction was still in its infancy or early stages. No clear model of state building—domestic or colonial—had yet emerged, and the colonial adventures these states began were still very much affected by the manner in which their respective domestic states were developing.

Likewise, at the turn of the century, a "new American state" was evolving that was the product of many compromises between political machines and reformers. Although this state had far stronger capacities than its predecessors did, its institutional structures remained affected by the persistence of fissiparous elements identified with the party system. The U.S. political system continued to be "fragmented, dispersed, and everywhere permeated by organized societal interests. The national government [lacked] such possible underpinnings of strong state power as a prestigious and status-conscious career civil service with predictable access to key executive posts; authoritative planning agencies; direct executive control over a national central bank; and public ownership of strategic parts of the economy."[128]

A Philippine parallel to this fragmented state could be seen in the two regimes, which had contrasting structures and even perspectives. The resemblance did not end there, as each regime resonated features of U.S. domestic political battles between machines and reformers, and the eventual integrated structure echoed the "patchworking" that characterized the late-nineteenth- and early-twentieth-century American national state. Although a more cohesive state eventually evolved in the United States, the colonial state in the Philippines did not follow suit. It maintained its patchwork character, because this became the convenient way to keep together the "series of societies" that made up the formal body politic called the Philippines. By maintaining the same decentralized, party-based patronage system, colonial officials—both Filipino and American—were able to establish a system that would become the enduring foundation of a resilient Filipino "cacique democracy."

NOTES

An earlier version of this essay was presented at the conference "Revisiting the Birth of our Century: The Meaning of 1898," Center for Latin American Studies, Tulane University, New Orleans, 30–31 October 1998. I thank the conference participants, as well as Donna J. Amoroso, Vince Boudreau, Anne L. Foster, and Julian Go, for their comments and criticisms. All shortcomings are mine.

1. Martin Shefter, *Political Parties and the State: The American Historical Experience* (Princeton, N.J.: Princeton University Press, 1994).

2. The classic text on the movement is Richard Hofstadter, *The Age of Reform: From Bryan to F.D.R.* (New York: Vintage Books, 1955). The Progressive Movement was, of course, not a unitary one. Its origins and the forces that composed it were diverse. What bound them together, however, was the commitment to reform politics and governance at the turn of the century.

3. See Kenneth Finegold, *Experts and Politicians: Reform Challenges to Machine Politics in New York, Cleveland, and Chicago* (Princeton, N.J.: Princeton University Press, 1995).

4. Stephen Skowronek, *Building a New American State: The Expansion of National Administrative Capacities, 1877–1920* (Cambridge: Cambridge University Press, 1982). The realignment was profound enough for Skowronek to assert confidently that, in this period, a "new" American state was being built.

5. The phrase "series of societies" is from Alfred W. McCoy and Ed De Jesus, eds., *Philippine Social History: Global Trade and Local Transformation* (Quezon City: Ateneo de Manila University, 1982), 4.

6. Despite their contrasting conclusions and viewpoints, studies by Filipinos and Philippinists share this assumption. See Peter W. Stanley, *A Nation in the Making: The Philippines and the United States, 1899–1921* (Cambridge, Mass.: Harvard University Press, 1974); Glenn Anthony May, *A Past Recovered* (Quezon City: New Day Publishers, 1987);

Teodoro Agoncillo and Milagros Guerrero, *History of the Filipino People* (Quezon City: R. P. Garcia, 1965); Renato Constantino, *The Philippines: A Past Revisited* (Manila: Tala Publishing, 1975); and Renato Constantino and Letizia Constantino, *The Philippines: A Continuing Past* (Tala Publishing, 1992).

7. Just how distinct these two regimes were can be gleaned by those who worked in them. See Cornelius C. Smith, *Don't Settle for Second: The Life and Times of Cornelius C. Smith* (Calif.: Presidio Press, 1977), 93. See also Leonard Wood, "Report of the Governor of the Moro Province, 1906," in *Report of the Philippine Commission, 1906* (Washington: Government Printing Office, 1906), 375 (hereafter, the Philippine Commission reports are cited as *RPC*).

8. See, for example, Walter LaFeber, *The American Search for Opportunity, 1865–1913*, vol. 2 (Cambridge: Cambridge University Press, 1993); Gabriel Kolko, *Main Currents in Modern American History* (New York: Pantheon, 1984); Martin J. Sklar, *The United States as a Developing Country: Studies in U.S. History in the Progressive Era and the 1920s* (New York: Cambridge University Press, 1992); Richard Drinnon, *Facing West: The Metaphysics of Indian-Hating and Empire-Building* (New York: New American Library, 1980); Amy Kaplan and Donald E. Pease, eds., *Cultures of United States Imperialism* (Durham, N.C.: Duke University Press, 1993).

9. Glenn Anthony May, *Social Engineering in the Philippines: The Aims, Execution and Impact of American Colonial Policy, 1900–1913* (Quezon City: New Day Publishers, 1984), xvii.

10. See, for example, Alfred W. McCoy, ed., *Philippine Social History: An Anarchy of Families: State and Family in the Philippines* (Madison: Center for Southeast Asian Studies, University of Wisconsin, 1993).

11. Resil Mojares, "The Dream Goes On and On: Three Generations of the Osmeñas, 1906–1990," in McCoy, *Anarchy of Families*, 315.

12. Frank Hindman Golay, *Face of Empire: United States–Philippine Relations, 1898–1946* (Madison: Center for Southeast Asian Studies, University of Wisconsin, 1998), 70. See also Michael H. Hunt, "Resistance and Collaboration in the American Empire, 1898–1903: An Overview," *Pacific Historical Review* 48 (June 1979).

13. Glenn Anthony May, "Civic Ritual and Political Reality: Municipal Elections in the Late Nineteenth Century," in *Philippine Colonial Democracy*, ed. Ruby R. Paredes (Quezon City: Ateneo de Manila University Press, 1989), 35.

14. For a more nuanced portrait of early-twentieth-century local politics, see Reynaldo Ileto, "The Municipal 'Boss' and His Critics in Southern Tagalog History," paper presented at Philippine Studies seminar, Sophia University, Tokyo, Japan, 12 May 2001; and, idem, "History and Criticism: The Invention of Heroes," in *Filipinos and Their Revolution: Event, Discourse and Historiography*, ed. Reynaldo Ileto (Quezon City: Ateneo de Manila University Press, 1998), 229–30.

15. Michael Cullinane, "Playing the Game: The Rise of Sergio Osmeña, 1898–1907," in Paredes, *Philippine Colonial Democracy*, 81.

16. Ibid., 84–98, 101. A "provincial fiscal" was the local official in charge of justice.

17. Ibid., 88.

18. Michael Cullinane, "Manuel L. Quezon and Harry Bandholtz: The Origins of Special

Relationship," *Bulletin of the American Historical Collection* 9 (January–March 1981): 79–90.

19. Idem, "The Politics of Collaboration in Tayabas Province: The Early Political Career of Manuel Luis Quezon, 1903–1906," in *Reappraising an Empire: New Perspectives on Philippine–American History*, ed. Peter W. Stanley (Cambridge, Mass.: Harvard University Press, 1984), 83. Cullinane writes that Quezon's friendship with the U.S. Army quartermaster Lieutenant Hunter Harris led to the latter's mobilizing "the U.S. Army transport system in the province to help bring [Quezon's] supporters to Lucena [voting center] at no personal expense." Ibid., 80.

20. Ibid., 80–81. Bandholtz's position as director of the Philippine Constabulary, which took over pacification duties from the U.S. expeditionary army, was likewise an asset in Quezon's rise to power.

21. Michael Cullinane, "*Ilustrado* Politics: The Response of the Filipino Educated Elite to American Colonial Rule, 1898–1907" (Ph.D. diss., University of Michigan, Ann Arbor, Mich., 1989), 420.

22. Idem, "Implementing the 'New Order': The Structure and Supervision of Local Government under the Taft Era," in *Compadre Colonialism: Studies on the Philippines under American Rule*, ed. Norman G. Owen (Ann Arbor: Center for South and Southeast Asian Studies, University of Michigan, 1971), 16. I owe this insight on the role of American-type elections in the shaping of the Philippine polity to Benedict Anderson, "Elections and Participation in Three Southeast Asian countries," in *The Politics of Elections in Southeast Asia*, ed. R. H. Taylor (Cambridge: Woodrow Wilson Center Press, 1996), 20–26.

23. *The Philippine Policy of the United States* (New York: Institute of Pacific Relations, 1939), 12.

24. Joseph Ralston Hayden, *The Philippines: A Study in National Development* (New York: Macmillan, 1942), 58–59.

25. Stanley, *Nation in the Making*, 269.

26. Paredes cogently notes that, "with their own history of patronage and clientelism, American colonialists appeared to have had little difficulty in mastering some essentials of Filipino politics." Ruby R. Paredes, "Introduction: The Paradox of Philippine Colonial Democracy," in idem, *Philippine Colonial Democracy*, 7.

27. Charles C. Bright, "The State in the United States during the Nineteenth Century," in *Statemaking and Social Movements: Essays in History and Theory*, ed. Charles Bright and Susan Harding (Ann Arbor: University of Michigan Press, 1984), 122. See also Wayne Morgan, ed., *Gilded Age* (Syracuse, N.Y.: Syracuse University Press, 1970).

28. Walter Dean Burnham, *The Current Crisis in American Politics* (Oxford: Oxford University Press, 1982), 96–100. See also Steven P. Erie, *Rainbow's End: Irish-Americans and the Dilemmas of Urban Machine Politics, 1840–1985* (Berkeley: University of California Press, 1988), 1–67.

29. Martin Shefter, "Party, Bureaucracy and Political Changes in the United States," in *Political Parties: Development and Decay*, ed. Louis Maisel and Joseph Cooper (Beverly Hills, Calif.: Sage Publications, 1978), 211–57.

30. Shefter, *Political Parties and the State*, 160. See also Samuel P. Orth, *The Boss and the*

Machine: A Chronicle of the Politicians and Party Organization (New Haven, Conn.: Yale University Press, 1919), 96–97, 100–109.

31. William Nills Ivins, *Politics and Money in Elections in New York City* (New York: Arno Press, 1970); Peter McCaffery, *When Bosses Ruled Philadelphia: The Emergence of the Republican Machine, 1867–1933* (University Park: Pennsylvania State University Press, 1993), 81–82, 86–93, 98, 113–44; Erie, *Rainbow's End*, 33–35.

32. Shefter, *Political Parties and the State*, 70.

33. One Filipino scholar on local politics, for example, wrote: "When the Americans moved in with their project of political democracy, they faced a native elite wise in the processes of power accumulation. Touched by imperial naiveté, the Americans' realization of this fact was surprisingly slow. *Responding to impulses within their own political tradition*, the practical imperative of using local intermediaries to govern the colony, as well as pressures from Filipinos, the Americans widened the field of 'politics' for the native elite." The author does not elaborate on what "impulses within their own political tradition" meant. Mojares, "The Dream Goes On and On," 314; emphasis added.

34. Golay, *Face of Empire*, 91–169; May, *Social Engineering*, 17, 42–43.

35. Henry F. Pringle, *The Life and Times of William Howard Taft* (Hamden, Conn.: Archon Books, 1964), 58–59.

36. Norman M. Wilensky, "Conservatives in the Progressive Era: The Taft Republicans in 1912," *Social Sciences* 23 (winter 1965): 3. When he became president, Taft refused to support congressional insurgents seeking to topple the "autocratic" rule of House Speaker James Cannon and continue with Progressive reforms on the grounds that he had a "gentleman's agreement" with the Republican leaders. The insurgency fizzled as a result. Golay, *Face of Empire*, 130. Golay cites Kenneth W. Hechler, *Insurgency: Personalities and Politics of the Taft Era* (New York, N.Y.: Columbia University Press, 1940), as his source.

37. As quoted in Stanley, *Nation in the Making*, 203, 207–9. Once in power, Harrison resorted to Tammany-like spoils practices, such as firing Republicans and anti-Filipino Americans in the bureaucracy and replacing them with his Filipino allies.

38. Golay, *Face of Empire*, 76–77. Taft considered himself the patron of the Federalistas, whom he treated as protégés.

39. Paredes, "Introduction," 7–9.

40. By the Harrison period, Filipinos had also mastered the art of machine politics, with Quezon and Harrison forming a lasting patronage relationship that led to the expansion of Filipino political influence within the colonial state. James C. Biedzynski, "The McIntyre–Quezon Conversation of 1913–1914," *Bulletin of the American Historical Collection* 13, no. 2 (1990): 69.

41. Benedict Anderson, "Cacique Democracy in the Philippines: Origins and Dreams," *New Left Review* 166 (May–June 1988): 11. Although Anderson speaks of "bosses" in this quote, I do not subscribe to the notion that Philippine politics is all "bossism." There are Filipino "bosses," no doubt, but elite politics also cannot simply be conflated under this term—even Anderson, cynical as he is about elite rule, still had to append the word "democracy" to his essay. An insightful critique of bossism and related theories is Reynaldo Ileto, "Orientalism and the Study of Philippine Politics," in *Knowing America's*

Colony: A Hundred Years from the Philippine War, Center for Philippine Studies Occasional Paper Series 13 (Honolulu: University of Hawai'i, 1999), 58–61.

42. Shefter, *Political Parties and the State,* 76.

43. James L. Sundquist, *Dynamics of the Party System: Alignment and Realignment of Political Parties in the United States* (Washington, D.C.: Brookings Institution, 1983), 172.

44. Charles W. Calhoun, "The Political Culture: Public Life and the Conduct of Politics," in *The Gilded Age: Essays on the Origins of Modern America,* ed. Charles W. Calhoun (Wilmington, Del.: Scholarly Resources, 1996), 186.

45. Skowronek, *Building a New American State,* 3–19, 39–162.

46. Ibid., 165–284.

47. As Skowronek describes it, the president "had never risen far above the status of a clerk during the heyday of party competition. The only truly national officer in American government and the ostensible head of the national administrative apparatus found his political and institutional resources hostaged to local party bosses in Congress." Ibid., 169. See also Calhoun, "Political Culture," 208.

48. Joel H. Silbey, *The American Political Nation, 1838–1893* (Stanford, Calif.: Stanford University Press, 1991), 236.

49. William E. Leuchtenburg, "Progressivism and Imperialism: The Progressive Movement and American Foreign Policy, 1898–1916," *Mississippi Valley Historical Review* 24 (December 1952): 483–504.

50. Stanley, *Nation in the Making,* 61–67. This description of how under his leadership the Taft Commission set itself to work hints at these Progressive schemes: "Within a few weeks, the [Taft] Commission was busy with plans to transform Manila into a healthy, habitable city and modern port; to build a summer capital to which Americans could flee the hot, dry season; to facilitate development of the colony's resources with all-weather roads and bridges, regional ports, and other 'public improvements'; and to modernize and extend public health services and facilities." Frank H. Golay, "The Search for Revenues," in Stanley, *Reappraising an Empire,* 233.

51. One author described the tax system being introduced as evidence of the Americans' "display[ing] a type of Progressive moralism, akin to that which stimulated Prohibition in the United States." Harry Luton, "American Internal Revenue Policy in the Philippines to 1916," in *Compadre Colonialism,* ed. Norman G. Owen, 136.

52. Stanley, *Nation in the Making,* 64.

53. Golay, "Search for Revenues," 238.

54. Hayden, *The Philippines,* 272.

55. Ibid., 273–74.

56. Ibid., 93–94.

57. Ibid.

58. Ibid., 101.

59. Ibid., 143. Hayden, a Republican, even conceded that the Democrats who were known to be notorious spoilsmen did not treat a Philippine assignment as spoils, allowing a certain degree of professionalism to thrive. Thus, "with rare exceptions the relatively small number of Americans who were brought out to the Islands after 1913 were technical men who [had] little regard for party political considerations." Ibid., 100.

60. Golay, "Search for Revenues," 244–45.

61. Idem, *Face of Empire*, 121, 125.

62. Ibid., 117.

63. Ibid., 126; emphasis added.

64. Ruby R. Paredes, "Origins of a National Elite," in idem, *Philippine Colonial Democracy*, 53, 56.

65. Luton, "American Internal Revenue Policy," 144–46.

66. Golay, *Face of Empire*, 156.

67. Ibid., 117.

68. Ibid., 139–42.

69. Ibid., 142–43, 151.

70. Crawford Young, *The African Colonial State in Comparative Perspective* (New Haven, Conn.: Yale University Press, 1994), 97.

71. See Julian Go's chapter in this volume.

72. Russel Roth, *Muddy Glory: America's "Indian Wars" in the Philippines, 1899–1935* (West Hanover, Mass.: Christopher Publishing House, 1981), 136, 151; Vic Hurley, *Swish of the Kris: The Story of the Moros* (New York: E. P. Dutton, 1936), 14–15; Rodney J. Sullivan, *Exemplar of Americanism: The Philippine Career of Dean C. Worcester* (Quezon City: New Day Publishers, 1992).

73. Philippine Commission Act 1876 created the "Mountain Province." Gerard A. Finin, "Regional Consciousness and Administrative Grids: Understanding the Role of Planning in the Philippine Gran Cordillera Central" (Ph.D. diss., Cornell University, Ithaca, N.Y., 1991), 76, 88. On the creation of Moro Province, see "An Act Providing for the Organization of the Moro Province," 1 June 1903, in "Acts of the Legislative Council of the Moro Province," 7 September 1903–31 August 1904, *Report of the Governor of the Moro Province* (Washington, D.C.: Government Printing Office, 1904), 113–31.

74. As one author puts it: "Race had long been at the 'center' of [the] American [expansionist] world view." Joseph A. Fry, "Phases of Empire: Late-Nineteenth Century U.S. Foreign Relations," in Calhoun, *The Gilded Age*, 264.

75. Frank Lawrence Jenista, *The White Apos: American Governors on the Cordillera Central* (Quezon City: New Day Publishers, 1987), 107–67.

76. The army was empowered to govern Moro Province for "the pacification of dissident elements, the establishment of law and the preparation of the Moros for their proper place in the body politic of the Philippines." Peter Gordon Gowing, *Mandate in Moroland: The American Government of Muslim-Filipinos, 1899–1920* (Quezon City: New Day Publishers, 1983), 72–73. Analogous rationales were given by Worcester, the main author of the Cordillera "Special Province Act": "to bring progress among the so-called 'wild tribes' so that they might one day join, if not lead the larger body politic." Finin, "Regional Consciousness," 57.

77. "Annual Report of Maj. Gen. George W. Davis, U.S. Army, Commanding Division of the Philippines," 1 October 1902–26 July 1903, *RPC* 1903, 39. On the Philippine Constabulary, see George Yarrington Coats, "The Philippine Constabulary, 1901–1927" (Ph.D. diss., Ohio State University, Columbus, Ohio, 1968).

78. W. Cameron Forbes, *The Philippine Islands*, vol. 2 (Boston: Houghton Mifflin, 1928),

445. See also Peter G. Gowing, "Moros and Indians: Commonalities of Purpose, Policy and Practice in American Government of Two Hostile Subject Populations," *Philippine Quarterly of Culture and Society* 8 (1980): 146–48. This comparison, however, was altered after David P. Barrows, chief of the Bureau of Non-Christian Tribes (created in 1901), observed the extent to which the "non-Christians" varied. Worcester, who was responsible for defining the various tribes of the Cordillera region, supported Barrows. See Dean C. Worcester, "The Non-Christian Tribes of Northern Luzon," *Philippine Journal of Science* 1, no. 8 (1906): 791–876; and idem, "Non-Christian Peoples of the Philippine Islands," *National Geographic*, vol. 2–4 (November 1913): 1206–7.

79. Finin, "Regional Consciousness," 79.

80. As quoted in Jenista, *White Apos*, 29–30.

81. Young, *African Colonial*, 76.

82. Taken together, the two special provinces occupied a total area of 39,223 square miles (7,200 square miles for the Cordillera and 32,023 square miles for Moro Province) out of a total Philippine area of 115,600 square miles.

83. Finin, "Regional Consciousness," 80–95. The Americans gave full attention to annual elaborate sub-provincial *canao*, or feasts, that combined "obligatory inspection duties" with what Worcester called a way of bringing about "the settlement of old difficulties between hostile towns" and an opportunity to talk about "future plans under the most favorable conditions." As quoted in ibid., 88–89.

84. Jenista, *White Apos*, 135–45. By the time roads and mountain trails were carved all over the Cordillera, the Americans were able to muster more than twenty thousand men, whose leaders wholeheartedly sent them to work the projects. Finin, "Regional Consciousness," 95–100.

85. "Report of the Governor of the Moro Province," 351.

86. Gowing, *Mandate in Moroland*, 56, 138–39, 194, 210–11, 332.

87. Douglas Thompson Kelley Hartley, "American Participation in the Economic Development of Mindanao and Sulu, 1899–1930" (Ph.D. diss., James Cook University of North Queensland, Townsville, Queensland, Australia, 1983), 38, 44–46.

88. Gowing, *Mandate in Moroland*, 221–22.

89. Finin, "Regional Consciousness," 103.

90. Francis Burton Harrison, *The Cornerstone of Philippine Independence: A Narrative of Seven Years* (New York: Macmillan, 1942), 124; Felix M. and Marie Kessing, *Taming Philippine Headhunters: A Study of Government and of Cultural Change in Northern Luzon* (London: George Allen, 1934), 102. Jenista quotes one of these officers, who declared: "I was alone in this station . . . and was veritable king over 15,000 to 20,000 savages and boss of fifty well-trained and disciplined non-Christian soldiers." As quoted in Jenista, *White Apos*, 232.

91. Jenista, *White Apos*, 48. The inhabitants of the Cordillera do not, of course, constitute a race.

92. Patricio N. Abinales, "State Authority and Local Power in Southern Philippines, 1900–1972" (Ph.D. diss., Cornell University, Ithaca, N.Y., 1997), 64–71.

93. Finin, "Regional Consciousness," 101; emphasis added.

94. Jenista, *White Apos*, 190–91, 254–55.

95. Forbes, *Philippine Islands*, 293–94.

96. Abinales, "State Authority and Local Power," 288.

97. Hofstadter, *Age of Reforms*, 265.

98. Skowronek, *Building a New American State*, 186–98 (on the civil service), 222–28 (on the army), 249–67 (on business regulation).

99. Ibid., 91.

100. Samuel P. Huntington, *The Soldier and the State: The Theory and Practice of Civil–Military Relations* (Cambridge, Mass.: Harvard University Press, 1957), 280; emphasis added.

101. Erie, *Rainbow's End*, 1–67.

102. Like Wood, Bliss was known for his administrative expertise. He was customs collector in Cuba and successfully negotiated the Cuban Reciprocity Treaty of 1902. As the governor of Moro Province, he studied Malay to communicate effectively with Muslim leaders. Later, he was appointed the U.S. military representative to the Supreme War Council in Europe and, after World War I, was a member of the American Commission to Negotiate Peace. Wayne W. Thompson, "Governors of the Moro Province: Wood, Bliss and Pershing in the Southern Philippines" (Ph.D. diss., University of California, San Diego, 1975), 5. See also Frederick Palmer, *Bliss, Peacemaker: The Life and Letters of General Tasker Bliss* (New York: Dodd, Mead, 1934).

103. *Mindanao Herald*, 3 February 1909, 3.

104. "Report of the Governor of the Moro Province," 356.

105. Finin, "Regional Consciousness," 104.

106. Harold Hanne Elarth, *The Story of the Philippine Constabulary* (Los Angeles: Globe, 1949), 86.

107. Even the leadership of Moro Province itself was subjected to these routines. After his term as the governor of Moro Province, Wood was "rotated" back to the United States and appointed army chief. In 1921, he returned to the Philippines as governor-general of the colony. Hermann Hagedorn, *Leonard Wood: A Biography*, vol. 2 (New York: Kraus Reprint, 1969), 392.

108. In 1906 alone, for example, the officials appointed district governors of Sulu, Lanao, and Cotabato (the areas considered most volatile) resigned to rejoin their military units in the United States. See "Report of the Governor of the Moro Province," 340. See also *Mindanao Herald*, 15 June 1907.

109. "Report of the Governor of the Moro Province," 356.

110. Thompson, "Governors of the Moro Province", 245.

111. Finin, "Regional Consciousness," 108–9.

112. *The Filipino People*, October 1912, 4–5. This pamphlet was published as part of Manuel Quezon's duties as Philippine Resident Commissioner to the U.S. House of Representatives. It is unsigned and printed in Washington, D.C.

113. Gowing, *Mandate in Moroland*, 245–46. See also Napoleon Casambre, "The Harrison Administration and the Muslim Filipinos," *Mindanao Journal* 1, no. 4 (1975): 54.

114. Skowronek, *Building a New American State*, 223–28, 235–41.

115. On the bureaucratic battles Wood had to fight, see James William Pohl, "The General Staff and the American Military Policy: The Formative Years, 1898–1917" (Ph.D. diss., University of Texas, Austin, 1967).

116. Abinales, "State Authority and Local Power," 182–97.

117. Charles Burke Elliot, *The Philippines to the End of the Commission Period: A Study in Tropical Democracy* (Indianapolis: Bobbs-Merrill, 1917), 95.

118. The term "ethnic juggling" is from James Mayall and Mark Simpson, "Ethnicity Is Not Enough: Reflections on Protracted Secessionism in the Third World," in *Ethnicity and Nationalism*, ed. Anthony D. Smith (Leiden: E. J. Brill, 1992), 8.

119. Thomas M. McKenna, *Muslim Rulers and Rebels: Everyday Politics and Armed Separatism in the Southern Philippines* (Berkeley: University of California Press, 1998), 86–112.

120. Finin, "Regional Consciousness," 109–12.

121. Cesar A. Majul, "Some Social and Cultural Problems of the Muslims in the Philippines," *Asian Studies* 14, no. 1 (1976): 91.

122. "Speech of Aluya Alonto on the Problem of Mindanao" (interpreted from Moro to English by Datu Marigan Saramain Alonto), 21 August 1934, in *Proceedings of the Philippine Constitutional Convention, 1934–1935* (Manila: Bureau of Printing, 1935), 420.

123. Charles Tilly, *Big Structures, Large Processes, Huge Comparisons* (New York: Russell Sage Foundation, 1984); Alexander George, "Case Studies and Theory Development: The Method of Structured Focused Comparison," in *Diplomacy: New Approaches in History, Theory and Policy*, ed. Paul Gordon Lauren (New York: Free Press, 1982), 43–68.

124. See esp. Martin Doornbos and Sudipta Kaviraj, eds., *Dynamics of State Formation: India and Europe Compared* (New Delhi: Sage Publications, 1997).

125. Young, *African State*, 76.

126. Romeo Cruz, *America's Colonial Desk and the Philippines, 1899–1934* (Quezon City: University of the Philippines Press, 1974), 19–23, 27. An interesting account of early American attempts to figure out the best way to govern the Muslims is Donna J. Amoroso, "Inheriting the 'Moro Problem': Muslim Authority and Colonial Rule in British Malaya and the Philippines," paper presented at the American Colonial State in Comparative Perspective panel, Association for Asian Studies Meeting, March 1997, Chicago, Ill.

127. Young, *African State*, 44.

128. Peter Evans, Dietrich Reuschmeyer, and Theda Skocpol, *Bringing the State Back In* (Cambridge: Cambridge University Press, 1985), 12.

JULIAN GO

The Chains of Empire: State

Building and "Political Education"

in Puerto Rico and the Philippines

In October 1899, General George W. Davis of the U.S. military government in Puerto Rico issued a seminal order: General Order No. 160. By that time, General Davis and his forces had been occupying Puerto Rico for more than a year. The war with Spain that had initially brought them to the island was finally over, and they now claimed complete control over the territory. General Order No. 160 proclaimed the establishment of municipal governments. It called for municipal elections with a restricted suffrage so that the new offices of mayor and councilor could be filled. It also arranged for the newly elected officials to carry out various duties, from policing to taxation and basic administration. Of course, the Puerto Ricans had already had municipal governments. The Spanish, during their three-hundred-year reign over the island, had originally set them up. But General Order No. 160 was supposed to mark something new entirely. It declared that the municipal governments were to be staffed exclusively by elected Puerto Ricans. The idea was that the Puerto Ricans, "for the first time in their history," should be given an opportunity to manage their own affairs and acquire practical education in the methods of modern governance. As General Davis stated, the new municipal governments were to serve as "a sort of kindergarten" in which Puerto Ricans could learn the ways of "popular government," Anglo-American style.[1]

That same year, halfway around the world and far into the Pacific, American military authorities issued a very similar order. General Order No. 43 in the Philippines also called for municipal governments. Literate and propertied Filipinos were to vote; the offices of municipal mayor and councilor were to be filled by elected natives; and the new officials were to carry out various administrative duties. Ostensibly, Filipinos thereby would be spared the "objectionable," "arbitrary," and "harsh" features of former Spanish rule and "for the first time . . . adopt representative control over their own civil affairs." As General E. S. Otis, who issued the order, put it, the new municipal governments—brilliantly colored with "the American spirit"—would give Filipinos the chance to "demonstrate a fitness for self-administration" and receive an "education" in the ways of democratic government.[2]

It should not be surprising that the general orders issued by the military governments in Puerto Rico and the Philippines were so similar. Both colonies were administered by the U.S. War Department, and Secretary of War Elihu Root was planning for both to be subjected to the same project of "practical political education." Through this project, Puerto Ricans and Filipinos would gain critical knowledge of, and practical experience in, Anglo-style political institutions. Under the United States' "strong and guiding hand," the colonized populations would receive a "course of tuition" and acquire the "character and habits of thought and feeling" necessary for "free self-government."[3] Puerto Ricans and Filipinos would be allowed to manage their own affairs with some measure of autonomy, while American administrators would supervise and direct them from above, providing "object lessons" in American models of government. In this way, the Puerto Ricans and Filipinos would emerge from their supposedly "rudimentary stage of political development" and be disciplined into the political image of their imperial master.[4] The two very similar general orders issued by the military authorities thus marked the beginning of this larger project, the beginning of a parallel attempt, in a sense, to discipline and democratize.[5]

Still, for all of its grandiose pretensions, the project of political education did not play out in either colony as initially planned. Nor did it unfold in exactly the same way in the two colonies. Despite the fact that it was to apply similarly to both, and despite its similar beginnings in the two colonies, the project eventually took on different forms in each, ultimately bringing about the construction of two very different colonial regimes. The task of this essay is to disclose and explain these divergent processes; to show why the project of political education in Puerto Rico and the Philippines was so altered over time that it diverged from its initial premises—and in fundamentally different ways in each colony.

The analysis affirms an existing and wide-ranging literature on colonial states and their projects. This literature stresses that colonial projects, whatever their designs, were rarely if ever realized in full. Across the imperial world, colonial-state builders and administrators pushed a range of projects, but once activated on the ground, those projects were often "deflected, or enacted farcically and incompletely."[6] Bruce Berman and John Lonsdale accordingly draw a distinction between colonial-state building and colonial-state formation. The first involves the "conscious effort [by planners and state builders] at creating an apparatus of control"; the second, by contrast, involves the "largely unconscious and contradictory process of conflicts, negotiations, and compromises [which] constitute the 'vulgarization' of power."[7] In a somewhat similar manner, Nicholas Thomas calls for analyses of colonial projects that grasp their "mediation" and "reformulation" in practice. He stresses that colonial projects "are often *projected* rather than realized" and so likens the enactment of colonial projects to the task of repairing an old car: "The cost and energy absorbed into surgery is never reflected in results, parts are replaced, but connections fail."[8] Political education in Puerto Rico and the Philippines is no exception to this literature. It was *projected* to set up a tutelary regime that would serve to teach Puerto Ricans and Filipinos the ways of American-style democratic government. Under American control, Puerto Ricans and Filipinos would vote in free elections, take up office, help devise legislation, and administer—first in the local (municipal) governments, and later in national legislative assemblies. As the native officials did this, and as they slowly learned their so-called "object lessons" in American-style governance, they would be given more autonomy. Local governments would be granted more duties and functions; the legislative assemblies would be allowed to devise laws "with less and less assistance"; and American control in general would slowly be loosened. "Free self-government in ever increasing measure"—this was the underlying principle of political education.[9]

Nevertheless, the project of political education unfolded in ways that transgressed its initial premises. As the extant literature on colonial projects would have it, political education was reformulated and modified once activated on the ground. Further, it was reformulated and modified in different directions and in distinct ways in each colony.

Political education in Puerto Rico took on a more restrictive and tightened form than initial plans dictated. American supervision over local affairs was intensified over time, and disciplinary mechanisms were tightened. This violated the original principle of "free self-government in ever increasing measure." Rather than offering more local autonomy over time (hence, more "self-government"), political education ended up creating a centralized colonial regime. Political education in the Philippines was much more lax than it was in Puerto Rico. American control and supervision was lightened, and disciplinary mechanisms were loosened over time. In contrast to Puerto Rico, a decentralized regime emerged. This pattern of decentralization followed the principle of "free self-government in ever increasing measure" but in actuality far exceeded it. Not only were the Filipinos given much more autonomy than their Puerto Rican counterparts; they were given autonomy far more quickly than had been initially planned. American administrators themselves later complained that they had gone "too far, too fast" in loosening supervision over local affairs.[10]

My analysis of these distinct patterns in political education thus affirms the existing literature on colonial states and their projects, but it also diverges significantly from it. Foremost, it diverges in its explanation of *why* colonial projects play out as they do. The existing literature most often highlights tensions within the colony to explain why projects were so often reformulated and modified in the process of their enactment. In contrast, and in keeping with the theme of the other essays in this volume, I show that such tensions internal to colonies were not the only determinants of political education. The different forms of political education in Puerto Rico and the Philippines were also determined by *translocal* tensions—that is, tensions that transcended the colonies and ran all the way up to and through the metropolitan state itself. In other words, the unpredicted and unforeseen character of political education in Puerto Rico and the Philippines was shaped by tensions that spanned the United States' entire chain of empire.

PROJECTS AND CHAINS

In a certain sense, of course, it is not entirely surprising that colonial projects were so often reformulated in practice. Indeed, the existing literature on colonial rule highlights at least two factors that served to complicate their completion. First, local populations did not always comply passively with the disciplinary dictates of colonial power. Through means subtle or blatant, quotidian or extraordinary, unwitting or concerted, they posed resistance, thereby complicating whatever designs colonial architects may have laid out. Consequently, confronted with the unpredictable and sometimes subversive actions of target groups, colonial-state builders often had to rework their plans.[11] Second, colonial agents themselves were not always unified in their goals. Administrators often enacted different colonial projects at the same time, and these projects were sometimes wracked with internal inconsistencies or contradictions. Administrators were thus compelled to perform all manner of patchwork. Sometimes they disavowed one project for the sake of another; at other times they subtly shifted the goals or operations of each project to mediate among competing imperatives.[12]

These factors were certainly present as political education was enacted in Puerto Rico and the Philippines. Local populations subjected to the project did not always act as passive receptors for the "object lessons" of political education. Moreover, administrators in both colonies planned a range of other projects besides political education: the construction of public schools, development of infrastructure, and American capital investment in agriculture. Both of these factors thereby complicated political education. They made for a host of tensions. Still, what is most striking is that the administrators in both colonies faced the same sort of tensions. In Puerto Rico as well as in the Philippines, local populations resisted the dictates of political education—and in very similar ways. Moreover, in both colonies administrators planned to enact the same contemporaneous projects besides political education, which is not surprising, as they were following the general state-building plans of Root (their supervisor in the War Department). This suggests that the different forms the project took were not solely the result of resistance from below or the competing imperatives of contemporaneous projects. Something more was going on.

Here, an understanding of what imperial chains are becomes crucial. By "chains of empire," I mean the multifaceted links and connections that colonial rule necessarily entailed. Together, these links and connections created a range of translocal tensions with which colonial administrators and planners had to cope. The first link in the chain of empire is that between colonizer and colonized. Colonial rule established lasting connections between peoples that previously were separate. At minimum, it placed agents of the colonial state and colonized peoples in direct and sustained contact with each other. Colonial-state administrators faced local populations over whom they were to rule and on whom they imposed their projects; local populations, in turn, faced a new colonial state to which they were to defer, at least in theory. Certainly, this link was wracked with conflict, as local populations resisted the efforts of colonizing agents. But it was a link nonetheless. In collaboration or in conflict, colonizer and colonized engaged each other. The actions of one thus shaped the actions of the other.

Such links within the colonies are almost too obvious, but they were concomitant with a series of other crucial links. While colonial states and administrators were connected to local populations, for example, they were also connected to the imperial center at home. They were accountable to a metropolitan-imperial state that commanded them from above. In turn, the metropolitan authorities themselves were accountable to other actors. On the home front, empire called forth a range of social forces. Imperialists and anti-imperialists, corporations and capitalists, even labor unions and religious groups—all of these domestic actors had their own agendas in relation to empire, and they often pressed them directly on the metropolitan-imperial state. Anti-imperialists pressured the state to loosen imperial control, while imperialists pressured to tighten it. Domestic labor unions, fearing the influx of cheap labor from the colonies, pushed the state to enact anti-immigration laws, while corporations sometimes pushed the opposite. Colonial rule was thereby part of an extensive series of connections that transcended particular actors and locales. It entailed a translocal, cross-colonial chain that linked colonized populations, colonial administrators, branches of the imperial state, and various social groups on the home front. Everyone was entangled, and the groups did not always pull in the same direction.[13] Colonial projects therefore were not only shaped by colonizing agents imposing their will on the colonized, however contradictory those impositions may have been. Nor were colonial projects shaped merely by the conflicts between colonial administrators and resisting local populations. Although these factors were certainly important, colonial projects were also shaped by the maneuvers of actors in the metropole, not least as those actors endeavored to realize their own distinct agendas in relation to empire. Projects on colonial ground were subject to the pulls and tugs of all of the actors in the chain of empire.

This was the case for political education in Puerto Rico and the Philippines. Political education in the two colonies was determined by translocal tensions running along America's chain of empire, not only by tensions or conflicts within each colony. No doubt, proponents of political education (such as the administrators on the ground and policymakers in the War Department) faced local resistance from below, and they certainly had to deal with the competing imperatives of their other projects. But they also had to deal with the metropolitan state and domestic actors pushing their agendas onto that metropolitan state. More specifically, proponents of the project had to deal with the U.S. Congress and the domestic groups it represented. The latter had particular plans for each colony, and as they struggled to realize their plans, they pulled the colonies in different directions. Ultimately, political education was pulled likewise.

By examining political education during military rule, then during the onset of civil rule (c. 1898–1901), one can see that the beginnings of the project were remarkably similar in the two colonies. Root and his administrators on the ground had similar visions of it, and they began to carry it out in similar ways. Further, they tied to it the same set of other projects, and in both colonies they faced the very same kinds of local resistance. It was only when the U.S. Congress and the domestic interests it represented exerted their influence on the colonies that the initially similar state-building trajectories began to diverge, ultimately bringing about a restrictive and tight form of political education in Puerto Rico and a lax and loose form in the Philippines.

MILITARY RULE: "A SORT OF KINDERGARTEN"

Political education in Puerto Rico and the Philippines began during military rule under the direction of Secretary of War Elihu Root.[14] In 1899, military commanders in both colonies issued their respective General Orders and thereby established municipal governments—the first step in the overall plan. Thereafter, state building proceeded in ways that were remarkably similar—at least, on certain counts.

First, in both colonies, the new municipal offices were quickly monopolized by the local elite: wealthy landowners, merchants, and, to a lesser extent, educated professionals.[15] In Puerto Rico, the first elections saw an overwhelming victory for the Federal Party, the party led by coffee and sugar *hacendados* (plantation owners) who had clamored for political autonomy from Spain and who now saw in U.S. rule new political opportunities.[16] For them, *America del norte* was the "State of States," the "Republic of Republics" that carried with it the flag of prosperity and progress.[17] They believed that American rule would bring unprecedented political blessings to the island. They also hoped that it would offer new markets for their sugar and coffee.[18] In the Philippines, the elite also took up local office. The difference was that some among the elite had already begun to resist American military domination, resulting in guerrilla warfare in many parts of the archipelago. Nevertheless, just as the rebels in certain provinces armed themselves, their wealthy and educated counterparts took office in the areas controlled by the Americans. In the so-called "pacified" areas, then, the Filipino elite were quick to partake of local governments, just as the elite in Puerto Rico were. And later, after the Americans' war of conquest had violently squashed Filipino resistance in different parts of the archipelago, many elite resisters dropped their arms. In the face of defeat, and also believing that U.S. rule would not displace them politically, these elites also began to participate in the new order.[19]

Second, with the local elite in each colony inserted into office, the military authorities in Puerto Rico and the Philippines began to activate the basic logic of political education. They subjected municipal affairs to their supervision and control. In Puerto Rico, U.S. military officers had the right to inspect local affairs and "report all errors of administration, mismanagement or failure of any kind on the part of Municipal Officers to administer the Government properly."[20] In the Philippines, military officers had similar powers, claiming the right to "exercise authority in exigencies."[21] The military authorities gave municipal governments some measure of autonomy, however, so they could carry out their various duties—formulation of local ordinances, collection of taxes, even municipal policing. In Puerto Rico, for example, General Davis determined that the towns should "be let alone and free to administer their own affairs."[22] In fact, when Davis received complaints from local native officials that

U.S. military officers were interfering too much with town councils, he swiftly reprimanded the officers.[23] In the Philippines, too, military authorities shied away from too much centralization, determined to give municipalities enough room to follow their own "impulse and initiative." The role of the local military agents was to be strictly "supervisory."[24]

The military governments in both colonies thereby tried to maintain a balance between central control and local autonomy. This was precisely the sort of balance for which Root had called in his outline for political education. There was to be just enough autonomy that the native officials could perform government functions and acquire experience, just enough control that they could perform properly and learn their object lessons adequately.[25] Of course, at this time the balance between central control and local autonomy was not yet regularized. The degree of autonomy that localities enjoyed and the intensity of control over local officials were not formally instituted. The role of military commanders was limited to building local governments and laying down the basic groundwork for the political education to come. They therefore exerted relatively little effort toward regularizing educative efforts in any systematic manner. Sometimes they handled abuses of power by native officials with scoldings. At other times, they removed guilty native officials from office completely. It was a precarious brand of political education—"a sort of kindergarten," indeed.[26]

The precarious balance between autonomy and control, however, did not undermine Root's basic plan. The American civil administrators were to soon take control from the military officials, and under their direction political education was to be enacted to its fullest. The relatively loose kindergartens of military rule were to be transformed into properly institutionalized schools of politics. Thus, as the civil administrators in both colonies took control in 1900, Root instructed them to institute the specific duties and functions of the municipal governments. This would firmly establish the degree of autonomy that municipalities initially would enjoy. By the same token, Root instructed the civil administrators to institute a system of surveillance and discipline to guide, teach, or punish native officials. The long-term view was that as the natives learned their lessons in governance, the civil administrators would slowly tip the scale toward autonomy—hence, "free self-government in ever increasing measure."[27]

During the first moments of civil rule, political education began to unfold very similarly in the two colonies, just as it had during military rule. Indeed, not only were the administrators in Puerto Rico and the Philippines charged with the same set of instructions from Root for instituting political education; they also faced very similar situations on colonial ground. Specifically, they both faced resistance from below, and they both planned to enact the same set of other projects besides political education.

On entering office in 1900, the civil administrators in both colonies quickly learned that the native officials were not strictly following their prescribed duties. In Puerto Rico, for example, administrators found that the Federals who were occupying municipal governments had been using their offices "merely as a means for furthering private ends." They had been deploying their institutional prerogatives "for the purpose of aiding their friends" and for "gratifying personal and political enmities."[28] Moreover, municipal *alcaldes* (mayors) were using local police forces "as a weapon to favor the political party to which he belonged"; moreover, they were engaging in financial fraud. It was "open and notorious that . . . public funds were not duly accounted for, expenditures were improperly made, and money was being stolen by municipal officials or diverted into improper channels."[29] The administrators in the Philippines discovered similar practices. Municipal officials were pocketing public funds for themselves, using the municipal police forces as their "personal servants" and "*muchachos*," and they were collecting "illegal taxes" to boot. Like their Puerto Rican counterparts, they were deploying office for their own "personal prerogatives."[30]

The political corruption among local officials was precisely what political education was supposed to uproot and replace. Corruption had been one of Root's major concerns, and it remained so for the administrators. It figured to them as the antithesis of democratic practice, the mark of political primitivity, just as did the political corruption of "ethnic bosses" in urban cities at home.[31] It stood as further proof that the Filipino and Puerto Rican elites were little more than "*caciques*" and "oligarchs"; that they were violating the "public trust" and thus had "little conception" of what liberty and free self-government truly meant.[32] The kinds of practices that the colonial administrators coded as "corruption," however, were more often than not manifestations of the patron–client relationships that had long structured political and social life in the two colonies. Under Spanish rule, political corruption had allowed the few natives who had held office to enhance and perpetuate their powers. Puerto Ricans and Filipinos had inserted resources of office into personalized circulations of exchange with commoners and peers to cultivate debts and, hence, to cultivate a network of friends and followers. Political corruption had been part of the very fabric of mercantilist governmentality in the colonies, articulating well with the Puerto Rican and Filipino elites' interest in enhancing their social and economic capital. Thus, in confronting corruption, the American administrators in both colonies were brushing up against a certain kind of agency on the part of the colonized, a certain kind of resistance.[33]

In the face of such resistance, the colonies' administrators nevertheless remained hopeful, confident that they could uproot corruption by regularizing political education. Administrators in Puerto Rico emphasized that experience and education under American rule would "rapidly" advance the "civic virtues" of the people. They stressed that "object lessons [would] be furnished" and that corruption would then subside.[34] One administrator even projected that "within five years American ideas will have been grasped to the extent that [the Puerto Ricans] will be able to navigate their own little government."[35] The members of the Philippine Commission affirmed similarly that they soon would be able to "teach" the Filipinos "the method of carrying on government according to American ideas." They reported that they were "by no means discouraged at the prospect of successfully fitting [the Filipinos] for self-government" and that, under their benevolent direction, the Filipinos would soon "become familiar with practical free government and civil liberty."[36] Despite the contingencies of resistance, then, administrators in Puerto Rico and the Philippines remained determined to fulfill the original principle of "free self-government in ever increasing measure."

At the same time, the administrators began planning a range of other state projects besides political education. These projects were all part of Root's larger vision of democratizing the colonies, fulfilling the United States' "unquestioned duty" to provide Puerto Ricans and Filipinos with "opportunities for . . . development in civilization."[37] The projects for the colonies were similar. One was to construct an extensive system of public schools for the masses. The schools would teach English, rudimentary academic skills, and especially civics lessons so that the "credulous" masses could learn how to exercise their rights against the "caciques" and "bosses."[38] This was the "civilizing" mission for the non-elite. As the elite of the colonies had political education, so would the peasant masses receive their own kind of education in public schools.

Another project was infrastructural development. The administrators planned to build new roads and railroads, irrigation works, and communication systems. Administrators were indeed appalled at the condition of the infrastructure in the two colonies. The situation was especially dire in the Philippines, largely due to the effects of war. But the Spanish–American War had had detrimental effects on infrastructure in Puerto Rico, as well. In any case, the colonies' administrators saw a desperate need to modernize existing infrastructure. The development of infrastructure would carry the colonies into the light of "civilization." To wit, administrators placed great emphasis on road building, because, as one of them put it, "there can be no civilization without means of transportation."[39]

The final project was economic development. Prefiguring modernization theories of democratization, Root stressed to administrators that economic prosperity was crucial for democratic state building. "If the people are prosperous and have an abundance of the necessities of life," he wrote, "they will . . . with patience be easily educated."[40] He particularly emphasized the role that U.S. capital investment should play, but not simply to please American capitalists. Espousing the theories of Charles Conant (a prominent economist whom Root enlisted as an adviser), Root stressed that U.S. capital investment would have a progressive and beneficial influence, both indirectly and directly. American capital would solidify private property and wage-based social relations; instill an individualistic labor ethic and secular modes of consciousness; and create wealth for the population as a whole.[41] On this the administrators agreed. Like Root, they were enamored of the ostensibly benevolent influence of American capital, especially if it was to be invested in agriculture. Governor Charles Allen in Puerto Rico wrote that American capital, with all of its "push and energy," would "proceed to make at least five spears of grass grow where one had grown before, to the immense and permanent prosperity of the island."[42] Philippine Governor William H. Taft wrote that with American capital would come the "moral improvement and the education of the people." Yankee capital would promote "Yankee ingenuity, Yankee enterprise, and Yankee freedom."[43] Thus, along with Root, administrators in both colonies called for the creation of central banks, efficient monetary systems on the gold standard, and reduced tariffs or even free trade between the United States and the colonies, along with other measures aimed at jump-starting economic growth and attracting capital investment.[44]

In short, political education at the onset of civil rule began to unfold similarly in the two colonies, just as it had during military rule. It was activated under similar local conditions.[45] The administrators in Puerto Rico and the Philippines faced the problem of "corruption," and in both colonies they planned to regularize political education so as to uproot it. Moreover, the administrators tied political education to the same set of developmental projects. They planned to build schools and roads, and they planned to develop the economy through the influx of "Yankee capital." Thus, not only was political education set to follow the same trajectory in Puerto Rico and the Philippines; so, too, was the larger process of development in "civilization." It was as if Root's initial visions of tutelary state building would be readily realized in both colonies.

The only problem was that Root and the administrators were not the only actors involved in directing colonial affairs. Initially they were. During military rule, for example, colonial affairs had been under the control of the metropolitan executive branch. The colonies were in the hands of the armed forces, and as commander-in-chief, President William McKinley had final say on all matters. As long as military rule was in place, only he could direct colonial affairs, and he had done so precisely by delegating responsibilities to the War Department and its head, Elihu Root. But civil rule was not to work that way. According to the U.S. Constitution, civil rule was subject to other branches of the metropolitan state—namely, the congressional branch. Although the War Department would still direct and administer the colonies, the U.S. Congress would have control over certain other areas of colonial affairs.[46] And when Congress, along with the domestic interests it represented, began to exert that control, the colonial administrations on the ground began to face very different situations. The chains of empire pulled them in different directions.

One of the most important areas of colonial affairs over which Congress had control was commerce between the United States and its new colonies. Only Congress could enact trade legislation. Only Congress could determine, for example, whether duties would be placed on goods to and from the colonies, and if so, at what rate. Of course, this was strictly an economic matter. It had no direct bearing on political education proper. But it was still linked to the overall plans of Root and the civil administrators. As noted, Root and the administrators were hoping that American capital would come to the colonies. To spark investment, they were hoping for a reduction in the existing Dingley tariffs on goods to and from foreign states. In their view, some kind of reduction in those tariffs would offer an incentive for U.S. capitalists to invest. It would especially offer an incentive for U.S. capital to set up large plantations.[47] But because Congress alone had the privilege of determining commercial policy, those plans were linked to forces over which Root and the administrators had little control.

Indeed, when the trade issue emerged in Congress, conflicting domestic interests began to maneuver. On one side, a group of capitalists joined Root and the administrators in their plans to attract U.S. capital. Sugar capitalists were especially vocal. As early as 1898 they had been expressing interest in investing in Puerto Rico. They had also expressed interest in the Philippines. Thus, Horace Havemeyer of the American Sugar Refining Company and his peers pressed for free trade.[48] Mining companies interested in investing in Luzon and wheat growers in the Northwestern states who were looking for new markets pressed for free trade, as well.[49] On the other side, domestic agriculturalists and workers urged Congress to keep tariff rates high. Because both Puerto Rico and the Philippines were sugar-producing countries, sugar-beet farmers in the United States were adamant about maintaining high tariffs. They even pressed for legislation that would limit the amount of land a U.S. corporation could hold in the colonies to prevent American sugar corporations from forming large-scale sugar haciendas. Tobacco farmers were likewise adamant about the tariff, fearing competition from Puerto Rican tobacco. Thus, the Beet Sugar Manufacturers' Association, the New England Tobacco Growers' Association, and the League of Domestic Producers all opposed free trade and lobbied for high tariffs on goods coming in from the colonies.[50] In this they were joined by the anti-imperialist groups brewing on the home front. Anti-imperialists also wanted high tariffs and restrictions on corporate land ownership. They hoped that this would halt possible economic exploitation of the colonies by the American trusts.[51] Such opposition to free trade made Root and the administrators nervous. Fearing that a high tariff would halt the influx of "Yankee capital," Philippine Governor Taft wrote to his fellow administrator Bernard Moses, "We are all on tenter-hooks of expectation as to the passage of the Spooner Bill [on tariffs]."[52]

In the end, Congress granted free trade for Puerto Rico. The Foraker Act of 1900 contained a stipulation that, although tariffs would remain at 15 percent of the existing Dingley rates, they could be declared null "whenever the [Puerto Rican] legislative assembly should enact and put into operation a system of local taxation sufficient to pay the expenses of the government."[53] A very different outcome for the Philippines followed. The 1901 Spooner Bill and the subsequent Philippine Tariff Act of 1902 provided only a 25 percent reduction in the tariff on goods coming from the Philippines—much lower than the 75 percent reduction for which administrators in the Philippines had called. Moreover, Congress restricted the amount of land that corporations could purchase there to 1,024 hectares (2,530 acres).[54]

A number of factors were at work in shaping the different stance that Congress took toward the two colonies. One was that U.S. capitalists were more divided on the Philippine trade issue than they had been on the Puerto Rico issue. Although some U.S. sugar capitalists had made plans to invest in the Philippines, other manufacturers and traders showed less interest. To them, the Philippines was too far away from the United States' traditional field of influence to make investment seem profitable, and the Philippine–American War had made it appear even less so. At best, the Philippines could serve as a gateway to the China market, not as a fruitful field for investment itself.[55] Business interests were more unified in their zeal for Puerto Rico. That colony was well within America's historical sphere of influence, and Puerto Ricans had not led a violent resistance movement against U.S. rule.[56] Another reason has to do with historical sequence: The trade issue for Puerto Rico was decided by Congress before it was worked out for the Philippines. Thus, by the time the tariff issue for the Philippines came up, free trade had already been declared for Puerto Rico. This made the anti-imperialists and agriculturalists more determined to restrict capital investment in the Philippines. They had already lost their case for high tariffs on Puerto Rico, and they were not about to lose again. They pressured Congress accordingly, and the U.S. sugar capitalists who had initially called for reduced tariffs on Philippine trade made little effort to stop them—perhaps because they were getting little support from other sectors of the business community, but most likely because they already had Puerto Rico as a fruitful field of investment.[57]

In any case, the overarching point should be clear: Even though Root and the administrators had similar visions and plans for the two colonies, other actors did not. Anti-imperialists, sectors of the business community, sugar-beet farmers—they all had their own, distinct agendas. And even though they were all maneuvering in the United States, far from the colonies, they were nonetheless linked to the colonies. The chain of empire connected their meeting rooms and platforms up to Congress, then out to the imperial periphery. The result was free trade for Puerto Rico and high tariffs for the Philippines. This had crucial and distinct implications for the colonial administrations. The Puerto Rico administrators were granted free trade, just as they had hoped. They therefore had the promising prospect of incoming U.S. capital, a key element contributing to the fulfillment of their developmental dreams. The administrators in the Philippines, by contrast, were not granted their desired economic policy by Congress. Their developmental plans were thus short-circuited. In all, the administrators in Puerto Rico and the Philippines were pulled in different directions by the chains of empire and therefore faced very different situations on the ground. As a result, they would begin to see and enact political education in ways that were very different from before.

THE PHILIPPINES: SPINNING THE "WHEELS OF DEVELOPMENT"

U.S. administrators in the Philippines, who were initially confident that they could teach Filipino officials American methods of government, were determined to make political education work. After they first entered office, then, they made efforts to tighten controls over local affairs. Foremost, they grafted onto the existing municipalities a system of provincial governments (akin to American states at home) and made it the duty of the provincial governments to inspect the municipalities under them. Provincial boards were to review municipal ordinances and annul undesirable ones, and the provincial governor was to make periodic inspections of municipal affairs. The board members and elected governor were Filipinos, but they were to be watched by Americans assigned to the boards as provincial treasurers. Those American treasurers would be crucial for surveillance. They were to ensure that the Filipino officials carried out their duties; they were also to ensure that the Filipino governor was properly inspecting the municipalities and reporting any corrupt activities he found. Moreover, the American treasurers were to keep tight reins on municipal finances. Finally, the Executive Bureau in Manila was to receive all complaints of corruption and ensure that the guilty were tried or reprimanded, depending on the nature of the offense.[58]

Through these measures the administrators sought a regularized pattern of surveillance that would uproot the local corruption that had become evident during military rule. The measures indicated just how serious the administrators were in following Root's plan for political education. But just as these measures were being instituted, the administrators received word from home that they would not get their desired tariff reduction. Their disappointment cannot be overstressed. They had placed great emphasis on providing incentives for so-called "Yankee capital," which in the long run was to bring "Yankee freedom" to the Philippines. In the short run it was to bring increased commercial activity and thereby feed state coffers so that infrastructure and public schools could be properly funded. In fact, Philippine Governor Taft had planned that the state funds for infrastructure and schools would come from land and local commercial taxes, revenues that were to have been increased by an influx of American capital investment.[59] So important was this plan that Taft had written to Root, "It would be like running on one wheel to develop this country without power to offer investments to capital."[60]

With the disappointment from Congress, however, Taft and the rest of the Philippine Commission members were indeed left with a dreaded "one wheel." Administrator Daniel Williams complained that the legislation enacted by Congress "effectually ties the hands of the Commission so far as development of the resources of the islands is concerned, without which development no general prosperity can be expected. . . . No action whatever was taken [by the metropole] to relieve us of our unfortunate currency muddle."[61] Taft complained likewise that Congress's decision to keep tariff rates high and restrict corporate land ownership "stops absolutely the investment of new capital."[62] He learned quickly that U.S. capital, like the U.S. Constitution, does not always follow the flag.

In the long term, the absence of U.S. capital investment contributed to the persistence in the pre-existing landed power of the Filipino elite.[63] But in the short term, it meant that the administrators faced a serious dilemma. How could they spin the "wheels of development" without American capital investment? To solve the problem, administrators such as Luke Wright and Cameron Forbes came up with specific strategies. First, because they could not rely on revenues derived from increased trade, they decided to turn to other taxes that had not initially been planned. One was a simple head tax, a reenactment of the Spanish *cedula*. The administrators originally had not planned to impose this tax, but they felt that they had no choice.[64] Another was a special tax whose receipts were to go for the construction of roads. That tax, too, originally had not been planned, as the administrators had hoped that road building could be funded by the revenues that capital investment and increased commerce would bring.[65] Both taxes were to provide the needed revenues that had been lost because of Congress's decisions, enabling infrastructural development and the construction of public schools.[66] This, then, was a modification of the original revenue plans, a new strategy for funding "development in civilization." But it came with a hitch: active collaboration with the local Filipino elite. The local elite were the only ones who could help collect the new taxes; they were the ones who could mobilize local populations.[67] The elite in the provinces and municipalities were especially important. As opposed to the urban elite (the merchant and professional class in Manila), the provincial elite were grand patron landlords who subsumed local peasants under their control. As the longstanding mediators between local populations and the central authorities in Manila during Spanish rule, only they had the capacity to carry out the new revenue plan. It is thus notable that, before the congressional disappointments, administrators had cultivated collaborative relations with the Manila's elite. But as the new taxation strategies were formulated, administrators disavowed them. They turned their attention to the provincial elite, cultivating new ties with them and offering them numerous concessions to enlist their support for the new strategy.[68]

The concessions resulted in a loose and lax form of political education. One concession was increased local autonomy. The administrators slowly but surely began to loosen their controls over the local governments. A crucial step taken in this regard was to remove the Americans from their positions as provincial treasurers. By 1906, nearly all of the treasurers had been removed and given a new office—that of public-works officer, indicative of the administrators' new emphasis on infrastructural development. The effect was crucial. With the American treasurer gone, financial affairs were in almost full control of Filipinos, with no direct American supervision. Relatedly, there were fewer Americans in the field to ensure that political corruption was watched and reported. Instead, the Americans on the provincial boards were to pay most of their attention to building infrastructure.[69]

A related concession was that the administrators became less insistent on punishing corrupt officials. When they did in fact find local-level corruption on the part of Filipinos, they were reluctant to punish. From 1903 to 1909, fewer than half of the Filipino officials found guilty of corruption were removed from office. The preferred sanction became a written or verbal scolding.[70] Even the officials removed from office were sometimes allowed to take up positions later, with little complaint from Americans. For example, when the Americans had to appoint officials to vacant positions, the positions were "distributed practically without regard to the previous political records of the recipients"—because, as Administrator Dean Worcester openly admitted, the Americans expected "cooperation" from the appointed officials in carrying out the new revenue strategy.[71] Some officials even came to rely on the very corruption that they initially had found so disturbing. Forbes sometimes turned a blind eye to the "illegal taxes" that many local Filipino officials had been collecting. Those illegal taxes, he had discovered, often went to the construction of roads and schools. The officials first collected illegal taxes as personal "tribute" (in Tagalog, *buwis*), just as officials had done in the Spanish days, and then used portions of them to provide returns to their community in the form of infrastructure. As long as such practices served the creation of infrastructure, they could be tolerated to some degree.[72] Further, after 1907, when the National Assembly was finally inaugurated, the Americans serving in the upper house sometimes allowed the Filipino delegates to pass "pernicious" bills structured as pork-barreling. Although this was contrary to the principles of political education, the Americans apparently found it useful: In return for allowing the delegates to pork-barrel, the Americans expected them to pass bills that would put more money into infrastructural development.[73]

This was all part of the administrators' new strategy aimed toward "getting things done" in the absence of Yankee capital.[74] Congress had pulled the Philippines into a situation in which the administrators had to turn to strategies and collaborative patterns that entailed decentralization and supervisory slackness. The overall result was lax and loose political education. The administrators tipped the projected balance between autonomy and control toward autonomy, far exceeding the original principle of free self-government in ever-increasing measure. Indeed, administrators later lamented this excessive decentralization, admitting that they had gone "too far, too fast" in loosening supervision and granting Filipinos so much autonomy.[75] But by then, it was too late. Doling out resources and concessions to the very "caciques" and "bosses" whom they initially had planned to discipline, the Americans at the apex of the colonial state had become less the tutors for democracy than the grand imperial patrons of a local patrimonial regime in formation (see Figure 1).[76]

PUERTO RICO: SWEETNESS AND STATE

The situation was very different in Puerto Rico. As noted, the U.S. Congress was more generous to the administrators there, granting them the free trade they desired. Administrators in Puerto Rico therefore faced the rather promising prospect of incoming U.S. capital. Their developmental dreams could in fact be realized. This situation had crucial consequences for the administrators' perceptions and actions. Most crucial was that the administrators saw local corruption on the part of Puerto Rican officials in a different and much more threatening light than did the administrators in the Philippines. Indeed, if the pillaging and pocketing of state funds were to continue, and if the local police forces could not be trusted to carry out the law, U.S. capital would face a hostile investment environment. The corruption on the part of the Federals in the municipal governments would stand as a serious threat to the sweet taste of sugar capital. During military rule, Commander Francis N. Mansfield had foreshadowed this in a report to the civil administrators. After acknowl-

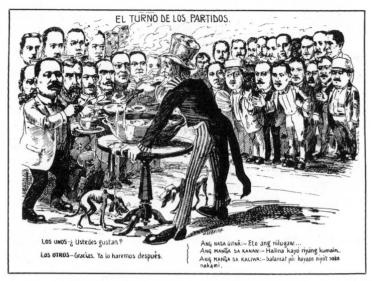

Figure 1. "Doling Out Favors." From Ruby R. Paredes, ed., *Philippine Colonial Democracy*, Southeast Asia Studies Monograph Series, no. 32 (New Haven, Conn.: Yale University Press, 1988), 64. Reprinted by permission of Yale University Press.

edging the need for capital investment, he urged: "The political situation must change before anything can be done. Civil government under present conditions [municipal corruption] would . . . discourage and prevent the introduction of new capital for investment."[77]

Of course, American capital was interested in arriving anyway, as has been shown. Nevertheless, the civil administrators were convinced that municipal affairs had to be cleaned up if American capital was to arrive in all of its promise. To be sure, the Foraker Act itself stressed that municipal finances in Puerto Rico had to be cleaned up. It declared that existing trade barriers would be declared null only when municipal finances were placed on a sound basis. Not surprisingly, after Congress passed the Foraker Act, administrators on the ground began calling for more direct American control over municipal finances. Administrator J. H. Hollander complained that, during military rule, too much autonomy had been granted to local governments and that this was "doctrinaire, premature and certain to result, if continued, in irregularity and confusion."[78] He complained, for example, that because Puerto Rican officials under U.S. rule had been able to collect "illegal taxes" without severe or systematic punishment, municipal finances were in complete disarray.[79] There was thus an "imperative and urgent need of revenue reform."[80]

Relatedly, the civil administrators began calling for a reorganization of the municipal police. The municipal police were being used by municipal mayors "as a weapon" against their "political enemies." They were also used as "organized mobs" to carry out political violence.[81] On one level, this violated the cherished principle that minority parties should be treated impartially. It likewise violated the principle that office was not to be deployed for personal or political ends. On another level, though, abuses of the municipal police force had implications for the prospect of incoming capital. The arbitrary use of police power, along with its associated violence, threatened life and property. Governor Allen complained that, because of the arbitrary use of police power by local officials, "citizens are not afforded the protection to life and property which they have the right to expect." He then stressed the importance of making "the American capitalist realize . . . that property is as well protected here as in the United States" and noted that "capital will come here and will come earlier if people can be assured of the protection of life and property, essential to prudent business methods."[82]

In short, the congressional legislation that called for free trade brought about a situation in which the corruption on the part of the Federals in the municipal governments had to be halted.[83] Subsequently, administrators enacted a strategy quite different from that which the Philippine administrators were enacting. With the aid of the Federals' enemies, the Republican Party (which had taken control of the legislative assembly), they began to enact a series of measures that centralized rather than loosened surveillance and control.[84] The first of these was the Hollander Act. The act stripped local governments of any significant tax-collecting functions, giving the central government the right to levy and collect all taxes, excepting local license taxes. It also set up an insular revenue bureau headed by Americans and made up of a salaried and permanent corps of revenue agents.[85] To add to the centralizing tendency, the jurisdiction of these collectors did not line up with municipal boundaries. Instead, the Hollander Act created separate districts to be supervised at the top by an American treasurer. Further, the Hollander Act created an intensive system of surveillance for detecting any fraudulent behavior on the part of local officials. It called for detailed registry books, a rigid system of assessment and payment schedules, and a hierarchical structure of internal control and supervision in order to locate and halt the "personal politics" and "bribery" that had marked earlier years.[86] Another law in 1902 solidified the system further, making all municipal finances subject to direct control of the insular treasurer, invariably an American. The law demanded

> the preparation of a code of regulations, setting forth in detail the precise manner in which the municipal treasurers and comptrollers should keep their books of account, deposit all funds, audit all claims and make all payments from the municipal treasury; the requirement of systematic reports, showing the actual financial transactions and conditions, and their subsequent compilation and analysis, so that operations might be clearly seen; and the organization of a system of inspection and audit by officials attached to the office of the treasurer, in order that the department might know whether its orders were being complied with and whether municipal affairs were being honestly and efficiently conducted.[87]

Such a system of surveillance and control contrasted markedly with the relatively lax system that the Philippine administrators set up. There, as we have seen, direct American control and surveillance over financial affairs was loosened rather than tightened, as the administrators gave local governments great leeway to collect taxes to make up for the projected loss of state revenue.

Another measure pushed by the American administrators dismantled nearly all of the existing municipal police forces. Both Puerto Rican municipal police forces and an American-led insular police existed during military rule; Governor Allen now suggested that the insular force be expanded and that it replace the existing municipal forces in all but the largest cities. The goal was to ensure "protection to persons and property and efficiency and economy of administration."[88] Thus, by 1902, nearly all the municipal police forces had been dismantled and replaced with the American-led insular force. Policing was thus "taken out of the hands of the municipal authorities and vested in the insular government . . . where it could be administered in a non-political manner."[89] The contrast with the Philippines is again worth noting: There, the municipal police forces were kept intact.[90]

By 1903, then, the American administrators had centralized in their own hands the critical state functions of taxation, financing, and policing. But this was not all. The Americans also began to punish local corruption on the part of the Puerto Rican officials in a systematic and sustained manner. When officials were found to be keeping their own police forces illegally, as was the case in Ponce in 1901, the Americans swiftly reprimanded them.[91] The Americans even replaced the municipal police forces in the largest cities, which had been spared in the 1902 legislation.[92] Further, the Americans were quick to punish financial mismanagement on the part of the local officials. After the Hollander Act was instituted, for example, they punished all those found guilty of fraud.[93] In addition, insular revenue agents often made unannounced inspections of municipal affairs, leading to the removal of guilty officials from office. Such was the case in 1903 and 1904 when insular agents swept through large municipalities such as Mayaguez, uncovered financial corruption, and dismissed incumbent mayors from office and dismantled their political machines.[94] Finally, the American governor-general consistently filled municipal vacancies with members of the political party that did not hold a majority of the council seats. That practice, instituted in the name of "impartiality" and respect for minority parties, set up a self-sufficient system of surveillance, as councilors of the minority party made haste to report any corrupt activities on the part of those councilors with opposing party affiliations.[95] Again, this practice stands in marked contrast to the Philippines, where administrators made little effort to achieve partisan balance and even appointed Filipinos to office who earlier had been found guilty of corruption.

Certainly, none of this was lost on the Puerto Rican political elite. Subjected to increasing controls, they soon leveled unprecedented criticisms against political education, no longer seeing in American rule the promise they had once seen (see Figure 2). Nevertheless, the American administrators remained relatively immune. In fact, in accordance with their centralized form of political education, they began to articulate a new discourse about it. In 1905, Administrator Edward Wilson wrote that the old pueblo ideal of municipal autonomy had to be dissolved for the sake of centralization, justifying centralization on the grounds that it was an evolutionary "Law of Nature." Centralization, he claimed, "is attended by increased intelligence."[96] Likewise, Administrator L. S. Rowe remarked that only through "a highly centralized administration" could Puerto Ricans be instilled with Anglo-American principles of government. He turned to examples of state centralization in France rather

GOMO SE EDUGA AL "NIÑO"

Según Mr. Lindsay estima
eres refractario al foete......

Pues mientras seas tan *zoquete*
no te lo quito de encima.

LA PRINCESA MATILDE

Figure 2. "How the 'Child' Is Educated," *Puerto Rican Herald*, 30 January 1904, 1243.
Original in Library of Congress, Washington, D.C.

than the Tocquevillan American towns about which Root had initially spoken.[97] Finally, Administrator William Willoughby acknowledged that the Americans' "exceedingly stringent" centralizing measures had "shorn" municipalities of "important classes of duties usually pertaining to local government," but he then claimed that "the necessities of the case . . . rendered such action imperative."[98] As has been shown, those "necessities" included not only corruption from below but also the fact that such corruption conflicted with what the administrators took to be the best interests of metropolitan sugar capital, the latter propped up by Congress.

In Puerto Rico, then, the administrators created a restrictive and intensified form of political education. Disciplinary mechanisms were regularized, and central controls were tightened. As was the case in the Philippines, this was an alteration of the initial principles of political education—just in the opposite direction. Whereas the Philippine administrators loosened central control, the Puerto Rico administrators tightened it. And whereas Root had called for "less and less [American] assistance" in accordance with Puerto Rican "capacity," the administrators tipped the balance toward more and more control. This despite the fact that administrators had initially predicted full municipal autonomy "within five years"—a prediction made before Congress's declaration for free trade and before the chains of empire pulled Puerto Rico into its peculiar position.

* * *

The story of political education in the U.S. empire thereby attests to existing scholarship on colonial rule and colonial projects. Political education was wracked with unforeseen complications, resulting in its two radically different forms. However, the story of political education also exceeds the existing scholarship on colonial rule, for the project was caught up in complications that existing scholarship has not yet fully elucidated or elaborated on. Most studies focus on resistance from below, logical contradictions, and competing imperatives among different projects as the key tensions that shaped the unpredicted outcomes of colonial projects. Such factors were certainly at work in regard to political education. Puerto Rican and Filipino officials did not act as docile students awaiting their "object lessons," and political education was in latent competition with the imperatives of infrastructural development and capital accumulation. Nevertheless, such tensions and complications internal to the colonies alone did not bring about the different forms of political education in the two colonies. As has been shown, the tensions and complications internal to the colonies were quite similar. In Puerto Rico and the Philippines, administrators faced corruption from below. In both colonies, they initially endeavored to enact the very same kinds of developmental programs. It was only when those factors internal to the colonies converged with the different stances taken by Congress that political education took on its particular forms, making any latent or logical contradictions in the project more manifest than they otherwise might have been. Political education became restrictive and intensified in Puerto Rico only after capital investment was propped up by Congress, thereby making the problem of corruption more pressing than ever. Political education in the Philippines became lax and loose only after Congress failed to prop up capital investment there—failure that stemmed from metropolitan political conflicts and that turned the goal of uprooting corruption into something that had to be sacrificed for the sake of infrastructural development. Ultimately, then, it was the tensions traversing the entire chain of American empire that shaped the way in which political education played out on the ground. Through this chain, local populations and civil administrators, the War Department and Congress, and anti-imperialists and sugar capital were all linked together.

This story, then, may help to clarify our picture of colonial states and their projects even as it complicates it. It suggests that colonial projects were wracked with tension not only because of their contradictory character or because of resistance encountered from below, but also because of the structure of colonial empire itself. Indeed, if one defines *colonialism* as a mode of formal political domination exercised by colonial states, then one of its key peculiarities certainly lies in the chains by which colonial populations, colonial states, and metropolitan actors were necessarily linked. Colonial domination was a formal extension of imperial state power; it occurred through colonial states that were always linked directly to metropolitan states. Thus, colonial rule was never simply a matter of a unified colonial state imposing its will on local populations; of local populations diametrically "resisting" this will; or even of conflicting imperatives and actions of colonizing agents on the ground. Colonial rule was also a matter of complex forces that transcended both the colonial state and the populations it ruled. It was a matter of an extensive series of connections that joined the fate of colonial populations on the ground to the actions of diverse metropolitan actors on the home front—a matter, in sum, of imperial chains in which all were entangled.

NOTES

This essay originally appeared in *Comparative Studies in Society and History* 42 (2000); reprinted with permission of Cambridge University Press. Research for this essay was funded by the International Pre-dissertation Fellowship Program of the Social Sciences Research Council and the American Council of Learned Societies (with funds provided by the Ford Foundation) and by the University of Chicago Council for Advanced Studies in Peace and International Cooperation (with funds from the John D. and Catherine T. MacArthur Foundation).

1. Headquarters Department of Porto Rico, "General Orders, No. 160," 1899, file 1286, entry 5, Record Group (RG) 350, Records of the Bureau of Insular Affairs, U.S. National Archives (NA). See also House Committee on Insular Affairs, U.S. Congress, *Committee Reports, Hearings, and Acts of Congress Thereto. U.S. Congress. House. Committee on*

Insular Affairs. Fifty-Sixth Congress, First and Second Session, 1900–1901 (Washington, D.C.: Government Printing Office, 1904), 222.

2. E. S. Otis, "Proclamation of January 4, 1899," in Cameron W. Forbes, *The Philippine Islands*, vol. 2 (Boston: Houghton Mifflin, 1928), 436–37; U.S. War Department (USWD), *Annual Reports of the War Department for the Fiscal Year Ended June 30, 1900. Report of the Lieutenant-General Commanding the Army. In Seven Parts. Part 2* (Washington, D.C.: Government Printing Office, 1900), 475, 477–78.

3. USWD, *Annual Reports of the War Department for the Fiscal year Ended June 30, 1899. Report of the Secretary of War. Miscellaneous Reports.* (Washington, D.C.: Government Printing Office, 1899), 24–25 (hereafter, the U.S. War Department annual reports are cited as *ARWD*).

4. Ibid.; Elihu Root to Mrs. Lowell, 11 February 1904, file 364–62, entry 5, RG 350, NA.

5. For an elaboration of the Americans' attempt to "discipline and democratize" in Puerto Rico and the Philippines, see Julian Go, "Transcultured States: Elite Political Culture in Puerto Rico and the Philippines during U.S. Colonial Rule" (Ph.D. thesis, Department of Sociology, University of Chicago, 2000), vol. 1, chap. 3.

6. Nicholas Thomas, *Colonialism's Culture: Anthropology, Travel, Government* (Princeton, N.J.: Princeton University Press, 1994), 106.

7. Bruce Berman and John Lonsdale, *Unhappy Valley: Conflict in Kenya and Africa, Book One* (London: James Currey, 1992), 5.

8. Thomas, *Colonialism's Culture*, 106. Frederick Cooper and Ann Laura Stoler have called for further studies that problematize rather than assume the "hegemonic operation" and "unity and coherence" of colonial states. See Frederick Cooper and Ann Laura Stoler, "Between Metropole and Colony," in *Tensions of Empire: Colonial Cultures in a Bourgeois World*, ed. Frederick Cooper and Ann Laura Stoler (Berkeley: University of California Press, 1997), 20.

9. For an overview of the plan, see *ARWD 1899*, 24–25. See also Truman R. Clark, " 'Educating the Natives in Self-Government': Puerto Rico and the United States, 1900–1933," *Pacific Historical Review* 42 (1973): 225–33; and O. Garfield Jones, "Teaching Citizenship to the Filipinos by Local Self-Government," *American Political Science Review* 28 (1924): 285–95.

10. Dean C. Worcester, *The Philippines Past and Present*, vol. 2, 2d ed. (New York: Macmillan, 1928), 968.

11. The literature on this is large, but see Frederick Cooper, "Conflict and Connection: Rethinking Colonial African History," *American Historical Review* 99 (1994): 1516–45, for a discussion of resistance in colonial Africa. See also, for other contexts, Eileen J. Findlay, "Love in the Tropics: Marriage, Divorce and the Construction of Benevolent Colonialism in Puerto Rico, 1898–1910," in *Close Encounters of Empire: Writing the Cultural History of U.S.–Latin American Relations*, ed. Gilbert M. Joseph, Catherine E. LeGrand, and Ricardo D. Salvatore (Durham, N.C.: Duke University Press, 1998), 139–72; Vicente L. Rafael, *Contracting Colonialism: Translation and Christian Conversion in Tagalog Society under Early Spanish Rule* (Durham, N.C.: Duke University Press, 1993); and Steve J. Stern, "Paradigms of Conquest: History, Historiography, and Politics," *Journal of Latin American Studies* 24 (1992): 1–34. For an illuminating discussion of the anthropological literature on resistance, see Sherry Ortner, "Resistance and the Problem of Ethnographic

Refusal," in *The Historic Turn in the Human Sciences*, ed. Terrence J. McDonald (Ann Arbor: University of Michigan Press, 1996), 281–304.

12. Berman and Lonsdale stress the contradiction between the imperatives of maintaining political legitimacy and capital accumulation. See Berman and Lonsdale, *Unhappy Valley*. A third possible reason is that actors arriving in the colonies from the metropole had their own distinct intentions and interests. Settlers, missionaries, plantation owners, and capitalists all had their own particular projects, which often conflicted with one another. Such conflicts made for a range of tensions, and each of their projects consequently suffered. On this point, see esp. John Comaroff and Jean Comaroff, *Ethnography and the Historical Imagination* (Boulder, Colo.: Westview Press, 1992), chap. 7; and Jane A. Margold, "Egalitarian Ideals and Exclusionary Practices: U.S. Pedagogy in the Colonial Philippines," *Journal of Historical Sociology* 8 (1995): 374–94.

13. My argument on chains of empire extends existing studies that allude to the place of the colonial state within larger imperial connections—most notably, Berman and Lonsdale, *Unhappy Valley*; Alice L. Conklin, *A Mission to Civilize: The Republican Idea of Empire in France and West Africa, 1895–1930* (Stanford, Calif.: Stanford University Press, 1998); and Joan Vincent, "Sovereignty, Legitimacy, and Power: Prologomena to the Study of the Colonial State," in *State Formation and Political Legitimacy*, ed. Ronald Cohen and Judith D. Toland (New Brunswick, N.J.: Transaction Books, 1988), 137–54. Unlike this literature, however, I examine specific practical and institutional links between colonial actors and metropolitan state branches and interests. In this I am directly informed by Berman and Lonsdale, *Unhappy Valley*, 152–54, although Berman and Lonsdale tend to reduce metropolitan–colonial relations to logical contradictions between the imperatives of accumulation and control, downplaying more complex contingencies such as the actions of colonized actors or political struggles of diverse agents in the metropole.

14. Elihu Root had been charged by President McKinley with formulating and supervising colonial policy. Root's War Department was in charge of the colonies in the absence of a colonial office and congressional legislation on the matter. Root articulated the project in the summer of 1899, informed by reports from military commanders and investigative commissions on the ground. Glenn A. May, *Social Engineering in the Philippines: The Aims, Execution, and Impact of American Colonial Policy, 1900–1913* (Westport, Conn: Greenwood Press, 1980), 5–8; Carmen I. Rafucci de Garcia, *El gobierno civil y la ley Foraker* (Río Piedras: Editorial Universitaria, 1981), 45–51. His basic plan is outlined in *ARWD 1899*, 24–30.

15. This was in accordance with Root's vision. He had called for property and literacy restrictions on the electorate and on office holding. Only later were the restrictions to be lifted. *ARWD 1899*, 24–30.

16. On the formation of this party and its sociological bases, ideology, and leadership, see Mariano Negrón Portillo, "El liderato anexionista antes y despues del cambio de soberania," *Revista del colegio de abogados de Puerto Rico* 33 (1972): 369–91; idem, "A Study of the Newspaper 'La Democracia,' Puerto Rico, 1895–1914: A Historical Analysis" (Ph.D. diss., State University of New York, Stonybrook, 1980), 37–49, 53–69; Angel Quintero Rivera, *Conflictos de clase y política en Puerto Rico*, 3d ed. (Río Piedras: Ediciones Huracán, 1981), 16–34.

17. "Manifesto de los dirigentes liberales invitado a la fundación del Partido Federal," *La Democracia*, 5 October 1899, 2.

18. Federal Party of Puerto Rico, "Programa del Partido Federal," in *Puerto Rico: Cien años de lucha política*, ed. Reece B. Bothwell Gonzalez (Río Piedras: Editorial Universitaria, 1899), 271–72. See also the points of view articulated by prominent members of the elite in Henry K. Carroll, *Report on the Island of Porto Rico; Its Population, Civil Government, Commerce, Industries, Productions, Roads, Tariff, and Currency, with Recommendations by Henry K. Carroll* (Washington, D.C.: Government Printing Office, 1899), 776–86.

19. Glenn May, "Resistance and Collaboration in the Philippine–American War: The Case of Batangas," *Journal of Southeast Asian Studies* 15 (1984): 69–90; Norman G. Owen, "Winding Down the War in Albay, 1900–1903," *Pacific Historical Review* 48 (1979): 557–89.

20. Headquarters Department of Porto Rico, "General Orders, No. 212," 1899, file 1069–2, entry 5, RG 350, NA. For specific practices by the military on this count, see Edward Berbusse, *The United States in Puerto Rico, 1898–1900* (Chapel Hill: University of North Carolina Press, 1966), 106; and Fernando Picó, *Cada Guaraguao . . . Galería de oficiales norteamericanos en Puerto Rico (1898–1899)* (Río Piedras: Ediciones Huracán, 1998).

21. Major-General E. S. Otis, "The Next Steps in the Philippines," *The Independent*, vol. 52, 1900, 2906; *ARWD 1900*, 478.

22. General George W. Davis to Elihu Root, 14 October 1899, Papers of Elihu Root, U.S. Library of Congress, Manuscript Division, 1899 D-H series, box no. 3.

23. Berbusse, *United States in Puerto Rico*, 95.

24. *ARWD 1900*, pt. 2, 476.

25. *ARWD 1899*, 27–29; see also William F. Willoughby, *Territories and Dependencies of the United States* (New York: Century Company, 1905), 15–16.

26. The quote is from General Davis in U.S. Congress, *Committee Reports, Hearings, and Acts of Congress Thereto. U.S. Congress. House. Committee on Insular Affairs. Fifty-Sixth Congress, First and Second Session, 1900–1901*, 222. The state-building practices of military authorities in Puerto Rico can be seen in "Report of the Military Governor of Porto Rico on Civil Affairs," in *ARWD 1900* (Washington, D.C.: Government Printing Office, 1902), pt. 13. For the Philippines, see *ARWD 1900*, 2:475–89.

27. On these plans for civil rule, see *ARWD 1899*, 28, and Worcester, *Philippines Past and Present*, 984.

28. Willoughby, *Territories and Dependencies*, 127, 167.

29. L. S. Rowe, *The United States and Puerto Rico* (New York: Longsman, Green, 1904), 145; William F. Willoughby, "The Reorganization of Municipal Government in Porto Rico: Political," *Political Science Quarterly* 24 (1909): 409–43, esp. 421, 431.

30. *ARWD 1901*, 1:20–21, 31. Michael Cullinane has discussed these kinds of practices on the part of the Filipino political elite in some detail. See Michael Cullinane, "Implementing the 'New Order': The Structure and Supervision of Local Government during the Taft Era," in *Compadre Colonialism: Studies on the Philippines under American Rule*, ed. Norman G. Owen (Ann Arbor: Center for South and Southeast Asian Studies, University of Michigan, 1971), 13–76.

31. John Buenker provides an overview of Progressive-era political culture in the United States that may be useful in contextualizing the administrators' views. See John D. Buenker, "Sovereign Individuals and Organic Networks: Political Culture in Conflict during the Progressive Era," *American Quarterly* 40 (1988): 187–204. Of course, as Patricio N. Abinales shows in his essay in this volume, administrators may have rallied against political corruption abroad, but they were no doubt familiar with it from home experience. I discuss this at greater length in Go, "Transcultured States," 1:3.

32. Such views are clear in the annual reports of the Philippine Commission and the reports of the governor of Puerto Rico during these years. For the Puerto Rican context, see Clark, "Educating the Natives"; for the Philippine context, see Cullinane, "Implementing the 'New Order.' "

33. For a more thorough discussion of these practices as resistance, see Julian Go, "Colonial Reception and Cultural Reproduction: Filipino Elite Response to U.S. Colonial Rule," *Journal of Historical Sociology* 12 (1999): 337–68.

34. Governor of Porto Rico, *First Annual Report of Charles H. Allen, Governor of Porto Rico (Covering the Period from May 1, 1900 to May 1, 1901)*, vol. 1 (Washington, D.C.: Government Printing Office, 1901), 98, 106.

35. George C. Groff, "A Successful Colonial Government," *The Independent*, vol. 52, January-March 1900, 102–5, 104–5.

36. *ARWD 1901*, pt. 1, 21.

37. Root, in *ARWD 1899*, 24.

38. William H. Taft, *Special Report of Wm. H. Taft, Secretary of War to the President on the Philippines* (Washington, D.C.: Government Printing Office, 1908), 27. On education in the Philippines, see Margold, "Egalitarian Ideals." For Puerto Rico, see Governor of Porto Rico, *First Annual Report* 1901, 49–52, 73–74 and, for an extensive analysis, Aida Negrón de Montilla, *Americanization in Puerto Rico and the Public School System 1900–1930* (Universidad de Puerto Rico: Editorial de Puerto Rico, 1975).

39. Charles Elliot, *The Philippines to the End of the Commission Government* (Indianapolis: The Bobbs-Merrill Company, 1917), 273. For specific infrastructural plans in Puerto Rico, see Carroll, *Report on the Island of Porto Rico*, 38; and Governor of Porto Rico, *First Annual Report*, 321. For the Philippines, see U.S. Philippine Commission, *Reports of the Taft Philippine Commission*, Senate doc. 112, 56th Cong., 2d sess. (Washington, D.C.: Government Printing Office, 1901), 71–77.

40. *ARWD 1899*, 30.

41. On Conant, see Carl Parrini, "Charles A. Conant, Economic Crises and Foreign Policy, 1896–1903," in *Behind the Throne: Servants of Power to Imperial Presidents, 1898–1968*, ed. Thomas J. McCormick and Walter LaFeber (Madison: University of Wisconsin Press, 1993), 35–66; and Martin Sklar, *The Corporate Restructuring of American Capitalism* (Cambridge: Cambridge University Press, 1988), 78–84.

42. Governor of Porto Rico, *First Annual Report*, 98–99.

43. Oscar Alfonso, "Taft's Views on 'The Philippines for the Filipinos,' " *Asian Studies* 6 (1968): 243.

44. Governor of Porto Rico, *First Annual Report*, 37–42, 59; Frank A. Golay, "The Search for Revenues," in *Reappraising an Empire: New Perspectives on Philippine–American*

History, ed. Peter W. Stanley (Cambridge, Mass.: Harvard University Press, 1984), 231–60, esp. 237.

45. My claim about similarity across local conditions is not intended to be all-encompassing. The Philippine–American War certainly made the Philippines very different from Puerto Rico on a number of counts. In speaking of similarity, I am referring only to the fact of political corruption, the administrators' hopes of uprooting it, and the ties between political education and other developmental projects. Later, I discuss how the war in the Philippines may have contributed to different outcomes in the two colonies in regard to political education.

46. For a brief discussion of some of the political developments leading to this distribution of imperial power, see May, *Social Engineering*, 4.

47. See, for the Philippines, U.S. Philippine Commission, *Fourth Annual Report of the Philippine Commission*, vol. 1 (Washington, D.C.: Government Printing Office, 1904), 8–10 (hereafter, the Philippine Commission reports are cited as *RPC*).

48. Lyman Jay Gould, "The Foraker Act: The Roots of American Colonial Policy" (Ph.D. diss., University of Michigan, Ann Arbor, 1958), 97; Richard E. Welch, *Response to Imperialism: the United States and the Philippine–American War, 1899–1902* (Chapel Hill: University of North Carolina Press, 1979), 82. For an informative discussion of U.S. sugar corporations in Puerto Rico and the web of interlocking directorates of which they were a part, see Cesar J. Ayala, "Finance Capital versus Managerial Control in a Colonial Sphere: United States Agribusiness Corporations in Puerto Rico, 1898–1934," *Research in Political Economy* 14 (1994): 195–219.

49. Margaret Leech, *In the Days of McKinley* (New York: Harper and Brothers, 1959), 490; Welch, *Response to Imperialism*, 82.

50. Luzviminda Bartolome Francisco and Jonathon Shepard Fast, *Conspiracy for Empire: Big Business, Corruption, and the Politics of Imperialism in America, 1876–1907* (Quezon City: Foundation for Nationalist Studies, 1985), 213, 242–43; Gould, *Foraker Act*, 92–93; Rafucci de Garcia, *El gobierno civil*, 76–77; *San Juan News*, 29 December 1899, 1.

51. See Welch, *Response to Imperialism*, chap. 5; Leech, *Days of McKinley*, 487–90.

52. William H. Taft to Bernard Moses, no. 16, 15 February 1901, in "Scrapbook of Philippines, Notes and Clippings," Bernard Moses Papers, microfilm 3550p, University of Philippines Library, Diliman (original at Bancroft Library, University of California, Berkeley).

53. As quoted in Governor of Porto Rico, *Annual Report of the Governor of Porto Rico* (Washington, D.C.: Government Printing Office, 1902), 9.

54. On this, see Bonifacio S. Salamanca, *The Filipino Reaction to American Rule 1901–1913* (Hamden, Conn.: Shoe String Press, 1968), 105–16. In Puerto Rico, the Foraker Act also put restrictions on land ownership, but the restrictions apparently went unnoticed, remaining throughout the American period a "dead letter." See Baily W. Diffie and Justine W. Diffie, *Porto Rico: A Broken Pledge* (New York: Vanguard, 1931), 75.

55. Welch, *Response to Imperialism*, 76.

56. Berbusse, *The United States in Puerto Rico*, 152; María Dolores Luque de Sánchez, *La ocupación norteamericana y la ley Foraker* (Río Piedras: University of Puerto Rico, 1980), 110. Countless U.S. businesses sent letters of interest to the U.S. consul in San Juan soon after acquisition; the National Manufacturers' Association and the New York Merchants' Association supported free trade. See ibid.; James L. Deitz, *Economic History of Puerto Rico: Institutional Change and Capitalist Development* (Princeton, N.J.: Princeton University Press, 1986), 104 fn. 71; Luque de Sánchez, *La ocupación norteamericana*, 110.

57. May, *Social Engineering*, 156; Whitney T. Perkins, *Denial of Empire: The United States and Its Dependencies* (Leyden: A. W. Sythoff, 1962), 211. Labor, moreover, was more fearful of job competition from Filipino immigrants than it was of competition from Puerto Ricans, not least because of the large number of Chinese Filipinos. Indicative here are the observations of Joseph Foraker himself. See Joseph B. Foraker, "The United States and Puerto Rico," *North American Review* 170 (1900): 464–71, esp. 470.

58. *RPC 1901*, 9–10. See also Cullinane, "Implementing the 'New Order,' " 19–23; Cameron W. Forbes, *The Philippine Islands*, 2 vols. (Boston: Houghton Mifflin, 1928), 1:154–56; and Taft, *Special Report*, 34.

59. Golay, "Search for Revenues," 237; *RPC 1902*, 1:7.

60. As quoted in Alfonso, "Taft's Views," 245.

61. Daniel Williams, *The Odyssey of the Philippine Commission* (Chicago: A. C. McClury and Co., 1913), 163.

62. As quoted in May, *Social Engineering*, 153.

63. By the 1920s and 1930s, the Filipino elite remained in clear control over landed and merchant capital. On this point, see Temario C. Rivera, "Class, the State and Foreign Capital: the Politics of Philippine Industrialization 1950–1986" (Ph.D. diss., University of Wisconsin, Madison, 1991), 67; for Filipino control over the sugar industry in particular, see Filomeno Aguilar, *Clash of Spirits* (Honolulu: University of Hawai'i Press, 1998), 207–8. Indeed, although free trade for the Philippines was finally declared for some Philippine goods in 1909 with the Payne–Aldrich Act, by that time U.S. capitalists had little interest in the archipelago, leaving the Filipino elite alone to benefit from it. See, for example, May, *Social Engineering*, 159–60.

64. Harry Luton, "American Internal Revenue Policy in the Philippines to 1916," in Owen, *Compadre Colonialism*, 129–56, esp. 144.

65. Forbes, *Philippine Islands*, 1:371–83.

66. Golay, "Search for Revenues," 238–39; Luton, "American Internal Revenue Policy," 144.

67. Forbes, *Philippine Islands*, 1:370–75.

68. Cullinane, "Implementing the 'New Order,' " 36; see also Worcester, *Philippines Past and Present*, 2:967–68. On the new collaborative pattern, see Michael Cullinane, "Ilustrado Politics: The Response of the Filipino Educated Elite to American Colonial Rule, 1898–1907" (Ph.D. diss., University of Michigan, Ann Arbor, 1989), 36; and Ruby R. Paredes, "The Origins of National Politics: Taft and Partido Federal," in *Philippine Colonial Democracy*, ed. Ruby R. Paredes (New Haven: Southeast Asia Studies Monograph Series, no. 32, 1988), 41–69.

69. *RPC 1907*, 1:44–45. This is not to say that the American administrators had no control at all. But the control was minor relative to Puerto Rico, as will be seen later.

70. Cullinane, "Implementing the 'New Order,' " 29.

71. Worcester, *Philippines Past and Present*, 2:967.

72. Forbes, *Philippine Islands*, 1:154–59, 259–60; *RPC 1913*, 14.

73. This is especially evident in the journal of Cameron Forbes. See, for example, the entry for 22 May 1909, "Journal of W. Cameron Forbes," vol. 3, fMS AM 1365, Houghton Library, Harvard University, Cambridge, Mass.

74. Cullinane, "Implementing the 'New Order,'" 37. An alternative explanation for the autonomy given to elites is that the Americans were hesitant to evoke their ire, especially considering the previous war. This does not explain, however, why the Americans initially made attempts to limit the power of local government and tighten supervisory control over the elite, even in the immediate aftermath of the war.

75. Worcester, *Philippines Past and Present*, 2:968.

76. On the "patrimonial" colonial regime, see Paul Hutchcroft, "Oligarchs and Cronies in the Philippine State: The Politics of Patrimonial Plunder," *World Politics* 43 (1991): 414–50, esp. 420–22.

77. United States War Department, Division of Customs and Insular Affairs, *Puerto Rico, Embracing the Reports of Brig. Gen. Geo. W. Davis, Military Governor, and Reports on the Districts of Arecibo, Aguadilla, Cayey, Humacao, Mayaguez, Ponce, San Juan, Vieques, and the Subdistrict of San German*, Divisions of Customs and Insular Affairs Circular no. 10 (Washington, D.C.: Government Printing Office, 1900), 87.

78. Governor of Porto Rico, *First Annual Report*, 145.

79. Ibid., 147.

80. Ibid., 192; report of Edward Lee, 16 July 1900, file 480, box 69, General Correspondence Series (GC), Reports, Fondo Fortaleza, Archivo General de Puerto Rico (hereafter, FF-AGPR).

81. Santiago Palmer to Governor of Porto Rico, 15 May 1902, file 11044, box 167, GC, Municipalities, FF-AGPR; see also complaints from various citizens to Governor Allen in file 542, box 111, GC, Municipalities, FF-AGPR. On "mobs" and policing, see Mariano Negrón Portillo, *Las turbas republicanas, 1900–1904* (Río Piedras: Ediciones Huracán, 1990).

82. Governor of Porto Rico, *First Annual Report*, 99; see also Governor Charles Allen to William McKinley, reproduced in Mariano Negrón Portillo, *Ruptura social y violencia política: Antología de documentos* (Río Piedras: Centro de Investigaciones Sociales, 1991), 164.

83. This is not to say that there is a necessary logical connection between capital investment and "good government." It is merely to say that they were historically connected in the imaginary of colonial administrators in both colonies. This connection is evident in the writings by adminstrators cited throughout this essay.

84. The Republicans were made up of professionals, workers, and merchants with ties to New York trading houses. Angel Quintero Rivera, "The Development of Social Classes and Political Conflicts in Puerto Rico," in *Puerto Rico and the Puerto Ricans: Studies in History and Society*, ed. Adalberto López and James Petras (New York: Halstead Press, 1974), 195–213, esp. 201. They had won the elections for the House of Delegates in 1900, and the American administrators held a majority on the Executive Council. The House of Delegates was part of Root's original plan for national legislatures in the colonies.

85. J. H. Hollander, "The Finances of Porto Rico," *Political Science Quarterly* 14 (1901): 553–81, 571–72.

86. Governor of Porto Rico, *First Annual Report*, 167, 177–80.

87. William F. Willoughby, "The Reorganization of Municipal Government: Financial," *Political Science Quarterly* 25 (1910): 69–104, 90.

88. Governor of Porto Rico, *First Annual Report*, 426.

89. Ibid., 402; Rowe, *United States and Puerto Rico*, 157; Willoughby, "Reorganization of Municipal Government," 409–43, 431–32.

90. Forbes, *Philippine Islands*, 1:205, 210.

91. Enrique Chevalier, Mayor of Ponce, to Governor of Puerto Rico, 29 October 1901, file 1433, box 95, GC, FF-AGPR.

92. Willoughby, "Reorganization of Municipal Government," 432.

93. Governor of Porto Rico, *First Annual Report*, 167. Unlike in the Philippines, detailed data on corruption were not collected.

94. See *San Juan News*, 25 April 1903–19 May 1903. See also file 97, box 96, Miscellaneous Correspondence, Government Series, FF-AGPR.

95. Clark, "Educating the Natives," 225–26.

96. Edward S. Wilson, *Political Development of Porto Rico* (Columbus: Fred. J. Heer, 1905), 151.

97. L .S. Rowe, "The Legal and Domestic Institutions of Our New Possessions," in *Proceedings of the Twenty-Second Annual Meeting of the Lake Mohonk Conference of Friends of the Indian and Other Dependent Peoples*, ed. Wm. J. Rose (Lake Mohonk: Lake Mohonk Conference, 1904), 38–43.

98. Willoughby, "Reorganization of Municipal Government," 431, 441–42.

PAUL BARCLAY

"They Have for the Coast Dwellers a Traditional Hatred": Governing Igorots in Northern Luzon and Central Taiwan, 1895–1915

Having seen an abstract of your article . . . on the Head-hunters in the Philippines I was greatly interested for the reason that we are having the same trouble . . . against similar savage head-hunters called "Ataiyal."—Ishii Shinji, Taiwan Bureau of Aboriginal Affairs, to David P. Barrows, Philippine Bureau of Non-Christian Tribes, 1 March 1911.[1]

Japan in [Taiwan] has for years been struggling, and without success, to control or subdue the aborigines of the mountains, a people of the same blood as [northern Luzon's] Igorots, of the same habits and traits, savage head-hunters, the terror of all the plainsmen of no matter what origin.—Lieutenant-Colonel Cornelis De Witt Willcox, professor, U.S. Military Academy, West Point, N.Y., January 1912.[2]

It was to the great centers of Europe and to national traditions of "internal expansion" that agents of the upstart Japanese and American Pacific empires looked for precedents, methods, and personnel to conquer and govern new territories. But one colonial problem in Taiwan and the Philippines—the pacification, education, and administration of hill tribes known to outsiders as headhunters—caused Ishii Shinji and Lieutenant-Colonel Cornelis De Witt Willcox to look locally for illumination and commiseration. Even before U.S. rule commenced in the Philippines, the popular digest *Littell's Living Age* suggested that the highlanders of each colony were "relatives," likening them to the ancient enemies of civility in the British Empire: "The most savage people of [Taiwan] are the mountaineers called Igorrotes. . . . They are headhunters, like their supposed relatives in Luzon. . . . They have for the coast dwellers a traditional hatred, like that of the highlander for lowlander, and their descents are like those of the Welsh and Scotch mountaineers of early days upon the more civilized people of the lowlands."[3]

The appellation *Igorrote* (also spelled *Igorot*) was coined by seventeenth-century Spaniards in reference to the inhabitants of northern Luzon.[4] Interestingly, the author of this 1895 article mistakenly placed Igorots in Taiwan, stretching the term's semantic range north of the Bashi Channel, the strait separating the Philippines from Taiwan. As shown in the epigraphs, well-placed Japanese and U.S. officials drew the same analogies. To all of these authors, headhunting in Taiwan and Luzon was embedded in a universal historical pattern of "traditional hatred" between preternaturally martial uplanders and their victims in the plains.

The first U.S. government inventory of the Philippines population conformed to this picture, reporting that "head-hunting is practiced by several of the peoples of North Luzon, some of whom have even been accused of eating portions of the bodies of their victims."[5] But within a decade of the U.S. invasion, the dominant timbre of American discourse on Igorots became one of requited paternal affection between ruler and ruled. "Traditional hatred" remained part of the story, but now the Filipinos in the plains and the ports, the vast majority of the archipelago's inhabitants, were blamed for provoking Igorot bloodlust. Philippines Secretary of the Interior Dean C. Worcester (1901–1912) made this typical statement:

> The average hill man hates the Filipinos on account of the abuses which his people have suffered at their hands, and despises them because of their inferior physical development and their comparatively peaceful disposition, while the average Filipino who has ever come in close contact with wild men despises them on account of their low social development and, in the case of the more warlike tribes, fears them because of their past record for taking sudden and bloody vengeance for real or fancied wrongs.[6]

Albert E. Jenks, chief of the Philippines Ethnological Survey, lent academic substance to Worcester's ideas in a 1904 issue of *The Outlook*. At first, wrote Jenks, the Igorots eagerly joined Emilio Aguinaldo's anti-American resistance, but they soon discovered that the *"insurrectos"* were as bad as, or worse than, the Spaniards, who had done little but exploit the Igorots and turn them against one another. After foolishly confronting American firearms with spears and axes, the Igorots manfully admitted defeat and began turning to U.S. agents and camp followers for medicine and mediation. Jenks anticipated that the Igorots would blossom under U.S. tutelage, as recipients of a "big American square deal." Like Worcester, he believed that Americans would finally give the neglected and abused mountain peoples their first taste of honest government.[7]

Scholarly studies of U.S. activities in the Cordillera have done little to alter the contours of the narrative bequeathed by participants such as Jenks and Worcester.[8] Frank Jenista, Ifugao subprovince historian, provides a telling example of the themes argued and illustrated in this volume. Calling on more sophisticated research methods and more than a half-century of hindsight, Jenista revived Jenks's and Worcester's version of history and applied it to other Southeast Asian colonial settings. He argued that Western officials were well disposed toward the hill tribes of Vietnam, Malaya, Borneo, the Philippines, and Burma because the mountaineers compared favorably to the duplicitous, complex, and overly refined populations of Southeast Asia's port cities. The hill tribes —Ibans, Kachins, Jarai, Semang, and Igorots—saw in Westerners the rare outsider whom they could trust. In language reminiscent of *Littell's Living Age* around 1895, Jenista concluded, "For at least the last five centuries of recorded history, Southeast Asians have been . . . divided into peoples of the hills and of the plains . . . [and] mutual antipathy between highlander and lowlander was the norm. Western colonial authority intruded into this Southeast Asian world and virtually without exception . . . developed relations with highland peoples that were largely congenial, in contrast to the inimical colonial relationships with lowland cultures."[9]

Jenista's assertion that colonizer–highlander relations were "largely congenial" finds strong echoes in Japanese colonial records and recent scholarship. Kabayama Sukenori, the first Japanese governor-general of Taiwan, declared in a well-publicized memorandum that Japan's government could and should improve on centuries of aborigine abuse at the hands of the Chinese.[10] The amount of early-twentieth-century Japanese journalism, literature, photography, anthropology, and film that portrayed Taiwan aborigines in romantic hues attests to the institutionalized belief that Japanese–aborigine relations had a certain warmth that contrasted with the hostile reception the Japanese received from Taiwan's wet-rice–growing Chinese population.[11]

That similar configurations of the mountaineer–lowlander–colonizer triad emerged in colonial Taiwan and the Philippines and have persisted in Japanese and U.S. historical memory should come as no surprise. They are products of a world historical epoch in which the transnational connections among colonizers were as important as, if not more important than, particular national traditions of conquest and imperialist discourse. In 1895, Taiwan was ceded to Japan as a condition of surrender in the Sino-Japanese War. Three years later, the United States wrested nominal control of the Philippine Islands from Spain. The term *"cession"* was used to describe transfers of sovereignty from Beijing to Tokyo, and from Madrid to Washington, but it took bloody wars to make these archipelagos into colonies. Japan's war against Republic of Taiwan forces lasted from August 1895 until March 1896; the United States fought a similar war against the Philippines Republic from February 1899 through March 1901. After crushing short-lived Taiwan and Philippines republics and setting up full-blown bureaucracies in the capitals, Taihoku (Taibei) and Manila, the new regional powers redoubled their efforts to extend government and infrastructure into the forbidding topography of the mountainous interiors.[12]

The earliest concerted Japanese and U.S. efforts among the mountaineers exemplify what James C. Scott has called the "high modernist" state's propensity to make hitherto "nonstate" spaces "legible" to the administrative centers of government. Qing dynasty and Spanish maps of upland Taiwan and Luzon depicted these interiors as scattered congeries of independent villages whose peoples fell under different rubrics meaning *"mountaineer," "pagan,"* or *"savage."* These terms denote a lack of attributes thought to constitute civility: appropriate clothing, use of chopsticks, wet-rice cultivation, baptism, and submission to taxation and labor drafts, among others. Such terminology is indicative of the early modern state's limited interest in and capacity for intervening in the warp and woof of daily life in the countryside. Japanese and U.S. government ethnologists replaced Qing and Spanish schema with colorful maps of the interior that aggregated the myriad villages into geographically contiguous but distinct "culture areas" or "tribes," according to perceived similarities in village social organization, architectural styles, religion, forms of personal adornment, language, physique, and

N

Taihoku | Kiirun
Toyen | Shinko
Shinchiku | Giran
Biyoritsu
Taichu
Shoka | Nanto
The Pescadores | Aboriginal District
Toroku
Kagi
Ensuiko
Tainan | Daito
Banshoryo
Hozan
Ako

Population of Administrative Districts

- under 1,000
- over 1,000
- over 3,000

Koshun

Map 1. Official Japanese map of Taiwan, 1905.

economic life.[13] These admittedly provisional maps provided administrators in Taibei and Manila with the rudiments of the kind of population data required by modern nation-states to conduct massive projects in education, sanitation, and labor mobilization (see Maps 1–4).[14]

One might well conclude from this brief accounting of connections, parallels, and coincidences that the Japanese in Taiwan acted and thought like Western colonizers, signaling their arrival as the first Asian member

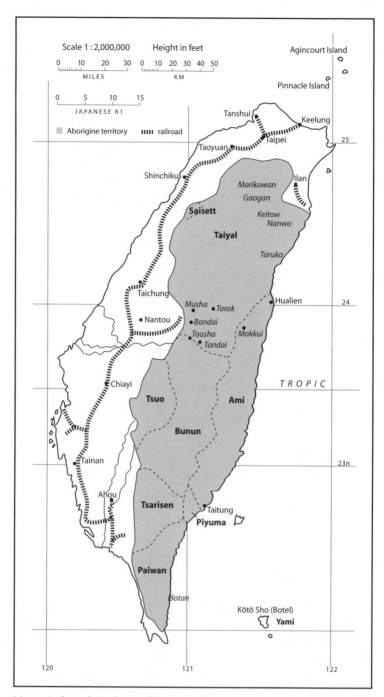

Map 2. Anthropological map of Taiwan, ca. 1910.

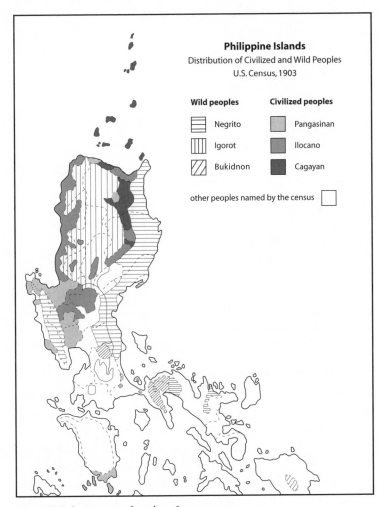

Philippine Islands
Distribution of Civilized and Wild Peoples
U.S. Census, 1903

Wild peoples   Civilized peoples

Negrito   Pangasinan

Igorot   Ilocano

Bukidnon   Cagayan

other peoples named by the census

Map 3. U.S. Census map of northern Luzon, 1903.

of the imperialists' club. Then again, Americans have imagined their Philippines adventure as a rupture with the past that produced a "sentimental imperialism." By comparing Japanese and U.S. rule in central Taiwan and northern Luzon, I will question the uniqueness of both imperialist endeavors and argue instead that Japan and the United States acted as fully modern colonial powers. They participated in what Louise Young calls "total empire," propelled by the sometimes conflicting dictates of domestic fantasy, economic calculation, and nationalist mass politics.[15] It makes more sense, as Laura Hostetler has argued in her study of Qing expansion in southwestern China, to think of these colo-

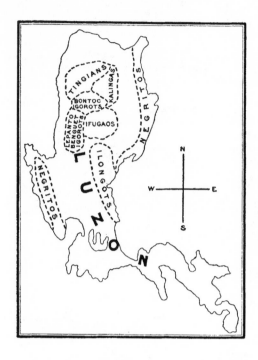

Map 4. U.S. anthropological map of northern Luzon, ca. 1907.

nial enterprises as manifestations of ideals, technologies, and institutions characteristic of a moment in world historical time than as primarily national or civilizational undertakings.[16]

Compared to their early modern predecessors, the Qing in Taiwan and the Spanish in Luzon, Japan and the United States were wealthy and technologically advanced. Unlike their fiscally straitened predecessors, when they suffered logistical and tactical setbacks they soon returned to the tasks at hand. Taiwan and the Philippines were annexed in an atmosphere of national competition, which presupposed a shared set of norms and goals. Under international law as construed by the modern nation-states, "underdeveloped" regions such as northern Luzon and central Taiwan belonged to no sovereign. These lands beyond the reach of Qing and Spanish dynasts threatened trade, resource exploitation, and national pride until conquered. Many articulate colonists who sought refuge in the study, administration, or representation of hill peoples betrayed an affinity with a diffuse "primitivist" ethos brought on by a sense that the iron cages of bureaucracy and routine were sapping civilization's vitality. In the early twentieth century, anthropology emerged as a profession whose members answered not to central governments but to only like-minded audiences of fellow adepts. Colonial ethnographers were often at the forefront of crafting images and informing discourse about the hill tribes. In a word, Japanese and American rule in these upland regions bore all of the marks of the intellectual, political, and legal culture of "high imperialism" in the Victorian era.[17]

There was little to differentiate U.S. and Japanese colonial apparatuses in terms of initial recorded perceptions of the upland populations of Luzon and Taiwan; self-proclaimed missions to build modern, efficient colonies; or use of indiscriminate and brutal force when resistance was met. However, the economic imperatives of colonizing the mountain interiors differed greatly. In Taiwan, the expense and bloodshed of military offensives were offset by the lucrative harvest of camphor trees, whereas in the Cordillera Central of northern Luzon, expectations of quick profits in the Igorot gold mines were disappointed by technical barriers that were not easily overcome by the U.S. colonial state or foreign capitalists.

The U.S. colonial state in the Philippines can be placed in global perspective by considering the Japanese conquest of Taiwan's upland populations to be structurally analogous to the United States' conquest of Luzon's Cordillera. By posing the question, "What would have happened had Americans in Luzon found an economic motive to dispossess Cordillerans or put their territory under foreign occupation?" it becomes possible to explain how turn-of-the-century Anglo-Americans— men steeped in a national tradition that produced Jim Crow and the Indian Reservation system—were able to govern with relative disinterestedness and little bloodshed a population they considered racially distinct and inferior. By analyzing Japan's policies toward Taiwan's aborigines during the first two decades of colonial rule (1895–1915), with special attention given to the strategic and economic imperatives of governing the uplands, and narrating the U.S. conquest of the Cordillera from 1900 to 1915 with reference to the Japan–Taiwan case, I will show that, after a series of striking parallels, the two cases parted about five years after the commencement of colonial rule. The reason for the divergence was not a lack of sympathy, fellow feeling, or romantic idealism on the part of Japanese colonizers. Rather, these sentiments were overwhelmed by economic considerations and the fierce armed resistance of Taiwan's upland peoples.

When the terms of surrender for the Sino-Japanese conflict were settled in April 1895, the image of perennial warfare between Taiwan's aborigines of the hills and Han Chinese of the plains was already a commonplace among literate Japanese. Japan's only armed foreign expedition since the Meiji Restoration had been conducted against a few Taiwan villages in May–December 1874. Japanese diplomats justified this invasion of Qing territory by claiming that southern Taiwan's hill people lived in a state of savagery beyond the pale of Chinese authority. This prolonged and costly military adventure, ostensibly carried out to avenge the murders of fifty-four Ryūkyūan seamen by headhunting aborigines, made the ferocity and isolation of Taiwan's hill tribes part of Japanese historical consciousness twenty years before annexation.[18]

When the Japanese took the reins of government in Taiwan (officially on 2 August 1895), they followed Chinese usage to classify its population into four broad categories: Haklo emigrants from Fujian; Hakkas from Guangdong; "tame" or "cooked" barbarians (*shufan*); and "wild" or "raw" barbarians (*shengfan*). The "tame–wild" opposition dates from the Song dynasty (C.E. 960–1279) and was first used to describe the Miao in southwestern China. During the Qing period in Taiwan (1683–1895), "wild barbarian" status was ascribed to hill peoples who generally resisted Qing rule, and "tame barbarian" was used to refer to those who cooperated with the Qing government or acculturated to Han folkways.[19] Toward the end of Qing rule, the terms *shanfan* (mountain barbarian) and *pingpufan* (plains barbarian) were in use, with roughly the same referents as the shengfan–shufan binary. By 1900, the Japanese taxed and governed those called shufan as they would Taiwan's Han Chinese inhabitants, the Hoklo and Hakka, thus codifying two administratively significant categories: Taiwanese (*hontōjin*) and mountaineers (*banjin, seibanjin*). The Japanese blanket term *seiban* (wild barbarian) connoted use of a non-Chinese language, shifting horticulture, hunting for subsistence, and residence in the mountainous territory that occupies the eastern two-thirds of Taiwan. Where the terms *banjin, seiban*, and *banzoku* appear in the Japanese sources, I use the term "*Taiwan aborigine*," a translation of *genjūmin* (*yuanzhumin* in Chinese), the term in current usage.[20]

From 1895 to 1902, the Japanese government concentrated its resources on putting down Taiwanese armed resistance in the plains. This seven-year war claimed about thirty thousand Taiwanese lives and involved fifty thousand of the one hundred fifty thousand Japanese troops sent overseas during the Sino-Japanese War.[21] Japanese sources rarely identified Taiwan aborigines as rebels during this period: The Japanese considered its counter-insurgency to be a war against Han Taiwanese. In the early years, top Japanese officials envisioned a future of mutually beneficial relations, and possibly an alliance, with the aborigines.

Throughout the period of resistance in the plains, the Taiwan government-general was assured of sufficient funds from Tokyo to finance its day-to-day operations and to build the basic infrastructure of a colonial government. Security and order were the watchwords of the day, cost be damned. But once the plains war reached its denouement, priorities were reordered to emphasize economic efficiency. The new enemies of the Japanese state in Taiwan were citizens and politicians back in Japan, who wanted to sell the financially burdensome colony back to China or to a European nation. In response to this fiscal and political challenge, the Taiwan government-general adopted measures that severely strained relations with large numbers of aborigines. In 1903, Japan's policy in the mountains was put on a military footing. By 1915, after very large expenditures and appalling death tolls of Taiwanese and Japanese had ended massed resistance, the Japanese state continued to garrison the upland villages with its colonial police force.

SEEKING ALLIANCES AND AVOIDING CONFRONTATION: EARLY JAPANESE POLICY

On 25 August 1895, less than a month into his term as Taiwan's first Japanese governor-general, Admiral Kabayama Sukenori warned his troops, "If we are to develop this island, we must first tame the savages. If upon meeting our men, they should think we are like the Chinese, they would certainly become an obstacle to our enterprise; this government must therefore adopt a policy of attraction and leniency."[22] Minister Resident (*benrikōshī*) Mizuno Jun, a crony of Kabayama's from the 1874 expedition to Taiwan, reinforced his superior's directive with a policy statement dated 31 August 1895. Like Kabayama, Mizuno blamed errant Chinese behavior for current and past violence along the aborigine border:

It is usual for the savages to be murderous, and they have made numerous attacks upon the Chinese. However, these attacks have been caused by a succession of swindles perpetrated by Chinese officials. Relations based on faithful dealings and trust have prevailed in their encounters with Westerners. . . .

Like the previous administration [Qing], we should establish a Pacification–Reclamation Office and gather the heads of the tribes together . . . to distribute cloth, tools, and hold feasts with drinking. If we add to this earnest and untiring moral instruction, we . . . can expect to harvest camphor trees in peace, produce camphor, manage the mountain forests, cultivate the savage lands, and build roads [in the savage territory].[23]

Pursuant to the goals spelled out by Mizuno's directive, an expedition headed by Hashiguchi Bunzō, chief of the Industrial Development Section, and Taihoku Prefecture's Governor Tanaka set out on 2 September 1895 to establish contact with the aborigines of Taikōkan (modern Dàxī), an area southwest of Taibei along the Danshui River. As a hub of the camphor industry, Taikōkan was strategically placed for monitoring Chinese–aborigine commerce and conflict.[24] En route, Hashiguchi's party met twenty-three Taikōkan villagers, to whom they distributed red cloth, blankets, tinned meat, and alcohol. Through the interpreter, Tanaka read a proclamation announcing that Japan had defeated China in a war and therefore was the island's new sovereign. Hashiguchi recorded that the aborigines were pleased to hear this, as they had been oppressed by the Chinese. After much persuasion and the distribution of additional blankets, Hashiguchi brought a party of six back to Taibei for a tour of government facilities. Accounts of this encounter were then widely disseminated and became emblematic of early Japanese hopes for an alliance of aborigines and the colonial government against resentful and rebellious Chinese lowlanders.[25]

Hashiguchi's observations about the events surrounding this expedition echoed Kabayama's and Mizuno's assessment of relations between the aborigines of the mountains and the Chinese-speaking Taiwanese of the lowlands. He regarded head-taking as a sad and cruel custom but one nonetheless that could be attributed to Chinese perfidy. He claimed that although the aborigines hated the Chinese and were still actively taking their heads, they harbored no ill will toward the island's new sovereign. Hashiguchi made much of a sentiment transmitted to him through his interpreter that the aborigines' ancestors had immigrated from far away and greeted the Japanese as long-lost relatives. However, Hashiguchi predicted that if droves of poor Japanese farmers and adventurers came to Taiwan seeking fortunes, relations with the aborigines would worsen.[26]

This fear of uncontrolled contact with Japanese of the baser classes, as well as the awareness that many old scores between the aborigines and Taiwan's Chinese inhabitants were still being settled, informed policies designed to isolate the aborigine territory from settlers, fortune seekers, and traders. On 31 March 1896, a special bureau called the *bukonsho*, or "Pacification–Reclamation Office," was established. It was charged with regulating intercourse among the Chinese, Japanese, and aborigines in the contested foothills, where camphor trees flourished. Eleven main outposts were built along the edges of the old Qing aborigine border, a great majority in the same locations as their Chinese predecessors (*fukenju*).[27] By an order dated 1 September 1896, all non-aborigines who crossed the border were required to possess permits issued by the Pacification–Reclamation Office.

The bukonsho fulfilled its mission to gather information about the distribution of highland villages and learned something of their political systems and social structures. Nevertheless, it came under fire for not being able to protect camphor harvesters from attacks outside the aborigine border. At the same time, it was ineffectual in stopping encroachments by settlers and tree-cutters on aborigine lands.[28] Japanese entrepreneurs began to call for more decisive action against the aborigines.[29] The office was abolished and replaced with branch offices in each of Taiwan's prefectures in June 1898.[30]

Camphor, traditionally used as an insect repellent and medicine, had been harvested in Taiwan since the seventeenth century, but two events, coincidentally occurring in 1858, increased its importance as an export commodity. First, the Englishman Alexander Parkes discovered a way to use camphor in the manufacture of celluloid, which meant that "combs, tobacco pouches . . . and indeed everything which had before been made of ivory, coral or tortoise-shell now came to be made of celluloid."[31] Second, the 1858 Treaty of Tianjin forced Taiwan's two major ports open to international trade as part of the settlement of the so-called "Arrow War." With demand up and foreign traders calling on Taiwanese ports, an influential comprador class emerged in Taiwan. After 1878, the export economy of camphor, tea, and sugar "absorbed about twenty percent of [Taiwan's] population."[32] Governor Liu Mingchuan made camphor a Chinese government monopoly in the late 1880s. The aggressive collection of the product increased warfare among immigrants from China, their descendants, and aborigines. During the last decade of Qing rule, Chinese losses from these battles were horrendous, contributing to the end of Liu's celebrated governorship.[33]

From May 1896 to the end of 1897, sporadic headhunting expeditions succeeded against Chinese Taiwanese, including a loss of twenty-three heads at Taikōkan on 13 September 1896.[34] This was the site of Hashiguchi's visit and the first place to have a Pacification–Reclamation Office installed. To counter an unprecedented outbreak of camphor-related violence toward the end of 1897, the Japanese state began to recruit and dispatch guards to defend camphor-harvesting and -processing areas in conjunction with the privately employed guards of landed Chinese gentry and Japanese camphor companies. Most of the 1,100 guards hired that year were Taiwanese residents in the border areas, working under Japanese police officers. The government-general launched a series of attacks against villages suspected of pillaging government installations and experimental camphor plots and killing camphor workers. These episodic thrusts and responses had mixed results. Aborigine villages were put to the torch, and whole companies of Japanese officers with their squads were routed and killed. Many battles were inconclusive.[35]

Perhaps the Japanese would not have pursued such a costly and bloody policy in subsequent years had not the world price of camphor, the colony's need for money, and Taiwan's lack of other quickly exploitable export items not combined to make the conquest of the mountains an imperative of Japanese rule on the island. In 1896, expenses related to war and civil government in Taiwan cost the Japanese National Treasury 11 percent of its annual budget. From 1895 to 1902, subsidies to Taiwan were about 7 percent of the Japanese national budget. By 1898, there were calls in Japan for the sale of the new colony back to China or to a European power.[36] In this atmosphere of crisis, the famous reforming team of Governor-General Kodama Gentarō and his Civil Minister Gotō Shimpei took charge of the colony in February 1898.[37] Gotō's short-term solution to the colony's financial problems was a government monopoly on opium, camphor, and salt. By instituting a government monopoly on camphor in June 1899, the Taiwan government-general received the profits from a lucrative export product. After the first year, which showed a loss for the monopoly, the camphor monopoly consistently supplied 15 percent to 25 percent of the Taiwan-generated revenue for the colonial state during the formative first phase of Japan's rule.

In 1900, the government-general started to cut off trade to the interior in salt and rifles by building an "aborigine border" (*bankai*). Japanese and Taiwanese troops, armed with mortars, were stationed along the camphor frontier. On 22 February 1900, all non-aborigines were forbidden to reside in or use land within this so-called aborigine border.[38] The same month, Kodama Gentarō repudiated the old Pacification–Reclamation Office philosophy, reasoning that "if we hold feasts for [the aborigines] and adopt a policy of attraction, it will take long months and years for them to reach a certain degree of evolutionary development; such slow and inconclusive measures should not be the basis for the urgent and pressing business of managing a new colonial possession; we must decisively and quickly eradicate all obstacles in our path."[39]

The years 1902 and 1903 saw the transition from a defensive posture toward the mountain aborigines to an offensive one. In March 1903, Kodama and Gotō convened a conference of all high-ranking officials on the island to discuss a plan to end the "Aborigine Problem." The resulting committee was chaired by a councilor in the Ministry of Civil Affairs, Mochiji Rokusaburō.[40] The "Mochiji line," as it came to be known, abandoned all pretenses to sympathy with the victimized noble savage. Mochiji endorsed Kodama's view that the mountain peoples should be subjugated quickly but urged that Japanese offensives be limited to areas that would bring in enough revenue to justify the expenditure of Japanese life and treasure.[41] From 1903 to 1909, Japanese police forces were accordingly concentrated along the fortified lines in the north, among the various branches of the tribe the Japanese called the "Ataiyal," where most of the camphor was being harvested. The "extension of the guard-line" and its "advance" became the dominant themes in government–aborigine policy through World War I. This moving cordon—a garrisoned line of stations, substations, and electric fences set within a two-hundred-meter-wide strip of scorched earth—constituted the outer limits of Japanese authority. The strategy was to cut off trade goods by prohibiting crossings without permits and to relocate surrendered villages "inside the line." The price of peace and resumed trade was surrender of firearms, submission to labor drafts, conscription in campaigns against other mountaineers, pursuit of new agricultural and stock-raising regimes, and presence of a Japanese police station in the surrendered village.[42]

The guardlines were manned and advanced by forces that varied between six thousand and seven thousand inspectors, engineers, laborers, guards, and police officers. A majority of these forces were Taiwanese guards.[43] By 1912, the lines contained 756 guard stations, 427 branch stations, and 196 superintendent stations, and extended to a total length of 226 miles.[44] For the five years from 1909 to 1914, the Taiwan government-general budgeted more than 15 million yen, or about $7.5 million dollars (6–10 percent of the colony's annual budgets), to push the conquest of the recalcitrant Ataiyal villages to completion.[45] In 1912, government forces suffered their heaviest losses of the fifty-year occupation—more than two thousand casualties—but by 1913, the Bureau of Aboriginal Affairs had begun to turn districts over to the jurisdiction of regular police offices. In 1914, Japanese army units garrisoned in Taiwan joined the offensive. More than twelve thousand men participated in the last push to conquer the Taroko branch of the Ataiyal on Taiwan's east coast, near Hualien.[46]

The Bureau of Aboriginal Affairs was disbanded in July 1915.[47] The 1909–1914 "five-year plan" dramatically reduced the number and scale of military encounters between the government-general and the highlanders. By 1922, annual counts of confiscated rifles had fallen to 109, and deaths attributed to the aborigines had fallen to sixteen. Despite the apparent success of the offensive, Japan's police maintained a significant presence among aborigine villages until their regime left in 1945. As late as 1931, the total number of police stationed in the interior remained at 4,671, for an average of one ranking officer for every 57.5 aborigines, compared with the 1:963 ratio that held in the Han Chinese–dominated plains, the areas under "regular administration."[48]

Not all Japanese officials abandoned the cause of the Taiwan aborigines after the camphor wars began in the late 1890s. Among critics of draconian measures, Japan's colonial ethnographers were especially vocal in trying to make Kabayama's vision a mainstay of policy.[49] But as the parliamentarian and public intellectual Takekoshi Yosaburō put it, for many Japanese, the wealth to be gained in the camphor forests tipped the balance in favor of dispossession and occupation:

Almost everybody who has come in contact with the savages declares that they are all quite capable of being raised from their present state of barbarism, and I am very strongly of the same opinion. But it is a question how much longer the Japanese authorities will be willing to pursue their present policy of moderation and goodwill, and leave nearly half the island in their hands. If there were a prospect of their becoming more manageable in ten or even in twenty years, the present policy might possibly be continued for that length of time, but if the process should require a century or so, it is quite out of the question, as we have not that length of time to spare. This does not mean that we have no sympathy at all for the savages. It simply means that we have to think more about our 45,000,000 sons and daughters than about the 104,000 savages.[50]

CONQUEST OF THE MOUNTAINS II:
U.S. IMPERIAL RULE IN NORTHERN LUZON

On 21 December 1898, the United States and Spain signed the Treaty of Paris, which made the United States sovereign in the Philippine Islands under international law. As was the case in Taiwan, many Filipinos did not recognize the legitimacy of the cession, provoking war. From 4 February 1899 to 21 March 1901, the United States battled the Philippines Republic. Americans declared continuing guerrilla resistance to have ended in July 1902 but relied on regular army troops to "maintain order" well into 1908. All told, estimates from these two phases of the war included about twenty thousand Filipino combatants and more than two hundred thousand Filipino civilians dead from causes related directly to the wars.[51]

Like their Japanese counterparts in Taiwan, the Americans inherited a practical ethnography of the Philippines from the previous rulers, the Spanish. The prominent division in Luzon, the largest of the archipelago's seven thousand islands and home to Manila, was between mountaineers and plainsmen.[52] The Spanish used the term *indio* to refer to Filipinos "wearing pants who attended mass, paid taxes, obeyed Spanish laws, and only went to war when the government told [them] to." Contrasted to the indio were the *tribus independientes* ("independent tribes)." The majority of Luzon's tribus independientes occupied the ridges and valleys of the Gran Cordillera Central. Spaniards called them *infieles* (pagans) and *Ygolotes, Tingues,* and *Mandayas* (these three words all denote mountain residence). By the end of the Spanish period, military commanders in the garrisons, or *camandancia* system, generally had replaced these terms with *Igorotte*. *Igorot* was the term that the Americans used to refer to the mountaineers of northern Luzon.

Much as the rise of camphor's value as a commodity after the 1858 Treaty of Tianjin brought Taiwan's aborigines notoriety in Qing annals, distant international affairs contributed to increased violence between the Spanish state and the Igorots. Thanks to Spain's alliance with France in a global war between the French and British empires, the British sacked Manila in 1762. The Tobacco Monopoly was instituted by the Spanish in 1781 to create revenue for a Manila treasury drained by the English occupation, the disruption of the galleon trade, and the declining fortunes of Madrid. The monopoly was a financial success, freeing the colony of dependence on the galleon trade and its subsidies from Mexico. In fact, Manila remitted monies to Madrid soon after the monopoly's creation.[53] Lowlanders and Igorots were united in their efforts to circumvent the monopoly's onerous restrictions in northern Luzon, a principal tobacco-producing region. Starting in the 1830s, a series of attempts to garrison the Cordillera were initiated to protect the tobacco monopoly from Igorot "smugglers" and to exact tribute from these previously ungovernable "pagans."

As the Spanish recruited lowland Christians to staff Cordillera-bound punitive expeditions and garrison forces, they exacerbated hostilities between indios and the Igorrotes. Spanish policies fomented deep divisions between highlanders and lowlanders during Spain's three-century rule on the islands. Before the Spanish occupation, it would have made little sense to think of Filipinos as a majority population of lowlanders defined by contrast to a mountain-dwelling minority known as "Igorots."[54] In a roughly parallel process, centuries of Dutch and Chinese rule in coastal Taiwan had created and intensified divisions between the mountain-dwelling, politically independent shengfan and the acculturated, wet-rice–growing Qing subjects, the shufan.

FALSE HOPES IN NORTHERN LUZON: U.S. GOLD MINING AMONG THE IGOROTS

During the 1899–1901 war against the Philippines Republic, there were a few episodes in which Igorots assisted on either side of battles or chases, but the war against U.S. occupation did not establish the Igorots as an ally or enemy of the Americans. However, rumors of mineral wealth in the Benguet area had spread among many of the American volunteers. Instead of shipping back to the United States, they made homes in the Benguet and Lepanto areas and became small-time miners. Many married into local society.[55]

During the seventeenth century, rumors of rich Igorot gold mines had brought Spaniards into the Cordillera, but they were successfully repulsed. By the nineteenth century, the Spanish had abandoned efforts to mine the ore themselves.[56] U.S. officials believed that they could succeed in tapping into this fabled store of wealth. In promotional literature for the large exhibit at the 1904 Louisiana Purchase Exposition in St. Louis, tales of Igorot gold and American practicality were used to advertise the economic potential of the new colony. The handbook's author argued that Spain's failure in the gold mines had been made irrelevant by the arrival of experienced Americans from the gold mines of the U.S. West.[57]

American hopes of taking large yields from these mines had diminished by the time the handbook rolled off the presses. While the U.S. Congress was drafting the Organic Act to put the Philippines government on a constitutional basis during the first half of 1902, repeated news of U.S. atrocities in Samar had changed public opinion on the colonial question. Congress decided to limit strictly the Philippine government's ability to exploit the islands. The Organic Act stipulated that "various reservations [be] imposed upon the disposition of mineral lands, including a provision that no party be permitted to hold more than one claim on the same vein or lode."[58] Most of the ore in the region was low grade, requiring expensive machinery and multiple lodes to extract profitable quantities of gold. With section 33 in place, limiting each company to one lode per claim, profitable mining by foreign companies was impossible. The *Reports of the Philippine Commission to the President* strongly urged the repeal of section 33 in each of its general recommendations for the years 1903 to 1907.[59]

In his July 1904 report, the governor of Lepanto-Bontoc stated that about one hundred fifty small claims had been staked in northern Luzon since the occupation had commenced, but that the intensive capital requirements for their profitable development drove off all but three or four claimants by the time of his writing.[60] Even after several rulings by the U.S. attorney general of the Philippines pulled the teeth out of these restrictions, climate and topography impeded development. The large plants established in Benguet were incapacitated by tropical storms in 1908. Capital proved difficult to attract because of the area's inaccessibility by road or rail. In 1909, the U.S. Supreme Court ruled that claims could not be filed legally on lands where Igorots could demonstrate de facto possession from previous use. In general, "the indigenous diggings were left to their rightful owners."[61] Although the oldest mining company in the region, the Benguet Consolidated Mining Company, finally began paying dividends in 1915, the first two decades of U.S. colonial rule has been judged a period of exploration and small beginnings for the mining industry. It was not until the 1930s that production technology, investment levels, and world demand all combined to make mining in the Cordillera a large enough venture to create significant Igorot–American friction.[62] But by the Great Depression, the bloodiest chapters in the United States' extension of its rule into the Cordillera had long passed.

EXTENDING U.S. GOVERNMENT INTO THE CORDILLERA

Besides the lure of gold, the Cordillera's potential as a site for a colonial hill-station drew American interest. During July and August 1900, Worcester (future Secretary of the Interior), fellow Philippine Commission member Luke Wright, and an escort of twenty-five constabulary soldiers headed north and inland to investigate Baguio's suitability as a U.S. summer capital that could serve as a haven from the heat and the anti-American sentiment of Manila. Like many Japanese officials in late 1890s Taiwan, Worcester saw the highlands and its residents as a possible bulwark against lowland insurrection. Worcester returned to Manila convinced of the Cordillera's strategic, aesthetic, and ethnographic bounty. He would eventually identify himself completely with the cause (as he imagined it) of the "non-Christian tribes."[63]

During the period of increased prospecting in Benguet and Lepanto, foreign miners in the area set up an informal system of government based on their experience in North American mining camps. According to Worcester and Wright, the residents of the Baguio area had shown no hostility to the miners, who had "been at work undisturbed for nearly a year." Judging the area free of the anti-American violence still raging throughout the islands (Emilio Aguinaldo had not yet been captured), Worcester and Wright seized an opportunity to put part of the Cordillera under civil authority, pre-empting its control by U.S. military officials. Benguet became the first province to be established under U.S. civilian rule in late November 1900.[64]

Thus began a form of U.S. rule that set the mountains apart conceptually and administratively from the lowlands. From the start, Worcester and the Philippine Commission treated the Cordillera as their private preserve. In this spirit, a clause placing the Muslim and pagan areas of the Philippines under the direct supervision of the Philippine Commission was built into the 1902 Organic Act. This meant that the Cordillera would not come under the legislative influence of the elected Philippine Assembly and that its governors would be American appointees instead of elected Filipinos. Following the November 1900 act establishing Benguet Province, a series of special acts passed from 1902 to 1905 formalized a system of indirect rule whereby Cordillerans would pay reduced or no taxes.[65]

In the southwestern part of the Cordillera, the Americans governed through locally elected village *presidentes* or by granting rival factions the status and resources needed to take positions of leadership in cases where established headmen would not cooperate. The village president's authority was symbolized by gold- or silver-headed (or pewter alloy) canes and brightly colored coats issued by the American provincial governor. The Americans acted as mediators in disputes that involved large sums of money or that took place among different settlements. They were also in charge of implementing the road tax, which eventually required all able-bodied males in the special administrative districts to work ten days per year on trail and road construction. This task often required the cooperation of village presidentes to procure the labor for the Americans. U.S. officials noted that Igorots in Lepanto and Bontoc had been accustomed to these burdens and that, in many respects, Spanish precedent proved—if not in theory, at least in practice—a good guide to provincial government in the highlands.[66]

In June 1901, Worcester made his second expedition to Benguet, this time traveling farther north to investigate reports of copper deposits in Lepanto. While in Baguio (site of the future hill station), he interviewed Samuel Kane, a former U.S. soldier turned prospector. Kane related credible firsthand accounts of bloody intervillage warfare occurring in

Banaue in Nueva Viscaya.[67] According to Philippines Constabulary reports from the northern and eastern parts of the Cordillera, these regions were unsafe for travel, commerce, and farming. These conditions presented a challenge to a U.S. approach based on low taxes and indirect rule. If the United States wanted to extend its authority throughout the Cordillera, force would have to be applied. Spanish expeditions into the Cordillera had been staffed by Christian lowlanders or by rival Igorot villages.[68] To stop intervillage violence, especially in the form of blood feuds and headhunting expeditions, the United States initially embraced this Spanish precedent.

On 18 July 1901, the Philippines Constabulary was established for the same reasons that Japan built its colonial police force. As guerrilla resistance dragged on after easily identifiable armies with unified command structures were defeated, professional soldiers became less effective agents of government control. The solution in both colonies was to create a well-armed civilian police force stationed locally but answerable only to Manila or Taibei.[69] Paralleling the Japanese conquest of Taiwan's uplands, the Philippines Constabulary established strongholds in areas on the border of the truly resistant and independent villages. With these anchors secured, hostile interior villages were then brought under surveillance. The pattern was repeated in each colony: Advance parties announced the terms of surrender to the new government. If a village decided to accept the new government (which meant cessation of headhunting and surrender of firearms), it would henceforth rely on the garrisoned constabulary forces for protection against neighboring villages. Often, enmity between villages was used, as in Qing and Spanish times, to recruit local forces against resistant villages. Recalcitrant villages faced campaigns of terror; dwellings, crops, and livestock were destroyed, and soldiers shot to kill.[70]

In one important respect, however, U.S. policy diverged from Japanese policy. By June 1902, the constabulary had enlisted Igorots in Lepanto-Bontoc to serve under U.S. officers. In that year, recruiting was under way in Ifugao, and by 1905 all non-Cordillerans were being phased out of the service in Ifugao. Unlike the Spanish before them—and unlike the Japanese in Taiwan—the U.S. did not bring lowlanders into the mountains in large numbers. Instead, they inserted themselves into local political and kinship structures to rule Igorots with Igorots. By 1917, there were Bontoc, Kalinga, Isneg, and Ifugao units of the constabulary;

very few Christian Filipinos remained in units assigned to the mountains. Although the Philippines Constabulary was capable of acts of brutality to establish themselves in a new region and to punish murders thought to be particularly heinous, these bursts of terror were followed by a withdrawal of forces and the incorporation of the defeated headmen into the leadership structure of the local constabulary.[71]

Like provincial governors, supervisors, and treasurers, U.S. Constabulary officers were greatly outnumbered in the Cordillera. In 1903, Levi Case was put "in charge" of forty thousand or so Ifugaos who had not yet recognized U.S. authority. Despite these odds, he and his successors were able to establish American presence in the region by greatly reducing, if not eliminating, intervillage warfare, supervising the construction of trails, and obtaining a monopoly over the use of violence in the region. This project was brought about in Ifugao with the aid of no more than sixty constabulary units in the force at any one time. The last large-scale confrontation with the constabulary in Ifugao was concluded in 1910.[72] From 1911 to 1915, there were only 26 killings in Ifugao and 103 for all of the Mountain Province, which had a population of about 300,000. And these were not casualties of the war of pacification. They are recorded in U.S. records with such comments as "dispute over deer," "quarrel over debt," "love affair," or "land dispute." Deaths of American and Philippine Constabulary officers were exceedingly rare in the Philippines and almost non-existent in the Cordillera. Nearly all entries in the constabulary reports related to headhunting concerning intervillage feuds; when constabulary units, who were mostly Igorots themselves in the Cordillera after 1905, engaged in weapons confiscation or armed searches in the Cordillera, they usually had no casualties at all.[73]

As the constabulary confiscated weapons and sealed alliances among formerly feuding villages, U.S. provincial governors set up administrations under the legislation designed by Worcester to keep the Igorot lands under his jurisdiction as secretary of the interior. These laws gave the provincial governor and subprovincial lieutenant governors wide latitude in selecting local officials. They were empowered to decide whether and how much to tax townships and provinces under their charge and to arbitrate local disputes without legal formalities. In 1908, Worcester pushed through legislation that redrew the provincial boundaries in northern Luzon to put the regions with large non-Christian populations under a single provincial government.

Mountain Province was divided into five subprovinces, reflecting Worcester's ethnological map of the region. By having one of his hand-picked men in each subprovince as a lieutenant governor, presiding over his own tribe, Worcester sought to bring the Cordillera under better control, without integrating mountaineers into the rest of the Philippines polity. Intramontane trade, travel, and diplomacy with and by Americans were encouraged, but Worcester steered policy toward isolating the region from contact with the lowlands. Aside from the trail-building endeavor and the suppression of intervillage warfare, the American government's work in the Cordillera was largely dedicated to maintaining its hill station at Baguio.[74] When Worcester resigned in 1913, the colonial state rested lightly on most Cordillerans, if it had touched them at all. Into the 1930s, there were still complexes of villages that did not pay taxes or otherwise recognize the American government in the southeastern areas of northern Luzon.[75]

As W. Cameron Forbes, a supporter of Worcester and former governor-general, would recall, it was politically risky to appropriate money for Mountain Province from the general budget. The Cordillera generated very little direct tax revenue. Igorots consumed few products, exported little, and so did not contribute much to consumption taxes or tariffs. Therefore, the Philippine Commission was always circumspect in its dealings with the assembly when appropriating money for the special provinces.[76] Dissatisfaction with the level of funding for his projects is a constant refrain in Worcester's writings. Instead of arguing that the economic development of the Cordillera could contribute to the wealth of the Philippines, he always presented funding requests in terms of a moral obligation to be exercised in favor of a people who had been victims of treachery, cunning, and violence throughout their long history of contact with lowlanders. In language highly reminiscent of that used by Kabayama, Mizuno, and Hashiguchi in Taiwan, Worcester articulated his rationale for a U.S. policy of segregating the Cordillera from the regular administration of the islands: "All the non-Christian tribes have two things in common, their unwillingness to accept the Christian faith and their hatred of the several Filipinos who profess it. Their animosity is readily understood when it is remembered that their ancestors and they themselves have suffered grievous wrongs at the hands of the Filipinos . . . [who] are absolutely without sympathy for the non-

Christian peoples, and have . . . shamelessly exploited them whenever opportunity has offered."[77]

In his popular *The Philippines Past and Present* (1914), a pot-boiling polemic written in response to Democratic Party campaign demands that the United States grant the archipelago political independence, Worcester warned that if the United States left, "there is every theoretical reason to believe that the Filipinos would adopt toward such hostile primitive peoples the policy of extermination which the Japanese have been so vigorously carrying out in dealing with the hill people of northern [Taiwan] who do not differ in any important respect from the hill people of northern Luzon."[78] Considering that his rhetoric could do little but antagonize members of the Philippine Assembly and their constituencies, it is easy to see how Worcester's requests for increased personnel and funding for Mountain Province fell flat and why his resignation was readily accepted by American officials who relied on the cooperation of Filipinos to implement policies and raise taxes.[79]

THE SPECTER OF HEADHUNTING REVIVED

Philippines Constabulary officers anticipated a reduction in personnel with the end of large-scale resistance in the plains. To maintain its numbers and budgets, its leaders began to press for a role in the pacification of the Igorots.[80] From 1905 to 1910 the constabulary was reduced from a peak of about seven thousand five hundred to a trough of four thousand.[81] In 1904, Director Henry T. Allen saw the troop reduction coming and urged that, if "it is desired to bring the remote tribes of northern Luzon . . . into proper relations with the government, this force [the constabulary] must be materially increased."[82] In the same report, J. S. Garwood, director of the fourth district (northern Luzon), couched the constabulary's efforts to raise its troop strength in terms of a bureaucratic turf war against Worcester's northern Luzon provincial governors. Garwood wrote that "at present there are vast districts where there is no recognized law except the savage customs of the people which have prevailed for centuries. . . . The real authority of a lieutenant-governor in one of the sub provinces does not have very great weight with these savages anyway. The headmen and others generally have come to constabulary officers, whom they recognize as the men in power." Garwood recommended that all civil government be dissolved and that the Cordillera be placed under constabulary martial law.[83]

In 1907, Thomas I. Mair, director of the fourth district, advocated an increased presence in the Cordillera, considering the constabulary's work in the plains to be nearly completed. Mair approved of Worcester's preference for diplomacy over force, but he departed from the powerful secretary of the interior and from fellow constable Allen by emphasizing the predatory activities of the Igorots. Unlike Worcester, whose calls for funding and manpower in the Cordillera invoked the noble savage and the history of Christian crimes against the Igorots, Mair appealed to the government's sense of obligation to its tax-paying merchants and farmers. Mair argued that more spending on the constabulary was justified in the Cordillera because lost acreage could be recovered if head-taking were stamped out and lowland merchants brought into the region to stimulate trade and industry.[84]

In 1908, with another large reduction of his bureau in sight, J. G. Harbord, acting director of the constabulary, brought the rhetoric of the headhunting menace to new heights, staking the constabulary's future on more aggressive measures in the Cordillera. Harbord's report makes no mention of past injustices inflicted on innocent highlanders by cunning lowlanders or past displacements from invasions led by the Spanish Instead, taking a page from the fourth district's director, Wallace Taylor, Harbord lumped the Igorots together with scalp-taking Sioux and Cheyenne in the United States and characterized the Kalingas, Gaddangs, and Apayaos (all Cordillerans) as wildmen driven by bloodlust. He wrote: "The menace to peace in this district is the raiding of Christian communities by the fierce warriors of the mountains and the taking of heads."[85]

The parallel with upland Taiwan here is instructive. As Japanese military and civil police officers were able to predict victory with confidence in the plains and ports, they began to argue for the importance of ending the headhunting menace from the uplanders. Moreover, the rights of the colonized agriculturists, petty entrepreneurs, and wage earners who bore the burden of colonial taxation were championed in an institutional climate dominated by the rhetoric of the noble savage. As has been shown, forces deployed specifically to deal with aborigines in Taiwan increased rapidly with the commencement of the 1909–1914 five-year plan. The amount of money spent on pacification made even the hard-line councilor Mochiji Rokusaburō pause. In northern Luzon, the same type of increase occurred, but on a very attenuated scale.

When Harbord wrote his 1908 report, he estimated that 240 constables were operating in an area in which more than 100,000 resided—that is, more than 400 residents per constable. Harbord's estimate was conservative: The ratio was probably closer to 1,000:1.[86] Kondō Masami estimated an analogous ratio of 57.5:1 for Japanese police and aborigines in upland Taiwan. From 1906 to 1909, the number of Philippines Constabulary dropped precipitously throughout the islands. The overall trend reversed in 1911, and by 1914 the number of constables in the District of Northern Luzon had returned to 1905 levels of about eight hundred men.[87] But unlike the push to the hills that occurred in Taiwan after resistance and banditry in the plains were reduced, the concentration of effort in northern Luzon did not present a qualitative shift in policy or method. The goals were still to establish diplomatic relations with powerful Igorot leaders and to recruit locals to staff the constabulary after open resistance had been countered with hut burning and gun confiscation.

In 1913, the constabulary faced its last major Cordilleran skirmishes in Apayao subprovince. The Americans still required the services of vigilantes to bring down a fugitive who had fired shots at the Lieutenant-Governor Norman G. Connor in 1915, which indicates the reluctance of the United States to garrison the area with its own people. Like the establishment of posts in the other regions of the Cordillera, the work in Apayao proceeded by fits and starts. From 1907 to 1915, a beginning was made toward incorporating Apayao into the colony, but the government appeared to be in no hurry to rush into a region that offered little in the way of immediate financial returns.[88]

Advocates of aggressive measures in central Taiwan presented statistical data to illustrate the staggering loss of life brought about by camphor-related violence in the foothills. American advocates of Igorot pacification, by contrast, were reduced to anecdotes that might cut either way. For every official who painted the Igorots as untamed beasts or waxed enthusiastic about reclaiming acreage for peaceful valley dwellers (C. E. Nathorst, Thomas Mair, and J. G. Harbord are examples), there was at least another who lauded the Igorots' courage and simplicity and blamed lowlanders for driving the Igorots into the hills (D. J. Baker, Crawford, and Allen, backed by the omnipresent Worcester, made this argument). Neither argument was persuasive enough to bring about a full-blown occupation of the Cordillera by tax collectors, constables, schoolmasters, and labor recruiters.

Howard Fry, a historian of Mountain Province, has hypothesized that the Americans were able to disarm Igorots with so little bloodshed because they entered into the politics of the Cordillera at a propitious time to play the role of mediators. Large quantities of rifles had entered the region during the 1896–1898 revolution and again during the 1898–1901 war of resistance against the Americans. This addition of lethal firepower raised the casualty rates in Cordilleran warfare to terrifying levels; some villages were being wiped off the map. These battles to the death, argued Fry, convinced many elders that Igorots had a stake in the constabulary's rifle-confiscation programs. Although resistance to disarmament could be fierce, it never generated confederacies that were large enough to take advantage of the small numbers of constabulary forces arrayed against them.[89]

As U.S. officials themselves acknowledged, and often regretted, their brand of indirect rule reinforced and even enhanced the political and economic power of leading clans and individuals in the Cordillera. From early on, ethnologists and provincial governors noted the remarkable degree of social stratification in Cordilleran society. For the more practical-minded, this was a blessing that provided the United States with a class of effective collaborators. In this aspect of government in the Cordillera, the U.S. state reproduced a prominent feature of its rule throughout the archipelago: dependence on and maintenance of a small socioeconomic elite by means of the politics of collaboration.[90]

* * *

Even if a certain amount of bias is allowed for in the American tally of Igorot casualties, one checks the most likely sources in vain for instances of U.S. fatalities in the Cordillera. Hence, the trope of Igorot–American compatibility has not rubbed up against any obvious and egregious counterexamples. This cannot be said for the Japanese case. Japan's extension of colonial administration into Taiwan's interior produced twenty thousand to thirty thousand casualties in its first twenty years. Two particularly bloody episodes captured international headlines: the 1909–1914 campaign to defeat the aborigines and the suppression of the

1930 Musha (Wushe) rebellion. The persistence of the belief that Japanese rule in Taiwan's uplands was benevolent and produced congenial relations between ruler and ruled raises questions about the operation of what Gananath Obeyesekere calls "mythmaking in the Pacific."[91] Even in the U.S. case, where the statistics do not impress and large battles are absent, one can discern, as Obeyesekere did, a dark undercurrent of violence and antipathy beneath the surface of resilient narratives of native–colonizer harmony.[92]

In archival research and interviews, the anthropologist Renaldo Rosaldo has found instances of U.S. brutality among Ilongots and Negritos, groups considered by U.S. rulers to be among the "non-Christian" tribes who lived in areas adjacent to the Igorot uplands.[93] Even Jenista's celebratory history of American–Igorot relations contains anecdotal evidence of U.S. disregard for Igorot life in the Cordillera.[94] One of the heroes of Jenks's 1904 article "Building a Province," the "Apo-medico" and lieutenant-governor of Lepanto-Bontoc Truman K. Hunt, built one of the thickest files in National Archives Record Group 350 (Bureau of Insular Affairs): the paper trail generated by his arrest for defrauding fifty Igorots whom he exhibited in the United States for great profit in 1905 and 1906. Hunt treated his employees so inhumanely that the U.S. Attorney General's office apprehended him after a nationwide chase.[95] Jenks himself, in private correspondence to his patrons at the Smithsonian Institution, admitted that he required the services of a "captured and roped guide" during his ethnological survey of Ifugao country.[96] Like the narrative pitting progressive Japanese and honest mountain-dwelling rustics against shady Qing officials and greedy Han farmers, the trope of American–Igorot congeniality provided a convenient rationale for colonial conquest.[97]

James C. Scott, a scholar of rural political economy, has argued that the "premodern state was, in many crucial respects, partially blind; it knew precious little about its subjects, their wealth, their landholdings and yields, their location, their very identity. It lacked anything like a detailed 'map' of its terrain and its people." In Scott's terminology, much of the premodern state's population was "illegible" to centralized, bureaucratized government.[98] In the late 1890s and early 1900s, the self-consciously modern American and Japanese states began to redraw the maps of northern Luzon and central Taiwan, announcing that the politically independent villages in the mountains would be made "legible" to officials in Manila and Taibei. By 1910, the bewildering variety of languages, political formations, and settlement patterns in both interiors had been catalogued in colonial censuses and schematized on ethnographic maps.

The international circulation of legal, technical, academic, and literary devices for dealing with the not-yet-legible rural populations of the world is enough to explain why these strikingly similar artifacts of colonial rule were produced in the first decade of the twentieth century by governments that were only marginally interested in one another's workings. Under government auspices, Ataiyals and Igorots were brought to Japan and the United States to witness the imposing structures, crowds, and machinery of modern cities in order to learn the benefits of submission and futility of resistance to their colonial overlords. To bolster a sense of participation and national pride at home, the colonial governments cooperated in staging exhibits of live Ataiyal and Igorots at the 1903 Osaka and 1904 St. Louis expositions.[99] Viewed as a "muddle of texts,"[100] icons, and discursive formations, then, the colonization of the mountain interiors of Luzon and Taiwan appears to us, as it did to many contemporaries, as a single historical drama played out in different localities. But one can hardly equate the fate of Cordillerans in the Philippines under U.S. rule to that of their supposed cousins in Ataiyal country under Japanese rule.

When Felix and Marie Keesing went to the Philippines in the early 1930s at the behest of the Philippines division of the Institute of Pacific Relations, their search of all pertinent U.S. records revealed that the population numbers for each Cordilleran tribe were unknown. The last census had been taken in 1918, and even its numbers were suspect.[101] It is safe to say that announced intentions to transform the Cordillera from a non-state space to a state space never materialized under U.S. rule.[102] By contrast, the 1920s saw the tribes of Taiwan's uplands become subject to annual population censuses at the household level in the total area under "special administration." One Taiwanese demographer has claimed that the data collected by the Japanese police among Aborigines make up the best long-run series of vital statistics on preindustrial village society available anywhere in the world.[103] By the late 1930s, after a series of land and timber surveys and several forced relocations of whole clusters of villages, the Japanese government had indeed made the non-Han population of Taiwan "legible" to the state.

The comparison of central Taiwan and northern Luzon reveals that culture alone, whether analyzed in terms of idealism and manliness by boosters such as Jenista or as colonial discourse by critics such as Vicente Rafael, is insufficient to explain the character of U.S. rule in northern Luzon.[104] Japanese annals provide examples of men like Jenista's "white Apos," who reportedly forged strong personal bonds with highlanders.[105] Yet these individuals could not stop the policies of dispossession and relocation that some have compared to the destruction of the Tasmanians.[106] As Japanese ethnographers and publicists elaborated and sold Ataiyal savagery and purity, the American colonial-discourse machine produced a number of well-circulated images, tropes, and human exhibits that essentialized and dehumanized Igorots.[107] Yet in practice, after an initial burst of energy and enthusiasm, American officialdom abandoned its plans to bring the Cordillerans under the kind of surveillance necessary to regulate their behavior. In a recent synthesis of scholarship on European colonialism in the modern era, Ann Stoler and Frederick Cooper argue that "imperial elites may have *viewed* their domains from a metropolitan center, but their actions, let alone their consequences, were not necessarily *determined* there."[108] Although national pride, primitivist discourse, and high modernity's pretensions to total control made aspects of these colonial projects nearly indistinguishable to the average Japanese or U.S. citizen circa 1900, the global political economy's relationship to local political conditions, social structures, and geography had a decisive impact on how imperial rule would be experienced in central Taiwan and northern Luzon.

NOTES

Research for this paper was made possible by a Social Science Research Council Japan Program Grant for Advanced Research, a University of Minnesota Graduate School Grant for Research Abroad, and a MacArthur International Pre-dissertation Fieldwork Grant. I thank Professors Edward L. Farmer, Bryon K. Marshall, Alfred W. McCoy, and David W. Noble for their guidance and inspiration. I also thank the two anonymous readers at Duke University Press for their helpful comments and suggestions.

1. Dean Conant Worcester Papers, box 1, "Correspondence 1907–1911," Bentley Historical Society, Ann Arbor, Mich.

2. Cornelis Willcox, *The Headhunters of Northern Luzon: From Ifugao to Kalinga, a Ride Through the Mountains of Luzon* (Kansas City, Mo.: Franklin Hudson, 1912), 278.

3. "Formosa and Its People," *Littell's Living Age*, 19 October 1895, 191.

4. Many regard "*Igorot*" and its many variant spellings as pejorative and nonscientific; the term has also been appropriated by some groups as a marker of resistance to a hegemonic Philippine national identity. The term's use was standard and widespread among Americans who wrote during the period covered by this paper, and its use will be retained throughout this essay with the understanding that "*Igorot*" may not have re-ferred to any specific collectivity whose members would have wished to be so labeled during this period. Igorots were ranked seventh in population in the 1903 census list of the archipelago's "tribes." The census counted 211,520 Igorots as 2.8 percent of a total population of 7,635,426 Filipinos. See U.S. Bureau of the Census, *Census of the Philippine Islands Taken under the Direction of the Philippine Commission in the Year 1903: Popula-tion*, 4 vols. (Washington, D.C.: Government Printing Office, 1905), 2:15–46. In 1984, an Igorot delegation to the United Nations' Working Group on Indigenous Populations reported that there were 600,000 Igorots out of a Philippines population of 50,000,000. See Fourth World Documentation Project, "Report by a Member of the Ibaloi People of the Philippines to the Working Group on Indigenous Populations, 1984: Review of Recent Developments in the Cordillera Provinces, Northern Luzon," available on-line from: ftp://halcyon.com/pub/FWDP/Eurasia/Ibaloi.txt.

5. "The Native Races of the Philippines," in Schurman Commission, *Report of the Philippine Commission to the President, January 31, 1900* (Washington, D.C.: Government Printing Office, 1900), 11–16 (hereafter, the Philippine Commission reports are cited as *RPC*).

6. *RPC 1910*, 75–76; *RPC 1900–1915*, 36 vols. The volume numbers refer to the volume within the set for a particular year. Where no volume number is indicated, only one volume for that year exists.

7. Albert Ernest Jenks, "Building a Province," *The Outlook*, 21 May 1904, 170–77; idem, "Address," *Report of the Thirteenth Annual Lake Mohonk Conference*, 23–25 October 1912, 200.

8. See Frank L. Jenista, *The White Apos: American Governors on the Cordillera Central* (Quezon City: New Day Publishers, 1987); Howard T. Fry, *A History of the Mountain Province* (Quezon City: New Day Publishers, 1983); Fred Eggan, "Applied Anthropology in the Mountain Province," in *Social Organization and the Applications of Anthropology: Essays in Honor of Lauriston Sharp*, ed. Robert J. Smith (Ithaca, N.Y.: Cornell University Press, 1974), 196–209; Kenton J. Clymer, "Humanitarian Imperialism: David Prescott Barrows and the White Man's Burden in the Philippines," *Pacific Historical Review* 45 (1976): 495–517; Karl L. Hutterer, "Dean C. Worcester and Philippine Anthropology," *Philippine Quarterly of Culture and Society* 6, no. 3 (1978): 125–56. Less approving are Renato Rosaldo, *Ilongot Headhunting, 1883–1974: A Study in Society and History* (Stan-ford, Calif.: Stanford University Press, 1980); Martin W. Lewis, *Wagering the Land: Ritual, Capital, and Environmental Degradation in the Cordillera of Northern Luzon, 1900–1986* (Berkeley: University of California Press, 1992); Gerard Anthony Finin, "Re-gional Consciousness and Administrative Grids: Understanding the Role of Planning in the Philippines' Gran Cordillera Central" (Ph.D. diss., Cornell University, Ithaca, N.Y., 1991). Some of this literature falls short of a frankly positive assessment of U.S. rule in the Cordillera. At worst, the Americans appear to have been misguided, lost, or ineffectual.

For an analysis critical of the historiography of U.S. Cordillera policy, see Rodney J. Sullivan, *Exemplar of Americanism: The Philippine Career of Dean C. Worcester*, Michigan Papers on South and Southeast Asia, vol. 36 (Ann Arbor: Center for South and Southeast Asian Studies, University of Michigan, 1991), 232–33. There is also a body of literature on U.S. discourse about Igorots. This work is more in keeping with the critical stance of colonial studies, although it touches little on political and economic conditions in the Cordillera itself. See Christopher A. Vaughan, "Ogling Igorots: The Politics and Commerce of Exhibiting Cultural Otherness, 1898–1913," in *Freakery: Cultural Spectacles of the Extraordinary Body*, ed. Rosemarie Garland Thomson (New York: New York University Press, 1996), 219–33; Robert Rydell, *All the World's a Fair: Visions of Empire at American Expositions, 1876–1916* (Chicago: University of Chicago Press, 1984); Benito M. Vergara Jr., *Displaying Filipinos: Photography and Colonialism in Early 20th Century Philippines* (Quezon City: University of the Philippines Press, 1995); Vicente L. Rafael, "White Love: Surveillance and Nationalist Resistance in the U.S. Colonization of the Philippines," in *Cultures of United States Imperialism*, ed. Amy Kaplan and Donald E. Pease (Durham, N.C.: Duke University Press, 1993).

9. Jenista, *White Apos*, vii.

10. Kabayama's advocacy of benevolence toward the aborigines is so entrenched in Japanese historical memory that he even appeared as "Kabayama Sukenori, the governor-general who set out to harmonize relations with the Taiwan Aborigines" (*Takasagozoku o yūwasaseyō toshita Kabayama sōtoku*) in a best-selling collection of nationalist "feel good" historical vignettes. Fujioka Shinobu, ed., *Kyōkasho ga oshienai rekishi* (Tokyo: Sankei shimbunsha), 139–41.

11. For example, Miyaoka Maoko, "Okada Shinkō 'Arisan banchōsasho' o yomu," *Taiwan genjūmin kenkyū* 3 (1998): 218–29, has confirmed celebratory narratives found in Japanese records with recent interviews in the Alishan region of Jiayi Prefecture in Taiwan. For a sketch of popular-culture images of Taiwan aborigines in Japan, see Leo Ching, "Savage Construction and Civility Making: The Musha Incident and Aboriginal Representations in Colonial Taiwan," *Positions* 8, no. 3 (2000): 795–818. For the anthropological tradition, see Paul Barclay, "An Historian among the Anthropologists: The Inō Kanori Revival and the Legacy of Japanese Colonial Ethnography in Taiwan," *Japanese Studies* 21, no. 2 (2001): 117–36.

12. Ōe Shinobu, "Shokuminchi sensō to sōtokufu no seiritsu," in *Teikoku tōji no kōkoku*, Iwanami kōza: Kindai Nihon to shokuminchi, vol. 2 (Tokyo: Iwanami Shoten, 1992), 3–11; Brian McAllister Linn, *The Philippine War 1899–1902* (Lawrence: University of Kansas Press, 2000). Before the United States set up administration in northern Luzon, Japanese officials made official inquiries about Native Americans and U.S. policy to inform Taiwan aborigine policy and continued to do so at least until 1906. U.S. consuls in Danshui began sending detailed reports to the State Department concerning Ataiyal attacks on Japanese camphor harvesters and Japanese colonial policy in early 1905. Davidson to Hill, 22 April 1899; Fisher to Loomis, 23 March 1905; Fisher to Bacon, 2 March 1906, all in "Despatches from U.S. consuls in Tamsui, 1898–1906," *File Microcopies of Records in the National Archives*, no. 117, roll 1 (Washington, D.C.: National Archives, 1947). In a popular photo album of Taiwan aborigines, Narita Takeshi introduced Taiwan as the island "next to the Philippines, only 5 or 6 hours by regular steamer from the Batan group" Narita Takeshi, *Taiwan seiban shuzoku shashinchō* (Tokyo: Nanten Shokyoku, 1995 [1912]). Direct comparisons such as Ishii's and Willcox's took longer to appear, attesting to the greater initial attention paid by each colonizer to the more prestigious English, French, and Dutch empires.

13. Based on evidence from the British Empire, Nicholas Thomas has referred to this type of colonial enterprise, "anthropological typification," as emblematic of modernity itself. See Nicholas Thomas, *Colonialism's Culture: Anthropology, Travel and Government* (Princeton, N.J.: Princeton University Press, 1994).

14. Paul David Barclay, "Japanese and American Colonial Projects: Anthropological Typification in Taiwan and the Philippines" (Ph.D. diss., University of Minnesota, Minneapolis, 1999).

15. Louise Young, *Japan's Total Empire: Manchuria and the Culture of Wartime Imperialism* (Berkeley: University of California Press, 1998). The argument here is that total empires involve citizens back home with affairs abroad, and that a dialectic between national identity and colonial enterprise is thus established. In Young's account, explanations of the timing and character of colonial regimes must take into account media, economy, ideals, domestic politics, and the international setting. Monocausal explanations do not work for total empires.

16. Laura Hostetler, *Qing Colonial Enterprise: Ethnography and Cartography in Early Modern China* (Chicago: University of Chicago Press, 2000). Hostetler argues against the commonplace that the Chinese borrowed Western concepts of space to generate their first modern maps. Rather, all cutting-edge early modern states, including France, hired the best international talent available to address the problems faced by centralizing early modern states.

17. I refer to the period roughly spanning 1871–1914. See Michael Adas, *"High" Imperialism and the "New" History* (Washington, D.C.: American Historical Association, 1993).

18. Sophia Su-fei Yen, *Taiwan in China's Foreign Relations, 1836–1874* (Hamden, Conn.: Shoe String Press, 1965); Edward H. House, *The Japanese Expedition to Formosa* (Tokyo 1875). The Japanese lost only twelve men in battle during these six months, but 525 more died of illness, mostly while waiting for negotiations to conclude. *Saigō totoku to Kabayama sōtoku* (Taihoku: Saigō totoku Kabayama sōtoku kinen jigyō shuppan iinkai, 1936), 471.

19. Laurence G. Thompson, "Formosan Aborigines in the Early Eighteenth Century: Huang Shu-ching's Fan-su Liu-k'ao," *Monumentica Serica* 28 (1969): 42; Emma Jinhua Teng, "Travel Writing and Colonial Collecting: Chinese Accounts of Taiwan from the Seventeenth through Nineteenth Centuries" (Ph.D. diss., Harvard University, Cambridge, Mass., 1997), 118; *Riban gaiyō* (Taihoku: Taiwan sōtokufu minseibu banmu honsho, 1912), 1, 59; John Robert Shepherd, *Statecraft and Political Economy on the Taiwan Frontier, 1600–1800* (Stanford, Calif.: Stanford University Press, 1993), 16–17, 398–403.

20. Hsieh Shih-Chung, "From *Shanbao* to *Yuanzhumin:* Taiwan Aborigines in Transition," in *The Other Taiwan: 1945 to the Present,* ed. Murray Rubinstein (Armonk, N.Y.: M. E. Sharpe, 1994), 404–19.

21. Ōe, "Shokuminchi sensō," 3–11; Harry J. Lamley, "The 1895 Taiwan War of Resistance: Local Chinese Efforts against a Foreign Power," in *Taiwan: Studies in Chinese Local History*, ed. Leonard H. D. Gordon (New York: Columbia University Press, 1970), 23–77.

22. *Riban shikō*, vol. 1–2 (Taihoku: Taiwan sōtokufu keisatsu honsho, 1918), 2.

23. Ibid., 3.

24. Ibid., 5.

25. Hashiguchi Bunzō, "Taiwan jijō," *Journal of the Tokyo Geographic Society* 17, no. 3 (October–December 1895): 321–22; *Riban gaiyō*, 50; *Taiwan dainenpyō* (Taihoku: Taiwan Keisei Shinposha, 1925), 14.

26. Hashiguchi, "Taiwan jijō," 321–22.

27. In 1722, the Qing instituted the earth-oxen trenches, earthworks, and stone pillars marking the territory beyond which Han were not to go and that mountain aborigines were not to cross. Various schemes were devised to guard this line, which shifted over the subsequent one hundred fifty years of Qing rule to reflect the reality of increased Han immigration and the expansion of territory under wet-rice irrigation.

28. Kojima Reiitsu, "Nihon teikokushugi no Taiwan sanchi shihai: tai kōzanzoku chōsashi, sono 1," *Taiwan kingendaishi kenkyū* 2 (1979): 5–10; *Riban shikō*, 9–21.

29. *Riban gaiyō*, 51.

30. *Riban shikō*, 97.

31. Takekoshi Yosaburō, *Japanese Rule in Formosa*, trans. George Braithwaite (New York: Longmans, Green, 1907), 171.

32. Ka Chih-ming, *Japanese Colonialism in Taiwan: Land Tenure, Development and Dependency, 1895–1945* (Boulder, Colo.: Westview Press, 1995), 35.

33. James W. Davidson, *The Island of Formosa: History, People, Resources and Commercial Prospects* (London: Macmillan, 1903), 406.

34. Chō Ryotaku and Ueno Keiji, *Forumosa: Taiwan Genjūmin no fūzoku* (Tokyo: Fuji Press, 1985), 163.

35. Kojima Reiitsu, "Nihon teikokushugi no Taiwan sanchi shihai: Musha hōki jiken made," in *Taiwan Musha hōki jiken kenkyū to shiryō*, ed. Tai Kuo Hui (Tokyo: Shakai shisōsha, 1981), 63–64; Formosa Bureau of Aboriginal Affairs, *Report on the Control of the Aborigines in Formosa* (Taihoku: Government of Formosa, 1911), 34–42.

36. E. Patricia Tsurumi, "Taiwan under Kodama Gentaro and Goto Shimpei," in *Papers on Japan*, ed. Albert Craig (Cambridge, Mass.: East Asian Research Center, Harvard University, 1967), 99–101.

37. Edward I. Chen, "Goto Shimpei, Japan's Colonial Administrator in Taiwan: A Critical Reexamination," *American Asian Review* 13, no. 1 (1995): 29–59.

38. Ōe, "Shokuminchi sensō," 9–10; *Riban gaiyō*, 62; Takekoshi, *Japanese Rule in Formosa*, 175; Chō and Ueno, *Forumosa*, 163–4.

39. Mochiji Rokusaburō, *Taiwan shokumin seisaku* (Tokyo: Fuzanbō, 1912), 378.

40. Mochiji's post put him within the inner circle of the central government; only ten other civil officials (including Gotō) shared Mochiji's rank of *chokunin*. Tsurumi, "Taiwan under Kodama," 115; *Taiwan dainenpyō*, 49.

41. Kojima, "Nihon teikokushugi (1981)," 50–52.

42. Ōe, "Shokuminchi sensō," 10.

43. *Report on Control of the Aborigines*, 45; *Riban gaiyō*, app. 4.

44. *Riban gaiyō*, app. 3.

45. *Riban shikō*, vol. 3 (Taihoku: Taiwan sōtokufu keimukyoku, 1921), 9–19.

46. *The Japan Yearbook* (Tokyo: Japan Yearbook Office, 1916), 708.

47. Ōe, "Shokuminchi sensō," 10; Mochiji, *Taiwan shokumin seisaku*, 392; *Taiwan jijō* (Conditions on Taiwan) (Taihoku: Taiwan Government General, 1916), 594–96.

48. Kondō Masami, "Taiwan sōtokufu no riban taisei to Musha jiken," in *Teikoku tōji no kōkoku*, ed. Ōe Shinobu et al. (Tokyo: Iwanami shoten, 1992), 35–58.

49. Barclay, "Japanese and American Colonial Projects," 187–223.

50. Takekoshi, *Japanese Rule in Formosa*, 230.

51. Stanley Karnow, *In Our Image: America's Empire in the Philippines* (New York: Ballantine Books, 1989), 139–94; W. Cameron Forbes, *The Philippine Islands*, 2 vols. (Boston: Houghton Mifflin, 1928), 1:224–27.

52. William Henry Scott, *The Discovery of the Igorots: Spanish Contacts with the Pagans of Northern Luzon* (Quezon City: New Day Publishers, 1974).

53. David Joel Steinberg et al., ed., *In Search of Southeast Asia: A Modern History* (New York: Praeger, 1971), 156–60.

54. Scott, *Discovery of the Igorots*, 1–5, 329–30.

55. T. K. Hunt, Samuel Kane, H. Walter Hale, and Phelps Whitmarsh, mainstays of early U.S. government in the Cordillera, all had their beginnings in this milieu. See Samuel E. Kane, *Life or Death in Luzon: Thirty Years of Adventure with the Philippine Highlanders* (Indianapolis: Bobbs-Merrill, 1933); Laurence L. Wilson, "Sapao: Walter Franklin Hale," *University of Manila Journal of East Asiatic Studies* 5, no. 2 (1956): 1–38; Jenks, "Building a Province," 170–77.

56. William Henry Scott, "The Spanish Occupation of the Cordillera in the 19th Century," in *Philippine Social History: Global Trade and Local Transformations*, ed. Alfred W. McCoy and Ed. C. De Jesus (Honolulu: University of Hawai'i Press, 1982), 39–56.

57. U.S. War Department, Bureau of Insular Affairs, *Official Handbook: Description of the Philippines* (Manila: Bureau of Public Printing, 1903), 48–50.

58. Peter W. Stanley, *A Nation in the Making: The Philippines and the United States, 1899–1921*, Harvard Studies in American–East Asian Relations, vol. 4 (Cambridge, Mass.: Harvard University Press, 1974), 89–90.

59. *RPC 1903*, 1:9; *RPC 1904*, 1:27; *RPC 1905*, 1:73; *RPC 1906*, 1:70–71; *RPC 1907*, 1:69.

60. *RPC 1904*, 1:519.

61. Lewis, *Wagering the Land*, 102.

62. Fry, *Mountain Province*, 74, 175; Winifred Lydia Wirkus, *History of the Mining Industry in the Philippines: 1898–1941* (Ph.D. diss., Cornell University, Ithaca, N.Y., 1974), 29–70.

63. Peter W. Stanley, " 'The Voice of Worcester is the Voice of God': How One American Found Fulfillment in the Philippines," in *Reappraising an Empire: New Perspectives on Philippine–American History*, ed. Peter W. Stanley (Cambridge, Mass.: Harvard University Press, 1984), 130–33; Sullivan, *Exemplar*, 144–47.

64. *Reports of the Taft Philippine Commission* (Washington, D.C.: Government Printing Office, 1901), 147; Fry, *Mountain Province*, 9–10.

65. Fry, *Mountain Province*, 9–10; Sullivan, *Exemplar*, 150.

66. *RPC 1904*, 1:519–29; Finin, "Regional Consciousness," 64–66; Wilson, "Sapao," 1–38; Daniel Folkmar, "The Administration of a Philippine Province," *Annals of the American Academy of Political and Social Science* 30 (July–December 1907): 115–22.

67. Jenista, *White Apos*, 24.

68. Scott, "Spanish Occupation," 53–54; Jenista, *White Apos*, 9.

69. Forbes, *Philippine Islands*, 203–4.

70. There are vivid accounts of these punitive expeditions in Jenista, *White Apos*, 43–45; Rosaldo, *Ilongot Headhunting*, 259–61.

71. Jenista, *White Apos*, 55–56; Rosaldo, *Ilongot Headhunting*, 259–63; Charles B. Elliott, *The Philippines: To the End of the Commission Government* (Indianapolis: Bobbs-Merrill, 1917), 173–75; W. E. Moore, "Law and Order in Philippines: Excellent Work of Native Constabulary," *The Globe* (Boston), 8 December 1912; Forbes, *Philippine Islands*, 213–14; *RPC 1915*, 124.

72. Jenista, *White Apos*, 35, 64, 88.

73. One constabulary officer had been killed in action while working among the hill tribes of northern Luzon from 1901 to 1935, and "twenty-three soldiers were slain and many were wounded, including five officers." Harold Hanne Elarth, *The Story of the Philippine Constabulary* (Los Angeles: Philippine Constabulary Officers Association, 1949), 136; *RPC 1915*, 118–20, for figures and quotes.

74. Fry, *Mountain Province*, 83–95; Finin, "Regional Consciousness," 76–81; Wilson, "Sapao," 5–9.

75. Lewis, *Wagering the Land*, 102.

76. Forbes, *Philippine Islands*, 593–94.

77. Dean C. Worcester, *The Philippines Past and Present*, vol. 2 (New York: Macmillan, 1914), 661.

78. Ibid., 671.

79. Fry, *Mountain Province*, 83–95.

80. For a discussion of *ladrones* (bandits), see Glenn May, *The Battle for Batangas: A Philippine Province at War* (New Haven, Conn.: Yale University Press, 1991), 63–64, 180–81.

81. Forbes, *Philippine Islands*, 227; Elarth, *Philippine Constabulary*, 133.

82. *RPC 1904*, 3:18.

83. Ibid., 3:116.

84. *RPC 1907*, 2:315.

85. *RPC 1908*, 2:368–69.

86. This is an unusually low estimate of the population of Mountain Province by an advocate of a stronger Cordillera policy; just two years earlier, the number 200,000 was given by Crawford; some estimates were as high as 300,000. The 800 men were not limited to Mountain Province. They were distributed among Isabela, Cagayan, Ilocos Sur and Norte, La Union, and Mountain Province. But given the much higher number of officers in the 1914 report, and the lack of operations reported on the coast or in the valleys, it is highly probable that the 1910–1914 period saw an increased constabulary presence in Mountain Province.

87. *RPC 1914*, 122.

88. Forbes, *Philippine Islands*, 227; Fry, *Mountain Province*, 63; *RPC 1913*, 97; *RPC 1914*, 73–74, 124; *RPC 1915*, 123–24; 134–35.

89. Fry, *Mountain Province*, 58–59.

90. Wilson, "Sapao," 7–8; Folkmar, "Provincial Administration," 120–21. For discussions of the politics of collaboration that characterized the political relationship between U.S. and Filipino officials, see Norman G. Owen, "Introduction: Philippine Society and American Colonialism," in *Compadre Colonialism: Studies on the Philippines under American Rule*, ed. Norman G. Owen (Ann Arbor: Center for South and Southeast Asian Studies, University of Michigan, 1971), 1–12; Michael Cullinane, "The Politics of Collaboration in Tayabas Province: The Early Political Career of Manuel Luis Quezon, 1903–1906," in Stanley, *Reappraising an Empire*, 59–84.

91. A reputable Japanese scholar recently claimed that Japan's aborigine policy was a success story obscured by the special pleading of left-wingers and Taiwanese nationalists in the postwar era. Mukōyama Hirō, *Taiwan Takasagozoku no kōnichi hōki: Musha jiken* (The Taiwan aborigine anti-Japanese uprising: The Musha incident) (Tokyo: Cho keizai kenkyu, 1999), i–ii, 26.

92. Gananath Obeyesekere, *The Apotheosis of Captain Cook: European Mythmaking in the Pacific* (Princeton, N.J.: Princeton University Press, 1997). Obeyesekere tackles a number of issues in this book. His convincing demonstration of how the violence toward South Sea islanders was bleached out of the published Euro-American accounts of Cook's voyages to Hawai'i are the most pertinent to this analysis.

93. See Rosaldo, *Ilongot Headhunting*; Renato Rosaldo, "Utter Savages of Scientific Value," in *Politics and History in Band Societies*, ed. Eleanor Leacock and Richard Lee (Cambridge: Cambridge University Press, 1982), 309–26; and Renato Rosaldo, "Imperialist Nostalgia," in *Culture and Truth: The Remaking of Social Analysis* (Boston: Beacon Press, 1989), 68–90.

94. Jenista, *White Apos*, 67, explains away Jefferson Gallman's intentional fatal shooting of an unarmed Ifugao as an act in accord with Igorot norms.

95. Bureau of Insular Affairs, Record Group (RG) 350, box 694, file 13847, U.S. National Archives and Records Administration (NA), Washington, D.C. Two of the fifty Igorots under Hunt's care died in the United States. He managed three troupes exhibited in New Orleans, Chicago, Minneapolis, Milwaukee, Boston, and Winnipeg, to name a few sites. According to this correspondence, the displays were popular and lucrative. Part of Hunt's downfall was caused by the cooperation of a rival showman who wanted to take over the "care" of Hunt's employees. U.S. War Department officials were eager to bring Hunt to justice for embarrassing the pro-retention Republican administration.

96. "We followed up the valley of this river, until in the town near Labuaguan our escort of ten native soldiers–who came from the Cagayan river, and are the poorest soldiers in the world–killed one man and wounded three others in the town. At this juncture we left most of our cargo to save our heads, and continued our hike with a captured and roped guide." A. E. Jenks to W. H. Holmes, 9 February 1903, BAE Letters Received, 1888–1906, box 11, "Jenks A. E., 1902–1904," National Anthropological Archives, Smithsonian Institution, Washington, D.C.

97. See Michael Stainton, "The Politics of Taiwan Aboriginal Origins," in *Taiwan: A New History*, ed. Murray A. Rubinstein (Armonk, N.Y.: M. E. Sharpe, 2000), 31–42.

98. James C. Scott, *Seeing Like a State: How Certain Schemes to Improve the Human Condition Have Failed* (New Haven, Conn.: Yale University Press, 1998), 2.

99. See Rydell, *All the World's a Fair*; Chō and Ueno, *Forumosa*; Matsuda Kyōko, "Pabirion gakujutsu jinruikan: seiki tenkanki ni okeru 'tasha' hyōshō o meguruchi," *Osaka Daigaku Nihongakuhō* 15 (1996): 47–70.

100. This is a phrase Nicholas Thomas uses in *Colonialism's Culture* to describe the cluster of concepts associated with the period of high imperialism.

101. Felix M. Keesing and Marie Keesing, *Taming Philippine Headhunters: A Study of Government and of Cultural Change in Northern Luzon* (Stanford, Calif.: Stanford University Press, 1934), 84.

102. This terminology is from Scott, *Seeing Like a State*.

103. Wang Jen-ying, *Population Change of Formosan Aborigines*, Academia Sinica Monographs, vol. 11 (Nankang, Taipei: Institute of Ethnology, 1967). These censuses were published as *Bansha kokō*.

104. Rafael writes, "Through the collection and classification of statistical data, [the census] kept watch over the population, mapping their social location and transcribing them as discrete objects of information and reformation," "White Love," 190. "Dressed in the 'tribal' attires for the camera's lens, images of their bodies are wrenched from their historical and social contexts. In their frozen state, they suggest the appearance of specimens undergoing different stages of tutelage," Ibid., 200. Although this language explicates the workings of a discourse, it is insensitive to the distance between colonial pretensions to control and its actual achievement.

105. Perhaps the best known was Mori Ushinosuke, whose last days were spent lobbying major Japanese newspapers to intercede in colonial policies to relocate aborigines.

106. Ōe, "Shokumin sensō," 13.

107. Ironically, a good counterpart to the texts discussed in Rafael, "White Love," is Mori Ushinosuke, ed., *Taiwan banzoku zufu* (Tokyo: Rinji Taiwan kyūkan chōsakai, 1918), a large collection of anthropological "types" assembled by a tireless critic of Japan's Taiwan aborigine policy.

108. Frederick Cooper and Ann Laura Stoler, "Between Metropole and Colony: Rethinking a Research Agenda," in *Tensions of Empire: Colonial Cultures in a Bourgeois World*, ed. Frederick Cooper and Ann Laura Stoler (Berkeley: University of California Press, 1997), 29.

VINCE BOUDREAU

Methods of Domination and Modes of Resistance: The U.S. Colonial State and Philippine Mobilization in Comparative Perspective

Relative to activity in colonial regimes across Southeast Asia, Philippine protest during the American period was distinct. Although many Filipinos were dissatisfied with the pace or terms of promised independence over the course of the American period, the promise itself sufficed to draw emerging national elites away from mass-mobilizing contention. The absence of national elites in protest movements left a distinct imprint on protest and mobilization during this period; it also shaped broader political alliances that would emerge under U.S. rule and beyond.

Hence, whereas nationalist student activists spearheaded resistance movements in Burma and Indonesia and provided an important push to Vietnamese nationalism, they remained marginal to Philippine nationalist protest from 1898 until the regime of Ferdinand Marcos (1965–1986). Coalitions between peasants and local intellectuals helped focus vast agrarian resistance movements such as the Burmese Saya San rebellion and Vietnam's 1908 tax rebellion; early-twentieth-century Philippine agrarian revolts, including the comparatively large Sakdal uprising in 1935, were mainly local affairs with weak national alliances and relatively parochial orientations.[1] Whereas the Burmese civil service applied sustained pressure for independence, Philippine bureaucrats seldom produced sharp or radical political demands, except when members of that service lost their positions. Although Philippine labor organizations did mount several important strike and protest waves under U.S. rule, their most important national connections were to electoral parties, and

Philippine labor never acquired the large-scale revolutionary stature that Burmese oil workers or the northern Vietnamese proletariat gained in their struggles. Neither, however, was Philippine protest under U.S. colonialism merely distinguished by the lack of resistance modes that were dominant elsewhere in Southeast Asian colonies, for it developed modes of activity, such as suffragist movements and heated electoral contests between recognized political parties, that were unique in the region.[2]

Distinct elements of U.S. colonial rule significantly shaped Philippine protest and resistance. Most particularly, without a coherent national elite leadership, Philippine protest tended toward limited and localized mass expressions or more civil demonstrations to demand broader voice or resources *within* existing or proposed arrangements. Where protest was most formidable, it required special circumstances that produced tactical alliances with national elites or with men who had held, but had been removed from, elite positions.

To make this argument, I take a comparative perspective that considers contrasts and comparisons between the Philippines and colonies in Burma, Indonesia, and Vietnam. According to one classic typology, colonists govern either directly, by bringing or creating their own administration, or indirectly through existing local authorities.[3] As will be shown, however, this distinction says comparatively little about how colonialism created and transformed administrative elites, about how such elites positioned themselves in relation to colonialism itself, or about the forces that pushed some toward anticolonial struggles and some toward collaborative interactions. Colonial administrations divided and reshaped Southeast Asian societies and in the process helped mold the colonial opposition, as well. To explain different patterns of resistance to colonial rule, then, I ask how local communities engaged that rule and how this engagement shaped modes of resistance and mobilization.

Three aspects of U.S. colonial practice worked unique influences on Philippine society in comparison with other Southeast Asian cases. First, the United States acquired a Philippine colony that had developed some coherence under Spanish rule—and in resisting that rule. More important, Americans could imagine the territory as a single package, defined as that which Spain had governed and the United States acquired by treaty. Questions of the retention or disposition of that territory, as both

Donna J. Amoroso and Patricio N. Abinales point out in this volume, soon led Americans to divide the Philippines into separate administrative districts and to think about Filipinos as differentiated. From the outset, moreover, U.S. Admiral George Dewy, head of the fleet which defeated Spain, and others seemed more interested in retaining Luzon than the entire archipelago.[4] Nevertheless, the U.S. administration regarded the puzzles attendant in acquiring a territory with a resident population differently from earlier colonial regimes. The initial model for the U.S. colonial project could be neither jungle exploration nor rolling conquest of nineteenth-century pre-national colonialism. Rather, it was the pacification of territory already acquired and the subsequent extension of governance over whatever territory the administration decided to retain.[5] Hence, whereas colonial powers in Indonesia, Vietnam, and Burma incrementally established dominion over colonial territory, constructed colonial states and social institutions piecemeal, and confronted questions of governance and representation only when compelled to by pressures against their rule, the United States dealt with these questions up front and arrived more quickly at the construction of integrated political institutions, including local security forces, representative assemblies, and a far-reaching civil service. Municipal governments were rapidly organized in the first years of U.S. rule in the Philippines, and a major consideration before the U.S. Congress in 1901 was the drafting of an "organic law or constitution" for the colonial government.[6]

This orientation, in turn, contributed to distinct ideas about representation, education, and the bureaucracy. Governing the Philippines raised questions about political responsibilities toward the islands' residents, not least because the question of colonial rule required justification at home beyond the economic exhortations of expansionist Republicans. The United States, as many have noted, approached the construction of governing institutions at least partly as a way to create a tractable political elite positioned and inclined to deflect and temper grievances generated by Philippine society under U.S. rule. These governing policies, discussed in more detail later, prevented potentially explosive nationalist alliances between political elites and the bureaucratic corps; encouraged political elites to recruit, socialize, and tame young college graduates; and placed many contentious decisions about bureaucratic hiring and promotion under Filipino, rather than American, authority.

The contrasts with other Southeast Asian cases are impressive. Dutch reforms in Indonesian educational and administrative policy increasingly placed aristocratic and upwardly mobile students together inside colonial schools and offices and outside them as unemployed, resentful graduates. When French schools in Vietnam began to produce their own Western-trained functionaries, local scholarly elites detached themselves from the larger educational system and provided important political and moral leadership to a nationalist movement of students and a growing class of "new intelligentsia." The destruction of the old Burmese court (the Hutladaw) in 1888 and of local authorities (*Myothugyis*) gave young Burmese graduates of British colonial schools a nationalist mistrust of British intentions (bolstered by the importation of Indian and Tamil bureaucrats) and a relatively free hand to assume leadership of the nationalist campaign. Quite obviously, of course, these policies, and the apparent persistence of colonial rule, provided nationalism with a more robust political vehicle. But it also produced models of protest and contention that outlasted the nationalist phase and shaped models of collective resistance into the independence period.

A third, ideological peculiarity underpins the distinctive arrangement of U.S. colonial institutions. America's colonial epoch began after its own Civil War helped dispatch the aristocratic ideology on which the U.S. South's plantation economy had rested. In its place, an orientation favoring individual rights and equality before the law linked to Northern industrialization and Western expansion captured Americans' imagination.[7] This orientation produced support for universal education, broad suffrage, and upward mobility, which did not sit well with Philippine agrarian elites who formed the political backbone of the Philippine Assembly: Most of the Philippine members of this new representative institution had far less liberal orientations and relied on more explicitly unequal social and political conventions designed to insure a docile labor force.[8] Not surprisingly, therefore, indigenous elites often labored to preserve their prerogatives against the grain of U.S. policy and inclination. Hence, from the outset, U.S. domination of the Philippines was somewhat at odds with local class domination, and local elites drew more fire and ire than Americans from upward-striving nationalists, particularly during moments of electoral competition and bureaucratic reorganization.

Although distinctive aspects of the U.S. administration set the Philippine regime apart, the entire arrangement also sat atop a society that in many ways was already distinct from the rest of Southeast Asia. In one respect, this distinctiveness consists in the recent Philippine revolutionary climax and the original connection that existed, however briefly, between arriving U.S. forces and elite Philippine nationalists. By 1898, the struggle against Spain had passed from its political to its military phase, and many of the nation's brightest leaders had given their lives in pushing the independence struggle to that point. In addition, by 1898 the logic of the revolution's military phase had placed particular burdens on Philippine society. In moving to open military struggle against a weakened Spain, Filipino revolutionaries shed important tactical and political advantages associated with secret societies, unions, and local mass organizations. For example, although the Katipunan ng Bayan had begun as a decentralized collection of social and secret forces based in Filipino neighborhoods, the war took soldiers out of these neighborhoods, forged them into an army (the revolution's first organization with national scope), and strained the more organic connection between local society and the resistance. After 1898, anticolonial forces faced a vigorous American adversary instead of the worn-out Spanish administration, and the Americans developed new tactics, such as concentration camps in Cavite, Batangas, and Laguna, that isolated revolutionaries from their social base.[9] Differences also began to emerge between the military under Emilio Aguinaldo's Cavite-based leadership and the Ilustrado movement's (a nationalist movement of the elite) Manila intellectuals—triggered largely when Americans offered incentives to the latter at a time that the revolutionary organization was still mainly unconsolidated.[10] Hence, in important ways the revolution paid for its early victory over Spain through substantial sacrifices in political capacities necessary to defeat the United States.

Moreover, the 1898 revolution took place about twenty years before anticolonialism had developed a substantial global political and organizational infrastructure, and this bit of timing had significant consequences. The decrepitude of the Spanish colonial regime, at war with the United States and already bereft of prime acquisitions in Latin America, accounted in substantial measure for Filipinos' early successes at the nineteenth century's close. But the Philippines' comparatively early revolutionary upsurge also segregated the Philippine struggle from some of the more important events in that global history, such as the impact (especially in Asia) of the Japanese victory over Russia in 1905 and of the Bolshevik Revolution in 1917.[11] These events pushed anticolonialists' resolve toward more resolute demands for self-rule rather than for expanded representation. Filipino nationalists in 1898 were therefore somewhat different from nationalists who soon emerged elsewhere in Southeast Asia. Those Ilustrados who did travel to Europe in the late 1800s entered a cosmopolitan milieu that differed substantially from that which Vietnam's Ho Chi Minh and Indonesia's Mohammad Hatta would discover a few decades later. Anticolonial questions in the late nineteenth century were still primarily creole questions, potentially resolved by imperialism's concessions to local elites' aspirations for greater standing within the colonial regime, although Filipinos and scholars still debate the precise balance between reformism and radicalism in prominent Ilustrado thinking.[12] But the more global anti-imperialism of nationalism's "third wave," and the supporting institutions of transnational movement and party organizations, had not yet clearly emerged. Hence, elite Filipino nationalists had little in the way of a global movement with which to counterbalance absorption into the U.S. system. If anything, the early conclusion of the revolutionary war against Spain, and clear strategies to supplant Spanish culture with Americanism, left the society plastic and defenseless in the face of U.S. efforts to develop a base in the archipelago.

PHILIPPINE COLLECTIVE ACTION
UNDER U.S. RULE: AN OVERVIEW

It is possible to divide Philippine protest and collective action under U.S. colonialism roughly into three periods. The first period corresponds to what O. D. Corpuz divides into two American wars: one against Muslims (Moros) in Mindanao, and the other against Christians in Luzon and the Visayas. Both began in 1899. The Moro wars lasted until 1912, and the Christian wars lasted until 1907. Filipinos at first engaged Americans in artillery battles along the railway corridor from Manila to Pangasinan, but heavy casualties soon forced them to switch to guerrilla tactics.[13] After the switch, the Americans shifted their attention to severing the connection between the guerrilla fighters and their mass base. In

Luzon, the United States built concentration camps that held entire provinces hostage to their soldiers' surrender. In the south, the army preferred to pound Muslim population centers into submission with artillery rather than imprison their residents.[14] After brutal tactics in both theaters had killed an estimated 13 percent of the archipelago's population, the United States forced surrender on the resistance.[15]

Even before this killing ended, some Filipinos began new forms of struggle and collective action, designed to secure positions within and under the U.S. regime rather than to displace that rule. As the Philippine–American War moved out of Manila and into the countryside, rapid capitalist expansion produced new activity among workers in Manila and would shortly do so in important secondary cities such as Iloilo and Cebu. At first, working communities fell back on autonomous forms of self-help organized among a *balangay* (community) of those practicing a similar trade; this occupational-membership basis fit new requirements of a society moving toward capitalist production and away from affective frameworks.[16] Before long, mutual-aid societies gave way to more outward-directed strategies of strikes and union politics. The U.S. regime, transporting ideas of rule and governance to its new colony, began a policy of limited toleration for mutual-aid associations (designed in part to win workers away from the more political strategy espoused by Isabelo de los Reyes) and in 1908 established an institution that would have been unheard of under the Spanish or, indeed, in other colonial regimes across the region: the Bureau of Labor.[17] This bureau, alongside Nacionalista Party efforts to win worker support in 1907 elections, legitimized labor politics and unions within limited economic and electoral parameters. Over the next several decades, workers' strikes largely reflected economic pressures on poor consumers, such as the ebb and flow of rice prices. More broadly, the advent of electoral politics opened the question of suffrage in various ways; encouraged by contact with American women, Filipinos began organizing the suffragist movement to lobby for the women's vote.[18] In both instances, unfolding representative opportunities encouraged urban populations to launch civic demonstrations designed to secure access to and standing in the new regime.

A much different, and more militant, struggle emerged frequently after 1923. A wave of small-scale peasant and worker-based rebellions began in the countryside, initially in reaction to central-state interference in local religious practices (the Colorum rebellion of 1923 in northeastern

Mindanao) and subsequently as capitalist expansion changed agrarian social relations and impoverished farmers in the countryside. In the cities, labor protest radicalized in the mid-1920s and 1930s and benefited from new educated and middle-class allies with axes to grind against Manuel Quezon's efforts to centralize and purge the state.[19] In both agrarian and rural rebellions, new themes entered the struggle. Mobilized and disaffected groups accused elites of betraying Philippine nationalist aspirations—something that suggests a diversification of nationalist perspectives beyond those of the national leadership. But it also suggests something that became increasingly prominent as independence drew near: The primary cleavages inflamed by nationalist debate did not separate American and Filipino adversaries; rather, they divided Filipinos. Tactically, the movements left behind the more civil modes of struggle within "pacified" territory during the century's first decades in favor of armed clashes with the constabulary that led predictably to one-sided defeats for activists. Rebellions from 1923 to 1935 were partly the fallout of political centralization that forged an increasingly closed and exclusive national elite. Agrarian rebellions were usually led by fairly parochial elites and tended to attract localized and limited support for violent outbursts rather than sustained struggles. Labor movements, and other, more urban modes of contention, often pulled together under former or aspiring members of the government bureaucracy who had been removed from or denied positions in the government. Urban protests, therefore, often were more center-directed and sustained, but they still levied their sharpest and most radical criticism against collaborating Filipino elites.

If Philippine collective action under U.S. rule is in many ways distinct from that in other Southeast Asian colonies, the utter absence of a truly integrative and national elite leadership for Philippine collective action is central to this difference.[20] The question is not so much why Filipino elites did not join a more radical nationalist movement against U.S. rule, for their more passive and patient activity makes perfect sense in light of the United States' promise of impending self-rule and the economic advantages elites enjoyed during the U.S. regime. Rather, how did the absence of broad and cross-class nationalist alliances set the tone for other forms of collective action and political contention? Without strong and national elite allies, demonstrations that began in the early 1900s, and continued through their more militant phase in the 1920s and

1930s, remained the limited affairs of small sections of society. Activists in these movements championed the explicitly segmented interests of people organized in bounded groups of women or workers rather than the more integrated demands framed as emanating from a Filipino nation. In the later popular movements of the 1920s and 1930s (and into the 1950s) rebellions never spread beyond their local points of origin—even in the broadest movement of all, the Sakdal Rebellion of 1935.[21] A reason may be that, beyond U.S. promises of Philippine self-rule, administrative and class divisions wrought on Philippine society by the structure of the American colonial state also greatly influenced mobilization and dissident patterns in the archipelago.

THE DISTINCTIVENESS OF U.S. COLONIAL RULE IN THE PHILIPPINES

In terms of world time, it makes sense to begin a consideration of the U.S. colonial state by setting it alongside Japan's burgeoning imperial efforts. Both countries walked onto the colonial stage as colonialism itself began to creak under the weight of its gathering obsolescence. In established colonial regimes, ambivalence appeared—or would shortly begin to appear—in a variety of colonial regimes, as suggested by the Netherlands' short-lived "enlightenment" policy in Indonesia; the socialist-driven reconsideration of the French position in Vietnam after World War I; and Britain's weakening capacities in India.[22] Despite such intimations of change, the United States and Japan viewed the acquisition of colonial territory partly as an emblem of political stature and thus overlooked this first shadow of tarnish. What distinguished the two regimes from each other, however, were their varying orientations and motivations for colonial acquisition. In late developing Japan, the state's competitive haste to enhance industrial production and accelerate national capacities required both vast external reserves of raw materials and a patriotic mission of expansion to deflect increased pressure on local populations. Pushed by these stimuli, Japanese imperialism developed into a strong state-led effort at domination and extraction that in most ways was utterly unconflicted and focused on overcoming competition from established colonial powers expanding through its Asian hinterland.

U.S. contrasts with the Japanese pattern lie rooted in America's comparatively earlier and more self-contained industrialization process. The

United States approached its colonial period without a serious shortfall of natural resources to spur a state-led mercantilist expansion and without the need to relieve social pressure from an overworked domestic society.[23] Instead, U.S. business desired a base from which to explore and exploit market opportunities in China, but this position was strongly supported by only a small circle of expansionist Republicans.[24] Thus, the United States' colonial enterprise required domestic justification elaborated in terms of other-directed missions, including a mission to govern justly, rather than as the mere acquisition of resources and markets. Acquisitive races with other large states to obtain a market share of China did not, therefore, strongly attract social support in the United States. America's political competition with rivals, primarily European rivals, was in fact more popularly expressed in the ironically *anti*colonial Spanish–American War. Hence, while President McKinley's operatic confusion over the Philippine question never quite rang true,[25] Americans (even powerful and politically involved Americans) did not agree about the purpose the colony would serve. In the pitched debates over retention, therefore, the justification for the Philippine colony was largely made in terms of the character of U.S. rule, and expansionist Republicans had a ready model for Philippine exploitation in the recently completed conquest of the American frontier.[26]

Lacking Japan's imperial drive and armed with its own individualist ideology, U.S. colonialism did not attempt to place economic activities under state auspices. The greatest U.S. colonial presence occurred during the Philippine–American War and fell off sharply immediately thereafter. Having attained military ascendency over the Filipino anticolonial resistance, the United States soon reduced its troops, and by 1903 the number of American soldiers in the country had fallen to 17,748 from a 1901 high of 71,528.[27] The maintenance of civil law and order passed from the U.S. War Department to a newly created Philippine Constabulary, with more localized staffing, command, and control. By 1904, only 345 American officers led 7,000 Filipino constables.[28] As the American fighting force underwent this transformation, the broader logic of U.S. control in the Philippines emerged. The state would separate colonial administration from accumulation and insure American society's untrammeled access to Philippine markets and productive resources. In setting up this system, the United States strove to establish laws and treaties regulating commerce and trade that insured American ascendency; to that end,

Americans dominated any governing body responsible for drafting these regulations.[29] In contrast, authorities charged with implementing and maintaining the rules were judged to have less discretionary power, and such posts could pass to Filipinos (suitably trained in the new U.S. educational system) through the much publicized Filipinization policy.

The educational system that prepared Filipino bureaucrats for their new responsibilities constitutes one of the most important elements of the American system. Soon after it gained control over the Philippines, the U.S. colonial government began an astoundingly broad effort at non-vernacular education, unprecedented in its number of both students and Americans deployed as teachers. In many cases, as Daniel Doeppers suggests, this stratum of Filipino bureaucrats came from middle- and lower-class families and approached these new opportunities armed exclusively with educational capital.[30] This, and the colonial state's decision to replace predominantly Spanish administrators with Filipinos, rendered educational attainment one of the great engines for upward mobility for middle- and lower-class Filipinos at that time. But perhaps of equal importance to the system's development was that educational institutions stood on a national, rather than international, framework. While young Indonesians, Vietnamese, and Burmese could acquire a passable administrative education in their own countries, those who aspired to advanced university education typically traveled to Europe. In the Philippines, several old Spanish colleges already existed to provide such education, and the Americans soon built others, such as the University of the Philippines (1908) on American University models—that is, not as mere training academies for administrators but as vehicles for providing higher, professional education. Some students still traveled abroad to study, but from the early 1900s, it became possible for local people to obtain advanced, professional degrees in the archipelago. Hence unlike their counterparts across Southeast Asia, many of the Philippines' twentieth-century leaders had not studied abroad for any length of time. Rather, they rose within domestic networks that continued to connect them to campus life even as they moved into government.

From 1901 onward, as the coercive American presence declined, the shock troops of U.S. colonialism arrived in robust numbers: Newspapermen, entrepreneurs, bankers, and lawyers flooded Manila and streamed into the provinces. They took charge of a massive effort to meet greatly expanded Western demand for tropical products such as sugar, copra, and abaca. They established the great sugar centrals, mapped out strategies for broader fruit production for export markets, and accelerated timber and mining operations. In these efforts, they worked hand in hand with the landed provincial elite who had been gathering power and productive resources during the last years of Spanish rule—an alliance rendered indispensable by legal restrictions on U.S. participation in the Philippine plantation economy, and, as Julian Go points, by some American ambivalence in the metropole about Philippine economic opportunities.[31] For these local elites, it was a time of great opportunity: Credit was readily available; new production strategies energized all types of industry; and formerly tight Spanish export controls were replaced with preferential access to the larger U.S. market and a more open orientation toward global trade in general.[32] Under the new American regime, local businessmen made a killing both by taking over industrial niches previously dominated by the Spanish and by rapidly acclimating themselves to the more freewheeling and liberal American system of trade and production.

Soon, two important alliances emerged between U.S. colonialism and Philippine society. First, the U.S. colonial state nurtured the new Filipino bureaucrat corps. This upwardly mobile civil service benefited from the comparatively egalitarian and democratic impulse of the United States' colonial administration. Second, the rush of American business planted entrepreneurial seeds among landed provincial elites who were awakening to the new possibilities of a global economy.[33] The *principalia* often drank deeply from the cup of capitalist practice but regarded the draft as a particularly aristocratic privilege. Such Filipino elites were often as wary of the administrative opportunities afforded their lower-class countrymen as they were eager themselves to participate in more aggressive capitalist accumulation. American businessmen sometimes also shared this mistrust of Filipino administration, and these quarters consistently raised the most pitched questions about Filipino preparedness for self-rule.[34] Hence, a tension existed in the regime's social base between mass-educated and upwardly mobile colonial bureaucrats from a new middle class and a revitalized and aristocratic principalia. These new political elites could take advantage of capitalist opportunities but were neither willing nor compelled (by the need to recruit mass support) to share power with the middle and lower classes.

The Philippine Assembly's institutional arrangement combined with the class tension at colonialism's social base to influence protest and mobilization under the U.S. regime. In part, the idea behind the Philippine Assembly replicated the United States' own bicameral pattern of regional representation: Its Filipino members came from across the archipelago and both protected regional interests and integrated regional elites nationally. But the evolution of the electoral system also insured the hegemony of landed interests over the newer working and administrative classes. Severe literacy and property requirements initially restricted the franchise to roughly 2 percent of the population. Elections began in 1902 with municipal-level contests that the local elite easily dominated, then used to establish patronage machines for larger contests. The Philippine Assembly's lower house was first elected in 1907, and broader bicameral contests followed in 1916.[35] Until then, Americans in the Philippine Commission formed the legislature's more powerful upper chamber. Beside insuring a tractable legislature, the system influenced the regard with which most assembly members viewed national political office. For landed elites, the important political and economic spoils existed in provincial agrarian realms. Hence, national office presented less an opportunity to accumulate power than insurance against national efforts to undercut local standing. Virtually everyone with a chance to win such elections also had an interest in keeping the national apparatus weak and unable to intervene strongly in local affairs.

The Philippine Assembly's distinct aspect was its position between society and the colonial state in importantly ambiguous relations to both power and national aspiration. Its members accommodated themselves to colonial rule, but its Nacionalista Party grounded recruitment on the demand for immediate independence. The assembly's independence debates, although tamed by their perch inside the U.S. colonial state, nevertheless drew attention from student activists and others who might otherwise have looked elsewhere for political leadership.[36] Moreover, the pageantry of periodic electoral competition gave these debates, demonstrations, and rallies a hothouse radicalism that both channeled dissent in directions that U.S. rule could accommodate and squarely fixed rival Filipino politicians, rather than American colonists, in the rhetorical crosshairs. Because assembly members held elected office, moreover, they constructed specific sorts of relationships with voting segments of Philippine society, and these relationships influenced dissent. In the first two decades of U.S. rule, for instance, workers pursuing mutual aid and socioeconomic unionism expended great efforts to link themselves to electoral machines.[37] Labor militancy outside electoral arenas could neither attract enough attention from assembly members to influence legislative debates nor distract national elites from these formal representative institutions. More political unionism would not emerge until disenchanted members of the bureaucratic elite broke ranks with representative government in the 1920s.[38]

The institutional and class divisions between the elitist assembly and upwardly mobile civil-service members also provided safety valves for the colonial regime. At first, there was little dissent within the civil service, for during the first two decades of U.S. rule, educational and career opportunities for middle- and lower-class Filipinos had never been better, and the bureaucracy remained quiescent. Yet comparative colonial experience suggests that such amity often changes, and a colonial bureaucracy whose training, expertise, or aspirations surpass their prospects can be explosive indeed. By the early 1920s, in fact, limitations on the colonial bureaucracy's ability to absorb college graduates did emerge when, for the first time, the administration was fully staffed. Faced with an overabundance of qualified bureaucratic personnel and still mistrustful of the bureaucracy's political aspirations, the national political elite began to pick and choose among aspiring administrators and advisers. Some of those passed over for work felt betrayed by the political elite and found in policy debates over independence and other matters a useful framework for advancing that criticism.[39]

By the early 1930s, an array of dissatisfied civil servants, some of whom had been moderate dissidents within the bureaucracy, had been shaken out of government service and began to explore alternative modes of amassing power. Several such men turned to mass society, where demands for social and political equity found expression as criticisms of local (rather than American) elites. Patricio Dionisio had vainly attempted to find government employment before he organized the Katipunan ng Bayan from factory workers and labor associations.[40] Quirico Abeto had been Quezon's minister of justice until he was forced from that position; he organized the Associated Federation of Labor (AFL), which soon took a hand in urban protests, as well. Benigno Ramos was another trusted Quezon aide who turned to mass-based collective action after a dispute with Quezon forced him from office. His newspaper *Sakdal* (to "accuse") rallied a mass movement that rolled to a bloody climax across Manila's provincial hinterland.[41] Each of these movements adopted anticolonial perspectives and often accused the ruling Nacionalista Party of pushing for a sham independence. But the focus of their collective action—and, indeed, their most forceful criticism—targeted Filipino leaders rather than the U.S. regime.

The relationship between the Philippine Assembly and the broader society, then, explains some peculiar aspects of political mobilization under U.S. rule. First, the absence of any significant national anticolonial movement or organization outside the political parties reflects the influence of the Americans' promise of self-rule, and the consequent efforts of Filipinos to concentrate on representative institutions that would secure position in that new dispensation. Those who may have been expected to construct a national political movement—such as labor-union members and the students who, by the late 1920s, periodically protested on university campuses—instead drew near party politics and often demonstrated in the service of party campaigns. Agrarian protest had virtually no cosmopolitan leadership: The electoral dynamic was overwhelmingly patronage-based, which quarantined mass communities from national politics and alleviated the need for national figures to work out a political posture that agrarian society would support. Even movements that would eventually develop into more national challenges, such as the Huk rebellion, began as local and mainly parochial collectives and achieved national stature only in the struggle against the Japanese occupation.[42] Electoral-party domestication within the colonial apparatus hence meant that the parties' links to mass society were domesticating, as well.

COMPARATIVE PERSPECTIVES ON THE
COLONIAL STATE AND SOCIAL RESISTANCE

To this point, I have attributed the distinctiveness of U.S. colonial practice primarily to the ways in which the early promise of eventual independence interacted with the construction of separate political and administrative classes to (especially) position politicians between the Americans and Philippine society. That the elite was *political* explains its efforts to build broad party support among university students, workers, and other potential dissidents and more individual electoral support in patronage-based provincial machines. That it was *aristocratic* explains limits on its political program, its unwillingness to continue the mass-mobilizing campaign of the Katipunan, and its disinclination to form united political fronts with an upwardly mobile colonial administration. Together, these aspects of representation under U.S. rule both channeled potential cosmopolitan nationalists away from extra-parliamentary movements and deprived local dissent of prominent and powerful national leaders. The reemergence of mass movements in the Philippines would wait for the development of a disaffected stratum of colonial bureaucrats with new grievances against the political elite in the 1930s. By reviewing alternative patterns of elite involvement in the colonial regimes of Indonesia, Burma, and Vietnam, one can see the impact of this Philippine pattern on larger politics of mobilization and dissent.

Indonesia

Through the early twentieth century, the Dutch indirectly ruled Indonesia via a pattern of parallel administration in colonial officials across the archipelago working alongside local aristocrats such as the Javanese *priyayi*. Working in the native bureaucracy, or *pangreh pradja*, gave local aristocrats both the greatest prospect for social mobility and an explicitly ennobled niche in the colonial structure that built on their prestige and authority.[43] As it gathered support among these aristocrats, this system also shielded peasants from direct exposure to Dutch rule and economic exploitation. Most farmers and plantation workers experienced a colonialism mediated by local authorities. By the end of the nineteenth century, however, changes were afoot in the relations between Dutch and Indonesian colonial society. In a move that highlights key differences between Dutch and American colonialism, the state-mandated cultivation system ended, and to increase production, more Dutch were placed directly in charge of tea, sugar, and coffee plantations.[44] After this change, Dutch reliance on Indonesian political intermediaries also waned, and more Dutch civil servants arrived in Indonesia to administer colonial rule directly. Increasingly direct forms of Dutch economic and political rule diminished the aristocracy's role as a buffer between the Dutch and local society. This helps explain the rise of nationalist sentiment—but not its form. To distinguish this form, one must look at the patterns of social alignments that were emerging at the time.

As indirect systems of Dutch rule in the archipelago were evolving, Dutch colonial officials began to fear the rise of pan-Islamic thought as wealthy Indonesians acquired education in the Middle East. To prevent this Islamic upsurge, and partly also to meet perceived needs for more capable local administrators, the state initiated several new educational programs. Over the next twenty years, the number and type of "native" schools expanded dramatically, principally through the opening of the First Class Native Schools in 1893, but then through the start of vocational schools and more tradition-based Muhammadiyah (1912) and the Taman Siswa schools (1922). In some measure, the bureaucracy's social base changed as more educated candidates from outside aristocratic families became eligible to work for the colonial regime.[45] Yet unlike the Philippines until the 1930s, the Indonesian state could not accommodate these newly trained local graduates. Far fewer jobs existed, because the newly trained had competition both from aristocrats who were already in the bureaucracy and from increased Dutch immigration.

Several elements of the Indonesian experience set it apart from events unfolding in the Philippines. First, it mattered greatly that, until the 1917 inauguration of the Indonesian Volksraad, the only avenue for Indonesian participation in colonial rule was the bureaucracy. When non-aristocratic families acquired access to new forms of education, they developed the basis for solidarity and common cause with existing, aristocratic members of the pangreh pradja. Initially, the juxtaposition of aristocrat and commoner bureaucrats created tension between the groups, but as educational attainment became the new standard for professional capacity, it blurred divisions between them.[46] When the bureaucracy's capacity to absorb these trained candidates for administrative service fell off, the resulting dissatisfaction had a far broader social base in Indonesia than in the Philippines. Moreover, that this increasingly dissatisfied bureaucracy existed before the Volksraad meant that an oppositional culture had already developed in the relationship between Indonesian elites and Dutch rule. Further, this oppositional culture found support in the contact that Indonesians who had studied in Europe made with Marxist and anticolonial organizations and parties there.[47] Even though the representative institutions of the Philippine Assembly at the outset were only slightly more fair than those of the Volksraad, they immediately generated far more support among Philippine elites.[48]

Finally, the less statist, free-market drive of U.S. economic activity in the Philippines from the outset cut rural elites in on the ground floor of capitalist opportunities. Reforms in the Dutch colonial system, in contrast, sought more efficient production and distribution and precluded similar Indonesian participation AND benefit. The more ambivalent tenor of Philippine anticolonial discourse, and the weakness of more general cross-class alliances behind that discourse, can in part be explained by the countervailing pull of elite prosperity that would be engendered by the severing of colonial ties. In Indonesia, there were far fewer countervailing forces. In fact, the narrower scope for elite participation in colonial enterprise promoted alliances between a dissatisfied bureaucracy and a mass society that was more directly encountering Dutch rule. Beyond the specific question of colonialism itself, these ties provided more fertile ground for mass–elite alliances in general; thus, little would prevent men with extensive landholdings, for example, from eventually taking up positions in the Indonesian Communist Party.

Burma

The British administration of Burma viewed the territory from the beginning as an ad hoc attachment to the more defined Indian colony and elaborated the colonial state in a piecemeal and open-ended process. It acquired first lower, then upper, Burma in a series of wars with the Burmese crown, and after victory eliminated the monarchy and lowland Burma's aristocratic power structure. The British abolished the traditional Burmese court, the Hutladaw, in 1888, then moved against local hereditary authorities, the Myothugyis. Colonial authorities faced the resulting power vacuum with several compensatory strategies, none of which were terribly well designed.[49] First, they opened educational institutions to train a new corp of bureaucrats selected from all class backgrounds in lowland Burma. Second, they imported Indian functionaries, trained in the Subcontinent's administrative schools, to work in Burma, and made broad use of the Indian army to control social relations in the countryside. Third, outside the lowland areas that most interested British authorities, they worked out several different administrative patterns that recognized or empowered local leaders of non-Burman nations in loose autonomy agreements. Groups such as the Karens and Shans received special advantages in their territory and were used extensively in colonial suppression of lowland Burmese rebellions.[50]

This irresolute pattern of administration betrays the status of colonial Burma in Britain's imperial designs: Burma lay between India, the jewel in the imperial crown, and China's inestimable riches, and was to be something between a way station and a supply depot for established and future colonial conquests. For these rather limited designs, the problem was less how to administer or govern Burmese territory than how to wrench it away from a stubborn monarchy capable of mobilizing its subjects; limit British liabilities in the less integrated and important frontier areas; and eventually harness the productive capacities of Burmese rice lands in the service of the empire. Once initial control was achieved, the British merely extended the governmental apparatus from neighboring India to stretch over Burmese territory, for this extension represented an expedient solution to the Burma question and one that matched Britain's idea of how Burma fit in the larger empire.[51] The resulting interaction between British colonialism and indigenous society produced a particular pattern of nationalist mobilization and conflict that differs from the other three cases in ways that reflect the interaction of this colonial apparatus and Burmese society.

The two great sources of trouble for Britain in colonial Burma were the newly educated young Burmese who formed the *a-so-ya-min* bureaucracy and a village-based and decentralized agrarian movement built on revivalist themes against colonial impositions designed to increase agrarian production. Unlike the Dutch or Americans (or, indeed, British policy itself in upland Burma), the British never tried to use lowland Burmese elites to buffer other forces in society. When they swept elite institutions aside, they cast modernizing and Westernizing students of colonial schools in a peculiar position. On the one hand, students absorbed new ideas about administration and political orientation from their studies. On the other hand, their prominence in a Burmese society newly deprived of established elites placed the students in the position of defending Burma against colonial pressure. At the same time, the reorganization in the countryside of Burmese agrarian life for production occurred directly through new colonial state agents, including Indian, British, and minority militia. Again, the vacuum left by the dissolution of the local Myothugyis meant that no legitimizing force stood between colonial power and society. But the end of the aristocratic presence in the countryside also deprived the Buddhist monks of support and placed them on the defensive during the agrarian squeeze. Not surprisingly, the colonial state's direct impositions on agrarian society created both peasant unrest and a traditionalist revival in the countryside. In both urban and the rural circles, the destruction of traditional elites, rather than their incorporation into the colonial effort, sharpened antagonisms between a Burmese society being forced through important changes and the colonial regime.[52]

Part of what made the bureaucratic stratum so explosive was its dual position as both the heir to precolonial Burma's national aristocracy and the beneficiary of that aristocracy's destruction. The reorientation of educational policy atop British colonial moorings, so soon after the abolition of the Burmese aristocracy, stirred dissent among students enrolled in the colonial schools. Students' demands for more Burmese educational curriculum and their enthusiastic participation in groups such as the Young Men's Buddhist Association (YMBA) reflected the dilemmas of a new elite caught between these two worlds. Yet such moves were not confined to urban areas or campuses, for the YMBA also expanded into the countryside and recruited many in village-level national associations and Buddhist societies. As these associations spread, they heightened the tension of students' dual position as new and national leaders of Burmese society and as defenders of an order threatened by imperialism. National campus protest seemed more at the head of a movement that stretched into the villages.[53]

Both urban and rural strata, however, had a second, importantly imperial wellspring for their resistance to British rule. The a-so-ya-min acquired power specifically as local (that is, Burmese) administrators in the British Empire. This sense of qualification, however, came into conflict with a colonial designation of their territory as linked to India. The point was driven home when the British brought bureaucrats, clerks, and soldiers from the Sub-continent to Burma. During the twentieth century's first several decades, the rate of Indian migration rose so that by 1931 more than one million Indians lived in Burma. Originally, Indian troops had been used prominently in pacification campaigns against resistant Burmese society after the last of the Anglo-Burmese wars. Thereafter, many assumed positions in the colonial bureaucracy but also evolved into economically powerful *chettyar* moneylenders.[54] These Indian functionaries created resentment among students and bureaucrats. Similarly, the Indian role in agrarian society, both in initial pacification campaigns and later as moneylenders, dispersed anti-Indian sentiment geographically. As the British began using resources siphoned from Burma in the administration of Indian colonies, urban and rural resentments on the issue rose and provided a common theme in nationalist struggles.

Together, these elements of British colonial policy help explain two aspects of Burmese engagement of the imperial regime: the almost total failure of attempts to recruit Burmese participation in parliamentary institutions, and the prominence of urban and educated youth in leading resistance against Britain. As in Indonesia, Burmese participatory institutions emerged as part of the British response to increased anticolonial sentiment in Burma and (more particularly) in India. As with the inauguration of the Volksraad, participatory avenues in Burma expanded at a time that opposition to British rule had already acquired significant momentum, and from the outset many identified these institutions as co-optive and unpatriotic. From the very beginning, figures in the nationalist movement urged electoral boycott, and at no time under British colonialism did Burmese electoral participation surpass 18 percent. Also, the main thrusts of national agitation in Burma were movements led by the colonial bureaucracy and students in schools designed to build that bureaucracy. In contrast, a political and conciliatory Philippine elite worked to tame a similar stratum of upwardly mobile students in the Philippines, and an older aristocratic elite provided initial leadership to younger Indonesian activists. Despite the importance of rural rebellion in Burma in the 1930s, therefore, it would be young nationalists of the 1917 footwear controversy (over Burmese demands that Europeans remove their shoes in Buddhist temples), the 1920 curriculum protests (a nationalist movement to gain more control over education), and the later, broader movements that led the struggle against the British crown.[55]

Vietnam

As in Burma, the French colonial state in Vietnam emerged piecemeal, through a series of territorial conquests that first established different patterns of rule across the country, then worked to unify those patterns in a single, centralized framework. Unlike the British, however, the French chose initially to work through the Vietnamese court, gradually imposing more confining restrictions on royal prerogatives until the monarchy had become almost entirely a tool of colonial control. To some degree, this effort benefited from the potential plasticity of mandarin alliances. Although they had pledged loyalty to the emperor, the mandarins also possessed a framework for shifting support between monarchs in Vietnam's history of dynastic struggle. Just as unique, the French conquest relied heavily on imported French administrators who occupied positions from the hierarchy's apex down to fairly low bureaucratic levels; with a vast reserve of its own colonial forces, and able early on to eat away at the structure of mandarin loyalties to the court, the French did not immediately confront monarchical authority in Vietnam. Instead, they outflanked it.[56] Soon many French settlers took up residence in Vietnam as government workers or as other employees. To the twin institutions of French administrators and mandarin collaborators the colonists added low-level clerks and functionaries trained in the Cochinchina Interpreter Schools, the graduates of which had little chance of climbing very high in the civil service. By the time the Vietnamese monarchy capitulated outright to the French, the issue of real control was largely moot.

The same education system that produced the mandarins, however, also spawned the first important social base of resistance to French rule: the scholarly elite. Only a few scholars achieved mandarin status; the examination system, however, trained many who did not earn the highest degrees but had substantial education nevertheless. Many such elites returned to small provincial cities or villages and began to teach and write, and they were distinct in Southeast Asia in two respects. First, they were sustained by a national and precolonial education system that remained independent from central authority. The system produced many teachers and scholars who perpetuated local patterns of study and learning that, although linked to the mandarinate's reproduction, developed independence from the national court, and eventually from the examination system itself.[57] In contrast, Philippine and Indonesian educational institutions depended almost entirely on central-state and (in the Philippines) church programs, and even the Burmese monastic educational traditions suffered greatly with the loss of central-state patronage. Second, in large consequence of the scholarly elites' autonomy from central power, they developed a far greater connection to grassroots Vietnamese society and. even before they had framed their politics in national terms, were concerned to broaden class participation in new political currents.[58]

At the outset, the contest between colonialism and the Vietnamese opposition divided society along fairly clear battle lines. The intrusion of

French imperial forces split the previously integrated provincial–capital links among court, bureaucracy, and educational institutions developed in early-nineteenth-century Vietnam. The French captured or outflanked most of that hierarchy's upper echelon and imported or created new, lower-strata functionaries who displaced more resistant and unruly provincial elites. The emerging colonial regime depended on widespread immigration and settler support (more intensely in directly ruled Cochinchina than in the northern provinces), a substantial army to compel complicity, low-level Vietnamese clerks and minor functionaries, and collaborating mandarins. On the opposition side stood provincial elites who were usually at the fringe of the bureaucracy and not sufficiently accomplished to have attained a mandarin position; they were sometimes supported by student circles and sometimes by a rural society with mounting grievances, but rarely by nationally prominent mandarins themselves set against the French. These early divisions accounted for the character of early resistance to French rule—such as the "writing brush war" between scholars on both sides of the colonial question in the 1860s, and the largely elite-driven "aid the king" movement that began in 1885.[59] As the French took over the monarchy, replaced lower bureaucrats with French officials, and recruited collaborators from among the mandarins, they also drove a wedge between increasingly heterogeneous sections of the elite: between provincial society and the court and between collaborating intelligentsia and those who advocated resistance.

These early forms of resistance in time gave way to broader reform movements that reflected changes wrought by colonialism. In the context of Vietnam's rapid integration into a global economic, political, and social empire, the structure of opposition and support grew more complicated. In Cochinchina, the reorientation and expansion of rice cultivation atop a capitalist framework created powerful Mekong Delta landlords who constituted a large component of the indigenous bourgeoisie and a stratum of smaller more nationalist local landlords closely tied to village life.[60] In addition, about ten thousand long-term French residents, or *colons*, lived in Vietnam, ad did a growing and volatile stratum of petit bourgeois.[61] In northern and central Vietnam, the colonial state built an urban economy that rested heavily on Vietnamese functionaries and more indirect forms of rule. In both instances, unfolding French colonial strategies markedly changed the terrain of struggle. In the

south, an increasing number of agricultural workers and petty functionaries came into conflict with French colons and francophile landlords in
a world that warped, rather than replaced, traditional village relations;
here religious-political movements such as the Cao Dai emerged.[62] In
northern and central Vietnam, a growing and restive class of petit bourgeoisie and proletariat found themselves ill equipped to break through
limits placed on their political power by a narrow and restrictive French
educational system and the domination of foreign and indigenous functionaries it empowered; here, more modern nationalist movement organizations and unions took shape.[63] In both sections of the country,
French administrative divisions of Vietnamese territory fragmented the
mobilization of protest and dissent.

These developments pushed anticolonial resistance beyond earlier
and more limited struggles among the scholarly elite. France's appropri-
ation of the Confucian hierarchy, as well as the limits of its own educational system, became increasingly obvious after 1900. Because established avenues of upward mobility had been captured by the colonial
apparatus, the scholarly resistance by then had metamorphosed into a
reform movement with a striking orientation toward broadening anticolonialism's social base and opening the way for more Western-
inspired learning.[64] By the early 1900s, the reform movement had new
supporters, too, for by then colonial society had created a restless layer of
educated young men and women who were underqualified for bureaucratic service, unwilling to take up manual labor, and disenchanted with
older norms of Confucian harmony. They joined the older scholarly elite
in framing dissatisfaction in terms of a quest for new models for struggle
and political rule, and they built movements to aid this search. The
reformers also believed in transmitting this new knowledge to all classes.
Some of the more prominent reform-oriented educational institutions
charged no tuition or provided scholarships for impoverished students;
reformers also advocated adopting romanized script in preference to
Chinese characters to render knowledge more accessible. Many looked
outside Vietnam for political models. The 1905 Japanese victory over
Russia influenced nationalist thinkers, as would the republican and
communist revolutions in China and Western Social Darwinism several
years later. Enthusiasm for these models lay behind a study movement to
Japan and an abortive military invasion by the Chinese-inspired restora-
tive society in 1915.[65]

As the reform movement developed anticolonial momentum, it connected political struggle and educational reform together in two distinct ways. First, education in Vietnam was tied only loosely to bureaucratic service, both because so many failed to find work in the colonial bureaucracy and because so many educators adopted anticolonial orientations and established their own schools. Even before reforms in 1916–1917 expanded access for Vietnamese to French schools, a broad and footloose circle of educated and semi-educated people concerned themselves as much with national political questions as with the workplace. Colonial education in Burma and Indonesia functioned more narrowly to meet administrative needs; it typically produced anticolonial resistance only when employment opportunities sharply fell off (Indonesia) or when the bureaucracy itself grew restive (Burma). In contrast, most former students in Vietnam did not work in the bureaucracy; education gave them a broader orientation and led them to consider more diverse questions of national governance and political power. Hence, former students who possessed enough education to read, write, and debate national politics became a potent opposition force because of a peculiar system that educated many but employed relatively few. Second, the search for new modes of knowledge, and for new ways to open that knowledge to broader sections of society, was a comparatively stronger theme in Vietnamese anticolonialism than elsewhere, because educators rather than students stood at its vanguard. Men such as Phan Boi Chau and Phan Chu Trinh amassed substantial reputations and followings during their decades-long search to design an educational system that would serve the anticolonial struggle.

The characteristic pattern of Vietnamese resistance to French rule lies in the centrality of this new stratum of intelligentsia and semi-educated people, their autonomy from the colonial bureaucracy, and their access to and interest in external models of struggle. For many, the Eastern Travel Movement (1905) was but the beginning of a process of travel, writing, organizing, and learning abroad. In Japan, China, and Hong Kong, Vietnamese nationalists connected with one another and with a growing international revolutionary and anticolonial movement. Nor was the attraction of liberation models culled from abroad confined to specific classes. Even children of the richest and most francophile families sent to France to study often returned with new awareness of the contradictions between domestic and imperial French politics and alive to new Marxist currents moving across Europe. Those who traveled overland to nearby Asian countries developed important organizational bases outside Vietnam, and beyond French control. With perhaps the most energetic anticolonial activity taking place *outside* the country, the Vietnamese movement, more than that in the Philippines, Indonesia, or Burma incorporated external models of national struggle: The Viet Nam Quoc Dan Dang (VNQDD) rigidly adopted the Kuomintang's Republican model, and socialism and Marxism soon gained footholds in organizations such as the Revolutionary Party of New Vietnam and the Association of Revolutionary Youth. Most important, however, the external settings provided a frame of reference and a period of incubation that lent immediately national perspectives to Vietnamese resistance movements. This, coupled with existing inclinations to develop mass followings for anti-French positions, helped generate resistance movements that had national centers of authority and a perspective that transcended the French administrative fragmentation of Vietnamese society.[66]

★ ★ ★

Although each case reviewed here stands apart from the others in important respects, there is considerable reason particularly to distinguish the engagement between Philippine society and U.S. colonialism. The combination in the Philippines of promised independence, economic and political concessions to new elites, and the creation of separate political and administrative classes early on scattered nationalist energies. The space for maneuver gained in those first years, at least partly (for the Americans) a lucky consequence of the revolutionary climax against Spanish rule, allowed the United States to establish a more responsive approach to governance—or, at least, an approach that was responsive enough to overcome skeptics in the United States and some dissidents in Philippine society. At the same time, this particular brand of U.S. colonial rule, set down toward the end of the creole nationalist period, made it more possible for U.S. colonists to co-opt Filipino nationalists. Having attracted important elements of the anti-Spanish movement to the American side, U.S. colonists needed to outflank not a nationalism running at flood tide but one that had ebbed considerably. In contrast, representative institutions in Indonesia, Burma, and Vietnam were a step behind, and they struggled to overtake, mobilized anticolonialism—and an anti-colonialism with new and more powerful global support and precedence that managed to hold national elites and mass followers firmly together. Dutch, British, and French struggles with colonial societies therefore encountered adversaries who stood atop socially broader and more powerfully adversarial coalitions. Liberal reforms in each of these settings never successfully undercut nationalism. Rather, they inspired vibrant and broadly based counteroffensives. Although it may be true that U.S. colonialism pursued some exceptional policies in the Philippines, therefore, profound differences between Philippine experiences and those of Indonesia, Burma, and Vietnam probably had more to do with the timing and global context of colonial rule, because these conditions influenced the political consequences of colonial practice. It is in this particular global context that the practices of U.S. imperialism exercised their special effect in the Philippines.

Flashpoints of local resistance against Dutch, British, and French rule all resulted from increases in the rate or directness of colonial economic exploitation that were triggered by growing demands for tropical products or the rising cost of empire. Peasant resistance on Dutch plantations after the cultivation system ended, Burmese resistance to increased rice exports to India, and the Vietnamese tax revolts in 1908 all occurred when a statist economic system attempted to raise revenues. In contrast, U.S. colonialism progressed under the cloak of social mission that was necessary in a recently, and still partly anti-imperialist, United States, and this mission motivated explicit restrictions on U.S. business activity in the archipelago. In any event, the most avid imperialists on the American side regarded the Philippines as a base for expansion elsewhere and so were willing to tolerate such restrictions to secure support for retaining the colony. In the Philippines, Americans largely worked to reorganize production, extend greater amounts of credit, and link Philippine agriculture to the world economy—activities that enabled Philippine elites to make a great deal of money. When economically statist colonial regimes created new elites (as in Burma) or worked through existing elites (as in Indonesia), they restricted the elites' economic opportunities. Such elites had comparatively less interest in buffering economic discontent that increased state extraction produced. Indeed, anti-imperialist political elites lent significant support to agrarian rebellions in each case. With rare and individual exceptions—notably, Pedro Abad-Santos's leadership of the Philippine Socialist Party—the Philippine political elite never championed grassroots complaints about colonial extraction.

Much has been said about the broad scope of educational opportunity in the Philippines under U.S. rule. Yet educational-policy changes also opened substantial opportunities for study in Indonesia and Vietnam. The distinctive impact of the U.S. educational system seems to lie in its content and more complete local elaboration. In Indonesia and Vietnam, most colonial schools imparted rather narrow administrative and bureaucratic skills. Those who wished for something more needed to cross over to European schools and, in many cases, travel out of the colony to the metropole. These study trips appear to have influenced twentieth-century Vietnamese and Indonesians in ways that recall the experiences of nineteenth-century Ilustrados traveling abroad. But the creole struggles with which nineteenth-century Filipinos found resonance differed from the anticolonial struggles of the twentieth century. In the Vietnamese case, foreign travel contributed both intellectual and organizational resources to the demand for national self-determination, particularly in the wake of post–World War I negotiations at Versailles. Even for Indonesians (who on the whole traveled abroad in smaller numbers and for shorter durations), the glimpse of a larger world introduced a new language of organizational and revolutionary modernity that invigorated politics. By that time, however, Filipinos were directing themselves more toward new educational opportunities *in* the Philippines that provided educational opportunities that were less narrowly administrative and more professional. Filipinos were able to attain an approximation of an American education on home soil, and elite political opportunity focused on climbing locally elaborated political networks. Thus, Filipinos were less exposed to anticolonial Marxist discourse than elites elsewhere in Southeast Asia. Hence, the United States' educational reforms not only kept many Filipinos apart from global nationalist movements, it also encouraged stronger integrative links between students and established representative institutions, which had broad political consequences down the line.

American economic and educational policies helped establish conditions under which the United States administrative design could work its characteristic effect. First, the United States planned from the outset to set up governing institutions in the Philippines or in those portions of the archipelago that it wanted to control and soon after placed the issues of self-government and representative institutions on the table. Because self-government and prosperity seemed within the grasp of elites early on, national electoral institutions were not saddled with the burden of diffusing an active nationalist movement. Instead, they could provide the framework for a new political and economic elite to emerge and grow strong. In contrast, all three of the other colonial regimes undertook representative reforms only when nationalism was cresting. It helped the Americans that the Philippine revolution divided in 1900 into two groups: wealthy elites willing to participate in American plantation capitalism, and soldiers for whom independence was less negotiable. Yet the initial U.S. framework that colonial control was a problem of governance helped insure that the self-interested collaborating elite would evolve into a political buffer against less satisfied members of colonial society. The recruitment of wealthy Ilustrados to the American side; the creation more generally of broad social opportunities for less powerful people; and the tendency (largely rooted within the Philippine elite) to keep political and administrative classes separate from one another all undercut the scope of subsequent nationalist struggle by converting the strongest potential nationalists into supporters of incremental transitions to independence. When voices rose to demand more comprehensive nationalist advance, they did so without strong national leadership and in patterns of mobilization that favored localized and limited, if often violent, modes of struggle.

Yet U.S. colonial policies did not succeed merely by empowering an elite allied with American interests—for indeed, the French had built a similar group with less political success in Vietnam. Rather, the United States created differentiated bases of support for its colonial regime in Philippine society. In important ways, the class and functional divisions between the civil service and the political elite prevented alliances between the two against U.S. interests. Indeed, by working through a political elite, the Americans were assured that many of the most volatile labor and agrarian movements in the 1920s and 1930s would be directed against Filipino politicians rather than U.S. colonialists. In contrast, Indonesia after educational reform and Burma after the monarchy's destruction suggest that too great a concentration of power in a state-constructed indigenous elite tends to sharpen the contrast between European and indigenous prerogatives, spurring nationalist mobilization. In Vietnam, by contrast, too large a segment of an autonomous elite existed outside the circle of colonial sponsorship. By creating an internally differentiated elite in the Philippines divided into administrators and politicians, who themselves needed to build constituency support (and, not incidentally, who attacked one another during elections), the United States prevented sharp oppositions between U.S. and Filipino power.

The consequences of interactions among these factors—of the United States' economic, educational, and administrative programs in the Philippines—should remind us of how vastly world time influenced colonial politics in these cases. By the time the Indonesian, Burmese, and Vietnamese anticolonial movements were gathering steam in earnest, it was virtually impossible to conceive of these struggles without Marxist referents. Ideas of a global, scientific workers' revolution were as inseparable from these later movements as they were alien to the 1898 Philippine revolution. Battles between French and Vietnamese forces raged across Asia, and both Burmese and Indonesians thought about great-power politics and the possibility of Japanese support for their anti-imperialist struggles. By the time these same global and Marxist currents entered Philippine political discussions, U.S. colonialism had already established (and segregated) political and bureaucratic institutions that pushed the likely audience for revolutionary politics a considerable way down the social scale. In most of Southeast Asia, the entrance of an explicitly Marxist framework of struggle attracted significant bourgeois attention and targeted local collaborators and (primarily) foreign occupying forces. By the time Marxism established a foothold in the Philippines, the new elite had gained such control over Philippine society that revolutionary politics concentrated far more on struggles among different Filipino classes.

The consequence of the absence of a marxist component to nationalist struggles for contentious politics in the Philippines, beyond even its influence on nationalism itself, has been profound. Most strikingly, patterns of rule that emerged under the Americans prevented any serious Marxist discourse from occurring among Filipino political elites and sparked a concomitant failure of leftist politics in general to find sponsorship among mainstream Philippine forces or institutions. In this way, some of the most important resources that social-movements scholarship associates with the spread and sustenance of political contention—national leaderships, access to mass media and social networks, institutional sponsorship[67]—have been unavailable to the Philippine left, except when the Marcos dictatorship attacked and alienated portions of that elite. Even then, however, leftist discourse was a rather thin veneer and quickly gave way to less inclusive, less participatory political modes after the dictatorship. More generally, larger measures of democracy in the Philippines have produced not expanded or more robust redistributive pressures or protest but, rather, the reverse. Hence, while populist periods in Indonesia and Burma often have been associated with robust parliamentary periods, representative government in the Philippines often has provided clearer opportunities for elites to distance themselves from mass pressures and return, once more, to patterns of insulated elite politics enabled by U.S. rule.

NOTES

1. David Sturtevant, *Popular Uprisings in the Philippines, 1840–1940* (Ithaca, N.Y.: Cornell University Press, 1976).

2. James S. Allen, *The Radical Left on the Eve of War* (Quezon City: Foundation for Nationalist Studies, 1985).

3. J. S. Furnivall, *Colonial Policy and Practice* (New York: New York University Press, 1956).

4. See Frank H. Golay, *The Face of Empire: United States–Philippine Relations, 1898–1946* (Quezon City: Ateneo de Manila University Press, 1998).

5. Ibid., 29.

6. Ibid., chap. 3.

7. Barrington Moore, *Social Origins of Dictatorship and Democracy: Lord and Peasant in the Making of the Modern World* (Boston: Beacon Press, 1966).

8. Bonifacio S. Salamanca, *The Filipino Reaction to American Rule, 1901–1913* (Hamden, Conn.: Shoe String Press, 1968), 185–90.

9. O. D. Corpuz, *The Roots of the Filipino Nation*, vol. 2 (Quezon City: Aklahi Foundation, 1989).

10. See Reynaldo Ileto, *Pasyon and Revolution: Popular Movements in the Philippines, 1840–1910* (Quezon City: Ateneo de Manila University Press, 1979); see also Jonathan Fast and Jim Richardson, *Political and Economic Revolution in 19th Century Philippines* (Quezon City: Foundation for Nationalist Studies, 1979).

11. In situating the end of Spanish colonialism in the Philippines in the context of the larger global decay of the Spanish regime, I have been influenced by conversations with Benedict Anderson; his discussion of the attraction that Indonesians felt to the global revolutionary flow have also contributed to my comparative perspective on this point. Benedict Anderson, "Rewinding Back to the Future," *Indonesian Democracy 1950s and 1990s* (Monash, Australia: Centre for Southeast Asian Studies, Monash University, 1992).

12. See, for instance, Floro Quibuyen, *A Nation Aborted: Rizal, American Hegemony and Philippine Nationalism* (Quezon City: Ateneo de Manila University Press, 1999).

13. O. D. Corpuz, *An Economic History of the Philippines* (Quezon City: University of the Philippines Press, 1997), 202–5.

14. James H. Blount, *The American Occupation of the Philippines* (New York: Knicker-bocker Press, 1913; repr. Quezon City: Malaya Press, 1968).

15. Luzviminda Francisco, "The First Vietnam: The Philippine American War, 1899–1902," in *The Philippines, End of an Illusion* (London: AREAS, 1973).

16. Melinda Tria Kerkvliet, *Mutual Aid and Manila Unions*, Wisconsin Papers on Southeast Asia, no. 7 (University of Wisconsin, Madison, 1982).

17. Daniel F. Doeppers, *Manila, 1900–1940: Social Change in a Late Colonial Metropolis* (Quezon City: Ateneo de Manila University Press, 1984), 118–19.

18. Antoinette Raquiza, "Philippine Feminist Politics: Disunity in Diversity?" in *Civil Society Making Civil Society*, ed. Miriam Coronel Ferrer (Quezon City: Third World Studies Center, 1997), 171–87.

19. Sturtevant, *Popular Uprisings*.

20. I make this remark, however, mindful that important nationalist individuals, such as Pedro Abad Santos and the labor leader Isabelo de los Reyes, did emerge from among the elite during this period.

21. Benedict Kerkvliet argues that, even in the 1950s, Huk rebels were never very effective outside their home provinces in Central Luzon. Benedict Kerkvliet, *The Huk Rebellion: A Study of Peasant Revolt in the Philippines* (Berkeley: University of California Press, 1977).

22. For more detailed reflections on the particular timing of Japanese imperialism, see Benedict Anderson, "Japan: 'The Light of Asia,'" in *Southeast Asia in World War Two: Four Essays*, ed. Josef Silverstein, Southeast Asia Studies Monograph Series, no. 7 (New Haven, Conn.: Yale University Press, 1966), 13–50.

23. In fact, Corpuz reports that U.S. investment in the Philippines was inadequate because the United States' domestic growth was attracting the most economic attention. Corpuz, *Economic History*, 244–46.

24. Walter LaFeber, *The New Empire: An Interpretation of American Expansion, 1860–1898* (Ithaca, N.Y.: Cornell University Press, 1963).

25. In an oft-quoted speech to a delegation of Methodist church leaders, President William McKinley explained U.S. policy in the Philippines in terms of mighty confusion and a divine inspiration to take up a civilizing mission: "I thought first we would take only Manila; then Luzon; then perhaps other islands also. I walked the floor of the White House night after night until midnight; and I am not ashamed to tell you, gentlemen, that I went down on my knees and prayed to Almighty God for light and guidance more than one night. . . . And one night late, it came to me this way—I don't know how it was, but it came: . . . that there was nothing left for us to do but to take them all, and to educate the Filipinos, and uplift and Christianize them. And by God's grace do the very best we could by them, as our fellow-men for whom Christ also died." General James Rusling, "Interview with President William McKinley," *Christian Advocate* (New York), 22 January 1903, 17.

26. Corpuz, *Economic History*, 220.

27. Ricardo Trota Jose, *The Philippine Army, 1935–1942* (Quezon City: Ateneo de Manila University Press, 1992), 15.

28. Ibid., 18.

29. Corpuz states that "the U.S. war secretary favored the Commission's views: that the islands were indeed a 'ready and attractive field for enterprise;' that mining laws, homestead and land laws, banking and currency laws, and general transportation laws were needed;" and, he added, "The great agency to bring industrial activity and awakening enterprise and prosperity and contentment to the country of the Philippines must be, not a military government, but the same kind of individual enterprise which has built up our country." Corpuz, *Economic History*, 221.

30. Doeppers, *Manila*, 59–68.

31. See Julian Go's chapter in this volume.

32. Doeppers, *Manila*, 9.

33. As Temario Rivera reports, "During [the American colonial period] a significant portion of the assets and investments in major agro-mineral export industries (particularly sugar milling and cordage, mining and logging/sawmilling) had already come under the ownership and control of a privileged landlord and merchant class. Further, commercial agricultural export production was largely controlled by Filipino landlords and compradores since earlier legislation limiting the size of landholdings for corporate planation agriculture dampened U.S. capital investment in large scale agriculture." Temario C. Rivera, *Landlords and Capitalists: Class, Family, and Sate in Philippine Manufacturing* (Quezon City: University of the Philippines Press, 1994), 25–26.

34. See for example, Harry B. Hawes, *Philippine Uncertainty: An American Problem* (New York: Century Company, 1929), chap. 10.

35. Aurora Catilo and Prosperpina Tapales, "The Legislature," in *Government and Politics in the Philippines*, ed. Raul De Guzman and Mila Reforma (Singapore: Oxford University Press, 1988), 139.

36. For an example of this, see Arturo Tolentino's account of the relationship that evolved between student activists (including himself) and commonwealth politicians such as Quezon and Roxas; Arturo Tolentino, *Voice of Dissent* (Quezon City: Phoenix Publishing House, 1990).

37. William Henry Scott, "The Union Obrera Democracia, First Filipino Labor Union," *Philippine Social Sciences and Humanities Review* 47, nos. 1–4 (January–December 1983); Kerkvliet, *Mutual Aid*. See also Doeppers, *Manila*, 124.

38. Doeppers, *Manila*, 123–36.

39. Theodore Friend, *Between Two Empires* (New Haven, Conn.: Yale University Press, 1965).

40. Sturtevant, *Popular Uprisings*; Brian Fegan, *Land Reform and Technical Change in Central Luzon: The Rice Industry under Martial Law* (Quezon City: Third World Studies Center, 1982).

41. Sturtevant, *Popular Uprisings*.

42. Kerkvliet, *Huk Rebellion*.

43. Heather Sutherland, *The Making of the Bureaucratic Elite* (Singapore: Heinemann Educational Books, 1979).

44. George M. Kahin, *Nationalism and Revolution in Indonesia* (Ithaca, N.Y.: Cornell University Press, 1952), 41–42. See also Ann Laura Stoler, *Capitalism and Confrontation in Sumatra's Plantation Belt* (New Haven, Conn.: Yale University Press, 1985).

45. Robert van Niel, *The Emergence of the Modern Indonesian Elite* (The Hague: Van Hoeve, 1970).

46. John D. Legge, *Intellectuals and Nationalists in Indonesia: A Study of the Following Recruited by Sultan Sjahrir in Occupation Indonesia*, Cornell Modern Indonesia Project (Ithaca, N.Y.: Southeast Asia Program Publications, 1988), 16–19.

47. See, for example, the account of life in exile in Mavis Rose, *Indonesia Free: A Political Biography of Mohammad Hatta*, Cornell Modern Indonesia Project (Ithaca, N.Y.: Southeast Asia Program Publications, 1987).

48. As Kahin explains, only 10 percent of the Indonesian population was allowed to vote to select 937 electors, who in turn would choose Volksraad members. But these 937 were supplemented by 515 electors appointed by the colonial government, and many Indonesians believe that the security apparatus coerced and intimidated voters. Kahin, *Nationalism and Revolution*, 40.

49. Daw Ni Ni Myint, *Burma's Struggle against British Imperialism, 1885–1895* (Rangoon: University Press, 1983).

50. Martin Smith, *Burma: Insurgency and the Politics of Ethnicity* (London: Zed Books, 1991), 41–44.

51. Mary P. Callahan, "The Origins of Military Rule in Burma" (Ph.D. diss., Cornell University, Ithaca, N.Y., 1995), 81–86.

52. Albert D. Moscotti, *British Policy and the Nationalist Movement in Burma, 1917–1937* (Honolulu: University Press of Hawai'i, 1974).

53. Robert H. Taylor, "The Relationship between Burmese Social Classes and British-Indian Policy on the Behavior of the Burmese Political Elite, 1937–1942" (Ph.D. diss., Cornell University, Ithaca, N.Y., 1974).

54. Furnivall, *Colonial Policy*, 116–21, 157–58. Indian moneylenders are called *chettyars*.

55. Moscotti, *British Policy*.

56. David G. Marr, *Vietnamese Tradition on Trial* (Berkeley: University of California Press, 1984), 24.

57. Ibid., 35–44; see also Hue-Tam Ho Tai, *Radicalism and the Origins of the Vietnamese Revolution* (Cambridge, Mass.: Harvard University Press, 1992), 12–20.

58. Nguyen Khac Vien, "Confucianism and Marxism in Vietnam," in *Tradition and Revolution in Vietnam* (Berkeley, Calif.: Indochina Resource Center, 1974).

59. Pierre Brocheux, *The Mekong Delta: Ecology, Economy and Revolution, 1860–1960*, Center for Southeast Asian Studies Monograph, no. 12 (Madison: Center for Southeast Asian Studies, University of Wisconsin Press, 1995).

60. "Indigenous bourgeoisie" is a slightly inexact translation of the Vietnamese term *tu san ban xu* as explained in Marr, *Vietnamese Tradition*, 26.

61. The first reliable census of colonial Vietnam is the 1937 count, which may be a bit outdated for discussions of the social base of resistance in the early twentieth century but nevertheless provides important indications of the class changes that were under way at the time. According to this census, Vietnam in 1937 contained about 10,000 working colons (in a total French population of 39,000); 10,500 members of the indigenous bourgeoisie; 55,000 small landlord families; and about 550,000 members of the mostly urban petit bourgeoisie. Marr, *Vietnamese Tradition*, 23–27.

62. Brocheux, *Mekong Delta*, 142–46.

63. Christine Peltzer White, "The Vietnamese Revolutionary Alliance: Intellectuals,

Workers and Peasants," in *Peasant Rebellion and Communist Revolution in Asia*, ed. John W. Lewis (Stanford, Calif.: Stanford University Press, 1974).

64. For example, see the discussion of the Tonkin Free School in Hue-Tam Ho Tai, *Radicalism*, 22–23.

65. Marr, *Vietnamese Tradition*, 35–44.

66. Ibid.

67. See Sidney Tarrow, *Power in Movement: Social Movements, Collective Action and Politics* (New York: Cambridge University Press, 1995).

CONTRIBUTORS

PATRICIO N. ABINALES is Associate Professor at the Center for Southeast Asian Studies, Kyoto University, and Southeast Asia editor of *Critical Asian Studies*. His new book is *Fellow Traveler: Essays on Filipino Communism* (2001).

DONNA J. AMOROSO wrote her dissertation on "Traditionalism and the Ascendency of the Malay Ruling Class in Colonial Malaya" (Cornell University, 1996). She works as an editor at Kyoto University's Center for Southeast Asian Studies.

PAUL BARCLAY is Assistant Professor of East Asian history at Lafayette College, Easton, Pennsylvania. He is working on a book-length study of Japanese and U.S. colonial rule in Taiwan and the Philippines.

VINCE BOUDREAU is Associate Professor of political science at City College, City University of New York. His most recent book is *Grass Roots and Cadre in the Protest Movement* (2002).

ANNE L. FOSTER is Assistant Professor of history at Saint Anselm College, Manchester, New Hampshire, where she also coordinates the Center for International Affairs at the New Hampshire Institute of Politics. She is working on book-length comparative studies of responses to rebellion and drug policy in colonial Southeast Asia.

JULIAN GO is Assistant Professor of sociology at the University of Illinois, Urbana-Champaign and Academy Scholar at the Academy for International Area Studies of Harvard University. His work has appeared in *Comparative Studies in Society and History* and the *Journal of Historical Sociology*.

PAUL A. KRAMER is Assistant Professor of history at Johns Hopkins University, Baltimore. His article "Making Concessions: Race and Empire Revisited at the Philippine Exposition, St. Louis, 1901–1905" appeared in *Radical History Review* (1999).

INDEX

Abad-Santos, Pedro, 282, 287 n.20
Abdullah (sultan), 146 n.42
Abeto, Quirico, 269
Abinales, Patricio, 30–31, 258
Aborigines: intercession efforts for, 255
n.105; Japanese policy, 254 n.91; Kaba-
yama and, 249 n.10; of Taiwan, 244–45.
See also Ethnic issues and groups; In-
digenous cultures
Accommodation, Filipino-American, 151,
153, 155
Accounting, 204
Acquisition of the Philippines: Anglo-
Saxonism and, 47, 57; debate sparked
by, 45; effect on U.S. colonialism, 4, 16–
17; Spanish legacy, 257–58; statehood
issues, 8; support for, 72–73; Treaty of
Paris, 35 n.3
Adams, George Herbert, 64
Adas, Michael, 17
The Administration of Dependencies
(Snow), 22
Administrative colonialism: administrative ethnography, 20; American treasurers, 198; annexation of Philippines
and, 72–73; colonial projects, 186; described, 10; expertise in, 180 n.102; interaction with other variables, 285;
mandarins, 276–77; military and, 167;
nationalist movements and, 281;
"patchworked" state, 31; population
ratios, 143 n.4; settler colonialism com-

pared to, 6, 68, 69; Taiwanese districts,
221; transfer of administrators, 20
Africa: African population, 48; colonialism in, 18, 162; consolidation of colonial
regimes, 43–44; indirect rule of, 21; Nigeria, 19, 21; South Africa, 61–63, 67–69
Agriculture: agrarian resistance movements, 256, 263, 270, 274–75; camphor
industry, 225, 228–30, 230–31, 243; capital investment in, 197; Chinese labor,
145 n.35; economic development, 266–
67; exports, 288 n.33; imperial policy
tours, 77; in Indonesia, 271; Malay culture associated wth, 130; in Moro region, 163; opium trade, 95–96, 98, 100,
101–6, 115 n.29; rice cultivation and export, 274, 282; sugar industry, 195–97,
208; tobacco, 195, 234; world economy
and, 282. *See also* Plantations and plantation colonialism
Aguinaldo, Emilio: British approach to,
62; Igorot followers, 218; Ilustrado
Movement, 260; leadership dismissed,
120; racial issues and, 71; resistance to
U.S., 237
"Aid the king" movement, 278
Albert, José, 101, 107, 108
Alcohol industry, 99–100
Allen, Charles, 193, 203, 204, 244
Allen, Henry T., 241
American Academy of Social and Political
Science, 10

"American Exceptionalism in an Age of International History" (Tyrrell), 42 n.74

American frontier, 265

Americanism, 65–66. *See also* Anglo-Saxonism

American League, 70

"America's Mission" (Bryan), 65

Amoroso, Donna J., 29–30, 181 n.126, 258

Anderson, Benedict, 14, 155, 286 n.11

Anderson, Stuart, 46

Anderson, Warwick, 15

Anglican Church, 48

Anglo-Americans: Anglo-American Society, 71; Anglo-Saxon racism, 53–54; Native Americans and, 6–7. *See also* Anglo-Saxonism

Anglo-Boer War: Philippine-American War compared to, 61–63; racial exceptionalism and, 45; U.S. response to, 66–67

Anglo-Burmese War, 275

Anglophobia: Germans, 64, 68; Irish, 64, 68; Philippine-American War and, 70; Venezuela boundary dispute and, 63–64; white settlement and, 69

The Anglo-Saxon Century and the Unification of the English-Speaking People (Dos Passos), 54

Anglo-Saxonism: American geopolitics and, 46; Americanism and, 65–66, 68; anti-imperialism and, 64–65; Boxall on, 72; British imperialism and, 47; colonial arguments, 58; critics of, 83 n.16; decline of, 69, 71; de-Saxonization, 70; divine providence and, 60–61; in fictitious works, 67–69; foreign policy and, 47; historical component, 57–58; hybridity, 49; Kramer's approach to, 28; magazine revolution and, 85 n.26; North American colonization, 52; in Philippines, 57; political component, 58; racial exceptionalism, 57, 66, 78; racial tensions, 48, 53–54, 72; rejection of,

51; Spanish imperialism compared to, 119; U.S. nationalism and, 50–51; "White Man's Burden," 73–74

Anglo-Saxon Review, 54

Annexation of Philippines. *See* Acquisition of the Philippines

Anthropology and anthropological maps, 222, 223, 224–25

Anticolonialism: "aid the king" movement, 278; comparison of, 281, 285; corruption and, 192; effect on colonial powers, 33; guerilla warfare, 189, 233, 261–62; Huk rebellion, 270; international movements, 280–81; local movements, 282; Musha (Wushe) rebellion, 245; political education and, 191; reform movements and, 279–80; revolutionary movements, 280–81; Spanish rule, 260, 281; Taiwan, 227; Vietnamese, 279; "writing brush war," 278. *See also* Anti-imperialism

Anti-imperialism: anglophobia and, 63–64; Anglo-Saxonism and, 65–66; Anti-Imperialist League, 63; chains of empire and, 187, 208; racial issues and, 45, 46–47, 86 n.34; republicanism and, 78; tariffs, 195–96, 197; U.S. annexation and, 63. *See also* Anticolonialism

Apayao subprovince, 242, 243

Appropriations, 29

Aristocracy: bureaucracy and, 275; in Burmese culture, 273; Civil War's effect on, 259; Filipino elites, 270–71; in Indonesian culture, 271; in Malay culture, 127, 128, 131; in Moro culture, 138; Vietnamese court, 276. *See also* Hereditary rulers; Monarchies

Army-Navy Club, 71

"Arrow War," 229–30

Aryans, 48

Asia, 18, 43–44

Assimilation, 19–20, 150

Associated Federation of Labor, 269

Association of Revolutionary Youth, 281

Revolution, 279; economic importance, 265, 274; in Filipino labor force, 214 n.57; in Malay States, 130, 142; opium trade, 94–98, 101–5, 107, 109, 111; on plantations, 147 n.67; rule of Taiwan, 234; Wood on, 139

Chinese Legation, 99

Cholera, 15, 111

Christianity: Catholicism, 48, 123; Christian-Muslim divisions, 126, 165; colonialism and, 19; Jesuits, 121–22, 123; in Luzon, 261; in Malay states, 120; missionaries, 29, 93, 97, 98–99, 104, 123, 141, 210 n.12; non-Christian minorities, 30–31, 126–27, 161–62; opium trade and, 98–99; in Philippines, 119; Social Gospel, 60; U.S. colonialism justified by, 287 n.25; Young Men's Christian Association (YMCA), 71. *See also* Religion

Citizenship, 7–8. *See also* Democratic values and democratization; Participation

Civil governance and civil service: Benguet area, 237; bureaucracies, 267; chains of empire and, 208; civilian regimes, 149; civil service, 157–58; class divisions, 269; corruption and, 191–94; in Indonesia, 271; opium trade and, 114 n.19; Organic Act, 237; political education and, 188; population ratios, 143 n.4; transition to, 12, 138; U.S. Army and, 168. *See also* Local governance and autonomy; Self-rule

Civility, 220

Civilizing mission of colonialism, 13, 149, 193

Civil society, 18

Civil War, 259

Classification of indigenous populations, 14, 119, 226, 255 n.104

Class tensions and divisions: census and, 15; comprador class, 230; Cordillera, 244; Indonesia, 272; opium use and, 94;

Philippine Assembly, 269; political and administrative divisions, 284; Vietnam, 289 n.61

Clientelism, 24, 26, 32. *See also* Patronage

Clifford, Hugh, 61, 74

Cochinchina, 103, 104–5, 277–78

Cochinchina Interpreter Schools, 277

Collaboration: American-Filipino, 150, 159; between imperial powers, 26; in municipal government, 151; resulting from Philippine-American War, 26–27; taxation and, 161, 199

Collective action: accommodation of, 33–34; Ramos and, 269–70; under U.S. rule, 261–64. *See also* Anticolonialism; Protest movements

"Colonial Government" (American Academy of Social and Political Science), 10

Colonialism and colonial rule: administrative colonialism, 6, 148; Anglo-Saxonism as justification, 58; arguments against, 87 n.41; chains of empire and, 208; civilizing mission, 13, 149, 193; colonial state-formation, 31; connection to metropole, 32; continental vs. overseas, 66; defined, 208; democratic values and, 26–27; distinctiveness of U.S. rule, 264–70; imperialism and, 3–11; legitimation of, 18–19; overseas, 10; plantation colonialism, 6, 147 n.67, 189, 195, 210 n.12, 267, 271, 282, 284; proliferation of, 18, 20; racial tensions and, 72; resistance to, 186, 270–81; scholarship on, 10–11; settler colonialism, 6–9, 44, 68, 78, 210 n.12; state building and state formation, 39 n.47, 184; unification of colonies, 53; U.S. exceptionalism, 2; U.S. governance of Cordillera, 236–41; variations of, 6. *See also* Anticolonialism

Colquhoun, Archibald, 73, 76

Commonwealths, 1

Communist Party, 273

Comparative methodology: absence of, 92–93; analysis of clientelism, 27; comparison of colonial systems, 25–26, 118–19; contributions to, 24; inter-imperial comparison, 32, 33–34; lacking in U.S. historiography, 24; paired-comparison, 171; Snow on, 22–23

Competition, among imperial powers: differentiation of imperial models, 22; economic competition, 55–56; effect on U.S. colonialism, 24–26; territorial competition, 20

Comprador class, 230

Conant, Charles, 193

Concentration camps, 260, 262

Conflicts. *See* Wars and conflicts

Confucianism, 279

Congress. *See* U.S. Congress

Connor, Norman G., 243

Constabulary (Philippines Constabulary): conflicts with hill tribes, 253 n.86; on Cordillera, 238; Ifugao units, 238–39; personnel shortages, 167, 241, 243; U.S. Department of War and, 265; Worcester and, 241

Constitutional issues, 59

Cooper, Frederick, 21–22, 247

Cordillera region: civilian police force, 238; federalism, 165; gold mines, 225, 235; Gran Cordillera Central, 233–34; headhunting practices, 241–44; languages of, 167; military rule, 163, 164; Philippine Constabulary and, 162; Progressivism in, 165; racism toward indigenous cultures, 163; segregation in, 240; size of, 179 n.82; "Special Province Act," 178 n.76; state building in, 161–67; Taiwan compared to, 32–33; tribal populations, 246; U.S. conquest of, 225; U.S. governance in, 236–41; violence in, 237–38

Corporations, 187

Corpuz, O. D., 261, 287 n.29

Corruption: civil governance and, 191–94; combating, 198; financial, 205; free trade and, 203; Hollander Act, 203–4; illegal taxes, 191; immigrant voters, 72; lack of punishment, 200; in local government, 205; opium trade and, 104–5; Philippines and Puerto Rico compared, 207–8; political education and, 213 n.45; political machines, 148; Tammany Hall, 154; in U.S. politics, 201

Cotabato, 136, 141

Court system, 149, 157

Courtwright, David, 94–95

Crime: Islam and, 140–41; opium smuggling, 96, 104, 105, 112; opium use and, 94–95; piracy, 129–30, 133, 134

Crow, Carl, 73

Cuba, 48, 58–59, 66–67

Culture and cultural issues: British rule and, 133; *canao* (feasts), 179 n.83; cultural kinship, 54; "culture system," 21; Malay culture and British rule, 128–29; Malays and capitalism, 130; Moro cultural identity, 123, 136–37; native customs, 19–20; northern Luzon, 247; origin myths, 55; racial issues and, 50

Curzon, George Nathaniel, 54

Datus (datos): alliances with, 124; American focus on, 138; aristocratic nature of, 128; authority of, 134–35; Dato Ali, 140; Dato Mandi, 137; Dato Piang, 137; datuship councils, 138; Davis on, 136; Pi's dismissal of, 144 n.16; protection from, 123; similarity to Malay rulers, 120; sultanate compared with, 137; U.S. rule and, 135, 140. *See also* Islam; Sultanate

Dauncey, Campbell, 71, 74, 76

Davao region, 126

Davis, George W., 122, 135, 182, 189–90

Decentralization, 185, 190, 201

Dekker, Edward Douwes, 115 n.33

Democratic Party: Boers and, 67–68; Filipinization and, 153; Hayden on, 177

Economic systems: British indirect rule, 128; Marxism, 281, 283, 285; monetary systems, 7; Organic Law and, 7; socialism, 282. *See also* Capitalism and capital investment

Education: Burmese bureaucracy, 276; Cochinchina Interpreter Schools, 277; colonial systems compared, 280; curriculum protests, 276; Filipinization policy, 265–66; French, 279; Indonesian native schools, 272; interaction with other variables, 285; mandarins, 276–77; opium use and, 108; in Philippines, 283; political, 32, 171, 183–86, 194, 197–201, 205–8, 213 n.45; public schools, 193; reform movements, 279–80, 283; support for, 259; Taman Siswa schools, 272; travel and, 283; universities, 266; Vietnamese, 278

Elections: Burmese participation in, 276; class tensions and, 268; elites, 151–52, 153, 170; municipal, 151–53, 182; Philippines, 151–52, 268; Progressives and, 149; protest movements and, 257; republican governance and, 170; self-rule and, 184; suffrage, 14, 182, 257, 259, 262, 289 n.48; Volksraad, 289 n.48. *See also* Participation; Suffrage

Elites and elite culture: accommodation, 155; agrarian, 259; autonomy of, 215 n.74; "bossism," 176 n.41; as buffer, 258; Burmese, 274–76; *caciques* and *caciquism*, 14, 155, 160, 163, 173, 191, 201; capital investment and, 199; civilizing missions and, 193; class issues and, 267, 269; clientelism and, 32; collaboration from Philippine-American War, 26–27; collective action, 263–64; corruption, 191–94; economic activities of, 214 n.63, 282; economic concessions to, 281; elections, 153, 170, 268; entrepreneurs and, 267; "ethnic juggling," 170; Filipino, 31, 42 n.82; *hacendados*, 189; Ilustrado movement, 260–61, 284; in-

digenous cultures and, 247; labor protests and, 263; landlords, 288 n.33; local politics and, 176 n.33; in Malayan society, 128, 131; Marcos dictatorship and, 285–86; marriage among, 54; Marxism and, 285; mass-elite alliances, 273; merchant class, 288 n.33; military and, 166; Moro ruling class, 141; in municipal government, 151–52, 189; nationalism and, 260–61, 287 n.20; patronage, 13–14, 24, 26, 31, 32, 148, 149, 153, 154, 155–56, 160, 170, 173, 175 n.26, 192; political education and, 205; political nature of, 270–71; protest movements and, 256, 257; provincial elite, 267; racial exclusion, 71; representative government and, 286; resistance to colonialism, 189; self-rule and, 283–84; Sergio Osmeña, 152; taxation and, 160, 161, 199; Vietnamese, 277–78

"Empires, Exceptions, and Anglo-Saxons: Race and Rule Between the British and U.S. Empires, 1880–1910" (Kramer), 27–28

England. *See* Britain and British Empire

English Club, 57, 71, 75

Enlightenment, 129

Entrepreneurs, 229, 267. *See also* Capitalism and capital investment

Epidemics, 15, 111

Ethical Policy, 103, 115 n.32

Ethnic issues and groups: Aryans, 48; Ataiyals, 217, 231–32, 246, 247, 249 n.12; Bontocs, 238; Celts, 48; Cheyenne Indians, 125, 242; Chinese immigrants, 94–98, 101–5, 107, 109, 111, 130, 139, 142, 147 n.67, 214 n.57; ethnic juggling, 170, 181 n.118; in Filipino politics, 171; Gaddangs, 242; Hakkas, 226; Haklos, 226; Hans, 226, 251 n.27; hill tribes, 225; Hindus, 126; Hoklos, 226; Hottentots, 69; Ibans, 219; Ifugaos, 238, 239, 245; Ilongots, 245; Irish, 51, 64, 68, 154; Isnegs, 238; Jarai, 219; Kalingas, 238–39,

161–62. *See also* Ethnic issues and groups

Missionaries: among Moro population, 123; conflicts with other colonial interests, 210 n.12; opium trade and, 29, 93, 97, 98–99, 104; Protestant, 141

Missionary Society, 99

Mizuno Jun, 106

Mochiji line, 231–32

Mochiji Rokusaburō, 243

"Models for Governing: Opium and Colonial Policies in Southeast Asia, 1898–1910" (Foster), 29

Modernization, 157, 177 n.50, 193. *See also* Infrastructure development

Monarchies: "aid the king" movement, 278; Burmese, 273, 274; Vietnamese, 276–77, 278

Monetary systems, 7. *See also* Economic development and commerce

Monopolies: camphor industry, 230–31; opium trade, 95–96, 101–6, 109–10; Sherman Anti-Trust Act, 156; tobacco industry, 234

"Moors," 122. *See also* Moro province and culture; Muslims

Morality issues, 112–13

Morgan, Henry Lewis, 144 n.19

Mori Ushinosuke, 255 n.105

Moro province and culture: American criticism of, 129; civilian rule, 168; classification of population, 119; conflict with Jesuits, 123; customs, 136–37; ethnographic histories, 137; federalism, 165; infrastructure, 163; Langhorne's account of, 118; legislative councils, 147 n.76; military rule, 178 n.76; "Moro Problem" described, 30; political education, 171; population, 37 n.27; Progressivism in, 165; size of, 179 n.82; state building in, 161–67; wars against, 261

Moses, Bernard, 196

Mountain Province, 161, 164, 240, 253 n.86

Mugwumps, 63

Muhammadiyah, 272

Municipal government: *alcaldes*, 191; corruption, 191; elections, 151–53, 182; establishment of, 182–83, 188–89; Foraker Act and, 202; Municipal Officers, 189; Philippines, 258; police forces, 204. *See also* Local governance and autonomy

Musha (Wushe) rebellion, 245

Muslims: animosity toward Manila, 170; Bates Treaty, 139–40; British indirect rule, 132; in British Malaya, 30–31; Christian-Muslim divisions, 126, 165; cultural customs, 126; direct and indirect rule of, 141–43; discriminatory views of, 162–63; Filipinization, 170; *kathis* (religious officials), 131; legal systems, 140–41; in Malay states, 30–31, 120–21; military force used against, 169, 262; in Mindanao, 119, 142; in Moro history, 137; nobility, 138–39; pan-Islamism, 271–72; traditional leadership, 124; U.S. attempts to govern, 181 n.126; U.S. misunderstanding of, 136

Mutual-aid societies, 262

Myothugyis, 259, 273, 274

Nacionalista Party: compared to American parties, 154; independence efforts, 268; integration of special provinces, 169; labor politics and, 262; local leadership, 153; opposition to, 270; Osmeña and, 152, 153

Narita Takeshi, 249 n.12

Nathorst, C. E., 243

National Assembly, 200–201

Nationalism and nationalist movements: Anglo-Saxonism and, 50–51; educational reforms and, 283–84; national-exceptionalist colonialism, 45; in Philippines, 260–61. *See also* Anticolonialism; Anti-imperialism

Native Americans: Anglo-Saxonism and, 48; Cheyenne Indians, 125, 242; Fil-

nance and, 170; restrictions on, 210
n.15. *See also* Elections

Party machines. *See* Political machines

Patchworked national state: effect on
Philippines colony, 149–50; Filipino
"turf wars" and, 160; sources of, 31;
U.S. and Philippines compared, 173

Paternalism: British rule and, 140; Muslim leadership and, 124; opium use
and, 29; racism and, 73–74, 161, 163;
U.S. Army, 121

Patrimonialism, 32, 158

Patronage: "cacique democracy" and, 173;
clientelism and, 24, 26, 32, 175 n.26;
corruption compared to, 192; origin in
Philippines, 153, 155–56; patchworked
state and, 149, 160; political machines
and, 148; political parties and, 154; republican governance and, 170; state
formation and, 31

The Pattern of Imperialism (Smith), 25

Payne-Aldrich Act, 214 n.63

Peking, China, 77

Pennsylvania Steel Company, 55–56

Pershing, John, 146 n.58, 163, 169

Phan Boi Chau, 280

Phan Chu Trinh, 280

Philippine-American War: Anglo-Boer
War compared to, 61–63; Anglo-Saxonism and, 59; capital investment
and, 196, 262; causes, 12; collaboration
resulting from, 26–27; effects of, 213
n.45; as expression of Anglo-Saxonism,
58; fictional accounts, 87 n.41; immigrant support for, 70; as "Indian War,"
9; Mahan on, 43; U.S. presence during,
265

Philippine Assembly: agrarian elites in,
259; elections, 268; Indonesian Volksraad compared to, 272; local leadership, 152–53; Moro involvement in, 171;
political mobilization and, 270; protest
movements and, 267–68; Worcester
and, 241

Philippine Civil Service Board, 76

Philippine Colonial Democracy (Paredes),
13–14

Philippine Commission: American domination of, 159; appropriations, 75; Bates
Treaty and, 140; civil service and, 157;
Cordillera region and, 237; critique of
Spanish system, 119; establishment of, 1;
funding for special provinces, 240; indirect rule of Malay States, 128; lower
house, 152; opium policy, 96, 98–100,
106, 109–10; Philippine Assembly upper house, 268; Philippine Commission
Act, 178 n.73; political education and,
192; *Report of the Philippine Commission*, 121–22; revenue plans, 160; tariffs
and, 198; use of Spanish divisions, 125

Philippine Socialist Party, 282

Philippines Constabulary: conflicts with
hill tribes, 253 n.86; on Cordillera, 238;
Ifugao units, 238–39; personnel shortages, 167, 241, 243; U.S. Department of
War and, 265; Worcester and, 241

Philippines Ethnological Survey, 218–19

Philippines: anthropological maps, 223;
anti-colonialism in, 281; capital investment in, 195; civil rule, 191–94, 204;
Commonwealth established, 153; corruption in, 191–94, 204; development
in, 197–201; distinctiveness of U.S. rule,
264–70; diversity within, 118–19; educational opportunity, 283; General
Order No. (43), 182–83, 188–89; hill
tribes, 219; merchant community, 56–
57; municipal governments established, 188–90; nationalism in, 260;
opium trade, 98, 101–6, 112; pacification of headhunters, 217; political education in, 188, 206–7; political elite,
282–83; Puerto Rico compared to, 189;
Puerto Rico contrasted with, 184, 185,
188; U.S. acquisition of, 1, 4, 8, 16–17, 35
n.2, 47, 57, 224, 257–58; Vietnam compared to, 277

Publishing industry, 54, 85 n.26

Puerto Rico: capital investment in, 195, 196; corruption in civil rule, 191–94; economic development in, 201–7; General Order No. (160), 182; municipal governments established, 188–90; Philippines compared to, 31–32, 189; Philippines contrasted with, 184, 185, 188; political education in, 188, 206–7

Qing Dynasty, 224, 226, 251 n.27

Quay, Matt, 154

Quezon, Manuel L.: American politicians compared to, 154; elite opposition to, 263; Moro involvement in, 171; on Muslim issue, 169–70; Muslim leadership and, 170–71; Nacionalista Party, 153; patronage and, 176 n.40; political machines and, 171; political power, 168–69; rise to power, 152; U.S. Army and, 175 n.19

Race and Rapprochement (Anderson), 46

Racism and racial issues: anti-imperialism and, 86 n.34; blood and culture, 50, 55; in censuses, 26; enlightenment ideas of, 129; exclusionist social institutions, 71; against Filipinos, 73–74; foreign policy and, 46; Indian reservation system, 225; indigenous cultures and, 163; Jim Crow, 225; language and, 50; paternalism and, 161, 163; race making, 46; race patriotism, 60; racial exceptionalism, 52, 57, 65, 66, 69, 76, 78; racial ideology, 46; racial rapprochement, 28, 46; separation of races, 164; unification of colonies and, 53; white settlement, 69. *See also* Anglo-Saxonism; Moro province and culture

Rafael, Vicente, 14, 247, 255 n.104

Ramos, Benigno, 269

Rangoon, 77

Reform movements: anticolonialism and,

279–80; education, 279, 283–84; judicial system, 157; political machines and, 148, 172; Progressivism, 166–67, 176 n.36; taxation, 157; U.S. Army, 166

Reid, Whitelaw, 55

Religion: Anglican Church, 48; Anglo-Saxonism and, 48; British rule and, 133; Buddhism, 274; Bureau of Non-Christian Tribes, 30; chains of empire and, 187; Confucianism, 279; conversion of indigenous cultures, 125; divine providence, 60; drug policy and, 93; Ghost Dance religion, 141; indigenous cultures and, 125, 141; interference in, 262–63; *kathis* (religious officials), 131; killing of Christians, 139; Malayan society, 127; millenarianism, 15; missionaries, 29, 93, 97–99, 104, 123, 141, 210 n.12; Moro religion, 122, 138; non-Christian tribes, 161–62; noninterference policies, 142; opium trade and, 98–99, 108; political implications, 141–42; Protestantism, 48, 99, 141; religious conflict, 165; religious courts, 131; secularism, 125; Social Gospel, 60; spiritual leadership, 129; U.S. colonialism justified by, 287 n.25. *See also* Christianity; Islam; Missionaries

Reports of the Philippine Commission to the President, 121–22, 235

Republicanism, 65, 78

Republican Party: Boers and, 68; business interests, 67, 215 n.84, 258, 265; loss of leadership, 169; "Old Guard," 154

Reservation system, 9

Revenue collection, 160. *See also* Taxation

Revolutionary Party of New Vietnam, 281

Reyes, Isabelo de los, 262, 287 n.20

Rice cultivation and export, 274, 282

Rivera, Temario, 288 n.33

Roads and road building, 193, 199. *See also* Infrastructure development

Robinson, Ronald, 14, 24

Rodgers, Daniel T., 25, 43

Roosevelt, Theodore: Anglo-Boer War, 67–68; Anglo-Saxonism, 50, 52–53; opium policy, 99, 100, 101, 110–11; on U.S. expansion, 58; *The Winning of the West*, 52, 58

Root, Elihu: capital investment and, 195; colonial policy, 4–5; development and, 194; opium policy, 92, 99–100; political corruption, 191, 198; political education, 183, 188–90; Progressivism, 166; restrictions on political participation, 210 n.15; state-building projects, 186, 192–93; tariffs, 196; U.S. mission in Philippines, 11–12; War Department under, 210 n.14

Rosaldo, Renaldo, 245

Rowe, L. S., 205

Royal Botanical Gardens at Kew, 77

Royal Commission on Opium, 102

Royalty, 131, 136. *See also* Aristocracy; Hereditary rulers

Rush, James, 104

Russia: Asian expansion, 60, 69–70; high imperialism, 17; Russo-Japanese War, 69–70, 261, 279

Saigon, 107

St. Louis Exposition, 246

Sakai, 126

Sakdal Rebellion, 264

Saleeby, Najeeb M., 137–38

Sarawak, 118

Saxton, Alexander, 49

Schurman, Jacob Gould, 77, 133

Schurz, Carl, 64–65

Science and technology: botany, 77, 91 n.70; celluloid development, 229; empire building and, 43–44, 55–56, 85 n.29; engineering, 55–56; imperial policy tours, 77; magazine revolution, 54, 85 n.26; resistance to, 15; steamships, 77, 132. *See also* Modernization

Scott, James C., 220, 245

Second Philippine Commission, 96

Secularism, 125

Seeley, John, 53

Self-help organizations, 262

Self-rule: American promise of, 270; capitalism and, 267; establishment of, 182–83; local autonomy, 185; provincial governments, 197–98; self-governing colonies, 143 n.5. *See also* Local governance and autonomy

Semang, Malaysia, 219

Separatism, 121. *See also* Anticolonialism; Anti-imperialism

Sepoy revolt, 64

Settler colonialism: administrative colonialism compared to, 6, 68; Anglo-Saxonism and, 78; economic component, 44; Philippines case compared to, 7; settlers, 210 n.12; Western frontier, 9; Willoughby on, 8

Shanghai, 107, 111–12

Shanghai Opium Commission, 93

Shans, 273

Shefter, Martin, 154

Sherman Anti-Trust Act, 156

Silbey, Joel, 156

Simpson, Mark, 181 n.118

Singapore: British indirect rule, 128; Dutch and British rule, 118; imperial policy tours, 77; opium trade, 107, 110, 112

Sino-Japanese War, 220, 226–27

Sioux Nation, 242

Skowronek, Stephen, 166

Slavery: in American South, 8; Anglo-Saxon defense of, 48; elimination of, 129–30; in Malay States, 128; in Moro culture, 123, 140; treaties on, 133–34; white slaves, 111; Wood on, 139

Slavic threat, 69–70

Smith, James F., 112, 152, 159

Smith, Tony, 25

Smoking Opium Exclusion Law, 93

Smuggling opium, 96, 104, 105, 112

Snow, Alpheus, 10, 22

Social Darwinism, 279

Social Engineering in the Philippines: The Aims, Execution, and Impact of American Colonial Policy, 1900–1913 (May), 13, 24, 150

Social Gospel, 60

Socialism, 282

Social movements, 270–81. *See also* Protest movements

Society for the Suppression of the Opium Trade, 102

South Africa, 61–63, 67–69

Sovereignty issues, 4

Spain and Spanish Empire: Anglo-Saxonism and, 59, 119; Beveridge on, 59; census of imperial territories, 26; Christian-Muslim divisions, 126; classification of provinces, 161; colonial governance, 10, 151; Cordillera, 234, 237–38; corruption in, 192; decay of Spanish regime, 286 n.11; failed military rule, 124; Filipino colonial state, 3–4; Filipino nationalism and, 260; former colonies, 132–33; framework for dealing with Moro population, 123–24; gold prospecting, 235; Hispanized Filipinos, 121; Igorots and, 218–19; influence in American politics, 72; Jesuit missionaries, 121–22; legacy of Spanish rule, 144 n.9, 149, 257; limitations of colonial power, 224; loss of Philippines, 220; Luzon, 224; Malay states, 120–21; Moro region, 30, 122–23, 137; Philippines purchased from, 1, 4; Propaganda Movement and, 89 n.58; Puerto Rico and, 182; revolts against, 151–52; tenuous control of the Philippines, 119; Treaty of Paris, 233; U.S. compared to, 137–38, 281; U.S. expansion and, 58. *See also* Spanish-American War; Spanish-Cuban-American War

Spanish-American War: anticolonialism and, 265; fictional accounts, 87 n.41; infrastructure destruction, 193; as source of Philippine-American War, 12; Treaty of Paris, 35 n.2

Spanish-Cuban-American War, 48, 58–59, 66–67

Specialization, 18

Special provinces, 178 n.76, 179 n.82

Spoils system, 148, 153, 160, 176 n.37

Spooner Bill, 196

Spurgin, William F., 96, 97

Sri Lanka, 143 n.4

Stanley, Peter, 153

State building: global perspective, 3; models for U.S., 172; in the regular provinces, 151–61; in the special provinces, 161–67; state formation compared to, 184

Statehood, 6–7, 8

Stead, W. T., 54

Steamships, 77, 132

Stevens, Joseph Earle, 57, 75

Stoler, Ann Laura, 21–22, 247

Straits Settlements: British indirect rule, 128; economic development, 130; grouping trade and, 102; imperial policy tours, 77; opium trade, 29, 107, 112; Philippine Commission report, 140

Stratemeyer, Edward, 68–69, 89 n.54

Strikes, 262. *See also* Labor and labor movements

Strong, Josiah, 60

Stuntz, Homer C., 98–99

Suffrage: efforts to expand, 262; in Indonesia, 289 n.48; protest movements and, 257; restrictions, 14, 182; support for, 259

Sugar industry, 195–97, 208

Sultanate: Abdullah (sultan), 146 n.42; aristocratic nature of, 128; Bates Treaty and, 136, 139–40; *datus* compared with, 137; decline of, 139–40; effect of colonial rule on, 141; indirect rule and, 120; in Malay culture, 131–32; Philippine Commission on, 128; police protection from, 123; Spain's influence on, 137; U.S. sovereignty and, 133–35; Wood on, 139

Sulu archipelago: Bates Treaty and, 134; legacy of Spanish rule, 144 n.9; Muslims of, 120–21; Philippine Commission on, 121–22; racial ethnic divisions, 126; Spanish rule, 132–33, 137; sultanate, 139, 141; traditional leadership, 136

Sumner, Samuel S., 135–36

Supreme Court, 7–8

Taft, William Howard: on Filipino politics, 153; free trade and, 198; goals for Philippines, 154; on modernization, 193–94; opium policy, 29, 99, 100–101, 106–7, 110, 114 n.23; Progressivism and, 157, 176 n.36; Second Philippine Commission, 96; Secretary of War post, 116 n.51; selection of Brent for Opium Committee, 116 n.43; support of Osmeña, 152; tariffs, 196; on U.S. mission in Philippines, 12

Taft Commission, 177 n.50

Tagalogs, 120, 200

Taikōkan region, 228

Taiwan, aborigines, 226–27, 231, 244–45; anthropological maps, 222; ceded to Japan, 220; Cordillera compared to, 32–33, 242–43; economic development, 225; headhunting practices in, 217–18; indigenous cultures, 249 n.12; Japanese colonial policy, 227–33; Japanese conquest, 225; Luzon compared to, 223; Philippines compared to, 3, 224; resistance to imperialism, 250 n.18

Takekoshi Yosaburō, 232–33

Taman Siswa schools, 272

Tammany Hall, 154

Tariffs, 95–96, 195–99. See also Taxation

Tasmanians, 247

Tattnall, Josiah, 55

Taxation: corruption and, 159, 204; development and, 199; duties, 195; Hollander Act, 203; illegal taxes, 191, 200, 202–3; insular revenue agents, 205; land seizures, 159; local, 196; Mair on,

242; Moro province, 140, 163; opium trade, 95–96, 97, 110; in Philippines, 9; Philippine Tariff Act, 196; porkbarreling, 200–201; Progressivism and, 177 n.51; reforms, 157; revenue collection, 160; road building and, 237; tariffs, 95–96, 195–99; tax revolts, 282

Tayabas Province, 152–53

Taylor, Wallace, 242

Technology. See Science and technology

Tennyson, Alfred, 71

Territorial government, 143 n.5. See also Local governance and autonomy; Selfrule

The Territories and Dependencies of the United States (Willoughby), 8

Teutons, 48, 68

"They Have for the Coast Dwellers a Traditional Hatred" (Barclay), 32–33

Thomas, Nicholas, 184

Tilly, Charles, 171

Tin mining, 130

Tobacco, 195, 234

Total empires, 223, 250 n.15

Trade: British trading companies, 19; camphor industry, 225, 228–30, 230–31, 243; Dutch trading companies, 19; imperial policy tours, 77; import economy, 113 n.6; sugar industry, 195–97, 208; tariffs, 95–96, 195–99; wealth in Malay culture, 129. See also Economic development and commerce; Opium and opium trade

Traditionalism, 274–75, 276

Transnational perspective, 24

"The Transvaal and the Philippines" (Mahan), 61

Travel: bridge building, 55–56; Eastern Travel Movement, 280; educational travel, 283; roads and road building, 193, 199; steamships, 77, 132

Treaties: acquisition of Philippines, 257–58; Bates Treaty, 133–34, 135, 136, 139–40; commerce and, 265–66; Malay culture and, 131; opium trade and, 97; Pangkor Treaty, 146 n.42; protectorate treaties, 131; Treaty of Paris, 4, 12, 35 n.2, 233; Treaty of Tianjin, 229

Trocki, Carl, 94, 111, 116 n.60

Turk, John C., 56

Turkey, 111

Tyrrell, Ian, 42 n.74

Unhappy Valley (Berman and Lonsdale), 210 n.13

Unincorporated territories, 7–8, 9, 37 n.25

Unions, 262, 268–69. *See also* Labor and labor movements

United Nations Working Group on Indigenous Populations, 248 n.4

United States: American frontier, 265; "America's Mission" (Bryan), 65; Beveridge on, 59; colonialism, 2; competition with other imperial powers, 22; conflicts with Japan, 41 n.73; cooperation with Britons, 55; domestic politics, 149–50; industrial power, 55–56; Japan compared to, 224, 264, 265; Philippines purchased from Spain, 1

University Club, 71

University of the Philippines, 266

Upton, Emory, 166

Urban economy, 278

U.S. Army: avoidance of Moro conflicts, 125; Bates Treaty and, 135; civil service and, 158; civilian governance and, 162, 168; indigenous populations and, 120, 162, 163; legacy of, 169; local governance and, 190; Moro assimilation and, 124; Muslim populations and, 121; personnel problems, 168; Quezon and, 175 n.19; reforms, 166; religious differences and, 162; rotation of officers, 168, 180 nn.107, 108

U.S. attorney general, 236

U.S. Congress: chains of empire and, 208; control over colonial affairs, 194, 195–

97; decentralization and, 201; free trade and, 201; opium tariff, 109; organic law and, 258; political education and, 188; Progressivism and, 161; revenue plans for Philippines, 161

U.S. Constabulary, 239

U.S. Department of State, 97, 249 n.12

U.S. Department of the Treasury, 97

U.S. Department of War: authority structure, 194; chains of empire and, 208; under Elihu Root, 210 n.14; Hunt and, 254 n.95; Philippine Constabulary and, 265; political education, 183, 188; tariff policy and, 97

U.S. Navy, 59

U.S. Supreme Court, 236

U.S.S. Bennington, 77

Venezuela, 63–64

Victoria (Queen of England), 55, 131

Vietnam: anticolonialism in, 281; autonomous elite, 284; censuses, 289 n.61; educational system, 283; elite role in colonialism, 276–81; French rule of, 264; hill tribes, 219; Philippines compared to, 258, 285; Philippines contrasted with, 259, 281–82; protest movements in, 257

Viet Nam Quoc Dan Dang (vnqdd), 281

Violence: headhunting practices, 32–33, 217–18, 228, 239, 241–44; killing of Christians, 139; in Luzon, 253 n.73; police power and, 203; political protest and, 270; Wounded Knee conflict, 141. *See also* Protest movements

Visayas, 120, 126, 261

Volksraad, 272

Voluntary engagement, 120

Voting. *See* Elections; Suffrage

Wars and conflicts: agricultural conflicts, 279; Anglo-Boer War, 45, 61–63, 66–67, 67–69; Anglo-Burmese War, 275; "Arrow War," 229–30; Civil War, 259;

Library of Congress Cataloging-in-Publication Data
The American colonial state in the Philippines : global
perspectives / edited by Julian Go and Anne L. Foster.
p. cm.—(American encounters/global interactions)
Includes index.
ISBN 0-8223-3101-2 (cloth)—ISBN 0-8223-3099-7 (pbk.)
1. United States—Foreign relations—Philippines. 2. Philippines—
Foreign relations—United States. 3. United States—Foreign
relations—1865–1921. 4. Philippines—Colonization—History.
5. Asia, Southeastern—Colonization—History. 6. Imperialism—
History—19th century. 7. Imperialism—History—20th century.
8. United States—Territories and possessions—History.
I. Go, Julian. II. Foster, Anne. III. Series.
E183.8P6 A46 2003   959.9′03—dc21   2002153862